Exam 70-632: *TS: Microsoft® Office Project 2007, Managing Projects*

S0-AEX-379

Objective	Chapter	Lesson
Configuring Tools and Options		
Set up Schedule options.	4	4
Set up Calculation options.	4	4
Set up Interface options.	1	1, 2, 3
Set up View options.	2 4	1 4
Set up General options.	4	4
Set up Calendar options.	4	4
Set up Security options.	4	4
Setting Up a Project		
Create and modify a template.	4	1, 2
Select a template.	1	1
Enter project information.	1 3	1, 2, 3 1, 2
Manage calendars.	1	3
Import and export data.	4	1
Estimating, Scheduling, and Budgeting Tasks		
Create a WBS.	2	1
Create and modify tasks.	1 2	2 1, 2
Estimate and budget tasks.	1 2	2 2
Sequence tasks.	2	2
Identify and analyze critical tasks and critical path.	2	2, 5
Manage multiple projects.	4	2, 3
Resourcing Project Plans		
Forecast time-phased generic skill or role requirements.	2	4
Create, modify, and use resource pools.	2 4	5 2, 3
Add, change, substitute, or remove resource assignments.	2	4
Predict durations and work calculations.	2	1
Optimize resource utilization.	4	2
Updating and Reporting on Project Performance		
Save and modify baselines.	2	3
Enter task updates.	3	1, 2
Reschedule incomplete work.	2 3	1, 2, 3 2
Track project progress.	3 5	1 1, 2
Analyze variance.	3 5	1 1, 2
Create, modify, and delete objects.	3 4	2 4
Create reports.	2 5	3, 5 1, 2

Note: Exam objectives are subject to change at any time without prior notice and at Microsoft's sole discretion. Please visit the Microsoft Learning Certification Web site (*www.microsoft.com/learning/mcp/*) for the most current listing of exam objectives.

Microsoft

MCTS Self-Paced Training Kit (Exam 70-632): Managing Projects with Microsoft® Office Project 2007

Joli Ballew and Deanna Reynolds
with Bonnie Biafore

PUBLISHED BY
Microsoft Press
A Division of Microsoft Corporation
One Microsoft Way
Redmond, Washington 98052-6399

Library of Congress Control Number: 2008923660

Printed and bound in the United States of America.

1 2 3 4 5 6 7 8 9   QWT   3 2 1 0 9 8

Distributed in Canada by H.B. Fenn and Company Ltd.

A CIP catalogue record for this book is available from the British Library.

Microsoft Press books are available through booksellers and distributors worldwide. For further information about international editions, contact your local Microsoft Corporation office or contact Microsoft Press International directly at fax (425) 936-7329. Visit our Web site at www.microsoft.com/mspress. Send comments to mspinput@microsoft.com.

Microsoft, Microsoft Press, Access, DirectX, Excel, Outlook, PivotChart, PivotTable, PowerPoint, SharePoint, Visio, Visual Basic, Windows, Windows Server and Windows Vista are either registered trademarks or trademarks of the Microsoft group of companies. Other product and company names mentioned herein may be the trademarks of their respective owners.

The example companies, organizations, products, domain names, e-mail addresses, logos, people, places, and events depicted herein are fictitious. No association with any real company, organization, product, domain name, e-mail address, logo, person, place, or event is intended or should be inferred.

This book expresses the author's views and opinions. The information contained in this book is provided without any express, statutory, or implied warranties. Neither the authors, Microsoft Corporation, nor its resellers, or distributors will be held liable for any damages caused or alleged to be caused either directly or indirectly by this book.

Acquisitions Editor: Ken Jones
Developmental Editor: Laura Sackerman
Project Editor: Melissa von Tschudi-Sutton
Editorial Production: nSight, Inc.
Technical Reviewer: Rozanne Murphy Whalen
Cover: Tom Draper Design

Body Part No. X14-71552

This book is humbly dedicated to all of the fearless project managers
who bring projects in on time and, maybe more important,
within budget to keep businesses running smoothly,
despite Murphy's Law.

About the Authors

Joli Ballew

Joli Ballew is a technical author, technology trainer, and Web site manager in the Dallas area. She holds several certifications, including MCSE, MCTS, and MCDST, and is a Microsoft MVP. In addition to writing, she occasionally teaches computer classes at the local junior college and works as a network administrator and Web designer for North Texas Graphics. She's written almost two dozen books, including *Degunking Windows* (Paraglyph Press, 2004), which was awarded the IPPY award for best computer book of the year in 2005; *CNet Do-It-Yourself Mac Projects* (McGraw-Hill Osborne Media, 2006); PC Magazine's *Office 2007 Solutions* (Wiley, 2006); *Breakthrough Windows Vista* (Microsoft Press, 2007); and *Windows Vista Home Networking* (Microsoft Press, 2007). Joli has also written a training manual similar to this book for Microsoft's MCDST certification entitled *Supporting Users and Troubleshooting Desktop Applications on a Microsoft Windows XP Operating System (Exam 70-272)* (Microsoft Press, 2004). In her free time, Joli enjoys golfing, yard work, exercising at the local gym, and teaching her cat Pico tricks.

Deanna Reynolds

Deanna Reynolds (MCTS) is an author and technical instructor living in Suffolk, Virginia. Since 1993, Deanna has been privileged to work with students traveling many different career paths on a multitude of software programs, including the entire Microsoft Office suite, project management, desktop publishing, and database development. Throughout her career, Deanna has led hundreds of computer productivity training sessions, from beginner through advanced levels. Most recently, Deanna's technical training has extended beyond the classroom to include more than 10 DVD-ROM courses.

Bonnie Biafore

Bonnie Biafore is a PMI-certified PMP (Project Management Professional) and award-winning author of more than a dozen books about project management, technology, and finance. In addition to writing *Project 2007: The Missing Manual* and *On Time! On Track! On Target!*, she manages projects as a contractor, provides instruction on project management and Microsoft Project, and produces technical documents for clients.

Contents at a Glance

Table of Contents

What do you think of this book? We want to hear from you!

Microsoft is interested in hearing your feedback so we can continually improve our books and learning resources for you. To participate in a brief online survey, please visit:

www.microsoft.com/learning/booksurvey/

What do you think of this book? We want to hear from you!

Microsoft is interested in hearing your feedback so we can continually improve our books and learning resources for you. To participate in a brief online survey, please visit:

www.microsoft.com/learning/booksurvey/

Acknowledgements

Although we would like to think we could put a book of this magnitude together all on our own, the reality is that this is a process which, much like any other project, is the result of hard work by an entire team of talented and dedicated professionals. After all, a book on Microsoft Office Project 2007 would not be complete without heartfelt thanks to both our project managers and fellow team members.

We would like to send out a very special thank you to those with whom we worked directly, including the following:

Laura Sackerman, our developmental editor, whose job it was to make sure we started this project off on the right foot, with the right words, and with a solid schedule. Thank you, Laura.

Melissa von Tschudi-Sutton, our project editor, whose job it was to make sure we completed this book on time and stayed true to the high standard that defines a Microsoft Press training kit. Melissa, your patience is unmatched. Thank you.

Bonnie Biafore (certified as a Microsoft Certified Technology Specialist and as a Project Management Professional by the Project Management Institute), our fearless technical reviewer and Real World contributor who brings true passion to the project management profession. Bonnie, thank you for the dedication and, of course, technical expertise you offered to this book.

A standing ovation and heaps of gratitude go to those whose names we know well (because we saw them over and over in the edits), but with whom we never worked directly, for making sure that our words flowed as we hoped they would and for ensuring that consistency prevailed, including Carol Whitney, project manager at the editorial production company nSight, Inc.; Rozanne Murphy Whalen, technical reviewer; and Joe Gustaitis, copy editor.

Finally, a special thanks to our tireless Studio B agent, Neil Salkind, Ph.D., and to our acquisitions editor, Ken Jones, for helping us to secure this fabulous writing opportunity. And, to our friends and loved ones, as always, for being supportive, loving sounding boards when we needed it most.

Introduction

This training kit is designed for team members, project leads, project managers, schedulers, or any user of Microsoft Office Project Standard or Professional 2007 who plans to take the Microsoft Certified Technology Specialist (MCTS) exam 70-632 to certify that he or she can build, maintain, and control well-formed project plans. We assume that before you begin using this kit you have a solid understanding of project management methodology as taught by the *Project Management Body of Knowledge (PMBOK)* and Microsoft Windows-based programs.

Many of the explanations in this training kit follow *PMBOK's* project management best practices. On the 70-632 exam you might be presented with a question that lists two or more possible correct answers. In these instances you need to know *PMBOK's best practice* in order to arrive at the correct answer. Where applicable, we have noted those best practices in the text.

By using this training kit, you will learn how to do the following:

- Configure tools and options
- Set up a project
- Estimate, schedule, and budget tasks
- Work with project resources
- Update and report on project performance

Hardware Requirements

The computer that you use to perform the practices requires Internet connectivity. Your computer should meet (at a minimum) the following hardware specifications:

- Personal computer with a 700-MHz or faster processor
- 512 MB of RAM or higher
- 1.5 GB of available hard disk space
- 1024 × 768 or higher resolution monitor
- CD-ROM or DVD drive
- Keyboard and Microsoft mouse or compatible pointing device
- Microsoft Windows XP with Service Pack (SP) 2, Windows Server 2003 with SP1, or later operating system

Software Requirements

The following software is required to complete the practice exercises:

- Microsoft Office Project 2007 Professional. Note: Professional Edition is preferable, but it is more expensive to purchase than Standard Edition. If you have Standard Edition, or would prefer to purchase Standard Edition, you will still be able to perform the exercises in this book.
- Optional: Microsoft Office Excel 2003 (or later). (You need this application to display Project visual reports.)
- Optional: Microsoft Office Visio Professional 2007. (You need this application to display Project visual reports.)

Using the CD

The companion CD included with this training kit contains the following:

- **Practice tests**   You can reinforce your understanding of Project by using electronic practice tests you customize to meet your needs from the pool of Lesson Review questions in this book. Or you can practice for the 70-632 certification exam by using tests created from a pool of 200 realistic exam questions, which give you many practice exams to ensure that you are prepared.
- **An eBook**   An electronic version of this book (eBook) is included for when you do not want to carry the printed book with you. The eBook is in Portable Document Format (PDF), and you can view it by using Adobe Acrobat or Adobe Reader.

> **Digital Content for Digital Book Readers:** If you bought a digital-only edition of this book, you can enjoy select content from the print edition's companion CD.
> Visit **http://go.microsoft.com/fwlink/?/LinkId=116279** to get your downloadable content. This content is always up-to-date and available to all readers.

How to Install the Practice Tests

To install the practice test software from the companion CD to your hard disk, do the following:

- Insert the companion CD into your CD drive and accept the license agreement. A CD menu appears.

NOTE   If the CD menu does not appear

If the CD menu or the license agreement does not appear, AutoRun might be disabled on your computer. Refer to the Readme.txt file on the CD-ROM for alternate installation instructions.

- Click Practice Tests and follow the instructions on the screen.

How to Use the Practice Tests

To start the practice test software, follow these steps:

- Choose Start/All Programs/Microsoft Press Training Kit Exam Prep. A window appears that shows all the Microsoft Press training kit exam suites installed on your computer.
- Double-click the lesson review or practice test you want to use.

NOTE Lesson reviews vs. practice tests

Select the (70-632) Microsoft Office Project 2007, Managing Projects lesson review to use the questions from the "Lesson Review" sections of this book. Select the (70-632) Microsoft Office Project 2007, Managing Projects practice test to use a pool of 200 questions similar to those that appear on the 70-632 certification exam.

Lesson Review Options

When you start a lesson review, the Custom Mode dialog box appears so that you can configure your test. You can click OK to accept the defaults, or you can customize the number of questions you want, how the practice test software works, which exam objectives you want the questions to relate to, and whether you want your lesson review to be timed. If you are retaking a test, you can select whether you want to see all the questions again or only the questions you missed or did not answer.

After you click OK, your lesson review starts.

- To take a test, answer the questions and use the Next, Previous, and Go To buttons to move from question to question.
- After you answer an individual question, if you want to see which answers are correct—along with an explanation of each correct answer—click Explanation.
- If you prefer to wait until the end of the text to see how you did, answer all the questions and then click Score Test. You will see a summary of the exam objectives you chose and the percentage of questions you got right overall and per objective. You can print a copy of your test, review your answers, or retake the test.

Practice Test Options

When you start a practice test, you choose whether to take the test in Certification Mode, Study Mode, or Custom Mode:

- **Certification Mode**   Closely resembles the experience of taking a certification exam. The test has a set number of questions. It is timed, and you cannot pause and restart the time.

- **Study Mode**   Creates an untimed test in which you can review the correct answers and the explanations after you answer each question.
- **Custom Mode**   Gives you full control over the test options so that you can customize them as you like.

When you are taking the test, the user interface in all modes is basically the same but with different options enabled or disabled depending on the mode. The main options are discussed in the previous section, "Lesson Review Options."

When you review your answer to an individual practice test question, a "References" section is provided that lists where in the training kit you can find the information that relates to that question and provides links to other sources of information. After you click Test Results to score your entire practice test, you can click the Learning Plan tab to see a list of references for every objective.

How to Uninstall the Practice Tests

To uninstall the practice test software for a training kit, use the Add Or Remove Programs option (Windows XP) or the Program And Features option (Windows Vista) in Windows Control Panel.

Microsoft Certified Professional Program

The Microsoft certifications provide the best method to prove your command of current Microsoft products and technologies. The exams and corresponding certifications are developed to validate your mastery of critical competencies as you design and develop, or implement and support, solutions with Microsoft products and technologies. Computer professionals who become Microsoft-certified are recognized as experts and are sought after industry-wide. Certification brings a variety of benefits to the individual and to employers and organizations.

MORE INFO   All the Microsoft certifications

For a full list of Microsoft certifications, go to *www.microsoft.com/learning/mcp/default.asp*.

Technical Support

Every effort has been made to ensure the accuracy of this book and the contents of the companion CD. If you have comments, questions, or ideas regarding this book or the companion CD, please send them to Microsoft Press by using either of the following methods:

- E-mail: tkinput@microsoft.com

- Postal mail at:
  Microsoft Press
  Attn: *MCTS Self-Paced Training Kit (Exam 70-632): Managing Projects with Microsoft Office Project 2007*, Editor
  One Microsoft Way
  Redmond, WA 98052-6399

For additional support information regarding this book and the CD-ROM (including answers to commonly asked questions about installation and use), visit the Microsoft Press Technical Support Web site at *www.microsoft.com/learning/supports/books/*. To connect directly to the Microsoft Knowledge Base and enter a query, visit *http://support.microsoft.coml/search/*. For support information regarding Microsoft software, connect to *http://support.microsoft.com*.

Chapter 1
Project Initiation

Successful projects often start with a concentrated planning phase. In project management circles this period of project planning helps you develop your project charter statement, goals, and a specific definition of success. Without these items it is likely your project will not succeed.

A project is always a temporary organization of related tasks that is set up to deliver one or more products or goals. Tracking those tasks in an electronic format can be crucial to determining the overall project cost and time (leaving it to the project manager to measure the quality outside of Microsoft Office Project 2007). Contained in a set start date or finish date, or both, the primary objective of project management is to ensure product delivery on time, within budget (cost), and to the stakeholder's expected quality.

Simply put, projects succeed through planning, quality controls, and regular communication. As the project manager, it's your job to make sure your project is a success. Project can assist you in this process by organizing the project tasks and milestones in a manageable format, helping you communicate project status to your project team members and stakeholders, and serving as a reference point for future projects that gives you an accurate snapshot of not only the time frame of a particular project but also the associated costs and effort.

The true challenge of managing projects involves making decisions about how and whether to make trade-offs among time, cost, quality, and scope. Balancing these four components is the key to successful project management. Project can help you monitor these components to ensure that your projects achieve the project objectives and come in on time, within budget, and at an agreed-upon level of quality. Much of the Initiation phase of project management happens in meetings and brainstorming sessions. This chapter gives you the information you will need to use Project for later phases and the information you will need to set up projects, tasks, and calendars in Project.

Exam objectives in this chapter:
- Set up Interface Options.
- Select a template.
- Enter project information.
- Manage calendars.
- Create and modify tasks.
- Estimate and budget tasks.

Lessons in this chapter:

Before You Begin

This chapter (and this book) assumes that the average reader is an experienced project manager. Following the Project Management Body of Knowledge (PMBOK), you'll see standard project management terms—many of which might already be familiar. Additionally, in keeping with PMBOK, this book has been organized into chapters that logically follow the standardized process groups: Initiating, Planning, Executing, Controlling, and Closing. All of this has created an environment conducive not only to understanding Project but also to a methodology with which project managers are already familiar.

Before you begin, you should:

- Understand common project management terms such as stakeholder, sponsor, tasks, scope, and milestone
- Have a familiarity with the Project Management Body of Knowledge (PMBOK)
- Understand common Windows functions including Save, Close, and New

---

Real World

Deanna Reynolds

More and more, I'm seeing project managers' assistants in the classroom looking to learn how to use Project right alongside their supervisors. I've even seen entire project teams in a classroom with their designated project manager. Unfortunately, these assistants and team members often have a difficult time understanding the flow of the Project software. That's because Project was developed from a project manager's viewpoint. Although many people have experience as project team members, they don't always understand the project process flow or key project management terms. To fully understand how a program like Project works, you should have a basic understanding of project management theory. With this fundamental knowledge baseline, using Project becomes second nature because you can often predict how the program will respond. That's not to say that non-project managers can't understand Project—they certainly can. However, for those with an underlying comprehension of project management theory, the learning curve for Project can be significantly reduced.

Lesson 1: Creating a New Project

Before you create your first project using Project, it's helpful to have a clear understanding of what Project can and cannot do. In a nutshell, Project is an electronic project management information system used to create schedules, calculate costs, and control changes in a project. Although Project can't take the place of your expert project management judgment, it can help you visually review your project plan and important milestones. Project is particularly adept at displaying the effect of project plan changes (such as changes made to the schedule and assignments) and comparing baseline and interim plans. This program is a project manager's ultimate electronic project planning and tracking tool.

Although Project can't meet with your project stakeholders to bring everyone to a consensus on the project scope and deliverables, it can help you by generating full-featured reports that you can use to effectively communicate with everyone involved in the project. Furthermore, throughout the lifecycle of your project, Project can help you anticipate potential changes to your project while tracking and communicating your project's current status to project team members and stakeholders.

Keep in mind, Project is simply a tool—not the actual project manager.

After this lesson, you will be able to:
- ■ Describe new features of the Project program.
- ■ Create a new project from a template and from an existing project.
- ■ Navigate the Project window and identify common elements.
- ■ Describe and access common Project views.
- ■ Enter initial project information.

Estimated lesson time: 90 minutes

Navigating the Project Window

At first glance, the Project window displays several familiar Microsoft Office elements. Although the Project interface doesn't display the Ribbon found in other Office 2007 programs, it does take full advantage of navigation features such as the Menu bar and task-specific toolbars. Figure 1-1 shows the default interface with the Standard and Formatting toolbars called out.

Standard Toolbar   Formatting Toolbar

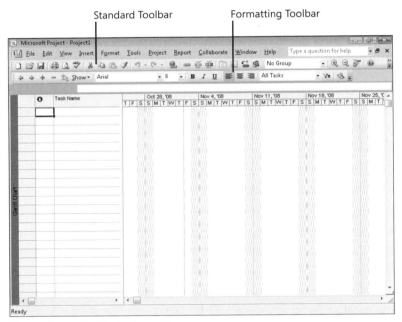

Figure 1-1   The Project interface

Toolbars

You might already be familiar with the Standard and Formatting toolbars because they offer many of the same features that other applications do. Using these toolbars, you can perform many tasks you're already familiar with (such as Save and Undo). You'll also have access to tasks specific to project management, including creating a task hierarchy, linking, and assigning resources.

In addition to the Standard and Formatting toolbars (which display by default), Project offers 12 additional customized toolbars to aid you in your work with the program, as follows:

- Collaborate
- Custom Forms
- Drawing
- Resource Management
- Tracking
- Visual Basic
- Web
- Analysis
- Compare Project Versions

- Network Diagram
- PERT Analysis
- Project Guide

The commands for the buttons found on each of these toolbars can also be found under various menu items; however, it's worthwhile to display those toolbars that contain commands you'll use most often as you work with Project.

NOTE Show additional toolbars

To show or hide any toolbar, right-click the Standard or Formatting toolbar and select or clear the desired element.

Project Guide Toolbar and the Project Guide Task Pane

One of the most common elements of the Project interface is the Project Guide. The Project Guide exists in two forms. The first is the Project Guide toolbar. The Project Guide toolbar contains five buttons and is shown in Figure 1-2, along with the Project Guide task pane.

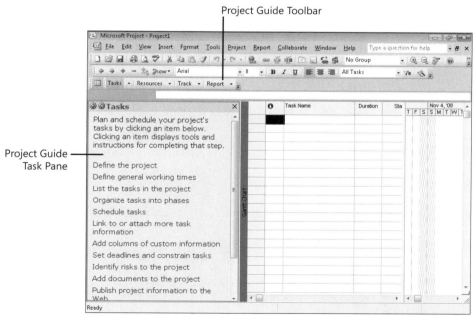

Figure 1-2 The Project Guide toolbar

The first button, when clicked, displays the Project Guide Tasks task pane (described below and shown in Figure 1-2). The remaining four buttons display a menu of activities sorted by category: Tasks, Resources, Track, and Report. Resources is selected in Figure 1-3. This toolbar acts as a mini-Menu bar, giving you access to many of the most common tasks related to project management in this program. Clicking any of these icons opens the desired view in the Project Guide task pane.

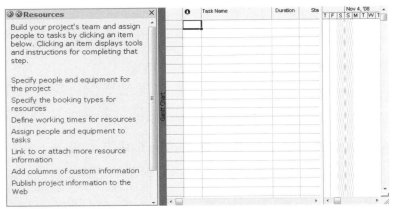

Figure 1-3   The Project Guide task pane offers quick links and wizards

The Project Guide task pane often offers wizards to guide you through tasks related to defining, managing, and tracking your new project. Two of the best features found on the Project Guide task pane are the Hint and More Information links located near the end of almost any displayed text. You can click either of these links for targeted Help text. Figure 1-4 shows the Help link related to listing tasks in a project.

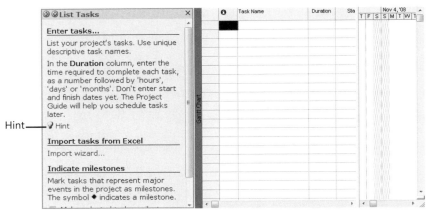

Figure 1-4   The Project Guide task pane offers quick links to help and hints

NOTE   **Project Guide toolbar and tasks pane**

One of the ways to display both the Project Guide toolbar and the Project Guide task pane is to open the Tools menu, choose Options to open the Options dialog box, and then click the Interface tab. In the Project Guide settings section, select the Display Project Guide check box. This way, each time you open Microsoft Project, the Project Guide toolbar and task pane will open as well. You can then toggle the Project Guide task pane on and off by clicking the Show/Hide Project Guide icon on the Project Guide toolbar. You can also view the Project Guide by opening the View menu and then choosing Turn On Project Guide.

Quick Check

- You want to use the Project Guide task pane to help you initiate your project, but it takes up too much of your screen. How do you toggle the task pane on and off?

Quick Check Answer

- Click the Show/Hide Project Guide icon in the Project Guide toolbar.

Features

Although the interface of Project hasn't changed dramatically from previous versions of the software, several key elements in the way the software works with projects have—for the better.

Exam Tip   When used independently (without the implementation of Project Server), both Project 2007 Standard and Project 2007 Professional offer the same upgraded features to you, the end user. This means that, when preparing for and taking the certification exam, you don't need to worry about the differences between the "Standard" and "Professional" versions. However, you might be asked questions related to features that are new to Project.

In addition to enhancing some preexisting areas by creating new templates, enabling multiple undo and redo levels, and allowing one-time exceptions to working times, other features are entirely new, such as change highlighting and visual reports.

Project Templates

Developed according to popular industry standards, Project offers 29 new built-in project templates. These templates include, among others:

- Annual Report Preparation
- Human Resource Information System Implementation
- Internal Readiness Training

- Security Infrastructure Improvement Plan
- Vendor Request For Proposal (RFP) Solicitation

For more information on using built-in templates to create your project plans, see the section entitled "Creating a New Project from a Template" later in this chapter.

To see all of the templates that come with Project, follow these steps:

1. Click File, and then choose New.
2. In the New Project task pane, shown in Figure 1-5, click On Computer.

Figure 1-5   Many templates are already available on your computer

3. In the Templates dialog box, shown in Figure 1-6, click the Project Templates tab.

Figure 1-6   The Project Templates tab of the Templates dialog box

4. Double-click any template to open it in Project.

Change Highlighting

One seemingly small change to a single task or resource can create a domino effect of change across many related tasks in terms of start/finish dates and task duration. With the new change highlighting feature, Project highlights changed areas on the Task or Resource Sheet. This way, when you make one change, you can see the ripple effect that the change might have throughout your entire project. By default, the change highlighting feature is enabled. You can disable this feature (or enable it again) by choosing View, Hide Change Highlighting (View, Show Change Highlighting) from the Menu bar.

For more information on change highlighting, see Chapter 3, "Execute, Monitor, and Control the Project Plan."

Exam Tip   With Change Highlighting turned on, you can see the effects of a change to your project before saving them. You can also turn off this feature. Make sure you know this before taking the exam.

Visual Reports

Nothing communicates project progress or costs better than a graph. The new Visual Reports in Project offer a wealth of graphical displays. Typically displayed in the form of bar and pie charts, these visual reports automatically compile and export the related project information to either Excel (as a PivotTable or PivotChart) or Visio (as a PivotDiagram). After the data has been exported, you have the option of displaying the data at different angles. Additionally, you can create your own customized visual reports.

For more information on visual reports, see Chapter 5, "Closing the Project."

Working/Nonworking Time

In Project, you've always had the ability to define both working and nonworking time for your resources, tasks, and project. However, in Project, you can now create one-time exceptions to the already predefined working times. Additionally, you can create alternative work week schedules for those working times that differ from week to week but still follow a somewhat regular working time pattern.

For more information on defining working and nonworking time within your project schedule, see the section entitled "Working with the Project Calendar" later in this chapter.

Multiple Undo/Redo

One of the new features not covered in depth in this book but worth mentioning is the option to use the Undo and Redo commands to retrace multiple steps. In Project you now have the option of setting your program preferences to undo or redo your last 99 steps. For more information on customizing Undo levels, see Chapter 2, "Project Planning."

Common Project Views

Although projects by their very nature are unique, project management typically follows the same set of processes (initiating, planning, executing, controlling, and closing). In implementing those processes into your project plan, Project offers a number of views—all of which you can access from the View menu.

However, project managers most often use eight views:

- Calendar
- Gantt Chart
- Network Diagram
- Task Usage
- Tracking Gantt
- Resource Graph
- Resource Sheet
- Resource Usage

The easiest way to access these views is from the View Bar. Figure 1-7 shows the View Bar in the Project interface. You add the View Bar by selecting View from the Menu bar and selecting View Bar. When displayed, the View Bar anchors to the left side of your Project window vertically and displays a related icon for each of these common views.

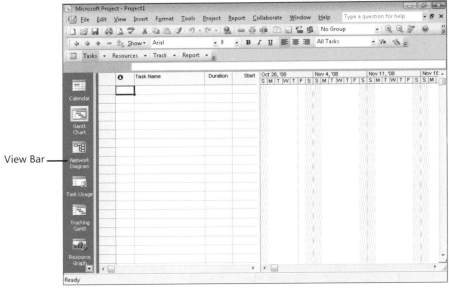

Figure 1-7 The View Bar offers quick access to the most popular project views

Exam Tip   In preparing for the exam, you'll want to be very familiar with the information each of these views provides. Although you probably won't be asked how to display a specific view, it is likely you'll be given a scenario in which you need to display certain information and asked which view provides the most accurate representation of the data.

Calendar

Typically, the Calendar view displays a month or week view of your project at a glance with upcoming tasks. You can very easily access the Calendar view by clicking Calendar on the View Bar, which is the first icon, as shown in Figure 1-7.

On the Calendar view individual tasks are represented as boxes with a thin, blue outline with higher-level, summary tasks in blue, bold text. You can also quickly note milestones by a darkly shaded box and durations are clearly spelled out next to both tasks and summary tasks.

Although monthly and weekly view buttons are clearly prominent in Calendar view (see Figure 1-8), you can click the Custom button to create a view that most accurately depicts the task timeline you need to see.

You can also view the Calendar view from the View menu by selecting Calendar. Figure 1-8 shows Calendar view.

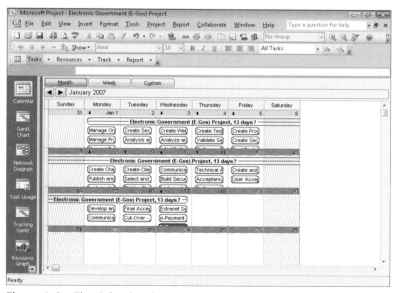

Figure 1-8   The Calendar view

Gantt Chart

The Gantt Chart is displayed by default when you launch Project and is widely considered the most common view. The Gantt Chart view is actually a combination of a visual Gantt Chart and the Entry table. The Entry table is displayed on the left side of the Gantt Chart view and is most recognizable by its spreadsheet-like appearance; however, you can choose to display various other tables with more relevant data based on the work you are currently doing. Figure 1-9 shows the default Gantt Chart view.

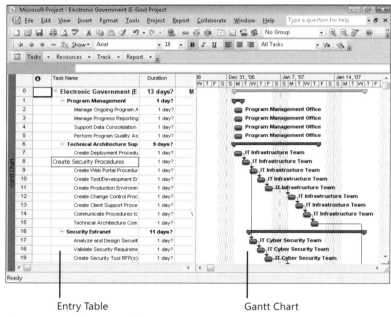

Entry Table   Gantt Chart

Figure 1-9   The Gantt Chart view contains two parts, the Entry table and the Gantt Chart

There are many Gantt Chart views, including:

- Bar Rollup
- Detail Gantt
- Gantt Chart
- Leveling Gantt
- Milestone Date Rollup
- Milestone Rollup
- Multiple Baselines Gantt
- PA_Expected Gantt
- PA_Optimistic Gantt

- PA_Pessimistic Gantt
- Tracking Gantt

You can locate these additional views from the View Bar and View menu. Taking full advantage of displaying both a table and a chart, the Gantt Chart displays bars that span a timescale. This view is particularly beneficial to a project manager when entering tasks and defining the project's initial work breakdown structure. After project work has begun, the Tracking Gantt view is often used to view the project schedule progress. You will work in many of these views throughout this book.

Tables   Tables control what task or resource information is presented in a sheet view. With tables, you can control the columns, or fields, that appear in the table. Additionally, you can drag the dividers between the field names to change the size of the columns as desired. When you first view the Gantt Chart, the Entry table might appear to have only two or three columns even though it has seven columns by default. To see the other columns, drag the divider to the right. See Figure 1-10. Optionally, you can scroll to the right (and left) using the horizontal scroll bar displayed at the bottom of the Entry table.

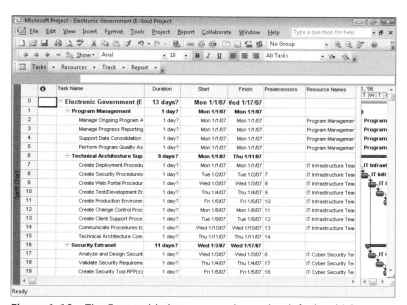

Figure 1-10   The Entry table has seven columns by default, which you can see by dragging the divider bar to the right

You can apply a different table to the Gantt Chart view by opening the View menu, and then choosing Table. This opens a submenu of available tables from which you can choose. This menu option is shown in Figure 1-11.

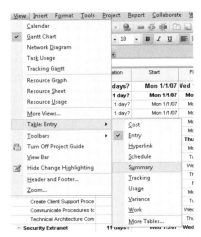

Figure 1-11   The View menu table options

MORE INFO   Project tables

The Entry table is just one of many tables you can use to display your project information. In fact, not only are there several additional tables from which you can choose by choosing View/Table/ More Tables, but tables are also fully customizable. For more information on customizing tables and creating custom fields (columns), see Chapter 4, "Team Collaboration and Multiple Projects."

Printing the Gantt Chart   When printing the Gantt Chart view, Project prints the view fairly close to what you see on the screen. This means that if two columns of the Entry table are displayed along with a timescale that displays task bars by week, that's the view that prints. However, if you modify the view to display three Entry table columns along with a timescale that displays task bars by quarter, that's the view that prints. As such, you'll want to modify your Gantt Chart view by positioning the divider bar and adjusting the timescale before opening the Print dialog box. Figure 1-12 shows the divider bar in dark black, which you can move by clicking and dragging.

Additionally, there are several printing options available in the Print dialog box, such as modifying the Gantt Chart legend (to help less experienced chart readers understand what they are looking at), customizing headers and footers, and forcing the first few columns of the Entry table to display on every printed page (particularly good for multiple page printouts). You'll learn more about this in the next exercise.

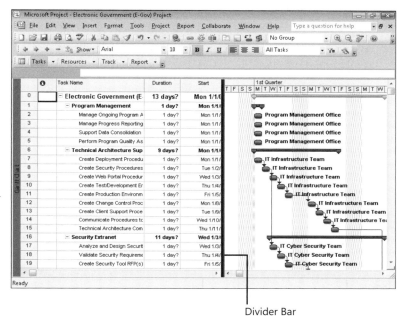

Divider Bar

Figure 1-12   Click and drag the divider bar to reposition it

In the following exercise, you'll open an existing template so you'll have some data to view and see what that data looks like in a Gantt Chart. (You might also want to find the Standard and Formatting toolbars and show and hide various toolbars to help familiarize yourself with the interface.)

To see what a Gantt Chart with a little data in it looks like and to change and print a Gantt Chart, complete the following steps:

1. Click File, and then choose New.
2. Under Templates, click On Computer.
3. Click the Project Templates tab.
4. Select the Annual Report Preparation template, as shown in Figure 1-13.
5. Click OK.
6. From the View menu, choose View Bar—unless the View Bar is already showing. (If desired, close the Project Guide task pane.)
7. From the View Bar, click Gantt Chart.
8. From the Format menu, choose Timescale.

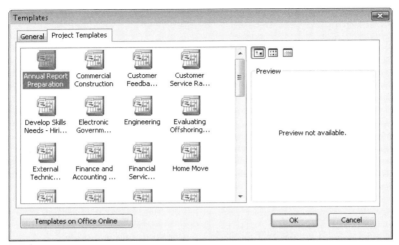

Figure 1-13   Choosing a template from the Project Template choices

9. In the Timescale dialog box, shown in Figure 1-14, under Middle Tier Formatting, in the Units window, change the view from the default of Weeks to Months.

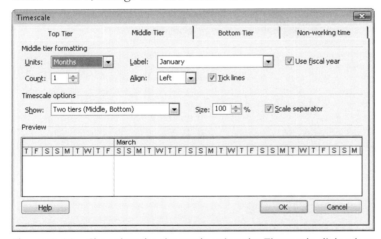

Figure 1-14   Changing the timescale using the Timescale dialog box

10. Click OK. Notice the new view. This is the view you'll print.

11. Click File and then choose Print. Note the options you have for printing. Options will vary depending on the printer.

12. Click OK to print or click Cancel to cancel printing.

13. Leave this project open to see what other views look like throughout this chapter.

MORE INFO   **Printing: a familiar task**

You print a Gantt Chart the same way you print any document. Select the printer and the print range (all or specific pages) and choose the number of copies to create. What you see will vary depending on your printer manufacturer. However, with Project's Print dialog box you also have the option to print data only for specific dates.

Network Diagram

Although the Gantt Chart view consists of a table and a chart, the Network Diagram view is based entirely on a chart. Unlike the Gantt Chart, which relies on a timescale to display the task bars, the Network Diagram displays project tasks in a flowchart format. Figure 1-15 shows a project open in Network Diagram view.

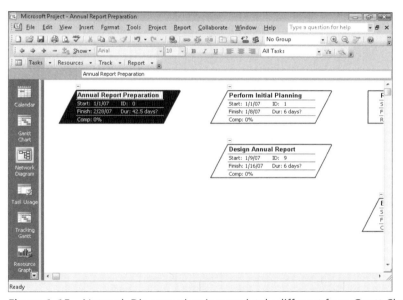

Figure 1-15   Network Diagram view is completely different from Gantt Chart view

The Network Diagram offers a view closest to the PERT (Program Evaluation and Review Technique) Chart. In Project you'll use the Network Diagram to work with tasks and task dependencies. For many project managers this is a familiar view and one they can work comfortably because it mimics a flowchart feel. Click View and then choose Network Diagram in any open project to see what a Network Diagram looks like. If you are working with the View Bar, you can also click the Network Diagram button to display this view.

Printing the Network Diagram   As you learned in the section on printing the Gantt Chart, the Gantt Chart printed size is closely based on the zoom level of the Gantt Chart. However, modifying the zoom level on the Network Diagram has no bearing on the size at which the diagram will print. To modify the printed size of a Network Diagram, you'll need to change your print settings in the Page Setup dialog box. After you open this dialog box, you have many of the same options you saw when printing a Gantt Chart, such as modifying the legend, customizing headers and footers, and adjusting the percentage level at which the diagram prints.

MORE INFO   Printing

Because preparing to print only involves clicking File and then Print and then configuring options specific to your printer, it does not need more explanation here. However, at the end of this chapter, there are several practice exercises—one of which involves printing a Network Diagram.

Quick Check

1. What view most closely relates to the project's tasks and task dependencies using the Program Evaluation and Review Technique? Is it the Network Diagram View, the Entry Table View, or the Task Usage view?
2. You like the Gantt Chart view, but have a need to see the projected costs of your project along with the Gantt Chart. Which table should you apply to show the projected costs for the project?

Quick Check Answers

1. Select the Network Diagram view and make any changes to the print preferences in the print dialog box before printing.
2. View the Gantt Chart and then apply the Cost table.

Task Usage

Closely mimicking the look of two side-by-side tables, the Task Usage view displays the Usage table on the left side of the view with a related timesheet view on the right. In this view you can work with your project's task assignments and see work or costs for each task according to a timescale you can customize. Click View, and then choose Task Usage in any open project to see the results. Figure 1-16 shows this view. If you have displayed the View Bar, you can also click the Task Usage icon to switch to this view.

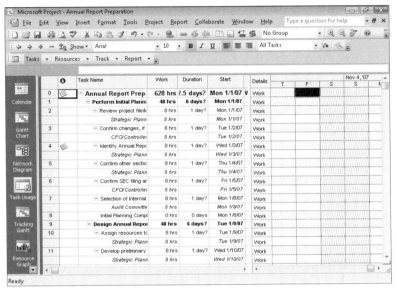

Figure 1-16   The Task Usage view

Tracking Gantt

Looking much like the Gantt Chart view, the Tracking Gantt takes viewing your tasks a step further by showing both the current task bars and the baseline bars for each task. This is the view you'll use when you need to compare the actual schedule (where you are today) with the baseline schedule (where you thought you'd be today). Figure 1-17 shows what a Tracking Gantt Chart looks like. To display the Tracking Gantt Chart, open the View menu and then choose Tracking Gantt in any open project.

MORE INFO   Setting baselines

To see the full effect of a Tracking Gantt Chart, you'll need to open a project file with a set baseline. For more information on setting baseline data on a project file, see Chapter 2.

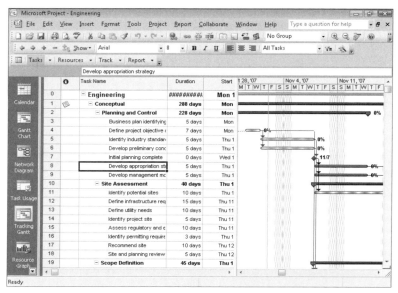

Figure 1-17   The Tracking Gantt Chart

Resource Graph

The Resource Graph is one of the best views for visually displaying resource overallocations for a single resource or a group of resources. The Resource Graph displays in a traditional bar chart format with blue bars representing work and red bars representing overallocation. To see what a resource graph offers, click View and then choose Resource Graph in any open project.

Resource Sheet

When you have a need to enter, edit, and review the project resources, you'll want to use the Resource Sheet. Displaying data in a table-like format, you can work with resources in much the same way you work with tasks in a table. Like in the Resource Graph, you can see overallocation in the Resource Sheet—easily identifiable by red text. To see what the Resource Sheet offers, click View and then choose Resource Sheet in any open project.

Resource Usage

Like the Task Usage view, the Resource Usage view is another assignment data view. In this view the Usage table (modified to sort the data by resource) is displayed on the left side of the view with a related timesheet view on the right. In this view you can work with your project task assignments and see work or costs for each resource according to a timescale you can customize. To see what the results look like, click View and then choose Resource Usage in any open project.

Exam Tip   In preparing for the exam, you'll want to be very familiar with the information each of these views provides. Take time now to look at each of the views, and make a note of what each view offers.

Quick Check

1. What view should you use when you need to compare the actual schedule (where you are today) with the baseline schedule (where you thought you'd be today)? Choose from Track Usage, Tracking Gantt, or Resource Usage.
2. You need to display, in chart form, resource overallocations for a single resource or a group of resources. Should you choose Resource Graph, Resource Sheet, or Resource Usage view?

Quick Check Answers

1. Tracking Gantt.
2. Resource Graph view.

Working with the Timescale

In several views the related data is displayed with a timescale. In Project the timescale is very similar to the zoom level of the project file. Rather than displaying a view at 50 percent or 100 percent (as you would see in Microsoft Office Word 2007 or Microsoft Office Excel 2007), you display many of the views in Project based on hours, days, weeks, months, quarters, and so on. There are several ways to modify the zoom level, and, as a result, the timescale in Project.

Zoom In/Zoom Out   Like most Microsoft Office programs, Project offers two zoom buttons for controlling the view level of your file. To zoom in or zoom out on the current project view, click the Zoom In or Zoom Out buttons located on the Standard toolbar. Figure 1-18 shows the Zoom In and Zoom Out buttons.

Figure 1-18   The Zoom In and Zoom Out buttons

View: Zoom   For a little more control over the zoom level of your view, you can open the Zoom dialog box by clicking View and then choosing Zoom from the menu.

In the Zoom dialog box you can choose to view your project file based on a selected time frame, including the following:

- 1 week
- 2 weeks
- 1 month
- 2 months
- Entire Project
- Custom

Timescale   On many of the views in Project (including, among others, the Gantt Chart view, Tracking Gantt Chart, Resource Graph, and Resource Usage Sheet), a timescale displays near the top of the view (and below the toolbars).

This timescale is an accurate representation of the current zoom level of the project file on which you are working. You can also modify the zoom level and the data that appears on this timescale by right-clicking the timescale and choosing Timescale from the shortcut menu, as shown in Figure 1-19.

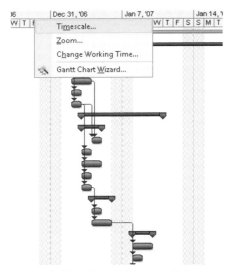

Figure 1-19   Timescale right-click options

After viewing the Timescale dialog box, you can choose how many tiers the timescale displays (one, two, or three) and what data appears on each tier.

Creating a New Project from a Template

During planning you can create your project file. One way to create a new file is to take full advantage of the 29 new templates added to Project. These templates (along with 12 from previous Project versions) cover a wide-range of topics, including the following:

- Commercial Construction
- Engineering
- Finance and Accounting System Implementation
- Human Resources Information System Implementation
- Managing Incoming Request for Quotes (RFQs)
- Marketing Campaign Planning
- New Business
- New Product
- Office Move
- Performance Reviews
- Software Development
- Vendor Request For Proposal (RFP) Solicitation

MORE INFO   **Project templates**

This is only a partial list of available templates. You can see all of the available predefined templates in the New Project dialog box by clicking the Project Templates tab.

Using a predefined template can save a tremendous amount of time in setting up a new project because each template already contains tasks and resources along with task relationships and resource assignments.

To create a new project from a template, follow these steps:

1. On the File menu, choose New.
2. In the New Project task pane, under Templates, click On Computer.
3. Click the Project Templates tab.
4. Select a template and click OK.

MORE INFO   **Templates on Office Online**

If you don't see the template you need in the On Computer section of the Templates options, you can click Templates on Office Online in either the Templates dialog box or the New Project pane and search for a template that more closely matches your current project.

Creating a New Project from an Existing Project

Even though projects are unique, often you'll have similar tasks and even more likely, similar resources, across projects. Rather than retyping all of the project information to create a new project file, you can create a new project file based on an existing project file.

When you create a project file based on a template, there are several constants, such as tasks and resources. When you create a project file based on an existing file, there might still be a little required cleanup work because existing project files often contain actuals, such as task progress, or extraneous information, such as constraints. You need to remove this data to allow the new project file to automatically reschedule.

MORE INFO   **Creating templates**

For more information on creating templates, see Chapter 4.

To create a new project from an existing project, follow these steps:

1. On the File menu, click New.
2. In the New Project task pane, under New, click From Existing Project.
3. Browse to the location of the existing project and click Create New.

NOTE   **Using project files earlier than Microsoft Project 98**

Before creating a new project based on an existing project that was created using Microsoft Project 98 or earlier, you first need to open the old file in Project and save it in the MPX file format.

When you create a new project based on an existing project that contains constraints, you'll need to adjust the dates right away. There is more than one way to do this, as with other Project tasks. Explaining this option lets you see one of them. To adjust the dates of an open existing project, complete the following steps:

1. Right-click the Standard toolbar and choose Analysis to show the Analysis toolbar.
2. Click Adjust Dates on the Analysis toolbar.
3. In the Adjust Dates dialog box, as shown in Figure 1-20, enter a new project start date.
4. Click OK.

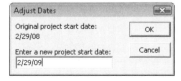

Figure 1-20   The Adjust Dates option

Quick Check

1. You are using an existing project from another department in your company to start your own project for moving to a new building. When you open it, the project doesn't have the right start date. How can you change the start date?

2. Your company has created a new product and is ready to initiate a project launch. You don't think you have an existing project to work from, but you also do not want to create a project from scratch. What should you do?

Quick Check Answers

1. Click Adjust Dates on the Analysis toolbar, and, in the Adjust Dates dialog box, enter a new project start date.

2. Create the project using the New Product Launch template.

Real World

Deanna Reynolds

As someone who has worked with projects, you understand that a project, by its very nature, is unique. In fact, that's the ultimate definition of a project and what distinguishes a project from a regular job activity. Just because a project is unique doesn't mean that similar tasks aren't performed from one project to the next and that the same people aren't working on multiple projects over a period of time. Just as you understand that projects are unique, you've probably also felt a certain sense of déjà vu as you work through (particularly initiating and planning) new projects. That's why the option of creating a new project from an existing project is available. This way you won't find yourself reinventing the wheel by creating an entirely new project. By creating a new project from an existing project, you can keep the constants that remain the same from one project to the next (such as a specific set of resources) and eliminate the repetitiveness of entering them each time you launch a new project file.

Exam Tip   You might see one or more questions on the exam related to applying lessons learned from previous projects to new projects. One way of accomplishing this is by creating a new project based on an existing project. Another option is to create a project file template you can use over and over again. For more information on creating a new project plan template, see Chapter 4.

Creating a New Project from a Blank Project

For total control over creating a new project file, you can create a new file based on the Blank project template. Of course, doing so means you'll have to enter every task, resource, and assignment.

When you create a new project file based on the Blank Project template, the start date of the project defaults to the current date. To create a new, blank project, click File, choose New, and then click Blank Project.

Entering Initial Project Information

After you've created a new project file, you can choose whether the project tasks and work are scheduled from a project start date or a project finish date. Additionally, you can define specific file properties.

Using the Project Guide as a means of accessing the most common tasks related to project management was discussed earlier in this chapter. One such task is defining the project by entering initial project information, such as the project start date.

To open the Project Guide and enter a start date, follow these steps:

1. Display the Project Guide task pane and toolbar as described earlier.
2. In the Project Guide toolbar, click Tasks, and in the task pane, shown in Figure 1-21, click Define The Project.

Figure 1-21   Define the project

3. Enter the date your project will begin. Click Continue To Step 2.
4. Select No when prompted to use Project Server and Project Web Access. Click Continue To Step 3.
5. Click Save And Finish.

MORE INFO   **Project Server/Project Web Access**

For the purposes of this book and the related certification exam, we have made the assumption that you will not be using Project Server or Project Web Access when working with your Project files. For more information on implementing enterprise solutions with Project Server or Project Web Access, consult the book entitled *Microsoft Office Project 2007 Inside Out*, by Teresa Stover (Microsoft Press, 2007).

Using the Project Guide task pane to enter initial project information gives you access to defining only the project start date. If you need to set a project to schedule from the finish date, you'll need to open the Project Information dialog box to make the change.

NOTE   **Scheduling from a project start date or finish date**

Typically, project management best practice tells project managers to schedule a project from the start date rather than the finish date. When a project is scheduled from the finish date, all tasks are automatically placed on the Critical Path, leaving no room for tasks to slip or project delays. Although the option to schedule from the project finish date is available, in nearly all cases a better option is to schedule from the project start date and set deadlines and constraints on the projects tasks and milestones.

To open the Project Information dialog box to modify a project finish date or a project start date, complete the following steps:

1. From the Project menu, choose Project Information.
2. In the Project Information dialog box (shown in Figure 1-22), choose to schedule either from the Project Finish Date or the Project Start Date.

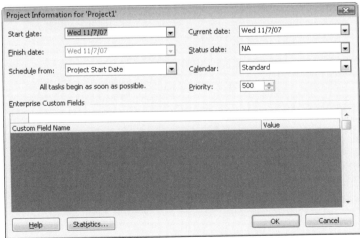

Figure 1-22   The Project Information dialog box

3. Next to Project Finish Date or Project Start date, enter a date.
4. Click OK.

MORE INFO   **Project status date and calendar**

The Project Information dialog box also contains fields related to the project status date and calendar. For more information on working with the project status date, see Chapter 3 and the following article: *http://office.microsoft.com/en-us/project/HA101487661033.aspx*. For more information on working with the project calendar, see Lesson 3 of this chapter, "Working with Calendars."

> ## Quick Check
> - You are planning a project that will start in one month. Where can you quickly configure the project's start date so that the tasks you enter will be based on that date and not the current date?
>
> ## Quick Check Answer
> - The Project Information dialog box.

Although entering a new project start date at the beginning of the project file creation process allows all new tasks to easily fall into the schedule, modifying this information after the project has begun doesn't automatically affect all tasks. For instance, if you have manually entered actual data, such as actual start or finish dates, the tasks with the manual data will not be rescheduled based on the new project start date. At the same time, tasks with constraints won't necessarily be affected either.

Exam Tip   On the exam you might be asked about defining the project start date or finish date, or both. You do this in the Project Information dialog box. It's helpful to keep in mind when considering different project management scenarios that scheduling a project from the finish date offers the least amount of flexibility because it typically places all tasks on the critical path.

PRACTICE Getting Started with Project 2007

In these practices you will review key elements of the Project interface, including how to access different views. You'll also review how to create a new blank project, a project from a template, and a project from an existing project file, as well as how to customize the project to meet your needs by entering initial project information. Finally, you'll review printing Gantt Charts and Network Diagrams.

► **Exercise 1   Set Up the Project Guide**

It's important for both passing the exam and working with Project to understand what the key interface elements are, how to navigate to them, and how to change them. One of the most commonly used options is the Project Guide and Project Guide task pane. In this exercise you'll review how to enable the Project Guide, use the Project Guide task pane, and toggle elements related to these on and off.

In this exercise you're going to use Project to start planning for an upcoming relocation to a new home in a new city. Project offers a template to help you. With the Home Move template open, you will explore the interface, the views, the View Bar, and the toolbars. After you're familiar with the interface, you'll be ready to move on to other tasks.

To complete this exercise, perform the following steps:

1. Click File and choose New.
2. In the New Project pane, below Templates, click On Computer.
3. In the Project Templates tab, select Home Move, and then click OK.
4. Scroll though the tasks in the Task Name field, and note how they are displayed in the Gantt Chart.
5. On the Menu bar, click Tools and choose Options.
6. Click the Interface tab.
7. Under Project Guide Settings, select the Display Project Guide check box if it is not selected. See Figure 1-23.

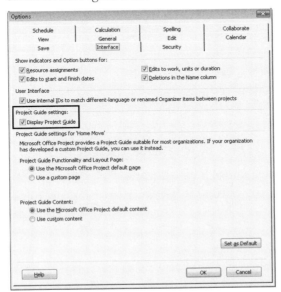

Figure 1-23   Setting the Project Guide to display automatically

8. Click OK.

9. Right-click the Standard toolbar and locate Project Guide. Select it to enable, clear it to disable. Enable the Project Guide. See Figure 1-24.

✔	Standard
✔	Formatting
	Collaborate
	Custom Forms
	Drawing
	Resource Management
	Task Pane
	Tracking
	Visual Basic
	Web
✔	Analysis
	Compare Project Versions
	Network Diagram
	PERT Analysis
✔	Project Guide
	Customize...

Figure 1-24   The toolbar shortcut menu offers many toolbars, including the project guide

10. On the View menu, choose View Bar to display the View Bar.

11. On the Project Guide toolbar, click the Show/Hide Project Guide button to enable and disable as desired. Enable the Project Guide task pane.

12. On the View Bar, click Calendar.

13. On the View Bar, click Task Usage.

14. Close the project file without saving changes.

▶ **Exercise 2   Work with Project Views**

In this exercise you'll enable some of the more common views and make notes about what is available in those views. In order to get a feel for how these views look when a project is open, you'll create a new project from a template before starting.

To complete this exercise, perform the following steps:

1. Click File, choose New, and, under Templates, select On Computer.

2. In the Project Templates tab, select the New Business template. Click OK (or double-click the template).

3. If the Project Guide task pane is open, close it. This will give you more screen "real estate."

4. From the View menu, choose Calendar. Make notes regarding what you see while using this view. See Figure 1-25.

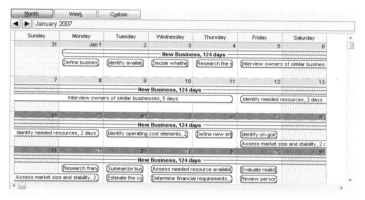

Figure 1-25   Using Calendar view

5. From the View menu, choose Network Diagram. Make notes regarding what you see while using this view.

6. On the View Bar (enable it if necessary), click Resource Graph. Make notes regarding what you see while using this view.

7. In the Resource Graph view, move forward through the different project resources using the horizontal scroll bar on the lower-left portion of the view until you see the Manager resource.

8. Using the horizontal scroll bar under the allocation bars (lower right portion of the view), scroll to view the different allocation bars for the Manager resource. Refer to Figure 1-26.

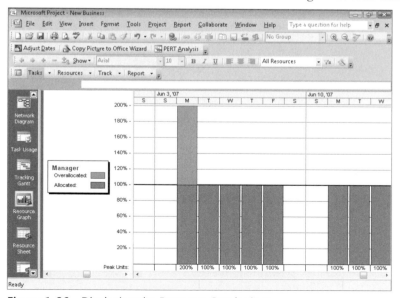

Figure 1-26   Displaying the Resource Graph view

9. From the View Bar, scroll down and click More Views. The More Views dialog box is shown in Figure 1-27.

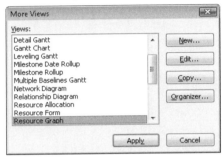

Figure 1-27   Locating more views using the More Views dialog box

10. In the More Views dialog box, select Bar Rollup. Click Apply.

11. Click the Scroll To Task button on the Standard toolbar (it's to the right of the Zoom In and Zoom Out icons) to jump to the first task in the project. Make notes regarding what you see while using this view.

12. From the View menu, choose Gantt Chart. Make notes regarding what you see while using this view. Note that this is the most commonly used view in Project.

13. Close the project file without saving changes.

▶ **Exercise 3   Create a New Project from a Template and Save It**

In this exercise you'll create a new project from a template, save the project under a new name (for use in Exercise 4), and enter initial project information using the Project Guide task pane. In the real world this is how you'll start many projects: You'll use an existing template as a starting point. Although saving a project is not a stated objective, of course, it's important to know how to do it!

To complete this exercise, perform the following steps:

1. Click File and choose New.
2. Under Templates, click On Computer.
3. Click the Project Templates tab.
4. Select the Annual Report Preparation template.
5. Click OK.
6. Click File and choose Save As.
7. In the Save As dialog box, shown in Figure 1-28 as it is in Windows Vista, change the file name to Annual Report 2008. Note the folder the file is saved in on your computer. You'll need to browse to that folder in Exercise 5.

Figure 1-28   Using the Save As dialog box to save a project

8. Click Save.

9. Enable the Project Guide task pane. (Right-click the Standard toolbar and select Project Guide from the drop-down list.)

10. In the Project Guide task pane, under Tasks, click Define the Project.

11. Under Enter Project Information, type a start date of **1/1/08**. See Figure 1-29.

Figure 1-29   Entering a start date using the Project Guide task pane

12. Click Continue To Step 2, also shown in Figure 1-29.

13. Accept the defaults in Collaborate on your project and click Continue To Step 3.

14. Click Save And Finish.

15. Save and close the project file.

▶ **Exercise 4   Start a New Project Based on an Existing Project**

In this exercise you'll create a new project from an existing project and schedule the project's start date to begin a month from the current date. You'll use the project you created in Exercise 3.

To complete this exercise, perform the following steps:

1. Click File and choose New.
2. Under New, click From Existing Project.
3. In the New From Existing Project dialog box, browse to the location of the project you saved in Exercise 3, Annual Report 2008.
4. Double-click the file to open it.
5. From the Project menu, choose Project Information.
6. In the Project Information dialog box, in the Schedule From drop-down list, select Project Start Date.
7. In the Start Date drop-down list, click the down arrow to access the calendar.
8. Use the right arrow in the calendar window to locate and select the date that is exactly one month from the current date shown.
9. Click OK.
10. Close the file without saving the changes.

▶ **Exercise 5   Print a Gantt Chart and a Network Diagram**

In this exercise you'll switch views between the Gantt Chart view and the Network Diagram view and modify a view to display the desired data to be printed. After you've configured what you want to print, you'll print the project plan.

To complete this exercise, perform the following steps:

1. Click File and choose New.
2. Under Templates, click On Computer.
3. Click the Project Templates tab.
4. Select the Annual Report Preparation template.
5. Click OK.
6. If necessary, display the View Bar.
7. From the View Bar, click Gantt Chart.
8. From the Format menu, choose Timescale.
9. In the Timescale dialog box, under Middle Tier Formatting, in the Units drop-down list, change the view from the default of Weeks to Months so more of the data can be printed.
10. Click OK.
11. Click File, and then choose Print. Note the options you have for printing. Options will vary depending on the printer.
12. Click OK to print or click Cancel.
13. Click View and choose Network Diagram.

14. Click File, and then choose Print.
15. In the Print dialog box, click Preview.
16. Note what your print job will look like, and change printer properties and preferences as desired.
17. Click Page Setup to change the printed page properties.
18. Click Close to close the Preview window.

Lesson Summary

- Project helps you organize project tasks and milestones, communicate project status, and save the project as a starting point for future projects.

- Standard, Formatting, and Project Guide toolbars are some of the most frequently used toolbars in Project. There are over a dozen toolbars, all available by right-clicking any open toolbar.

- Project offers 29 new templates. These range from Annual Report Preparation to Vendor Request For Proposal Solicitation. Using a predefined template can save a tremendous amount of time because the template already contains much of the information you initially need to create, including tasks, resources, task relationships, and resource assignments.

- Instead of retyping all of the project information to create a new project file, you can create a new project file based on an existing project file. Additionally, you can create a new project file from the Blank project template.

- After you've created a new project file, you can choose whether the project tasks and work are scheduled from a project start date or a project finish date by opening the Project Information dialog box. From this same location you can modify a project's start or end date.

- New features and enhancements include the ability to apply multiple undo and redo levels, allowing one-time exceptions to working times, and the ability to actively see project modifications through change highlighting and visual reports.

- You can print Gantt Charts and Network Diagrams, and each offers print options, including what dates to print.

Lesson Review

You can use the following questions to test your knowledge of the information in Lesson 1, "Creating a New Project." The questions are also available on the companion CD if you prefer to review them in electronic form.

NOTE Answers

Answers to these questions and explanations of why each answer choice is correct or incorrect are located in the "Answers" section at the end of the book.

1. You open Project to create a new project for your company regarding event planning and execution. You want to use the Project Guide task pane to help you initiate the project. However, when you right-click the Standard toolbar, Project Guide is not available. How can you enable the Project Guide? (Choose all that apply.)

    A. Choose Turn On Project Guide from the View menu.

    B. Change the view from Gantt Chart to Calendar. Because the Gantt Chart is so large there is no room for the Project Guide task pane.

    C. From the Insert menu, choose Turn On Project Guide.

    D. Select the Enable Display Project Guide check box on the Interface tab in the Options dialog box.

2. John is in charge of putting together the company's presence at the 2008 electronics industry tradeshow. It's the first time his company will be involved in a tradeshow. He does not want to start a new project and have to input common tasks like reviewing tradeshow fees, obtaining sponsor approval, and determining payment options, among other things. Which of the following can he use to get started? (Choose all that apply.)

    A. Use an existing tradeshow project on his company's server.

    B. Use the Project template Tradeshow Planning, Execution, and Wrap-Up.

    C. Access Microsoft Office Online and look for an appropriate template there.

    D. Use the Project Guide task pane to initiate the project and type the start date.

3. You are in charge of setting up a project for internal readiness training for getting employees trained on using the new phone system you plan to install in three weeks. Your boss suggests you use the Project template named "Internal Readiness Training." How do you access this template?

    A. Click File, choose New, and from the New Project task pane, click On Computer. Click the Project Templates tab and select the Internal Readiness Training template.

    B. On the Project Guide toolbar, click Resources, and from the Project Guide task pane, click Specify Template. Click the Project Templates tab and select Internal Readiness Training.

    C. From the Project menu, choose Project Information. In the Project Information dialog box, select the template to use.

    D. Click File, choose New, and from the New Project task pane, click Blank Project. Import the Internal Readiness Training template.

4. Which would you select to create a new project with total control so that you can enter every task, resource, and assignment yourself?

    A. A template from Office Online

    B. An existing project

    C. Any project under the Project Templates tab in the Templates dialog box

    D. A blank project

5. You need to print a Gantt Chart to show your boss how much you've achieved over the last month in relation to your project's timeline. However, each time you print the Gantt Chart, you do not get the desired results. You want the chart to fit on one page, in Landscape view, and with the results only from the last month showing. What do you do?

    A. Format the Timescale as Days. Before printing the document, select the dates you want to print in the Timescale options in the Print dialog box. Use the printer's advanced properties to select Landscape view.

    B. Format the Timescale as Years. Before printing the document, select the dates in the Timescale options in the Print dialog box. Use the printer's advanced properties to select Landscape view.

    C. Format the Timescale as Months. Print the document using Landscape view using your printer's properties page. Project's Print feature will make the Gantt Chart fit on the printed page by default.

    D. Adjust the zoom level of the displayed Gantt Chart to display the date range you want to print all in your window. Before printing the document, select the dates in the Timescale options in the Print dialog box. Use the printer's advanced properties to select Landscape view.

6. You need to print a network diagram of your entire project. Unfortunately, each time you click Print and accept the default settings from the Print dialog box, the data you want to print doesn't print on a single page. How can you solve this problem?

    A. Modify the print settings in the Print dialog box.

    B. Modify the zoom level on the Network Diagram to match the size at which the diagram will print.

    C. Modify the Network Diagram legend in the Project Information dialog box.

    D. Turn off the Project Guide task pane, and then print with the Print dialog box defaults.

Lesson 2: Working with Tasks

As most project managers will probably agree, tasks are the heart of any project. In fact, breaking a project's scope down into manageable work packages (each typically lasting between 8 and 80 hours) is one of the first rules of project management. Another key element of project management is allotting the appropriate amount of time to each task. Ideally, you would have the time parameters for any given task written down in a handy file; however, the project stakeholders typically rely on you as the project manager to obtain accurate estimated task durations from knowledgeable resources.

This lesson covers the basics of adding tasks to a project file and working with the Task Information dialog box to add and modify tasks. It also explains task durations and how to use the Program Evaluation and Review Technique (PERT) method to estimate them. Understanding the PERT method and learning a simple calculation can go a long way toward helping you understand how Project works behind the scenes to help you schedule and manage your project-related tasks.

> **After this lesson, you will be able to:**
> - Add work packages to your project file.
> - Use the Task Information dialog box to add and edit task information.
> - Add and estimate task durations.
> - Define project milestones.
>
> **Estimated lesson time: 120 minutes**

> **Real World**
>
> *Deanna Reynolds and Joli Ballew*
>
> Some of the most successful students of Project are those who come in with a good working knowledge of Office Excel. That's because the two programs have a lot of similarities, especially when it comes to moving around the interface.
>
> For instance, Project is loaded with tables that display just about every field (column) imaginable related to project management. The beauty of these tables is they present a familiar working environment for experienced Office Excel users. This means that if you use Office Excel, you probably have quite a bit of experience with tables already.
>
> Similarly, in both programs you can type and enter text, press the Tab key to move between columns, personalize the interface by configuring only the columns you want to see, and stretch the columns to see the data you need quickly. You can also create custom views in both programs, as well as sort and filter data.

Adding Tasks

Before you can assign resources to do the project work, you need tasks. Before you can determine how long your project will take and how much it is projected to cost, you need tasks. Essentially, before you begin any sort of project management execution, you need to break your project's scope down into manageable work packages known as tasks.

Initially, creating tasks in Project might force you to work based on past experience and assumptions. In project management these assumptions are often temporary decisions you make to account for information you haven't yet received. As you add your first tasks to a project file, don't worry about having exact durations or every task the project might need. In fact, don't even worry about whether or not you're entering tasks in the correct order. Adding tasks later, rearranging tasks, and modifying existing tasks is where the flexibility of this program really shines through.

MORE INFO   Rearranging tasks

For more information on reordering, modifying, inserting, and deleting tasks in your project plan file, see Chapter 2.

Granted, more than just typing tasks into an electronic format goes into initiating and tracking a project, but you have to start somewhere. In fact, Chapter 2 discusses applying the decomposition process to tasks you've entered in your project plan in greater detail. This lesson concentrates on adding new tasks to get your project plan started.

NOTE   Decomposition

In project management *decomposition* is the process of breaking down the project's work packages into more detailed tasks so that accurate task durations can be estimated.

In Project entering tasks is typically done in Gantt Chart view on the left side of the window in the Entry table. To enter a task in Gantt Chart view, follow these steps:

From the View menu, verify that Gantt Chart is selected.

NOTE   Turn On Project Guide

If you don't have a lot of experience using Project, from the View menu choose Turn On Project Guide. With the Project Guide displayed, click the Tasks button to obtain information about adding tasks, organizing tasks into phases, scheduling tasks, and linking to task information. The Project Guide is not only a great learning tool but also an excellent project management tool.

Select the first cell in the Task Name column and type a descriptive name for the first task. Press Enter. Notice that after typing the task name, the default duration of 1 day is automatically entered, as is a start date. Task durations are discussed further later in this lesson.

NOTE   Missing columns in the Entry table?

If you can't see the Duration, Start, and Finish columns in the Entry table of the Gantt Chart, drag the divider to the right or close the Project Guide, or both.

In the second Task field, type a detailed name for the task. Press Enter. Figure 1-30 shows an example.

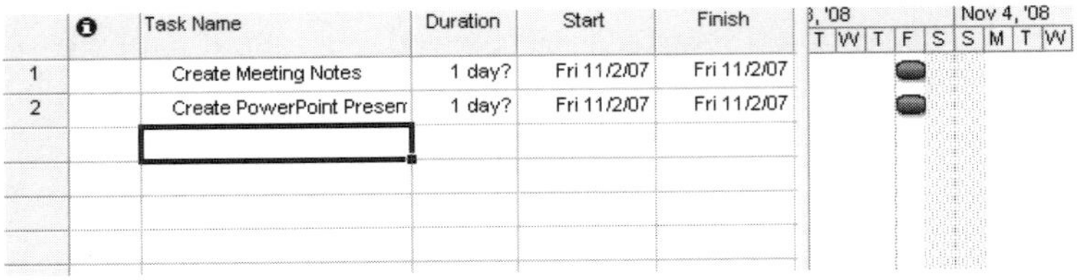

	❶	Task Name	Duration	Start	Finish	
1		Create Meeting Notes	1 day?	Fri 11/2/07	Fri 11/2/07	
2		Create PowerPoint Presen	1 day?	Fri 11/2/07	Fri 11/2/07	

Figure 1-30   Type a description of the task in the Task Name column

---

MORE INFO   Importing tasks

You can also add tasks to the current project by importing the data from an existing source such as a Microsoft Office Excel spreadsheet or a Microsoft Office Access database table. Each of these import options is described in detail in Chapter 4.

As you enter initial project tasks, don't worry about the original task order. Task order is something that's easily modified later using techniques such as Cut, Copy, and Paste.

MORE INFO   Working with task durations

As you enter your first tasks, notice that the default task duration automatically fills in as "1day?", as shown in Figure 1-30. On closer examination, you can see that the duration is actually an estimate, as indicated by the question mark. Later in this chapter we'll look at modifying and estimating task durations.

As you add tasks in the Gantt Chart view using the Entry table, you might notice that Project actually fills in more than just the Duration field automatically. The Entry table contains additional fields (columns) that track each task's start date, finish date, predecessors, and resources. Of these additional fields, the Start and Finish Date fields are automatically populated, initially, based on the task's duration.

There are several ways to view the additional columns. One is to move the slider at the bottom of the Project interface to the right. The other is to drag the divider bar that is between the Gantt Chart and the Entry table to the right.

Figure 1-31 shows all eight columns in the Entry table. They include:

- **Task ID**   A unique number that is assigned to each task in a project. The Task ID is the far left column in the Entry table.
- **Task Indicator**   When constraints, hyperlinks, notes, or recurring patterns are added to a task, indicators are placed in the Task Indicator column. These indicators contain handy tooltips you can view simply by resting your mouse pointer on top of a specific icon.
- **Task Name**   The name you give any task. As the project progresses, your project team members and stakeholders might have access to the project data, including reports. As such, you'll want to enter task descriptions that are somewhat meaningful to anyone else who might see the project information.
- **Duration**   The amount of time you expect it will take to complete the task. Duration is typically entered in hours, days, weeks, or months.
- **Start**   The date the task will start. Typically, the start date is automatically set based on defined task relationships.
- **Finish**   The date the task will end. Typically the finish date is automatically set based on the start date and assigned task duration.
- **Predecessors**   Tasks that must start or finish before the selected task can start or finish.
- **Resource Names**   The name of a resource, whether people, equipment, or materials, assigned to complete a task.

	🛈	Task Name	Duration	Start	Finish	Predecessors	Resource Names
1		Create Meeting Notes	1 day?	Fri 11/2/07	Fri 11/2/07		
2		Create PowerPoint Presen	1 day?	Fri 11/2/07	Fri 11/2/07		

Figure 1-31   By default, the Entry table contains eight columns

Real World

Bonnie Biafore

Communicating the work that a task represents can be challenging. Overly brief task names often aren't informative, and long names either get in the way or are cropped by the width of a column in a view. Ideally, task names should identify the result and the action taken to produce it (or the scope and the action performed). Using both a verb and a noun in a task name is the simplest way to convey both of these elements—for example, "build staircase" or "tally survey results."

A task name without a verb can lead to confusion about the work being done. For example, a task name like Survey doesn't tell the assigned resources whether they are supposed to design survey questions, gather survey answers, or report the results. Action verbs are better for describing work more clearly. For example, design, format, calculate, and print are more specific than produce or analyze.

Because most projects include work packages as well as several layers of summary tasks, you can make your task list easier to read by using a different name format for summary tasks. Because summary tasks span several activities, you can use a verb that encompasses all the work being done, such as Prepare Report to summarize researching, writing, formatting, and printing a report. Another option is to use the "ing" form of a verb for summary tasks, such as Preparing Report.

When you first begin adding tasks to a new project, you'll notice that every task you enter begins on the same date. Also, the task start date always matches the project start date. In fact, if you don't enter any task durations, the tasks also all finish on the same day due to the default new task duration of one day. This is only an indication that you've just begun working on your project file.

Although you do have the ability to enter information directly into the Start and Finish fields shown in Figure 1-31, doing so adds constraints to the project tasks that you might not have intended. As you begin creating your project file, allow Project to fill in these fields for you based on the program's default settings and any durations you enter in the Duration column. After you create task relationships, add resources, and specify task constraints, the Start and Finish fields will adjust automatically. Overwriting these fields with your own dates will only stop Project from performing these automatic project adjustments.

Adding Recurring Tasks

Each task you enter typically occurs just once during the project life cycle. Occasionally, you will have project tasks that occur periodically (multiple times) throughout a project, such as a project status meeting. Another great use of recurring tasks is adding regular project progress checkpoints.

For tasks that occur multiple times, you can create a recurring task. Doing so eliminates the repetitive typing of entering the same task multiple times. Recurring tasks are typically project-related tasks that always have the same duration and occur weekly, monthly, or at a regular, defined interval.

To create a new, recurring task, complete the following steps:

1. On the View menu, choose Gantt Chart, if this view isn't already displayed.
2. Select the task row where you want the recurring task to appear in the Entry table.
3. From the Insert menu, choose Recurring Task. The Recurring Task Information dialog box is shown in Figure 1-32.

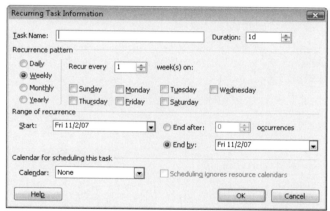

Figure 1-32 The Recurring Task Information dialog box

4. In the Task Name box, type the task name.
5. Set the Duration of the recurring task and, under Recurrence Pattern, select your chosen option.
6. Choose a task frequency and select the check box for the day of the week the task should occur. You can select multiple days of the week if you like.
7. Under Range Of Recurrence, enter a start date for the first occurrence of this recurring task.
8. Select End After or End By.
   a. For End After, type the number of occurrences—for instance, **12**.
   b. For End By, enter the date you want the recurring task to end—for instance, **4/18/ 2008**.
9. Under Calendar For Scheduling This Task, select a calendar if you want to apply a calendar to the task or select None, as shown in Figure 1-33. For more information on working with calendars and assigning a calendar to a task, see Lesson 3, "Working with Calendars."

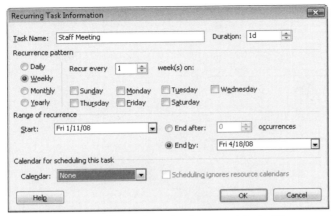

Figure 1-33 Modifying the calendar associated with a recurring task

---

NOTE **Same task, irregular occurrence**

For tasks that are repeated throughout the project life cycle but do not happen on a regular or definable schedule, you'll need to enter those tasks individually either by typing or using the Copy command. The recurring task command works only with tasks that follow a regular interval schedule.

You can quickly identify a recurring task on the Entry table (in Gantt Chart view) by its indicator icon located in the column to the left of the task name and to the right of the ID column. See Figure 1-34.

Recurring Task icon

Figure 1-34 Identify a recurring task by this icon

NOTE **The Indicator column**

In the Entry table, several icons might be present in the Indicator column, including icons indicating task constraints, notes, and hyperlinks, as well as the recurring task icon.

Quick Check

1. You want to ensure that you start your project off correctly. You've defined the project, created a task list, and made a list of recurring tasks. What steps can you take in Project to begin your project file?

2. The project stakeholders have asked for a status meeting every two weeks throughout the lifecycle of the project. How can you account for this meeting in your project schedule?

Quick Check Answers

1. Enter the project's tasks (including recurring tasks) into the Task Name column using descriptive task names. At this stage you're only placing the defined work packages in the project file.

2. Create a recurring task that occurs every two weeks to mark the progress meetings.

Using the Task Information Dialog Box

When you create new tasks, you'll typically enter them directly into the Entry table. Using the Entry table, you can also change the duration and start and finish dates, create predecessor tasks, and add resources. This is a good place to start.

You can also access and configure these same options from the Task Information dialog box. In the Task Information dialog box you can work with advanced task information as well. Instead of focusing immediately on changing the task information from the Entry table, go ahead and access that and more from the Task Information dialog box.

There are several ways to open the Task Information dialog box (shown in Figure 1-35):

- Double-click any task.
- Right-click any task and, from the shortcut menu, choose Task Information.
- Use the Shift+F2 key combination.
- Click the Task Information icon on the Standard toolbar.
- From the Project menu, choose Task Information.

As shown in Figure 1-35, the Task Information dialog box contains six tabs, all related to managing tasks after they've been entered. As you work on your project, you'll find yourself accessing the Task Information dialog box often for various reasons. Consequently, it's important to be familiar with every tab. For example, to work in-depth with a chosen task's predecessors, you'll open this dialog box and click the Predecessors tab. Or to specify a date that a task must finish by, you can open this dialog box and click the General tab.

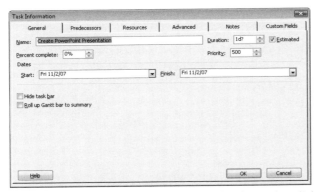

Figure 1-35 The General tab of the Task Information dialog box

As different concepts are introduced throughout this book, you'll see references to opening and working with the Task Information dialog box. Below is a breakdown of each tab and where to find additional information in this book, if applicable.

General

In the General tab, shown in Figure 1-35, you can access basic task information such as the task name, duration, and the start and finish dates (all of which are also accessible on the Entry table). Also, you can track a task's progress by filling in the Percent Complete box and you can designate a task's priority level (between 0 and 1000).

Predecessors

In the Predecessors tab, shown in Figure 1-36, you can access basic task information such as the task name and duration. This tab, however, is specifically designed to display and modify the selected task's relationships with other project tasks. For more information on setting and working with task relationships, see Chapter 2.

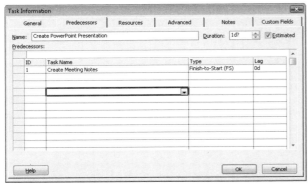

Figure 1-36 The Predecessors tab of the Task Information dialog box

Resources

In the Resources tab, shown in Figure 1-37, you can access basic task information, such as the task name and duration. This tab, however, is specifically designed to display and modify the selected task's resources, their work units, and task cost based on information that has been added to the project's resource sheet. For more information on creating and assigning task resources, see Chapter 2.

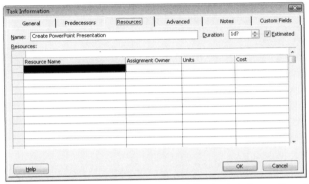

Figure 1-37   The Resources tab of the Task Information dialog box

Advanced

In the Advanced tab, shown in Figure 1-38, you can access basic task information such as the task name and duration. Additionally, you can access several advanced task options such as task constraints. For maximum control over project scheduling, you can set each task to Fixed Duration, Fixed Units, or Fixed Work from the Task Type drop-down list, assign a specific calendar to an individual task, and set the preferred earned value method. For more information on working with task constraints, setting the task type, and setting the preferred earned value, see Chapter 2. For more information on assigning a specific calendar to an individual task, see Lesson 3 in this chapter, "Working with Calendars." This tab also has check boxes for marking the selected task as a milestone (regardless of the task duration), employing effort-driven scheduling, and ignoring resource calendars.

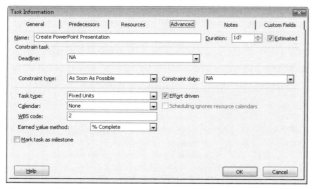

Figure 1-38   The Advanced tab of the Task Information dialog box

Notes

In the Notes tab, shown in Figure 1-39, you can track memos and add text that you need to record about a task that doesn't logically fit into one of the many fields. Additionally, you can use the Notes tab to add manual notes for individual tasks. You can also access basic task information, such as the task name and duration. For more information on creating task notes, see the section of this chapter entitled "Defining Task Acceptance Criteria."

Figure 1-39   The Notes tab of the Task Information dialog box

Custom Fields

In the Custom Fields tab, shown in Figure 1-40, you'll view and assign values to custom task fields, enterprise custom fields, outline codes, and enterprise outline codes. From this tab you'll be able to only edit the displayed values. In order to edit or create the custom fields, you'll need to access the Custom Fields dialog box. For more information on creating custom fields, see Chapter 4.

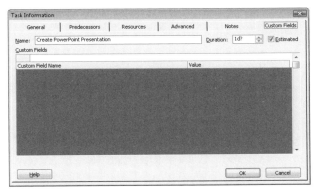

Figure 1-40   The Custom Fields tab of the Task Information dialog box

Quick Check

1. Which tab in the Task Information dialog box do you choose to work with task constraints?
2. Which tab in the Task Information dialog box do you choose to track a task's progress by filling in the percent complete box and enter a task's priority level?

Quick Check Answers

1. The Advanced tab.
2. The General tab.

Working with Task Durations

A task's duration is the amount of time between a task's start and finish date and is measured in time units, such as hours, days, weeks, and months. Essentially, a task's duration is the estimated amount of time the task will take to complete.

By default, new tasks are entered with an estimated duration of one day. You can easily change this duration by selecting the duration cell, entering a new duration, and pressing the Enter key. As you enter new durations, if you choose to enter simply a number without a duration code (shown in the tables below), Project assumes that the duration unit is days and enters the word "day" after your typed number.

NOTE **Quickly enter the duration for several tasks**

You can quickly enter the same duration for several tasks by selecting several task duration cells, opening the Task Information dialog box, and then typing the duration. This applies the duration you've just typed into the duration cells of all selected tasks. You can also use this multiple cell selection method to modify other information found in the Task Information dialog box.

Standard Durations

By default, Project calculates durations according to a standard working calendar. This means that eight hours is equal to one working day; one week is equal to 40 hours; and one month is equal to 20 working days (four weeks at five days each week). Often, this is easy to remember by thinking of Project's default calendar as a standard, 40-hour work week where an employee works 8:00 A.M.–5:00 P.M. with a one-hour lunch.

MORE INFO   **Scheduling tasks**

This type of scheduling works well for many tasks. In Project you do have the option of scheduling tasks across different sets of working hours. Scheduling tasks across different hours is covered in Lesson 3, "Working with Calendars."

Because Project offers interchangeable durations, you can enter your task durations in minutes, hours, days, weeks, or months. Table 1-1 offers a duration code table with standard duration codes recognized by Project.

Table 1-1   Durations and Duration Codes

Duration	Duration Code
Minutes	M, Min, Minute
Hours	H, Hr, Hour
Days	D, Dy, Day
Weeks	W, Wk, Week
Months	Mo, Month

Elapsed Durations

In Project, a standard working day begins at 8:00 A.M. and finishes at 5:00 P.M., allowing for a one-hour lunch from noon until 1:00 P.M. This means that the remainder of each day (midnight–8:00 A.M. and 5:00 P.M.–midnight) is designated as nonworking time. But there might be times when you need to schedule your project tasks across this nonworking time. For these times you can use elapsed durations.

You use elapsed durations when you need tasks to span a continuous 24-hour period, including weekends and holidays, to account for needed space between one task and the next, such as needing to allow for paint to dry or concrete to harden. To designate a task's duration and to take advantage of this type of continuous effort, simply add the letter "e" in front of the duration code, as shown in Table 1-2.

Table 1-2   Elapsed Durations and Elapsed Duration Codes

Duration	Elapsed Duration Code
Hours	eH, eHr, eHour
Days	eD, eDy, eDay
Weeks	eW, eWk, eWeek
Months	eM, eMo, eMonth

Automatic Update of Desired Durations

When entering task durations, you can use any of the duration codes shown in the previous tables. For the sake of continuity, Project automatically updates the codes you entered to one standard code applied to all tasks. For example, you can enter task durations as 1d, 1dy, or 1day, and in every case Project adjusts the duration to "1 day." You can, however, mix and match different duration types in the same project file. For instance, in one file you could use days, weeks, and months, depending on the tasks. It's only the reference to each of those time units that Project standardizes.

Exam Tip   You might see questions on the exam related to calculating a task's duration. Unless specific working hours have been identified in the question scenario, assume that the answer relies on Project's default working times of 8 hours each day and a 40-hour work week. Just make sure to watch for scenarios that indicate a task needs to span nonworking time on an irregular basis—in this case you'll need to use elapsed durations.

Quick Check

- Your team members work from 8 A.M. to 5 P.M. each day. They also get an hour off for lunch. Will Project's Standard calendar work for this project, or do you need to manually input your employees' lunch hour?

Quick Check Answer

- The standard calendar states that the company's working day begins at 8:00 A.M. and finishes at 5:00 P.M. and employees get a one-hour lunch from noon until 1:00 P.M. So the Standard calendar will work in this instance.

Change Default Duration Codes

You can change the default duration codes for the current project file in the Options dialog box by following these steps:

1. From the Tools menu, choose Options.
2. In the Options dialog box, shown in Figure 1-41, click the Schedule tab.

3. Under Scheduling Options For, in the Duration Is Entered In drop-down list, select a duration unit.

4. If you want to use the same setting for all future projects, click Set As Default. Click OK to save your changes.

Figure 1-41   Setting schedule options in the Options dialog box

Setting the default duration code for your project file modifies only what Project uses for each duration unit in your project. Throughout your project file you can use any combination of duration units to specify each task's length. You are not required to use only the duration you select in the Scheduling Options duration options.

Change the Duration of a Task Using Gantt Bars

You know you can change the duration of any task using the Entry table and the Task Information dialog box. But you might not know that you can change the duration of a task by dragging from the right edge of any task shown in the Gantt Chart bars.

To see how this works, create a task in the Entry Table and view the Gantt Chart. Select the Gantt Bar for the task you want to change the duration of and drag the bar to the right. In Figure 1-42 the task Prepare Meeting Room is being dragged in the Gantt Chart to change the time from one day to three days. Notice the Finish and Duration information in the resulting pop-up box.

Figure 1-42 Change a task's duration by dragging a Gantt Bar for any task

---

Quick Check

■ Name three ways you can change the duration of a task.

Quick Check Answers

1. Double-click the task and make the change in the Task Information dialog box.
2. Change the duration in the Entry Table.
3. Drag the Gantt Bar for the task to the right.

Estimating Task Durations Using the PERT Formula

Coming up with accurate task duration estimates is an age-old project management dilemma. Luckily, we have a couple of tools at our disposal to estimate task durations. One of these tools is built into Project–Program Evaluation and Review Technique (PERT) Analysis.

PERT Analysis uses a weighted average of three duration estimates to calculate an estimated duration for a task. This is a great tool when you don't have a specific duration but do have duration estimates from reliable sources. Who are reliable sources? A reliable source is anyone (or anything) with experience working with this type of task, including, but not limited to, skilled project managers, the people who will be performing the work, and even the data logs of a resource like a machine (to find out how fast the equipment can get the job done).

Real World

Joli Ballew

A local T-shirt printing facility recently acquired the contract for printing hats, T-shirts, and sweatshirts for the winner of next year's high-school championship football game. The shirts and sweatshirts must have the winning team's entire season on the back, including each game played, who they played, the final scores, and the winner and score of the final championship game.

The big game is played on a Friday night, and the project stakeholders want 5,000 T-shirts, 2,000 sweatshirts, and 2,000 hats to be available and for sale Monday morning at the winning high school.

Although the project can be defined, tasks entered and organized, and resources assigned, the shirts can be printed only as fast as their presses will allow—after the big game is over. Only by calculating exactly how many T-shirts can be printed each hour, by each press, on a 24-hour around-the-clock weekend schedule with a full crew can the project manager determine if more presses need to be added, if work needs to be contracted out, or if other additional print facilities need to be rented for the weekend.

The moral of the story? Sometimes you can move only as fast as your equipment will let you, and knowing how fast a machine can perform work (or the machine's specifications) can be a reliable resource!

Manually Calculate Task Duration

You can use the Estimated Duration formula to manually calculate a task's duration the same way Project would. To properly estimate task durations (either manually or using Project), you'll need access to three numbers:

- Expected time
- Most Pessimistic time
- Most Optimistic time

With these three numbers, you and Project can create accurate task estimate durations. Each of these numbers holds a weighted average in Project.

- The Most Optimistic and Most Pessimistic times each hold a weight of one (or 16.66 percent each).
- The Expected Time holds a weight of four (or 66.67 percent).

NOTE **Is manual calculation necessary?**

Although you might think that understanding how to manually calculate a task's duration isn't important (because you can have Project do it for you), it really is something you need to know. You should be able to tell by looking at the results of the PERT analysis if the duration is approximately where it should be. You can know this only if you know how to calculate the task duration manually.

When plugged into the following formula, you can calculate estimated durations just like Project:

Estimated Duration = ((Optimistic + Pessimistic + (4*Expected))/6

Exam Tip   Even though Project offers a PERT Analysis feature that performs the estimated duration calculation, you might be asked to manually calculate task duration estimates using the same PERT Analysis formula that Project uses behind the scenes.

Quick Check

1. You are given the following information about a specific task's duration:
    - ❏ Most Optimistic = 10 days
    - ❏ Most Pessimistic = 20 days
    - ❏ Expected = 15 days

    Using the formula for Estimated Duration, how many days can you expect the task to take? (You'd likely guess somewhere around 15 days, but do the math!)

2. You are given the following information about a specific task's duration:
    - ❏ Most Optimistic = 8 days
    - ❏ Most Pessimistic = One month
    - ❏ Expected = 3 weeks

    Using the formula for Estimated Duration, how many days can you expect the task to take? (It's not the Expected Duration!)

Quick Check Answers

1. Because Estimated Duration = ((Optimistic + Pessimistic + (4*Expected))/6, plugging in the numbers offers the following for the Estimated Duration:

    ```
    = ((10 + 20 + (4*15))/6
    = ((30 + (4*15))/6
    = (30 + 60)/6
    = 90/6
    = 15 days
    ```

    The number for Estimated Duration is not always the Expected Duration, but occasionally it is.

2. Before you began, you should have changed the Most Pessimistic time to 20 days and the Expected time to 15 days. When working a mathematical equation such as this, it's imperative to use the same units of time (that is, you never mix months with days in the same equation). That being said, because Estimated Duration = (Optimistic + Pessimistic + (4*Expected))/6, plugging in the numbers offers the following for the Estimated Duration:

    ```
    = ((8 + 20 + (15*4))/6
    = ((28 + (15*4))/6
    = (28 + 60)/6
    = 88/6
    = 14.67 days
    ```

Automatically Calculate Task Duration

After you get the hang of manually calculating task duration estimates, you're ready to move to using Project's PERT Analysis feature. The calculation you worked with when manually calculating estimated durations is the same calculation that Project uses. This means that you'll still need access to three numbers: Expected Time, Pessimistic Time, and Optimistic Time.

To begin, you'll need to display the PERT Analysis toolbar. You do this by clicking View, choosing Toolbars, and choosing PERT Analysis. Figure 1-43 shows the PERT Analysis toolbar.

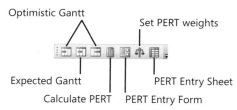

Figure 1-43   The PERT Analysis toolbar

Quick Check
■ What three things must you have to properly estimate task durations using PERT?
Quick Check Answer
■ Expected Time, Most Pessimistic Time, and Most Optimistic Time.

After you display the PERT Analysis toolbar, you can use the Pert Entry Form button to calculate estimated task durations based on the most optimistic, most pessimistic, and expected durations you enter.

To calculate an estimated task duration using the PERT Analysis toolbar, follow these steps:

1. On the PERT Analysis toolbar, click the PERT Entry Form button.
2. In the PERT Entry dialog box, shown in Figure 1-44, type a number for the Optimistic, Expected, and Pessimistic Durations.
3. Click OK.

When you use the PERT Entry Form to estimate and then enter estimated durations for your project's tasks, those durations are added to your project file under PERT Analysis fields. In fact, you can view those fields using one of the first three buttons on the PERT Analysis toolbar.

Exam Tip   Remember that Project uses the time units interchangeably. This means that when you use the PERT Analysis formula to determine an estimated duration, your answer on paper might be 80 hours but the only answer on the exam that matches might be two weeks. Watch out for interchangeable durations such as this on the possible exam answers.

Figure 1-44   Using the PERT Entry dialog box to calculate a task's duration

---

Real World

Bonnie Biafore

Similar to task durations defined using different units, estimates that you receive from different people might not be measured in the same way. You must make sure that you know what the estimates you receive represent. If your IT department says that it takes four days to install a new server, is that four days for one person, two days each for a systems engineer and a network engineer, or some other combination? If another estimator tells you a task takes 30 days, does that mean 30 work days or a duration of one month?

Before you enter task durations in Project, find out what your estimates truly represent: estimated work hours or days, estimated duration, or estimated duration and estimated resources. Then you can define the task duration in whatever units you want.

View PERT Analysis Results

As noted earlier, when you use the PERT Entry Form to estimate and then enter estimated durations for your project's tasks, those durations are added to your project file under PERT Analysis fields. In fact, you can view those fields using one of the first three buttons on the PERT Analysis toolbar.

There are three options, Optimistic Gantt, Expected Gantt, and Pessimistic Gantt:

- **Optimistic Gantt**   This button displays the Gantt Chart along with the PA_Optimistic Case table. The Opt Duration fields of any task that uses the PERT Form calculation is displayed and the project's Gantt Chart is updated to reflect the most optimistic outcome.
- **Expected Gantt**   This button displays the Gantt Chart along with the Entry table. The Exp Duration fields of any task that uses the PERT Form calculation is displayed and the project's Gantt Chart is updated to reflect the expected outcome.

- **Pessimistic Gantt** This button displays the Gantt Chart along with the PA_Pessimistic Case table. The Pes Duration fields of any task that uses the PERT Form calculation is displayed and the project's Gantt Chart is updated to reflect the most pessimistic outcome.

NOTE Viewing the PA fields

You might need to move the Gantt Chart divider bar to the right to display the fields in the Gantt Chart table. When you click these PERT Analysis toolbar table buttons, you might not see an immediate change in the table data. If this happens, drag the divider bar to the right to display the newly added columns.

After you've entered PERT Analysis figures in the PERT Entry form, you can apply those calculation results to your Entry table by clicking the Calculate PERT button on the PERT Analysis toolbar. If you choose to enter task durations in this way, Project will overwrite any durations and Start or Finish dates you have entered for tasks utilizing the PERT Analysis form.

NOTE PERT vs. CPM

By default, Project calculates based on the Critical Path Method (CPM), which forecasts the project's total duration by analyzing the least amount of task scheduling flexibility. In project management you can use the PERT Analysis method for estimating task durations and CPM to manage task importance by defining task relationships and constraints. This way, CPM and PERT can work hand-in-hand.

Using the Set PERT Weights button on the PERT Analysis toolbar, you can modify the default weights given to any of the formula variables. However, for the purposes of the certification exam, be sure you understand the default values and use those in any calculations you're asked to perform.

Creating a Milestone

Throughout a project's life cycle, you'll most likely have built-in checkpoints. These checkpoints can define different areas, such as the end of phases, the passing of a set amount of time, or any other criteria that you, as the project manager, define. Deciding on milestones, their dates, and what happens if milestones are missed is part of your job as a project manager, and it is a difficult task. However, creating a milestone in Project is easy.

Create a Milestone with a New Task

To create a milestone in Project, follow these steps:

1. Create a new task in the Entry Table.
2. Type a descriptive name. You want the task to serve specifically as a marker for a checkpoint (milestone).

Set the duration of the task to zero days in the Entry table. Figure 1-45 shows an example of a task with a duration of zero, thus, a milestone.

Figure 1-45   A milestone is represented by a diamond in the Gantt Chart and a duration of zero days

As you can see from Figure 1-45, milestones are displayed visually on the Gantt Chart as diamonds. This makes milestones easily recognizable as a project checkpoint and easy to locate in any Gantt Chart.

Create a Milestone from an Existing Task

Although modifying a task's duration to zero days automatically denotes that task as a milestone in Project, you can mark a task of any duration as a milestone, displaying the same diamond shape.

To mark a task of any duration as a milestone, follow these steps:

1. Select a task in the Entry Table.
2. Double-click the task to open the Task Information dialog box.
3. In the Task Information dialog box, click the Advanced tab.
4. Select the Mark Task As Milestone check box.
5. Click OK.

After you have denoted a task as a milestone, it appears in the Gantt Chart as a diamond on the task's scheduled finish date.

Exam Tip   You might see one or two questions on the exam related to the best practice for defining a milestone in your project schedule. Although a task of any duration can be marked as a milestone, project management best practice indicates that to achieve this result you should create a task specifically for the purposes of acting as a milestone by setting that task's duration to zero (0) days. Setting a task's duration in this way automatically denotes the chosen task to "milestone status" and creates a diamond shape on the Gantt Chart for easy visual reference.

> **Quick Check**
> - You need to create a milestone for a project you're creating. Should you use an existing task or create a new one? What is the best practice regarding this?
>
> **Quick Check Answer**
> - Create a new task, name it descriptively, and set the duration to zero days.

Defining Task Acceptance Criteria

Defining task relationships and constraints will be discussed in greater detail in Chapter 2. This lesson concentrates on tracking the task acceptance criteria as defined in your project scope statement. The criteria are all of those little things you, as the project manager, need to remember about an individual project, phase, or task. Many of these little details aren't necessarily measurable in terms of budget or time, but they are important to ensure that the project is successful.

In Project you can use the Notes feature to help you and your project team members keep track of all of the little things that aren't easily tracked elsewhere in your electronic project file.

To add notes to any task, complete the following steps:

1. Select a task in the Entry Table.
2. Double-click the task to open the Task Information dialog box.
3. In the Task Information pane, click the Notes tab.
4. Type notes as desired, and then click OK.

NOTE   **Adding notes**

A quick way to jump to the Notes tab of the Task Information dialog box is to select the task to which you want to add the note and then click the Task Notes button on the Standard toolbar.

After a note has been added to a task, a note indicator is added to the related task's indicator column. By resting your mouse over the top of the note indicator, you can see the text of the note in a tool tip. See Figure 1-46.

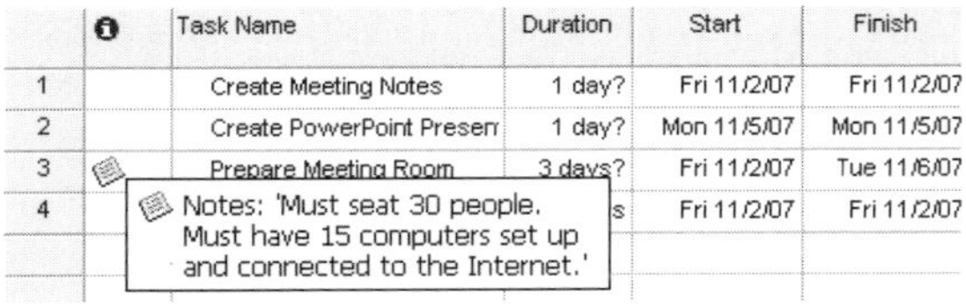

	❶	Task Name	Duration	Start	Finish
1		Create Meeting Notes	1 day?	Fri 11/2/07	Fri 11/2/07
2		Create PowerPoint Presen	1 day?	Mon 11/5/07	Mon 11/5/07
3		Prepare Meeting Room	3 days?	Fri 11/2/07	Tue 11/6/07
4		Notes: 'Must seat 30 people. Must have 15 computers set up and connected to the Internet.'	s	Fri 11/2/07	Fri 11/2/07

Figure 1-46   The Notes pop-up

NOTE   Tool tip text

If the note is extremely long, the tool tip text might be cut off. To view the entire note, simply double-click the note indicator icon to open the Task Information dialog box to view the full text of the long note.

Notes aren't just valuable on the screen—they can be printed as well. To print notes, follow these steps:

1. On the File menu, choose Page Setup.
2. From the Page Setup dialog box, click the View tab.
3. Select the Print Notes check box.
4. Click OK to apply this to future print jobs or click Print to print now.

PRACTICE Working with Tasks

In these practices you will review what you've learned in this lesson. The first practice is to add tasks to your project file. The second is to use the Task Information dialog box to edit task information. The third and the forth are to add and estimate task durations. The fifth and sixth are to define project milestones.

▶ **Exercise 1   Add Tasks to a Project File**

In this exercise you'll add tasks to a project file, create a recurring task, and save the file for Exercises 2 and 6.

To complete this exercise, perform the following steps:

1. Open Project. Create a new, blank project and display the Gantt Chart, if necessary.
2. Select the first cell in the Task Name column, and type **Hold Sales Meeting**. Press Enter.
3. Enter a second task name, **Perform Sales Review**. Press Enter.
4. From the Insert menu, choose Recurring Task.
5. In the Task Name box, type the task name **Hold Review Meeting**.
6. Under Recurrence Pattern, select Weekly.
7. Leave Recur Every 1 Week(s) as is.
8. Under Recurrence Pattern, select the Friday check box.
9. Select End After, and type 12 for number of occurrences.
10. Under Calendar For Scheduling This Task, select Standard.
11. Click OK.
12. Click File, and then choose Save.
13. In the Save As dialog box, name the file and note the location of the saved file. Leave the file open for Exercise 2.

▶ **Exercise 2   Use the Task Information Dialog Box**

In this exercise you'll use the Task Information dialog box to edit data for an existing task. Complete Exercise 1 before working on this exercise.

To complete this exercise, perform the following steps:

1. Open the file used in Exercise 1, if it isn't open already.
2. Double-click the task Hold Sales Meeting.
3. In the Task Information dialog box, from the General tab, change the duration from 1d? to 1d by using the up spinner arrow to move to 2d, and the down spinner arrow to move back to 1d.
4. From the Notes tab, type **Make sure room is big enough for 20 people.**
5. From the Advanced tab, for Calendar, select Standard.
6. Click OK.

▶ **Exercise 3   Manually Estimate Task Durations**

In this exercise you'll manually estimate task durations using the Estimated Task Duration formula. For this exercise use the following data:

- Most Optimistic = 10 days
- Most Pessimistic = 20 days
- Expected = 12 days

To complete this exercise, follow these steps:

1. Write down the Estimated Duration formula: ((Optimistic + Pessimistic + (4*Expected))/6.
2. Make sure all values use the same duration—in this case days.
3. Input the data for Most Optimistic, Most Pessimistic, and Expected values: ((10 + 20 + (4*12))/6.
4. Add 10 + 20: ((30 + (4*12))/6.
5. Multiply 4*12: ((30 + 48))/6.
6. Add 30 + 48: 78/6.
7. Divide 78 by 6: 13.
8. Note that the Expected Duration is 13 days.

▶ **Exercise 4   Automatically Calculate Task Duration**

In this exercise you'll verify that 13 days is the correct value you manually calculated in Exercise 3. Complete Exercise 3 before working through this exercise. For this exercise use the data given here:

- Most Optimistic = 10 days
- Most Pessimistic = 20 days
- Expected = 12 days

To calculate an estimated task using the PERT Analysis toolbar, follow these steps:

1. Click View, choose Toolbars, and choose PERT Analysis. (Don't click PERT Analysis if there's already a check by it–it's already showing.)
2. On the PERT Analysis toolbar, click the PERT Entry Form button.
3. In the PERT Entry dialog box, enter 10d for Optimistic, 12d for Expected, and 20d for Pessimistic.
4. Click OK.
5. On the Pert Analysis toolbar, click Calculate PERT.
6. Click Yes to continue.
7. Note 13 days on the Entry table.

▶ **Exercise 5   Define a Project Milestone**

In this exercise you'll create a project milestone by creating a new task.

To complete this exercise, perform the following steps:

1. Create a new task in the Entry Table named **Meet Marketing Deadline**. Press Enter.
2. Set the duration of the task to zero days in the Entry table.

▶ **Exercise 6   Define a Project Milestone from an Existing Task**

Although it is not recommended that you create a project milestone from an existing task, there might be instances where you need to do so.

To complete this exercise, perform the following steps:

1. Select the Sales Review task in Entry Table.
2. Double-click the task to open the Task Information dialog box.
3. In the Task Information pane, click the Advanced tab.
4. Select the Mark Task As Milestone check box.
5. Click OK.
6. Verify that there is now a diamond in the Gantt Chart for the task.

Lesson Summary

■ Tasks are the basis of any project. Tasks help break down the work into manageable pieces. You must assign tasks before you can determine how long a project will take, how much it will cost, and what resources are needed.

■ The Entry table contains fields that allow you to easily track each task's start date, finish date, duration, predecessors, and resources.

■ The Task Information dialog box contains six tabs, all related to managing the tasks you create. You access the Task Information dialog box to change the task duration, the task type, select a calendar, mark a task as a milestone, change a start or finish date, and more.

- A task's duration is the estimated amount of time the task will take to complete and is measured in minutes, hours, days, weeks, or months. Elapsed durations are used when your tasks span a continuous 24-hour period, including weekends and holidays.

- Project's default calendar is the Standard calendar, which schedules tasks based on a 40-hour work week in which a resource works 8:00 A.M. – 5:00 P.M. with a one-hour lunch.

- The formula for calculating a task's duration manually is Estimated Duration = ((Optimistic + Pessimistic + (4*Expected))/6.

- Using the PERT Analysis toolbar, you can calculate an estimated task duration based on the most optimistic, most pessimistic, and expected durations you enter.

- Milestones are generally checkpoints. Defining milestones, their dates, and what happens if milestones are missed is part of a project manager's duties. You can create a milestone by setting the duration of a task to zero days.

Lesson Review

You can use the following questions to test your knowledge of the information in Lesson 2, "Working with Tasks." The questions are also available on the companion CD if you prefer to review them in electronic form.

NOTE   Answers

Answers to these questions and explanations of why each answer choice is correct or incorrect are located in the "Answers" section at the end of the book.

---

1. You need to create a new task with a duration of seven days. Your current project file is configured to use the Standard calendar. What is the correct way to input the task and set the duration to seven days?

   A. Create the task in the Entry Table and set the duration to one week.

   B. Create the task in the Gantt Chart by right-clicking and selecting New Task. Set the duration to seven days.

   C. Create the task in the Entry table and set the Duration field to seven days.

   D. Create the task in the Entry Table and set the Duration field to one week.

2. You previously created a new task with a duration of 5 days, but after much thought you decide you need to change the duration to 10 days, as well as change the calendar type, and add notes to the task with your reasons for extending it. The notes you write will help determine acceptance criteria for the task. Which of the following do you do to make all of these changes? (Choose all that apply.)

   A. Using the Entry Table, double-click the task you want to change, and in the Task Information dialog box, make the desired changes.

    B. Double-click the bar for the task in the Gantt Chart, and in the Task Information dialog box, make the desired changes.

    C. Using the Entry Table, right-click the task you want to change, choose Task Information, and in the Task Information dialog box make the desired changes.

    D. Select the task in the Entry Table and use the key combination Shift+F2 to open the Task Information dialog box and make the desired changes.

3. You previously created a new task with a duration of 5 days, but after much thought you decide you need to change the duration to 10 days, as well as change the calendar type. Where in the Task Information dialog box can you change the duration of the task and the calendar type? (Choose all that apply.)

    A. Change the duration from any tab; change the calendar type from the Advanced tab.

    B. Change the duration from the General tab; change the calendar type from the Advanced tab.

    C. Change the duration from any tab; change the calendar type from the Resources tab.

    D. Change the duration from the Predecessors tab; change the calendar type from the Advanced tab.

4. You are in charge of making sure that the project for creating and launching a new Web site for your company goes according to schedule. You want to schedule a meeting to occur every Thursday from 1 to 2 P.M. so you can hear from the head of each department regarding his or her progress. What do you need to do in Project to account for this meeting in the project schedule?

    A. Create a task called Staff Meeting in the Entry Table and right-click it to open the Task Information dialog box, where you can schedule the task to recur as often as desired.

    B. Create a task called Staff Meeting in the Entry Table, right-click it, and select Recurring Task Information. This opens the Recurring Task Information dialog box, where you can input the task information desired.

    C. From the Project Menu, choose Project Information, and in the Project Information dialog box, input the task name, recurrence pattern, and related information.

    D. From the Insert Menu, choose Recurring Task and input the task name, recurrence pattern, and related information.

5. You need to identify when a set of tasks end for a phase in your project. You create a task in the Entry Table named Milestone Submission. What else do you need to do to make this task a milestone? (Choose all that apply.)

    A. Do nothing. Naming the task with Milestone in its name is all you need to do.

    B. Right-click the task icon in the Gantt Chart and choose Mark Task As Milestone.

      C. In the Task Information dialog box for the task, from the Advanced tab, select the Mark Task As Milestone check box.

      D. Change the duration of the task to zero days.

6. You need to decide how long a task will take and you have three expert opinions. One is the most optimistic (15 days), one is the most pessimistic (28 days), and one is how long you expect the task to take (17 days) after taking into consideration your team's abilities and its past project experiences. Unfortunately, you're nowhere near a computer or calculator and your client needs an answer right away. You'll have to calculate the duration manually. What duration do you give your client?

      A. 18.5 days

      B. 17 days

      C. 17.5 days

      D. 24 days

7. You need to quickly determine the duration of a task. Which one of the following should you select from the PERT Analysis toolbar to get started?

      A. Expected Gantt

      B. Calculate PERT

      C. PERT Entry Form

      D. PERT Entry Sheet

Lesson 3: Working with Calendars

For every project there must be a project calendar. The project calendar defines the high-level working time in which tasks for the project can be performed. This lesson covers working with the project calendar in many forms, including modifying and copying an existing project calendar, creating a new project calendar, and setting default calendar options.

After this lesson, you will be able to:

- Customize and set the base project calendar.
- Define default working times for the Standard, Night Shift, and 24-Hour calendars.
- Modify an existing project calendar.
- Copy an existing project calendar.
- Create a new project calendar.
- Assign a calendar to a task or group of tasks.
- Set default calendar options.

Estimated lesson time: 45 minutes

By default, Project assigns the Standard base project calendar to every project. The Standard project calendar is one of three project calendars available with each new project. Each of the available base calendars is described in Table 1-3.

Table 1-3   Available Project Calendars

Calendar	Characteristics
Standard	The Standard calendar is the default base calendar for all new projects with a working time defined as Monday through Friday, 8:00 A.M. until 5:00 P.M., with a one-hour lunch from noon until 1:00 P.M. each day. This defined working time creates eight hours of working time across five days a week totaling a 40-hour work week.
24-Hour	The 24-Hour calendar schedules tasks across seven days a week, 24 hours each day. In other words, no nonworking time is defined on the 24-Hour calendar. In this calendar time is measured as elapsed durations.
Night Shift	The Night Shift calendar considers a typical night-shift working time frame of 11:00 P.M. until 8:00 A.M. with a one-hour lunch from 3:00 A.M. until 4:00 A.M. each of five working days. This calendar defines working hours commonly known as the "graveyard shift" and, like the Standard calendar, creates eight hours of working time across five days a week totaling a 40-hour work week.

Any of these three calendars (or any calendars you create) can be applied in three places. You can apply any of these calendars to the entire project, individual tasks, or individual resources, as follows:

- **Project**   The project calendar applies scheduling to tasks and resources across the entire project and includes exceptions for nonworking time, such as company-wide holidays or staff meetings that don't pertain to the active project.
- **Tasks**   The calendar you apply to a task (or a group of tasks) specifies working time and exceptions that pertain only to the tasks in which the calendar is assigned.
- **Resources**   Each individual resource or group of resources can work from a customized calendar. This type of scheduling is particularly helpful in tracking individual personal time off and customized flex schedules of individuals and departments.

Conceivably, you could assign all three of these calendars to various areas of your project schedule. As you work with calendars (in this lesson and in future lessons related to both tasks and resources), keep in mind that there are essentially two calendar sets. The first is the actual calendars (Standard, Night Shift, and 24-Hour) and the second is where those calendars are assigned (Project, Tasks, and Resources).

Quick Check

- Which of the three project calendars should you assign to a machine that works all day and all night?

Quick Check Answer

- The three project calendars are Standard, 24-Hour, and Night Shift, any of which can be assigned to projects, tasks, or resources. For this scenario you need to assign the 24-Hour calendar because the machine works 24 hours a day.

Working with the Project Calendar

Initially, the project calendar assigned assumes that your project tasks will be completed over a standard 40-hour work week. Those 40 hours are scheduled across five working days, specifically Monday through Friday, thus designating 8:00 A.M.–5:00 P.M. with an hour off for lunch as "working time." This is because the default base project calendar for all new projects is the Standard calendar.

NOTE   Working vs. nonworking time

There are a couple of high points you'll want to take away as you work through this lesson on calendars and working versus nonworking time. First, working time is any time work is, or can be, performed on a task. If your project resources are all involved in the same staff meeting each week and that meeting isn't directly related to the project, this is a good example of scheduling the time the staff members are in a meeting as nonworking time. Second, nonworking time is now classified in Project as "exceptions."

At any point during your project you can assign any one of the three base calendars that are available to all new projects: Standard, Night Shift, and 24-Hour. To change the calendar assigned to an open project, follow these steps:

1. Open any existing project. You can also open any project template.
2. On the Project Menu, choose Project Information.
3. In the Calendar drop-down list, click the down arrow, as shown in Figure 1-47.

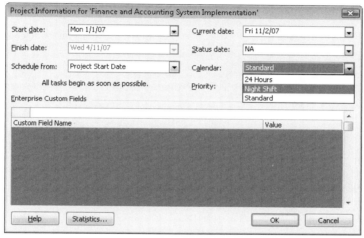

Figure 1-47   Using the Calendar option to select the desired calendar for a project

4. Select one of the following: 24 Hours, Night Shift, or Standard (Project Calendar).
5. Click OK.

MORE INFO   Project planning

Although you can assign calendars to the project, individual tasks, and resources, this lesson focuses solely on working with the project base calendar and assigning a calendar to an individual task. For more information on working with resource calendars, see Chapter 2.

Project Information Dialog Box

In the steps you use to change the project base calendar, you're required to open the Project Information dialog box. In the Project Information Dialog box you can modify the project's start and finish date, the current date and project status date, as well as the base project calendar. Refer to Figure 1-47, shown previously.

Also in the Project Information dialog box you can modify the project-level priorities. You can set a project's priority to any number between 0 and 1000, with 500 being the default. The higher the number, the higher the priority. The priority number you enter in the Project Information dialog box tells Project how readily tasks in the current project are delayed when resources are leveled across multiple projects. Figure 1-48 shows the Priority box. Use the up and down spinner arrows to change the number, or type your own.

Figure 1-48   The Priority option

MORE INFO   **Resource leveling**

For more information on leveling and working with multiple projects, see Chapter 4.

You can also set individual task priorities in the Task Information dialog box using the same 0 to 1000 scale. Overall, when a project's resources are leveled to address overallocation (a common issue when using one set of resources from a resource pool in several projects), Project will consider project-level priorities, which are set in the Project Information dialog box, over task-level priorities, which are set in the Task Information dialog box.

Exam Tip   You might see a question on the exam with a scenario that places you in the role of managing multiple projects. In this scenario you might be asked how to designate one project as more critical than another even though both projects use the same resources. In this scenario the more critical project should be set with a higher priority (1000) than lower-level projects. You do this in the Project Information dialog box.

Modifying an Existing Project Calendar

Often you will come across times where one of the default project calendars simply does not meet your task scheduling needs. During these times you can modify the existing project calendars. This way, you can add customized nonworking times (exceptions), such as company-wide holidays.

> **Real World**
>
> *Deanna Reynolds*
>
> Over the past several years, allowing employees to work flex schedules has become increasingly popular. I've even seen companies shut down on Friday afternoon as many employees head out early after working extended hours Monday through Thursday. If everyone involved in a project is off on a certain day, then definitely create a working time exception. However, if a day off, even though regular, affects only a couple of project team members, you'll create exceptions on individual resource calendars, not the project calendar. As such, flex-time exceptions are best suited for resource calendars while company holidays should be noted on the project calendar.

In Project 2003 you could make changes to working and nonworking times for a day or set of days first by highlighting the day(s) you wanted to change and then making the change to the working time. In Project you create exceptions to define nonworking time. These exceptions can be one-time occurrences, such as a company holiday, or recurring exceptions, such as weekly staff meetings.

To create a one-time exception, follow these steps:

1. On the Tools menu, choose Change Working Time.
2. In the Exceptions tab, in the Name field, type a name for this exception.
3. In the Start Field, type or select a start date from the drop-down calendar. If desired, select a finish date.
4. Click OK to apply this exception to the Standard (Project Calendar).

To create a recurring exception and to set working times, a recurrence pattern, and a start and end date, complete the following steps:

1. On the Tools menu, click Change Working Time.
2. In the Exceptions tab, in the Name field, create a new exception by typing an exception name. See Figure 1-49.

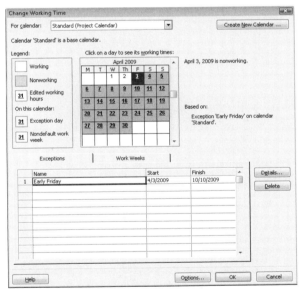

Figure 1-49   The Exceptions tab

3. In the Start box, click the down arrow, and, using the calendar, select the start date of this exception. If desired, select a finish date.
4. With the exception selected, click Details.

5. In the Details dialog box, shown in Figure 1-50, under Set Working Times for These Exceptions, select Working Times.

6. In the first row of From and To boxes, input the first range of working times for this exception.

7. In the second row of From and To boxes, press the Delete key or enter a second range of working times for this exception. (For example, early release Fridays would have one row of working time from 9:00 A.M. to noon.) See Figure 1-50 for an example.

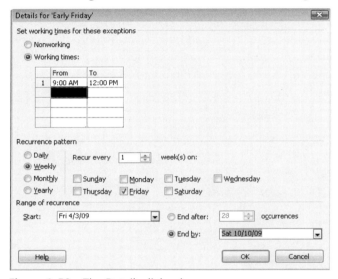

Figure 1-50   The Details dialog box

8. Under Recurrence Pattern, shown in Figure 1-50, select a desired recurrence.

9. Set your desired exception recurrence settings.

10. Under Range Of Recurrence, set your start and finish date ranges. Again, see Figure 1-50.

11. In the End After ___ Occurrences, set the number of occurrences to your desired number.

12. Click OK. Click OK to close the Change Working Time dialog box.

Exam Tip   If you have experience with Project 2003, you'll notice that the steps for changing working time exceptions have been changed. Take note of this change because you might be asked a question about defining nonworking time. For instance, you might be asked how to mark every Friday in a given month as nonworking time. You'll need to know that this is done in the Exceptions tab and not by clicking the Friday column header.

Quick Check

■ You need to create an exception for the company picnic that's being held next Friday at corporate headquarters. What type of exception should you make to the project calendar?

Quick Check Answer

■ A one-time exception.

As you create exceptions to the base project calendar, you can see those exceptions visually on the Gantt Chart. Days that have been designated as "nonworking" are shown with a gray bar similar to what you see across Saturdays and Sundays when the Standard calendar is applied to the project.

To see exceptions that involve partial working hours, you'll need to increase the zoom on the Gantt Chart to display task bars across hours instead of days as shown in Figure 1-51. You can do this by clicking the Zoom In button on the Standard toolbar or by using the key combination Ctrl+/ to zoom in (and Ctrl+* to zoom out).

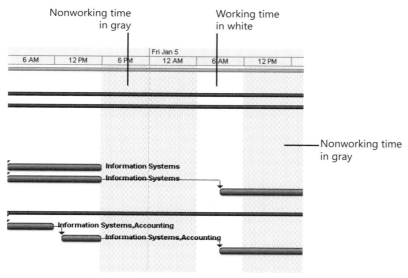

Figure 1-51   Exceptions during partial working hours

Exam Tip   When you read through the questions on your exam, remember that you might see the terms "nonworking time" and "exceptions" interchangeably. As such, we've worded this book the same way. Essentially, "nonworking time" and "exception" is the same thing.

Copying an Existing Project Calendar

When you know you'll be making widespread changes to a project calendar, such as the addition of several holidays or other nonworking days (exceptions), you can choose to copy an existing calendar, save it under a new name, and make your changes to the new calendar. This method leaves the original default calendars in place as backups should you need them again.

To copy an existing project calendar, follow these steps:

1. Open the project you want to copy the new calendar to.
2. On the Tools menu, choose Change Working Time.
3. Click the Create New Calendar button, as shown in Figure 1-52.

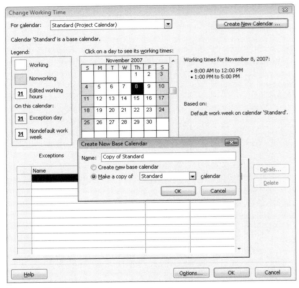

Figure 1-52   Copying a calendar

4. In the Name box, type a name for the new calendar.
5. From the Make A Copy Of drop-down list, select the calendar you want to copy.
6. Click OK.
7. Create exceptions on the new calendar.
8. Click OK.

Creating a New Project Calendar

Project also offers the option to create a brand-new calendar from scratch. This is a viable option when none of the three default calendars comes close to meeting your project task scheduling needs.

To create a new calendar, complete the following steps:

1. Open a new project.
2. Click Tools, and then choose Change Working Time.
3. In the Change Working Time dialog box, click the Create New Calendar button.
4. The default name of the calendar is Copy Of Standard. Change it to another calendar name that suits your needs.
5. Select Create New Base Calendar, as shown in Figure 1-53.

Figure 1-53   Creating a new base calendar

6. Click OK to return to the Change Working Time dialog box.
7. Create exceptions or changes to the work week on the new calendar. If you change the work week, you'll set the working times using the Details dialog box shown in Figure 1-54.

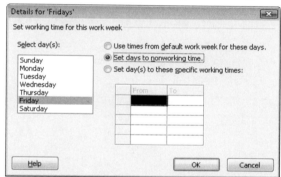

Figure 1-54   Configuring your new Calendar

8. Click OK.
9. Click OK, and then click OK again.

NOTE   Plan ahead

If your project is currently scheduled to reach completion by March 15, schedule your working time exceptions through April 15. This way you won't have to modify your calendar each time the project finish dates slips.

> **Quick Check**
> ■ You need to create a calendar that represents your company's unique working hours. What two options do you have for creating this calendar?
>
> **Quick Check Answer**
> ■ Modifying an existing calendar or creating your own from scratch.

Applying a Calendar to a Task

Earlier, this chapter discussed creating new project calendars and customizing existing calendars, but there can only be one project calendar. Remember, the project calendar defines task scheduling across the entire project.

Occasionally, you'll have a task that needs to take into account scheduling considerations that fall outside the defined project calendar. In this instance modifying the project calendar with the task's scheduling constraints is likely to affect the scheduling of other tasks.

To address this issue, you can create or assign a specific calendar for an individual task or set of tasks.

To assign a base calendar or a calendar you created to a single task or a recurring task, complete the following steps:

1. On the View menu, choose Gantt Chart, if it is not already selected.
2. Double-click the task, and in the Task Information dialog box click the Advanced tab.
3. In the Calendar list, select the calendar that you want to use the task. See Figure 1-55.

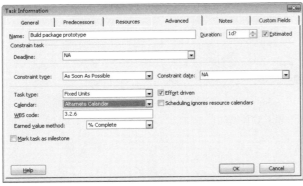

Figure 1-55   Creating a new base calendar

4. If you do not want the resource calendar to change the scheduling of the task, select the Scheduling Ignores Resource Calendars check box.
5. Click OK.

> ### Real World
>
> *Deanna Reynolds*
>
> Project's default calendar working times of Monday through Friday, 8:00 A.M.–5:00 P.M., with an hour for lunch, certainly reflects a commonly used working and scheduling environment. However, consider a project for a company-wide software rollout. One of the tasks that needs to be accomplished to bring this project to completion is the installation of new software. Installing the software during regular working hours will most likely result in company-wide downtime, which is something the stakeholders want to avoid. This means that the only option is to perform the installation task during non-working hours. This is a perfect opportunity to employ a custom task calendar. This way you can override the project default calendar for this one task. Another option is to employ a specific resource calendar. Doing so allows you to create custom working times by resource to ensure that you are accounting for time off for resources that might have worked all night on the installation.

Setting Default Calendar Options

If you find yourself modifying the default project calendar for every project you create, you have a couple of options to save yourself project planning time in the future. First, you can create customized calendars and then store those calendars in the Global.mpt. Global.mpt is the file in which all new blank projects are based. Alternatively, you can click the Calendar tab in the Options dialog box and modify the default settings. Let's first look at customizing a calendar and adding it to the Global.mpt.

To modify a default project calendar, follow these steps:

1. Create a new calendar.
2. From the Tools menu, choose Organizer.
3. Click the Calendars tab.
4. Select the calendar you created in the right pane, and then click Copy. See Figure 1-56.
5. Note that the new calendar is now listed in the Global.MPT pane of the Organizer's Calendars tab. Click Close.

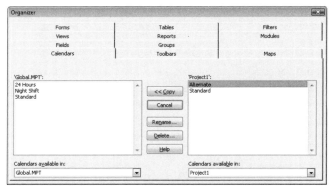

Figure 1-56   Modifying a project calendar

Your second option for modifying working times is to use the Calendar tab located in the Options dialog box, which is shown in Figure 1-57.

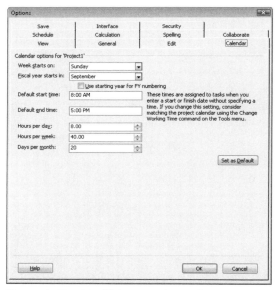

Figure 1-57   Modifying a project calendar using the Options dialog box

Here you can change the default start and end time for tasks, as well as the typical hours per day and per week and working days per month. The numbers in this dialog box are applied to all tasks in which you've specified a start or finish date but haven't specified a time. However, the project management best practice is to allow Project to schedule task start and finish dates.

To modify working times using the Options dialog box, follow these steps:

1.   Click Tools, and then choose Options.

2. Select the Calendar tab.
3. Make changes as desired using the down arrows by each option. Note that you can also set this as the default by clicking the Set As Default button. If you decide to modify the settings on the Calendar tab, those settings will be in effect for the current project only, unless you click the Set As Default button. Clicking this button will ensure that these settings are applied to all new projects based on the Blank project template.

PRACTICE Working with Calendars

In these practices you will reinforce what you've learned in this lesson. For the most part, you'll be creating a new project, with tasks and durations. In the first practice you'll select a base calendar for a project, just like you would in the workplace. The second practice is to copy an existing calendar, and the third is to create a new calendar from scratch. Finally, the fourth practice is to assign a calendar you've created to a single or recurring task included in your project.

NOTE Practice exercises

Perform these practices in order because each depends on the one before it.

▶ Exercise 1   Select a Base Calendar for a Project

In this exercise you'll create a new, blank project and select a base calendar for it. You need to select a calendar that represents your project's needs most closely, and for this project you'll choose the Night Shift calendar. To complete this exercise, follow these steps:

1. Create a new project based on the Blank project template.
2. Click Project, and then choose Project Information.
3. From the Calendar drop-down list, select Night Shift, and then click OK.
4. Click File, choose Save, and name the project Night Shift.

▶ Exercise 2   Copy an Existing Calendar

Your boss is very happy with how you modified the Night Shift calendar to meet your project's needs. He wants to copy the calendar to use for himself. You need to copy your calendar under a new name and add it to the Global.mpt file. To complete this exercise, follow these steps.

1. With your project open, click Tools, and then choose Change Working Time.
2. Select Night Shift (Project Calendar) in the For Calendar window if it isn't already selected.
3. Click Create New Calendar.
4. Name the calendar Copy Of Night Shift.
5. Select Make A Copy Of Night Shift Calendar.

6. Click OK to close the Create New Base Calendar dialog box. Click OK again to close the Change Working Time dialog box.
7. Click Tools, and then choose Organizer. Click the Calendars tab.
8. Under Night Shift, select Copy Of Night Shift.
9. Click Copy.
10. Click Close.
11. Send your boss a copy of the Global.mpt file.

Your boss can now create a new project using Project and use Copy Of Night Shift from the Calendar drop-down list.

► **Exercise 3   Create a New Calendar**

You are starting a new project and need to create a new calendar. You need a calendar to use for your temporary workers. None of the existing calendars are close to meeting your needs so you want to create a new calendar from scratch. To create a new calendar, perform the following steps.

1. Click Tools, and then choose Change Working Time.
2. Click Create New Calendar.
3. In the Create New Base Calendar dialog box, select Create New Base Calendar.
4. Name the calendar Temporary Workers. Click OK.
5. Select the Temporary Workers calendar in the For Calendar drop-down list.
6. Create the following exceptions in the Exceptions tab:
   a. Default Start Time: 8:00 A.M
   b. Default End Time: 8:00 P.M
   c. Days Per Week: Monday through Friday
7. Click OK to close the Change Working Time dialog box.

► **Exercise 4   Assign a Calendar to a Task**

You need to assign the Temporary Workers calendar to the task of readying the new warehouse for a large inventory shipment. The shipment is due in six weeks, and you'll use the new workers and the new calendar to get everything ready. To do this, follow these steps:

1. In your open project, in Gantt Chart view, for Task Name, type **Ready Warehouse**.
2. Press Enter.
3. Change the duration to five weeks. To do this, in the Duration window, type **5 wks**.
4. Double-click the task to open the Task Information dialog box.
5. Click the Advanced tab.
6. In the Calendar window drop-down list, choose Temporary Workers.
7. Click OK.

Lesson Summary

■ There are two calendar sets. The first set contains actual calendars (Standard, Night Shift, and 24-Hour), and the second set refers to where those calendars are assigned (Project, Tasks, and Resources).

■ Working time is any time work is or can be performed on a project-related task. Non-working time is time that is not related to a task or project, which has nothing to do with whether the employee is actually at work or not.

■ Regarding calendars, you can modify the existing project calendars, copy an existing calendar, or create a new calendar to suit your project's specific needs.

Lesson Review

You can use the following questions to test your knowledge of the information in Lesson 3, "Working with Calendars." The questions are also available on the companion CD if you prefer to review them in electronic form.

NOTE Answers

Answers to these questions and explanations of why each answer choice is correct or incorrect are located in the "Answers" section at the end of the book.

---

1. You want to use Project's standard working times for tasks with defined start and finish dates but not defined times. Which two options offer a place where can you make all of the changes?

    A. By clicking Tools, choosing Options and then selecting the Calendar tab.

    B. In the Change Working Time dialog box, by clicking Options.

    C. In the Project Information dialog box, under Calendar.

    D. In the Task Information dialog box, under Calendar.

2. You need to apply a calendar to a project that meets your project's specific needs. The days, hours, and work weeks you need for the project are not like any other project you've encountered. Which one of the following should you do?

    A. Apply Project's Alternate calendar to the project.

    B. When creating the new project, select Templates on Office Online and download a calendar that meets your needs.

    C. Create a new calendar from scratch.

    D. Use the Project Information dialog box to change the Standard calendar's hours and times.

3. The working times for your latest project, Taking Inventory, are from midnight to 6 A.M. for the next two weeks. You don't want to create a calendar from scratch. What is the quickest way to accomplish this?

    A. Modify the 24-Hour calendar in the Change Working Time dialog box and apply this calendar to the project.

    B. Copy the Night Shift calendar in the Change Working Time dialog box and apply this calendar to the Taking Inventory task.

    C. Copy the Standard calendar in the Change Working Time dialog box and apply this calendar to the project.

    D. Modify the Night Shift calendar in the Organizer dialog box (from the Calendar tab) and apply this calendar to the Taking Inventory task.

4. You created a calendar that you use when taking inventory twice a year. The calendar's name is Inventory. The Inventory calendar allows working days on Saturday and Sunday only, in eight-hour shifts from 8:00 A.M. to 5:00 P.M. In an unrelated project you have a task that can only be performed on weekends—that is the only time the machine that is needed to perform the task is available. The machine can run 24 hours a day. You've already copied the Inventory calendar to the existing project. Which of the following represent valid next steps? (Choose two. Each correct answer is a complete solution.)

    A. Modify the Inventory calendar in the Change Working Time dialog box, and then apply it to the task using the Task Information dialog box.

    B. Select the Inventory calendar in the Task Information box, and then make changes to the calendar in the Change Working Time dialog box.

    C. Select the Inventory calendar in the Project Information dialog box, and then make changes to the calendar in the Change Working Time dialog box.

    D. Modify the Inventory calendar in the Change Working Time dialog box, and then select the calendar in the Project Information dialog box.

Chapter Review

To further practice and reinforce the skills you learned in this chapter, you can perform the following tasks:

- Review the chapter summary.
- Review the list of key terms introduced in this chapter.
- Complete the case scenarios. These scenarios set up real-world situations involving the topics of this chapter and ask you to create a solution.
- Complete the suggested practices.
- Take a practice test.

Chapter Summary

- When setting up interface options, you can hide and show toolbars, hide or show the Project Guide, and toggle the Project Guide's Task pane on and off.
- You can set up and configure a new project in a number of ways, but the Project Guide is generally best for new Project users.
- Templates provide a starting point for many projects. Templates come preconfigured with tasks, resources, working times, start and finish dates, and more.
- After a project has been created, you can enter project information in many ways. The most common include the Project Information dialog box, the Task Information dialog box, the Entry table, and the Gantt Chart.
- Project comes with three calendars: Standard, Night Shift, and 24-Hour. You can apply these calendars to tasks, projects, and resources. You can also create calendars from scratch and copy or modify existing calendars.
- Tasks are the building blocks of any project. You generally enter tasks using the Entry table. You can modify tasks using the Task Information dialog box, and you can apply calendars to them, among other things.
- You can estimate and budget tasks from the Entry table or in the Task Information dialog box. In the Task Information dialog box you can select a calendar, add notes, change the start and finish dates, and set estimated durations, priorities, predecessors, resources, and more.

Key Terms

Do you know what these key terms mean? You can check your answers by looking up the terms in the glossary at the end of the book.

- calendar
- decomposition
- duration
- exception
- Gantt Chart
- milestone
- Network Diagram
- PERT formula
- project
- project calendar
- Project Guide
- recurring task
- Resource Graph
- Resource Sheet
- Resource Usage View
- task
- task calendar
- Task Usage view
- template
- timescale
- Tracking Gantt

Case Scenarios

In the following case scenarios you will apply what you have learned about using Project in this chapter, including setting up a project and working with both tasks and calendars. You can find answers to these questions in the "Answers" section at the end of this book.

Case Scenario 1: Managing a Software Roll-out Project

You're a project manager for a company gearing up for a company-wide software roll-out. The scope of this project includes, among many variables, the successful implementation of a company-wide software upgrade. During this roll-out, the stakeholders have made it very clear that company employees should experience zero downtime. For you this means scheduling actual software installation during times that are typically reserved for employee time off. Answer the following questions:

1. During the meetings with the project stakeholders, you've learned that this company has managed successful software roll-out projects in the past. How can you use the lessons learned from previous projects when creating your new project file?

2. You've created the initial project plan and the project stakeholders would like to see a printed timeline of the project. Which view can you print and distribute?

3. In your project schedule you'll need to account for a weekly project status meeting that involves several key members of your team. Assuming this status meeting is related solely to this software roll-out, how would you account for this time in your project schedule?

Case Scenario 2: Scheduling a Project

You've just been assigned the project management responsibilities for a large construction project. Over the next 18 months you'll be responsible for making sure that the new building construction is finished on time, to scope, and within budget. Answer the following questions:

1. Even though the construction project is on a tight schedule, there are about five company holidays in which no work will be performed on any of the project tasks. How do you account for these days in your project schedule?

2. To build some slack into the schedule, you decide to make every Friday a half working day by scheduling work for only four hours. How would you reflect this reduced working time in your project schedule?

3. Of all of the tasks on your project schedule, only one will require your workers to work around the clock to ensure that everything is completed properly. How can you meet this scheduling requirement so that it reflects appropriately on your project schedule?

Case Scenario 3: Task Durations

As an experienced project manager, you already know that estimating task durations can be tricky. Fortunately, you also understand the PERT formula. Using the PERT formula and your knowledge of task durations, answer the following questions.

1. Task: Hang Wallpaper. There seem to be varying opinions on how long it will take to hang wallpaper in the new conference room. For instance, the project stakeholders have said they would like the task completed in six hours, but when you give that time frame to the wallpaper contractors, they think you must be kidding. And to give themselves some extra time to account for errors and long breaks, they've asked for 14 hours to complete the work. Although you can't base the entire task duration on previous work, you know from similar projects that similar tasks for rooms close to the same size that this task could most likely be finished in seven hours. Use the PERT formula to determine a task duration for hanging wallpaper.

2. Task: Phase 1 Checkpoint. Phase 1 consists of eight tasks. In order for Phase 1 to be completed, the related tasks must be completed. At the end of Phase 1 you've entered a task designed to act as a marker to designate the end of Phase 1. What is the duration of the Phase 1 Checkpoint?

3. Task: Order Conference Room Equipment. Ordering the conference room equipment can take anywhere from one to four weeks, although typically the furniture arrives within 10 business days. Use the PERT formula to determine a task duration for ordering conference room equipment.

Suggested Practices

To help you successfully master the exam objectives presented in this chapter, complete the following tasks. It is best to work through all of these exercises.

- **Practice 1: Set Up Interface Options**   Learning more about setting up interface options will help you refine Project by making available the toolbars, Project Guide, and other options you'll need access to regularly. To learn more about interface options, open a Project template and click each option in the View menu one at a time to study what happens to the interface and project information.

- **Practice 2: Select a Template**   To learn more about available templates, in the Project Guide, under New Project, click Templates On Office Online. Browse through the available templates and become aware of what is available online for Project.

- **Practice 3: Enter Project Information**   For more information on entering project information, visit the Project home page at Microsoft.com and look for Project training courses. Courses range from a few minutes to almost an hour. Work through as many online courses as you can.

- **Practice 4: Create and Modify Tasks**   At this stage you'll want to be comfortable with entering and editing tasks. For this, practice adding tasks and working with durations. Remember, you can modify task start and finish dates. However, this is discouraged because doing so disables Project's ability to automatically schedule tasks for you.

- **Practice 5: Estimate and Budget Tasks**   When estimating and budgeting tasks, start with some research. Ask others or check online to help you estimate how long tasks will take and how much they will cost. After you have the necessary data, use the PERT formula to help you. Learn more about estimating and budgeting tasks in books specifically created for project managers. To be a successful project manager, you need to know more than just how to use Project; you need to understand project management theory, too.

- **Practice 6: Manage Calendars**   Make sure you know the difference among Project calendars, Resource calendars, and Task calendars, and when and why they should be applied. You can find out more at Microsoft.com.

Take a Practice Test

The practice tests on this book's companion CD offer many options. For example, you can test yourself on just one exam objective, or you can test yourself on all the 70-632 certification exam content. You can set up the test so that it closely simulates the experience of taking a certification exam, or you can set it up in study mode so that you can look at the correct answers and explanations after you answer each question.

MORE INFO   **Practice tests**

For details about all the practice test options available, see the "How to Use the Practice Tests" section in this book's Introduction.

Chapter 2
Project Planning

According to the Project Management Body of Knowledge (PMBOK), the Project Planning phase is easily the most time-consuming part of project management. It covers many aspects. While you are working in the Planning phase, you will be involved in several facets, including cost and resource budget planning, setting resource requirements, risk planning, assigning resources to tasks, building a schedule, and communicating project plans.

Although much of a project's Initiation phase happens in the conference room, a great deal of the Planning phase can take place in the Microsoft Office Project 2007 program. In this phase you will begin to see the power of this program's ability to help you build a work breakdown structure (WBS), transform that WBS into a project schedule, assign resources to tasks, and then analyze the resulting project critical path. Project displays project changes "on-the-fly," showing you the results of any project plan changes immediately. This instant display allows you to try out several project scenarios and explore the overall effect on the project plan before choosing your solution.

Not surprisingly, the one characteristic that makes Project so good at predicting work hours and task durations is also the one that seems to take the most time to learn—effort-driven scheduling. For this reason, much of this chapter has been devoted to the explanation of effort-driven scheduling, coupled with real-world scenarios.

Exam objectives in this chapter:
- Set up View options.
- Create a WBS.
- Create and modify tasks.
- Estimate and budget tasks.
- Sequence tasks.
- Identify and analyze critical tasks and critical path.
- Forecast time-phased generic skill or role requirements.
- Create, modify, and use resource pools.
- Add, change, substitute, or remove resource assignments.
- Predict durations and work calculations.
- Save and modify baselines.
- Reschedule incomplete work.
- Create reports.

Lessons in this chapter:

Before You Begin

As you begin this chapter related to the Planning phase of your projects, you will continue to see standard project management terms—many of which might already be familiar. Before you begin, you should:

- Be able to create a new project based on a predefined template, an existing project, or a blank project
- Understand how to set up initial project information, including the project start date and initial tasks
- Be comfortable navigating between common project views, including Gantt Chart View, Network Diagram, and various tables

---

Real World

Deanna Reynolds

Project 2007 cannot help you in coming up with workable tasks for your project plan. This is where you get to use your project management expertise. One option, although it might seem somewhat archaic, is an old paper-based method of organizing your project scope into smaller, more manageable work packages—and it relies on Post-It™ notes. Simply write each task you can think of on individual sticky notes, sticking each to a nearby wall or door as you write. After you have finished your task brainstorming session, you can begin to logically group sets of tasks by rearranging the notes. Finally, you can create additional notes that mark the beginning and end of each group of tasks. This is an example of bottom-up planning.

Lesson 1: Working with Tasks

A large part of being an effective project manager is excelling at the ability to take a large project scope and break it down into manageable work packages. This is often where the familiar project management question "Just how do you eat an elephant?" comes in. The answer, of course, is "One bite at a time."

Those bites are your project work packages, deliverables, or tasks. In the last chapter you learned about adding tasks to a project plan file. This lesson takes those tasks that you already know how to enter and begins to organize them into phases that define a WBS, complete with WBS numbering.

> **After this lesson, you will be able to:**
> - Define a work breakdown structure (WBS).
> - Outline tasks.
> - Insert, copy, and move tasks.
> - Display WBS numbers.
> - Customize WBS numbers.
> - Display project summary information.
>
> **Estimated lesson time: 45 minutes**

Organizing Tasks

As you learned in the previous chapter, entering tasks is fairly straightforward. Luckily, moving, copying, and inserting tasks are just as simple at this step in the project management process because relationships have not yet been defined. There are actually several methods for performing each of these functions; however, in this book we will focus on those that represent the "best practice" application with only a passing reference to other techniques.

Exam Tip   Exam 70-362 focuses on the best practice answer to each given question. In other words, you will not need to know all the ways a task can be moved, but you will need to know that the best practice for moving a task is dragging. In this instance, dragging to move a task is important because using the Cut and Paste commands causes the Task Unique ID field to be renumbered, which can ultimately cause problems if you integrate the project with other applications. It's generally best to drag the entire task row because you have to move an entire task row if there is any other data associated with the task.

Moving Tasks

To verify that Project is enabled for cell drag-and-drop and to move a task using drag-and-drop, follow these steps:

1. On the Tools menu, choose Options.
2. In the Options dialog box, click the Edit tab.
3. Under Edit Options For Microsoft Office Project, verify that the Allow Cell Drag And Drop check box is selected.
4. Click OK.
5. In a new, blank project, under Task Name, type **Drag and Drop Practice**, as shown in Figure 2-1.

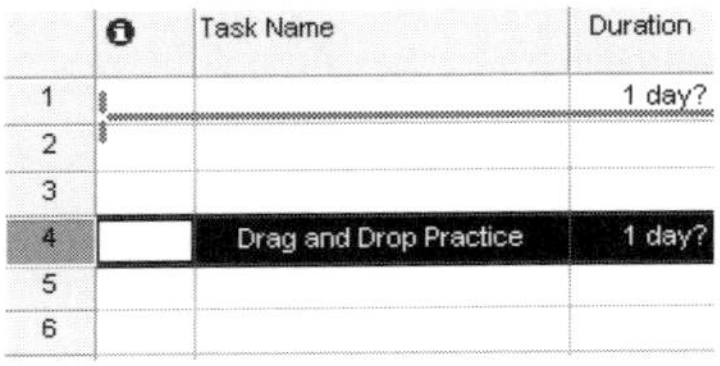

Figure 2-1   Enter a task, and then practice dragging it

6. Select the ID cell, the cell on the far left that shows the task's ID number (so that the entire task row is selected), and then position the pointer over the ID cell to get the four-headed arrow.
7. Drag the task to a new row in the Task Name column.

MORE INFO   **Moving tasks with relationships**

Moving tasks when relationships have been defined can cause problems in your project plan. Tasks and relationships are covered more in depth later in this chapter.

Other methods for moving tasks include the following:

- Right-clicking the Task ID column for the task, choosing Cut Task from the drop-down menu, repositioning the mouse in a new row's Task ID column, right-clicking the cell, and choosing Paste from the drop-down list.
- Selecting the task by clicking the Task ID column and using the Cut Task option from the Standard toolbar. The icon is a pair of scissors, as in other programs. Then repositioning the mouse in a new row's Task ID column and using Paste from the Standard toolbar. The Paste icon is a clipboard.
- Selecting the task by clicking on the Task's ID column you want to cut and using the keyboard shortcut for Cut (Ctrl+X), repositioning the mouse in a new cell, and using the keyboard shortcut for paste (Ctrl+V).

MORE INFO   Moving tasks

For more information on moving and copying tasks in Project, consult the following book: *Microsoft Office Project 2007 Step by Step.*

Copying Tasks

Unlike moving, there really is no clear cut "best practice" when copying tasks. Here is a list of all of the acceptable copy methods:

- To copy a task, in the task ID column name, right-click and choose Copy Task. As with cutting, you can perform this in a variety of ways, including using the Standard toolbar Copy Task button, using the key combination Ctrl+C, and using Copy Task from the Edit menu.

- To copy multiple contiguous tasks, select the first task by clicking the Task ID number, hold down the Shift key, and select the last task in the same manner. Then use any available method to copy them. To copy noncontiguous tasks, select the first task, hold down the Ctrl key, and select the second task. Repeat to select more tasks. Use any acceptable method to copy the tasks.

- To copy multiple contiguous tasks and their information, select the first task's ID number, hold down the Shift key, and select the last task's ID number. Then use any acceptable method to copy them. To copy noncontiguous tasks, select the first task's ID number, hold down the Ctrl key, and select the second task's ID number. Repeat to select more tasks. Use any acceptable method to copy the tasks.

TIP   Adjacent vs. nonadjacent cells

In Project you can select several adjacent cells simply by positioning the mouse pointer inside the first cell in the range you want to select and then clicking and dragging down to the last cell in the range. Additionally, you can use your keyboard in conjunction with your mouse by selecting the first cell in the range, holding down the Shift key, and selecting the last cell in the range. In order to select nonadjacent cells, you need to use keyboard key Ctrl plus the mouse. In other words, select the first cell, and, while holding Ctrl, continue to select additional cells.

Inserting Tasks

There are a couple of available methods for inserting tasks. Far and away the most universally acceptable way to insert a task is to simply use the Insert key on the keyboard. However, you can also insert tasks from the Insert menu. Let's look at both.

To insert a task using the Insert key on the keyboard or the Insert menu, complete the following steps:

1. Position the mouse in the Entry table in the cell below where you want to insert a task. You can select the Task ID number, the Task Name, the Duration, or any other Entry table cell in the task.

2. Press the Insert key on the keyboard or choose Insert and choose New Task. The Insert menu is shown in Figure 2-2.

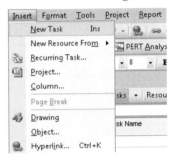

Figure 2-2 Insert a task using the Insert menu

3. Fill in the task's information.

NOTE Using keyboard shortcuts

On the Insert menu shown in Figure 2-2, note that Ins is next to New Task. This is the keyboard shortcut—in this case the Insert key. At the bottom, see Hyperlink. The keyboard shortcut for entering a hyperlink is Ctrl+K.

Deleting Tasks

There are a couple of available methods for deleting tasks. The most universally acceptable way to delete a task is to simply use the Delete key on the keyboard. However, you can also delete tasks from the Edit menu. Let's look at both.

To delete a task using the Delete key on the keyboard and using the Edit menu, follow these steps:

1. Select the ID number cell for the task you want to delete. The entire task should be highlighted.

2. Press the Delete key on the keyboard or choose Edit, and then choose Delete Task.

Notice that in step 1 you selected the entire task to delete by selecting its Task ID number cell. If you select only the task name and press Delete, Project displays the delete indicator in the Indicators column. When you see this indicator, shown in Figure 2-3, you will need to click the indicator and choose to delete the entire task or just the task name.

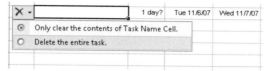

Figure 2-3 The Delete indicator shows when you delete from the Task Name and not the Task ID number

---

Quick Check

1. What is considered the best practice for inserting a new task?
2. Which key on the keyboard would you press to allow you to select a noncontiguous range of tasks?

Quick Check Answers

1. Select the new task position, and then press the Insert key on the keyboard.
2. Ctrl.

Undo and Redo

New to Project is the ability to undo multiple edits—up to 99 levels. You can undo your last edit by clicking the Undo button on the toolbar or by choosing Edit and Undo *<last command name>*. You can perform either of these actions up to 99 times. However, if you need to undo multiple levels, it is best to click the arrow next to the Undo button on the Standard toolbar and decide how far back you would like to go. This is shown in Figure 2-4. You drag your mouse over the edits you would like to undo.

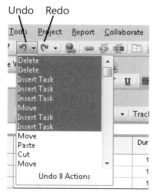

Figure 2-4 Performing a multiple undo

You can also redo edits in the same manner. You can click once on the Redo icon on the Standard toolbar to redo one edit or use the down arrow beside it to redo multiple edits. Alternately, you can choose Edit and Redo *<last command name>* from the Standard menu bar.

Exam Tip   For exam 70-632 you will need to be aware of this new multiple Undo feature, how many levels you can undo, and how to modify the number of Undo levels tracked by Project.

Changing the Default Number of Undo Levels   Even though Project allows up to 99 levels of Undo, by default, the program tracks only the last 20 actions. You can modify this number to suit your needs by entering any number between 1 and 99. Follow these steps:

1. Choose Tools, and then choose Options.
2. Click the General tab.
3. Under General Options For Microsoft Office Project, change the number of Undo Levels to the desired number. See Figure 2-5.

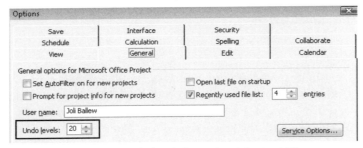

Figure 2-5   Change undo levels from the default of 20

TIP   Save feature

While you are in the Options dialog box, click the Save tab. Configure Project to automatically save your project frequently.

---

4. Click OK.

Outlining the Project Plan

If you have a general idea of project organization but have not yet developed detail level tasks, you will begin your planning using the *top-down method*. This means that you have a good idea of your high-level organization, which will turn into summary tasks in Project. Later you will add the details, project tasks, and subtasks.

For a project plan that has all of the detail tasks but has not yet been organized into a high-level plan, you will use the *bottom-up method*. With this planning method, you start with a highly detailed task list, or subtasks, and create logical groups to represent summary tasks.

When your tasks have been entered and organized, you can begin setting up those tasks into a workable outline. You do this by demoting (indenting) tasks that you want to define as subtasks and, if necessary, promoting (outdenting) tasks that you want to define as summary tasks. (The Formatting toolbar offers the Indent and Outdent buttons to make this easy to do.) At this stage you will implement your preferred approach to organizing your project plan into your chosen task groups (top-down or bottom-up) and then begin to indent and outdent your chosen tasks to organize your project tasks.

Exam Tip   On Exam 70-632 you might be given a project planning scenario for which you will need to determine whether the project manager used top-down or bottom-up planning in order to determine whether you need to create subtasks or summary tasks. Although these planning methods are not specific to Project, understanding key project management theoretical concepts such as these will help you as you take this exam.

Using the Bottom-up Method

We will start by creating an outline using the bottom-up method.

Figure 2-6 shows a recently started project. You can see all of the detail tasks. You already know how to create a new project and add tasks, so getting to this point is easy. As the project is further refined, one of the first things that needs to be done is to insert a few tasks that will act as summary tasks. You can do this by using the Insert key. As you know, to insert a task using the Insert key, select the cell below where the task should go and press Insert on the keyboard. See Figure 2-7 and compare it to Figure 2-6 to see what has been added.

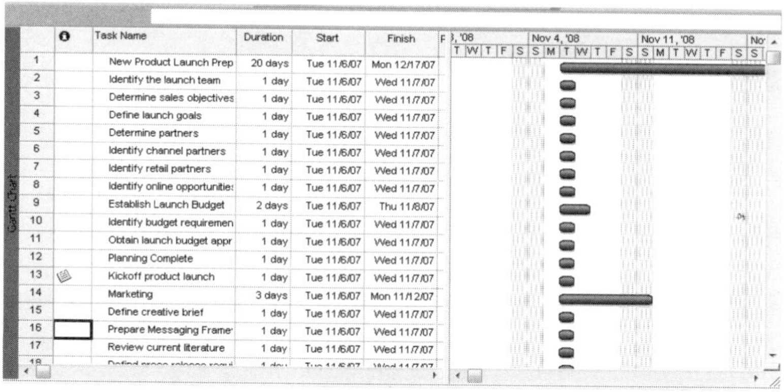

Figure 2-6   Projects often start with a detailed task list

Now that the summary tasks have been added (as shown in Figure 2-7), you can begin to create the outline structure. Notice that the durations of the summary tasks have not been updated. This is because a summary task's duration, start date, finish date, and a variety of other calculated fields are derived from the data contained in the subtasks. This will be changed when you indent the subtasks. Figure 2-8 shows how the indent process changes the information in the Entry table.

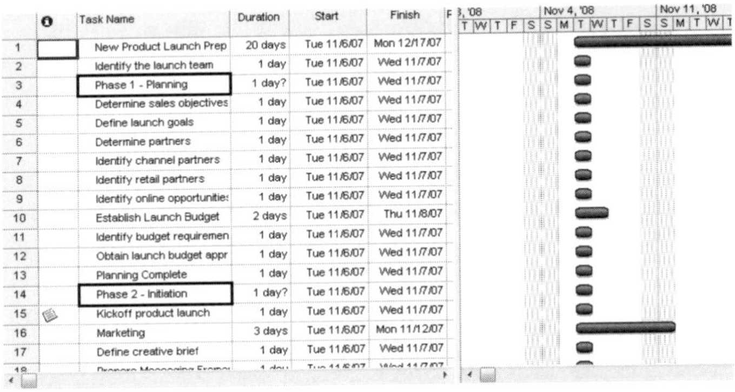

Figure 2-7   Insert phases to further define the project

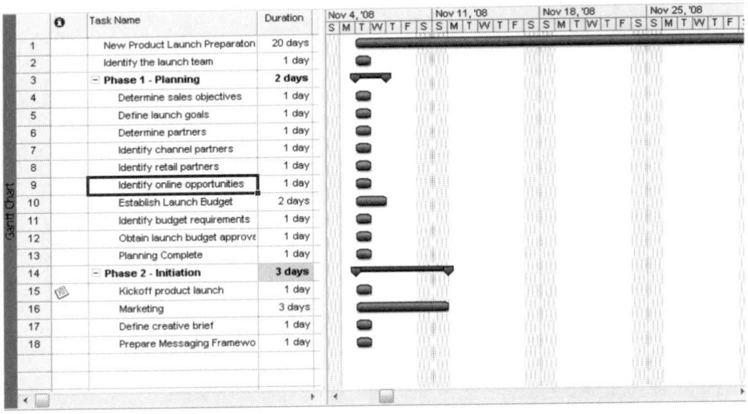

Figure 2-8   Use the Indent button to create subtasks

Look at each of the summary tasks in Figure 2-8. Note how the summary tasks' durations are equal to the length of the longest subtask. After task relationships are defined, the summary task duration will automatically update to represent the total duration of all subtasks.

Multiple Summary Tasks

Each project can have multiple outline levels creating several summary tasks. As shown in Figure 2-9, here the project is defined in phases, which are entitled Define Sources of Customer Feedback, Determine Data Analysis Methods, Design Custom Issue Response Process, and others.

1	– **Develop Customer Feedback Collection Processes**	**$3,880.00**
2	– **Define sources of customer feedback**	**$2,040.00**
3	Identify sources of voluntary customer feedback	$680.00
4	Identify sources for solicited customer feedback	$680.00
5	Determine internal and competitive sources of custom	$680.00
6	Determine Data Collection Methods	$280.00
7	– **Determine Data Analysis Methods**	**$840.00**
8	Determine appropriate data analysis method	$0.00
9	Develop a plan and a schedule for performing analysi	$0.00
10	Incorporate the developed analysis schedule into this	$0.00
11	Design of Feedback Collection and Analysis Process COI	$0.00
12	– **Design Customer Issue Response Process**	**$720.00**
13	Design method for following up with customer issues	$144.00
14	Identify resources responsible for working with unsa	$144.00
15	Define issue resolution process	$144.00
16	Designate resource as being accountable for resolvir	$144.00
17	Define customer follow-up process	$144.00
18	Design of Customer Issue Response Process COMPL	$0.00
19	– **Design Customer Feedback Monitoring Process**	**$2,960.00**

Figure 2-9   Summary tasks can be custom names

Notice how the summary tasks have a – sign to the left. This means they are high-level tasks with associated subtasks. Often, a subtask is also a summary task.

Not only do these summary tasks represent cumulative subtask data, but each contains its own outline indicator allowing the subtasks to be collapsed (hidden) or expanded (displayed), using + and – signs on the screen.

Using the Top-down Method

Now that you understand summary tasks and subtasks and you have seen them in action from a bottom-up methodology, let's look at approaching a similar project using the top-down method. In Figure 2-10 you can see only tasks that represent phase or summary level information.

	❶	Task Name	Duration	Start
1		Phase 1 - Initiation	1 day?	Tue 11/6/07
2		Phase 2 - Planning	1 day?	Tue 11/6/07
3		Phase 3 - Execution	1 day?	Tue 11/6/07
4		Phase 4 - Control	1 day?	Tue 11/6/07
5		Phase 5 - Close	1 day?	Tue 11/6/07

Figure 2-10   Planning a project using the top-down method

Working from the top down, use the Insert key to add details under each task, and then use the Indent button to demote the subtasks under each phase task. Figure 2-11 shows what has been added to the project shown in Figure 2-10, using the top-down planning method.

	ⓘ	Task Name	Duration	..., '08	Nov 4, '08	Nov 11, '08
1		− Phase 1 - Initiation	**2 days**			
2		Marketing	2 days			
3		Kickoff product launch	2 days			
4		− Phase 2 - Planning	**2 days**			
5		Determine sales objectives	2 days			
6		Determine partners	2 days			
7		− Phase 3 - Execution	**2 days**			
8		Marketing	2 days			
9		Sales	2 days			
10		− Phase 4 - Control	**5 days**			
11		Sales	2 days			
12		Hire and train sales staff	5 days			
13		Final quality review	4 days			
14		− Phase 5 - Close	**5 days**			
15		Launch product	5 days			

Figure 2-11   Insert tasks to further define the project

Thus far, we have used only the Indent button to develop our project plan outline. However, several additional buttons are on the Formatting toolbar that are designed specifically for your work in outlining your project. Figure 2-12 shows these buttons.

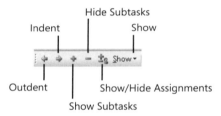

Figure 2-12   Use these formatting buttons to change how you view the project

The formatting buttons are explained here. To use them, first select a task:

- **Outdent**   Click this to move a subtask (or multiple selected tasks) up a level.
- **Indent**   Click this to make the selected task a subtask. The task above it will become a summary task and will be displayed in bold.
- **Show Subtasks**   Click this to show subtasks for the selected summary task.
- **Hide Subtasks**   Click this to hide subtasks for the selected summary task.
- **Hide Assignments**   Click this to hide assignments.
- **Show**   Click this to show tasks at a specified level.

MORE INFO   Working with tasks

For more information about working with tasks, read the following articles at Microsoft Office Online:

http://office.microsoft.com/en-us/project/HA101154011033.aspx?pid=CH100666521033

http://office.microsoft.com/en-us/project/HA101130691033.aspx?pid=CH100666551033

http://office.microsoft.com/en-us/project/HA101980911033.aspx?pid=CH100666621033

Project Summary Task

Summary tasks provide helpful total information both on the Entry table and on the Gantt Chart as a summary bar. You can display this same information for the entire project by displaying the project summary task.

To show the Project Summary task, complete the following steps:

1. Choose Tools, choose Options, and click the View tab.
2. Under Outline Options, select the Show Project Summary Task check box. See Figure 2-13.
3. Click OK.

Figure 2-13 Show the project summary task on the Entry table and Gantt Chart

---

TIP Attaching project level documentation

You can attach additional files that pertain to your project to the project summary task. Because most projects have so many related files, this is often not feasible. Doing so might greatly increase your overall file size. Even though you might have an entire folder structure within the project file, you can consider attaching the project charter to the summary tasks to make it easily accessible. For more information, refer to the following book: *Microsoft Office Project 2007 Inside Out.*

After the project summary task is displayed, you will see it added as the top task in your project plan; however, there is something special about this project summary task. Not only does it display the total project duration with start and finish dates, it is assigned the task ID number "0." The project summary task name is derived from Project's file name. You can modify this task name by double-clicking the task name and making the desired changes in the Task Information dialog box.

Quick Check

1. What type of information is displayed with the project summary task?
2. Adding detail level tasks first, then inserting project phases is an example of what type of project planning method?
3. How many levels of Undo are now available in Project? What is the default number of Undo levels in any new project?

Quick Check Answers

1. Project Name, Project Start Date, Project End Date, and Total Project Duration.
2. Bottom-Up.
3. There are 99 Undo levels available in Project. Of those, only 20 are available by default.

Defining the WBS

Creating an outline of tasks is the first step in Project in creating a WBS. The next step is to assign the detail level WBS codes. With WBS codes, each level of an assigned number represents summary tasks, subtasks, work packages, and so on. For example, a typical WBS code is 2.4.1, where "2" represents the phase (or summary task), "4" represents the fourth activity of the second phase, and "1" represents the first deliverable of the fourth activity in the second phase of the project. Figure 2-14 shows an example.

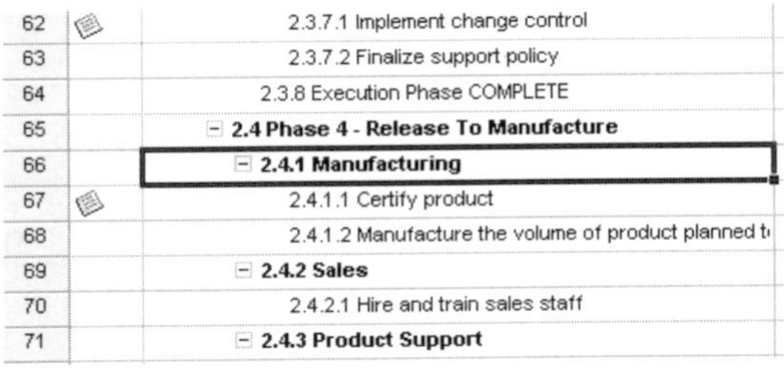

62		2.3.7.1 Implement change control
63		2.3.7.2 Finalize support policy
64		2.3.8 Execution Phase COMPLETE
65		⊟ **2.4 Phase 4 - Release To Manufacture**
66		⊟ **2.4.1 Manufacturing**
67		2.4.1.1 Certify product
68		2.4.1.2 Manufacture the volume of product planned t
69		⊟ **2.4.2 Sales**
70		2.4.2.1 Hire and train sales staff
71		⊟ **2.4.3 Product Support**

Figure 2-14   WBS codes help further define the project's tasks

Typically, you can use Project's default outline numbers as your WBS codes. To display the default outline numbers, follow these steps:

1. Choose Tools, choose Options, and click the View tab.
2. Under Outline Options For *<Project Name>*, select the Show Outline Number check box. Click OK to save your change.

Occasionally, you might need to use customized WBS codes based on your organization's coding scheme. Doing so requires some customization in creating new WBS codes as well as in modifying the displayed table to view the customized codes.

Custom WBS codes can include ordered numbers, upper and lowercase letters, and unordered characters. You can have only one set of WBS codes. To define your own WBS codes, follow these steps:

1. Choose Project, choose WBS, and choose Define Code.
2. Enter a Project Code Prefix if required. This will be necessary if you need to distinguish this project's numbering system from other projects in your organization.
3. In the Sequence drop-down list, select from Numbers (Ordered), Uppercase Letters (Ordered), Lowercase Letters (Ordered), or Characters (Unordered).
4. In the Length drop-down list for this sequence, select the length limit, if you have one.
5. In the Separator drop-down list for this sequence, select the separator. The choices include a period, a dash, a plus sign, or a slash.
6. Select the Sequence field in the second row. Repeat steps 3–5. Continue in this manner until all codes are input. Figure 2-15 shows an example.

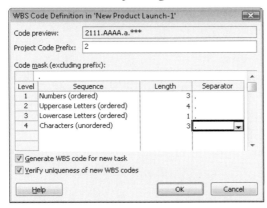

Figure 2-15   Create your own WBS code

After you have defined your custom WBS numbers, you will need to display those numbers on the project file. To display your custom WBS numbers, follow these steps:

1. Right-click the Task Name column heading in the Entry table.
2. From the shortcut menu, choose Insert Column.
3. In the Field Name drop-down list, select WBS.
4. Click OK.

> **MORE INFO**   **Creating custom WBS codes**
>
> Creating custom WBS codes is an advanced topic. For additional information related to working with custom WBS codes, refer to the following book: *Microsoft Office Project 2007 Inside Out.*

> **MORE INFO**   **Work breakdown help**
>
> For more information, visit *http://office.microsoft.com/en-us/project/HA102171211033.aspx?pid= CH102202741033*. Additionally, the Project Management Plan template, available at *http:// office.microsoft.com/en-us/templates/TC010774551033.aspx?pid=CT101172331033*, might prove quite useful.

PRACTICE Working with Tasks

In these practices you will review the skills you learned in this lesson. Each of these practices has to do with working with tasks. Because tasks are the building blocks of any project, it is important that you are comfortable with anything that is task-related.

The first exercise is to set up view options, including showing the Project Summary Task. The second is to create a unique WBS outline system, and the third is to create a WBS, add and group tasks, and modify them.

▶ **Exercise 1   Configure View Options**

You need to create a single task that summarizes the duration, work, and costs related to all the tasks in your project. You would also like to apply numbers that indicate the position of the task in the overall outline of the project. To complete this exercise, you must show the project summary task and the WBS numbers.

1. Choose File, choose New, and click On Computer.
2. In the Templates dialog box and the Project Templates tab, select Commercial Construction, and then click OK.
3. Choose Tools, choose Options, and click the View tab.
4. Under Outline Options For Commercial Construction, verify that the Show Project Summary Task check box is selected. If it is cleared, select it.
5. Under Outline Options For Commercial Construction, select the Show Outline Number check box.
6. Click OK.
7. Leave this file open for Exercise 2.

▶ Exercise 2   **Create a Unique WBS Outline System**

You are not happy with the default outline that was applied to the Commercial Construction project you created in Exercise 1. You want to define your own system that contains letters as well as numbers. Perform the following steps to complete this exercise:

1. With the Commercial Construction project open from Exercise 1, choose Project, choose WBS, and choose Define Code.
2. Do not enter a Project Code Prefix.
3. In the first Sequence drop-down list, select Numbers (Ordered).
4. In the second Sequence drop-down list select, Uppercase Letters (Ordered).
5. In the third Sequence drop-down list, select Numbers (Ordered).
6. In the fourth Sequence drop-down list, select Lowercase Letters (Ordered).
7. Click OK.
8. Right-click the Task Name column. Choose Insert Column from the shortcut menu.
9. In the Field Name drop-down list, choose WBS from the list.
10. Click OK to add the custom WBS numbers to the Entry table. Note that the numbering in the WBS column is different from that in the Task ID column.
11. Choose File, and choose Save As. Save the file as Commercial Construction 2.

▶ Exercise 3   **Add a WBS and Work With Tasks**

You are creating a new, blank project to help you manage your personal tasks in the construction of a new home. You need to add tasks and a WBS and position the tasks appropriately.

You will add these items to your task list: Approve Final Product, Final Walkthrough, Review Tasks, Apply For Permits, Receive Foundation Permit, Receive Framing Permit, Framing, Install Joists, Complete Roof Framing, Exterior Finishing, Install Brick, Install Siding, and Final Acceptance.

In this exercise you will add these tasks in the order presented and then indent and outdent as needed, as well as cut, copy, and paste. Although cutting, copying, and pasting tasks is not an actual test objective, it is still important to know how to do it.

To complete this project, perform the following steps:

1. Choose File, New, and click Blank Project in the New Project pane.
2. In the first Task Name field, type **Approve Final Product**. Press Enter.
3. In the second Task Name field, type **Final Walkthrough**. Press Enter.
4. Repeat steps 2 and 3 until you have input all items listed in the scenario (in the order presented).
5. Drag the mouse over the Task ID numbers for tasks 1, 2, and 3. They are in the wrong position and need to be moved. Approving the final product is the last thing you do, not the first.

6. Drag these tasks below Task 12: Install Siding.

7. Select the Task Name, "Receive Foundation Permit," and click the Indent button on the Formatting toolbar. This makes the task a subtask.

8. Repeat step 7 for the following tasks because they are also subtasks: Receive Framing Permit, Install Joists, and Complete Roof Framing.

9. Select the Task Name "Install Brick," hold down the Ctrl key, and select Install Siding, Approve Final Product, Final Walkthrough, and Review Tasks.

10. Press Alt+Shift+Right Arrow to indent the selected tasks.

11. Right-click the ID Number field for the task Final Acceptance, and choose Delete Task.

12. Select the Task Name "Approve Final Product," and click the Outdent button on the toolbar.

13. Choose File, choose Close. Do not save the file.

Lesson Summary

- Tasks are the basis of any project. Understanding how to manipulate them by using the Cut, Copy, Paste, Insert, and Delete commands is essential.

- Project now has 99 undo levels, but the default setting remembers only the last 20 steps.

- The two approaches to outlining a project are top-down and bottom-up.

- Summary tasks help you outline and manage your project by allowing you to group tasks and view them appropriately.

- You can use the default WBS numbering system or create your own using the WBS Code Definition In *<Project Name>* dialog box.

Lesson Review

You can use the following questions to test your knowledge of the information in Lesson 1, "Working with Tasks." The questions are also available on the companion CD if you prefer to review them in electronic form.

NOTE   Answers

Answers to these questions and explanations of why each answer choice is correct or incorrect are located in the "Answers" section at the end of the book.

---

1. You want to create a task to summarize the duration, work, and costs related to your department's current project. You also need to apply a distinct number to each task. What do you need to do to create this task?

   A. Create a summary task in the Zero Task ID field of the Entry table and enable outline numbering.

    B. Outdent the first summary task in the Entry table to make it the project's summary task and enable WBS numbering.

    C. Show the project summary task and enable outline numbering in the Options dialog box.

    D. In the WBS Code Definition In *<Project Name>* dialog box, create a code mask. Then, in the Project Information dialog box, select the Show Project Summary Task check box.

2. The default WBS outline structure does not meet your needs. You want to create your own outline structure from scratch. When creating a specific outline structure for your project, which of the following represents a valid outline structure? (Choose all that apply.)

    A. 51.A.1.a.

    B. 25.*.5.c.

    C. Tab_124_Tab_a42

    D. 25.M.44444.A

3. You need to make a summary task a subtask. It is in the correct position in the Entry table and you have selected the Task Name field. What do you do now? (Choose three. Each answer represents the entire solution.)

    A. From the Edit menu, choose Indent.

    B. Click the Indent icon on the Formatting toolbar.

    C. Hold down the Alt+Shift+Right Arrow key combination.

    D. Right-click and choose Indent Task from the drop-down list.

4. You are starting a new project in Project. You have decided on all of the major project phases but are not sure yet what tasks will be required for each phase. What project method are you using to decide on your project's task list?

    A. The top-down method

    B. The bottom-up method

    C. The top-up method

    D. The bottom-down method

5. You have defined the phases and tasks for your next project and are ready to input those into Project. You need to create a WBS structure for your project. How can you create the WBS in Project? (Choose two.)

    A. Open a template that closely matches the phases and tasks in your project and edit that template to suit your needs.

    B. Choose Insert, choose WBS, and modify as necessary.

    C. Choose Tools and then Options. In the View tab, select the Show Outline Number check box.

    D. Open a new blank project, enter tasks into the Entry table, and then define them as summary tasks or subtasks.

6. Your boss needs a summary of your project. He doesn't need specifics, just a high-level understanding of the project work, defined by its phases. Which one of the following would be appropriate to give him?

    A. A list of the tasks in your project

    B. The code mask you created for your WBS outline

    C. A list of the summary tasks in your project

    D. The project summary task

7. Your project is quite large and takes up a lot of space on your computer screen. Because of this, you need to display tasks in a manner that will allow you to move quickly among them. After your tasks are grouped, what two icons will you use most often from the Formatting toolbar to achieve this?

    A. Outdent and Indent

    B. Hide Assignments and Show Assignments

    C. Link Tasks and Unlink Tasks

    D. Show Subtasks and Hide Subtasks

Lesson 2: Task Relationships

The last lesson focused on defining the initial project WBS. However, defining the WBS is only the first step in developing your project schedule. In fact, you probably noticed that all your tasks begin on the same day and no one task depends on the start or finish of any other task in the project. That is where task relationships come in.

If you are an experienced project manager, you might understand relationships more readily by thinking of the process of sequencing activities. Project managers often use either the Precedence Diagramming Method (PDM) or the Arrow Diagramming Method (ADM) to define the order of activities in a network diagram. With Project you can use a similar method through the assignment of task relationships, constraints, and deadlines.

In this lesson you will work specifically with activity sequencing by learning about the four task relationships types, applying those relationships to specific tasks, and using task constraints, as well as task deadlines, to be sure your tasks (and, ultimately, your projects) finish on time.

After this lesson, you will be able to:
- Describe task relationships.
- Assign task relationships.
- Work with lag and lead.
- Describe and assign task constraints.
- Describe and assign task deadlines.

Estimated lesson time: 90 minutes

Working with Task Relationships

Developing your initial project work packages and determining accurate estimated durations for those tasks can be a time-consuming process, and there is no doubt that time spent in those areas is necessary. Proper project planning will only serve to make sure your projects run smoothly. However, without task relationships, your tasks all start on the same day—that is simply not a realistic project schedule.

Real World

Deanna Reynolds

A "workaround" that people new to project management sometimes try is to manually enter start and finish dates for each task in the Entry table. This way, tasks start on the day the project manager assumes is correct. Although this approach might display what appears to be an accurate Gantt Chart, that chart is accurate only until project work begins. When you begin to manually modify a task's start and finish dates, you prevent Project from doing what it was intended to do—create a project schedule based on tasks and their durations. Through this automatic scheduling, when a change occurs in one task, you can immediately see the domino-effect of change throughout the entire project schedule in the form of the new Change Highlighting and an updated Gantt Chart. When the Start and Finish Date fields have been manually overwritten, each time one task changes the project manager is forced to go through all affected tasks and enter new start and finish dates. Instead, you can utilize Project's task relationships and constraints to define task start and finish dates without impeding the automatic scheduling of the software.

Prior to the introduction of project scheduling programs, project managers were forced to hand draw their activity sequencing in the form of flowchart diagrams. Now, with Project, you can use task relationships to electronically create similar sequencing. As an added benefit, when you use task dependencies to schedule your project tasks, the software will calculate the amount of float you have and, in turn, keep track of the critical path.

Exam Tip   The terms "task dependencies," "task relationships," and "links" are all used interchangeably within Project. As such, you might see all three terms on your certification exam and in this book.

Types of Task Relationships

As you enter tasks, by default no relationship between any tasks exists. This creates a project plan file that looks a little like the example in the Figure 2-16.

As you can see, there really is no project schedule. All tasks begin on the same day, and the entire project length is equal to the length of the longest task (three days). However, after you begin defining task relationships, the project takes on a whole new flow.

	❶	Task Name	Duration		Dec 31, '06	Jan 7, '07
0		− Vendor Request For Proposal (RFP) Solicitation2	**3 days**			
1		− RFP Criteria	**2.5 days**			
2		Review criteria to determine if formal RFP process is requ	2 days			
3		Inform procurement of need to create RFP	2.5 days			
4		− RFP Solicitation Process	**3 days**			
5		− Define Requirements	**2 days**			
6		Interview users to understand their product and serv	1.5 days			
7		Document requirements	2 days			
8		Define criteria for evaluation of the responses	1 day			
9	📝	Identify the evaluation team	1 day			
10		− RFP Creation	**2 days**			
11		Obtain template from procurement for RFP format	1 day			
12		Draft RFP	2 days			
13		Review RFP with procurement and subject matter exp	1 day			
14		Refine RFP	1 day			
15		RFP content ready to release	0 days		◆ 1/1	
16		− Market research	**3 days**			
17		Identify potential companies with appropriate product	3 days			
18		Determine if preliminary request for interest/informatic	1 day			
19	📝	Solicit RFI responses (if needed)	2 days			

Figure 2-16   When you enter tasks, no relationships are configured by default

There are four types of relationships in Project:

- Finish-to-Start
- Finish-to-Finish
- Start-to-Start
- Start-to-Finish

When you create a relationship between two tasks, both a predecessor and a successor are defined. The predecessor task is the task that must begin or reach completion before another task (the successor) can begin or finish. This means that the successor ultimately depends on the start or finish of the predecessor task.

MORE INFO   Task drivers

After you have defined relationships, a task's predecessor(s) becomes a task driver. You learn more about task drivers later in this chapter in Lesson 5, "Final Project Planning Steps."

The following pages look at each of the relationship types.

Finish-to-Start (FS)   In a Finish-to-Start relationship, the predecessor task must reach completion before the successor task can begin, as shown in Figure 2-17.

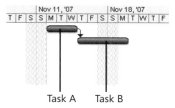

Figure 2-17   A Finish-to-Start relationship

Finish-to-Finish (FF)   In a Finish-to-Finish relationship, the predecessor task and the successor task reach completion at the same time. Thus the completion date is determined by whichever task finishes later, as shown in Figure 2-18.

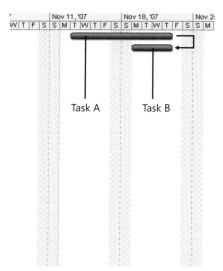

Figure 2-18   Task B (the successor) can reach completion as soon as Task A (the predecessor) reaches completion

Start-to-Start (SS)   In a Start-to-Start relationship, the predecessor task and the successor task begin at the same time, as shown in Figure 2-19.

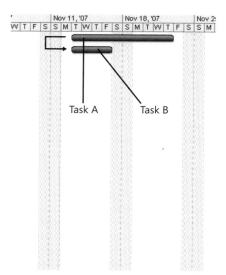

Figure 2-19   Task B (the successor) can begin as soon as Task A (the processor) begins

Start-to-Finish (SF)   Although a Start-to-Finish relationship is rarely used, it is available. In this relationship the successor task can finish when the predecessor tasks starts, as shown in Figure 2-20.

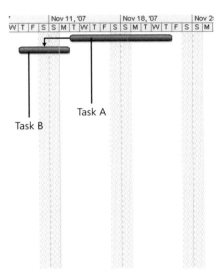

Figure 2-20   Task B (the successor) can finish when Task A (the predecessor) starts

Of the four relationship types, Finish-to-Start is the default and most commonly used. This relationship type creates a project flow that allows each successor task to begin after its predecessor task has finished.

Exam Tip   Task relationships are covered extensively in the certification exam. You will need to be very familiar with each of the task relationships and how each defines tasks as predecessors and successors. You will also want to understand how applying different types of relationships to a project file can affect the project schedule. For instance, you might be given a scenario in which you need to shorten the project schedule by two days. Of the answers, you might be asked which relationship between defined tasks would achieve the desired result.

After relationships have been assigned, you can see a more accurate representation of your project in terms of appropriate activity sequences and total project duration, as shown in Figure 2-21.

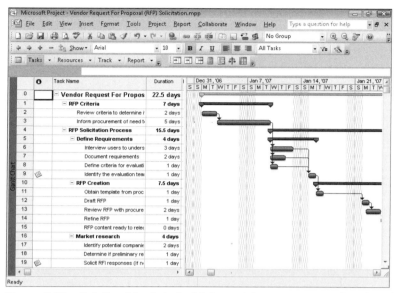

Figure 2-21   Relationships help build the activity sequences and project duration

---

Real World

Bonnie Biafore

Tasks linked to one another are referred to as successors and predecessors, but the dependency in a task relationship is about control, not which one comes first. A task dependency specifies how one task controls when the other task occurs. The predecessor task controls the successor task.

Finish-to-Start task dependencies are easy to understand because the control involved is timing. One task follows the other in chronological order. If the other types of dependencies give you trouble, you can identify the one you need by asking a series of questions:

What does this task need in order to start? This question helps you find the predecessors to a task, which is usually easier to think about. When you answer this question, you know the two tasks you must link together.

Does the start or finish of the predecessor task control the successor? This question helps you identify the first half of the task dependency type. For example, if the answer is "finish," the dependency type is either Finish-to-Finish or Finish-to-Start.

Does the predecessor task control the successor's start or finish? This question completes the selection of the dependency. For example, if your answer to the first control question is "finish" and the answer to this question is "finish," the dependency is Finish-to-Finish.

> ## Quick Check
> 1. What are the four types of task relationships?
> 2. What is the most common type (and the default)?
>
> ### Quick Check Answers
> 1. Finish-to-Start, Finish-to-Finish, Start-to-Start, Start-to-Finish.
> 2. Finish-to-Start is the default relationship type and the most commonly used in project management.

Applying Task Relationships

Now that you know which options are available for linking tasks to create predecessors, successors, and an overall project flow, let's look at the steps for defining these relationships in your project plan.

Because the Finish-to-Start relationship is the default task relationship in Project, you can use the Link Tasks tool on the Standard toolbar to create this task dependency. To create a Finish-to-Start relationship between two tasks using the Link Tasks tool, follow these steps:

1. Select the two (or more) tasks you want to link.
2. On the Standard toolbar, click the Link Tasks button.
3. Note the blue arrow linking the tasks in a Finish-to-Start relationship.

NOTE Link Tasks shortcut

If the Link Tasks button isn't quite fast enough for you, you can also use the keyboard shortcut combination Ctrl+F2 to link selected tasks using the default task relationship, Finish-to-Start.

Another quick way to create a Finish-to-Start relationship between two tasks is by using the drag-and-drop method. To create a link between two tasks using this method, follow these steps:

1. In the Gantt Chart, position the mouse over the predecessor task's Gantt bar so that it shows a four-headed arrow.
2. Click and drag (making sure the pointer is a four-headed arrow) from the predecessor task to the successor task, as shown in Figure 2-22.

NOTE Applying task relationships

Using the same drag-and-drop method, you can create a Finish-to-Start relationship in the Network Diagram.

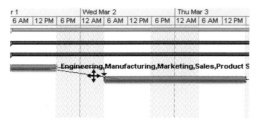

Figure 2-22   Use the Gantt Chart to define a task relationship by dragging from one task's Gantt bar to another

Because the Finish-to-Start relationship is the default, you can see there are several ways to achieve the same effect. However, to initially create any other type of relationship, there is only one surefire way—the Task Information dialog box.

To create a task relationship using the Task Information box, complete the following steps:

1. Double-click the successor task to open the Task Information dialog box.
2. In the Predecessors tab, select the first Task Name cell. In the Task Name drop-down list, select the predecessor task for this task.
3. Select the first Type cell.
4. In the Type drop-down list, review the types of task relationships available.
5. Select Finish-to-Finish, as shown in Figure 2-23.

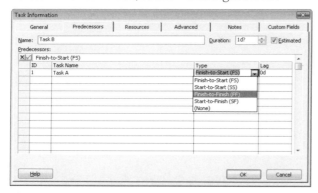

Figure 2-23   Defining task relationships in the Task Information dialog box

6. Click OK.

After you become comfortable with defining task relationships, you can enter task predecessors directly on the Entry table in Gantt Chart view. As you can see in Figure 2-24, task relationships are listed in the Predecessors column as numbers. These numbers are the Task ID numbers that define task predecessors.

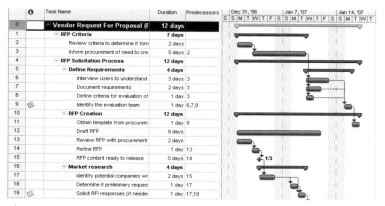

Figure 2-24 Task relationships are listed in the Predecessors column of the Entry table

In Figure 2-24 you can see that Task 13 is the predecessor for Task 14 and that Tasks 6, 7, and 8 are all predecessors for Task 9. From this graphic we can also infer that all task relationships are Finish-to-Start because only numbers appear.

By modifying the task relationships slightly to include other relationship types, we can see how those additional relationships are differentiated in the Predecessors column in Figure 2-25.

	❶	Task Name	Duration	Predecessors
0		⊟ **Vendor Request For Proposal (F**	**20 days**	
1		⊟ **RFP Criteria**	**7 days**	
2		Review criteria to determine if forn	2 days	
3		Inform procurement of need to cre	5 days	2
4		⊟ **RFP Solicitation Process**	**13 days**	
5		⊟ **Define Requirements**	**4 days**	
6		Interview users to understand	3 days	3
7		Document requirements	2 days	3
8		Define criteria for evaluation of	1 day	3
9	📝	Identify the evaluation team	1 day	6,7,8
10		⊟ **RFP Creation**	**5 days**	
11		Obtain template from procurem	1 day	9
12		Draft RFP	4 days	11SS
13		Review RFP with procurement	2 days	12FF
14		Refine RFP	1 day	13
15		RFP content ready to release	0 days	14
16		⊟ **Market research**	**4 days**	
17		Identify potential companies wi	2 days	15
18		Determine if preliminary reques	1 day	17
19	📝	Solicit RFI responses (if neede	1 day	17,18

Figure 2-25 Change task relationships and change predecessor notation

Notice that the predecessor for Task 12 is Task 11 with the "SS" notation. This abbreviation tells us that not only is Task 11 the predecessor but also a Start-to-Start relationship has been defined. For Task 13, the predecessor is Task 12 and a Finish-to-Finish relationship has been defined as indicated by the abbreviation "FF."

Table 2-1   Task Relationship Abbreviations

Relationship	Abbreviation
Finish-to-Start	FS (or none)
Start-to-Start	SS
Finish-to-Finish	FF
Start-to-Finish	SF

To use the Entry table to create these types of relationships, follow these steps:

1. Move the slider to display the Predecessors column in the Entry table in the Gantt Chart view.

2. For any task, type the predecessor task ID number in the related Predecessors field on the Entry table.

3. Add the two-character abbreviation for the relationship type.

Quick Check

1. What is a predecessor task?
2. What is a successor task?
3. Name four ways to link tasks with a Finish-to-Start relationship.

Quick Check Answers

1. A predecessor is a task whose start or finish date determines the start or finish date of a successor task.
2. A successor is a task whose start or finish date is driven by its predecessor task.
3. Click the Link Tasks icon on the Standard toolbar. Drag and drop between task Gantt bars in the Gantt Chart. Use the Task Information dialog box. Press Ctrl+F2.

Order of Task Selection   When you drag to select tasks on the Entry table and then click the Link Tasks button on the Standard toolbar, the tasks are automatically linked in order, beginning with the task with the lowest Task ID number, regardless of whether you drag from the last task to the first or from the first task to the last when you define your selection. However, you can select multiple tasks at the same time by selecting the tasks you want to link by using either the Shift key (to select a contiguous range of cells) or the Ctrl key (to select a noncontiguous range of cells) and then clicking the Link Tasks button on the Standard toolbar. In this case the task predecessors and successors are defined based on the order in which you selected the tasks in the first place.

For instance, consider the example in Figure 2-26.

Figure 2-26   Tasks are currently unlinked

Selecting Task 3, then Task 4, and clicking the Link Tasks button will create a Finish-to-Start relationship that defines Task 3 as the predecessor and Task 4 as the successor. See Figure 2-27.

Figure 2-27   A Finish-to-Start relationship between Tasks 3 and 4

However, selecting Task 4, then Task 3, and clicking the Link Tasks button will create a Finish-to-Start relationship that defines Task 4 as the predecessor and Task 3 as the successor. See Figure 2-28.

Figure 2-28   A Finish-to-Start relationship between Tasks 4 and 3

NOTE   **Linking considerations**

When defining your task relationships, always remember to link "like with like." This means that summary tasks should be linked to summary tasks and subtasks should be linked to subtasks. However, summary tasks should *not* be linked to subtasks. This means that in order to keep a project flow across phases in your WBS, you can define a relationship between the last task of Phase 1 and the first task of Phase 2. But do not link the last task of Phase 1 to the Phase 2 summary task. You should link only similar task types. One option that project managers can employ is to create a milestone task at the beginning and end of each phase to create cross-phase linking.

Modifying Task Relationships

After initial task relationships have been defined, you can easily modify them in the Task Information dialog box by accessing the Predecessors tab (this is the same place you access when you create a task relationship other than a Finish-to-Start). However, you might find it easier to make the change directly within the Network Diagram or Gantt Chart view using the Task Dependency dialog box.

You can open the Task Dependency dialog box simply by double-clicking any link line on the Gantt Chart or Network Diagram, as shown in Figure 2-29.

Figure 2-29   The Task Dependency dialog box

To modify an existing task dependency using the Task Dependency dialog box, complete the following steps:

1. Double-click the link line between any two tasks.
2. In the Task Dependency dialog box, shown in Figure 2-29, open the Type drop-down list.
3. Select a new type from the drop-down list.
4. Click OK.

NOTE   Quickly create a task relationship

To create a task relationship other than Finish-to-Start, another option is to create the relationship using any of the shortcut methods and then double-click the link line and change the link type. This bypasses having to open the Task Information dialog box.

Deleting a Task Dependency

Take another look at Figure 2-29. You will notice that the Task Dependency dialog box also offers a Delete button. When you click this button, the chosen task relationship is removed from the project plan.

When you use the Delete option to remove a task link, only the specific task dependency is removed from the project plan. If you would prefer to remove all task dependencies related to a specific task, you can use the option to unlink tasks. However, the unlink command might not work exactly as you initially expect it to. Although the Link command links only the selected tasks, the Unlink command unlinks every task linked to the selected task(s). This option is found both on the Standard toolbar and under the Edit menu.

Next, look at Figure 2-30—specifically Task 16. Notice the two dependencies related to that task.

Selecting the task and then clicking the Unlink button on the Standard toolbar causes two changes to occur automatically, which can be seen in Figure 2-31.

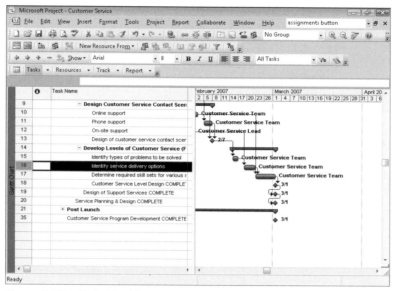

Figure 2-30   Task 16 with two task dependencies

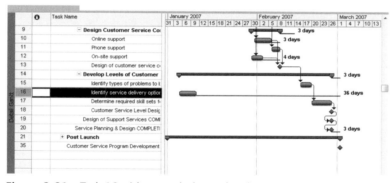

Figure 2-31   Task 16 without task dependencies

To unlink tasks using the Unlink button on the toolbar, select the task and click the Unlink button.

Quick Check

■ What is the difference between using the Delete button in the Task Dependency dialog box to remove a task link and clicking the Unlink Tasks button on the Standard toolbar?

Using Lag and Lead

In addition to using task relationships to define your project schedule, you can modify when a relationship goes into effect using Lag and Lead options. As you create relationships, you will see the Lag box in both the Task Dependency dialog box and the Task Information dialog box. Lag and lead time are both entered in the Lag box.

Real World

Deanna Reynolds

To understand lag and lead time, let's look at a real-world example. Consider the following project tasks:

■ Remove Furniture (1 Day)
■ Prep Walls for Painting (2 Days)
■ Paint Walls (1 Day)
■ Replace Furniture (1 Day)

In this example you can feasibly create Finish-to-Start relationships between each of these four tasks to create a five-day project. However, as you review the project schedule, you realize you cannot paint the walls immediately after the prep work has finished. If repair work, such as filling holes, needs to be completed, you will need to allow time for the spackle to dry. In this case you would add one day of lag time to the link between the Prep Walls for Painting tasks and the Paint Walls task. This way, you tell Project to wait (or lag) one day after the completion of the Prep Walls for Painting task prior to beginning the Paint Walls task. You have now extended your project plan to six days. To make up for that time, you decide the wall prep work can begin when half of the furniture has been cleared from the room. In this case you would add −50% lead time to the link between the two tasks to give the successor a head start (or lead) by allowing it to begin with the Remove Furniture task is 50 percent complete. You have now reduced your project to 5.5 days by entering a negative number. Finally, you really cannot load the furniture back into the room until the paint has fully dried. In this case you need to add some buffer time between the end of the Paint Walls task and the beginning of the Replace Furniture task. Because you are looking for a delay between two linked tasks, this qualifies as lag time and is entered as a positive number. Let's assume you add one day of lag time to the link between the Paint Walls task and the Replace Furniture task. Your total project plan time is now 6.5 days.

Lag Time

Lag time is any amount of time you need to account for between the completion of the predecessor task and the start of the successor task or the start of one task and the start of another. This always depends upon the type of assigned task dependency. However, in every case lag time inserts a delay between two tasks and is always entered as a positive number.

Figure 2-32   Lag time denotes extra time needed between tasks

In Figure 2-32 notice the three-day buffer between the completion of Task 11 and the beginning of Task 12. This is lag time. You will see lag time denoted on both the Gantt Chart and in the Predecessors column in the Entry table. In Figure 2-32 you can see that the lag time has been entered as a duration based on days. You can use any duration time to define your lag time. Additionally, you can use a percentage to designate that a successor wait a length of time equal to the percent entered based on the predecessor task duration. For example, if the predecessor task is two days and a lag time of 50 percent is entered, the total time between tasks is equal to one day (typically eight hours).

To enter lag time, follow these steps:

1. Create a relationship between two tasks.
2. Open the Task Information dialog box for the successor task.
3. View the Predecessors tab.
4. Enter a positive number or a positive percentage in the Lag column next to the task's predecessor.
5. Click OK.

If you decide later that the lag time is too long, perhaps that only two days are needed for the boss to approve the procurement template instead of three, you can change the lag time in a number of ways. You can open the Task Information dialog box again and use the Predecessors tab, or you can edit the lag time in the Task Dependency dialog box or in the Entry table.

To change the lag time using the Task Dependency dialog box, double-click the link in the Gantt Chart between the tasks to open this dialog box and change the lag time as appropriate. To change the lag time in the Entry table, select the Predecessors column for the task and change the number after the + sign to the number you want the lag time to be.

Exam Tip   For the certification exam you might be asked to calculate new project or task durations based on whether lag or lead time is added to a task relationship. To increase your own comfort level with these predictions, create a sample project file and make lag and lead changes to see how the program responds. Be sure to account for nonworking time and commit to memory that lag time is always entered as a positive number and lead time is always entered as a negative number.

Lead Time

Lead time is a head start you give a successor task. You will use lead time whenever you want a successor task to begin partway through the work of the predecessor task.

Figure 2-33   Lead time is extra time you give a successor task

As you can see in Figure 2-33, a lead time of −50% has been added to Task 12's Finish-to-Start relationship with Task 11. In this case the time was entered as a percentage. You can also enter lead time as a negative number. This negative number (or percentage) tells Project that Task 13 can begin at a time equal to 50 percent of the duration of Task 12 (or after one day). Lead time creates overlapping Gantt Chart bars, also shown in Figure 2-33.

Real World

Bonnie Biafore

One technique that project managers use to shorten a project schedule is called *fast-tracking*, which means that tasks that originally were scheduled to occur one after the other now overlap or even run concurrently. Projects typically have tasks that can overlap with no problems. For example, one person can paint the walls of one office while someone else moves the contents of another room in preparation for painting.

Fast-tracking is not risk-free. A decision made for a predecessor task could affect work that has already been completed in an overlapping successor task—for example, when a construction project begins construction before the design is complete.

Because fast-tracking can introduce risk into a project, it's important to choose tasks for fast-tracking that deliver results—that is, a shorter overall schedule. Tasks on the critical path, by definition, shorten the duration of a project. If you can overlap the longest tasks on the critical path, you obtain the shortest project duration with the fewest schedule changes and risks. To fast-track tasks, all you have to do is add lead time to the link between two tasks.

NOTE Lag and Lead time—there is only one box

Even though there are technically two functions—lag and lead time—both of these numbers are entered in the Lag box in Project. You enter lag time as a positive number and lead time as a negative number. Think of lag time as a buffer or "wait time" and lead time as a "head start" for the project tasks.

To enter lead time, follow these steps:

1. Create a relationship between two tasks.
2. Open the Task Information dialog box for the successor task.
3. View the Predecessors tab.
4. Enter a negative number or a negative percentage in the Lag column next to the task's predecessor.
5. Click OK.

If you decide later that the lead time is incorrect, you can change the lead time in a number of ways. You can open the Task Information dialog box again and use the Predecessors tab, or you can edit the lead time in the Task Dependency dialog box or in the Entry table. Remember, you add lead time in the Lag column or text box.

To change the lead time using the Task Dependency dialog box, double-click the link in the Gantt Chart to open this dialog box and change the value in the Lag field as appropriate. To change the lead time in the Entry table, select the Predecessors column for the task and change the number after the - sign to the number you would like the lead time to be.

Quick Check

- Lag time is always written as a _____ number or percentage, while lead time is always written as a _____ number or percentage. (Use "positive" and "negative" to fill in the blanks.)

Quick Check Answer

- Lag time is always written as a positive number or percentage, while lead time is always written as a negative number or percentage.

Using Task Constraints

Task constraints are conditions you place on the start or finish date of a selected task. Project has eight constraint types with varying degrees of flexibility. In fact, some constraints are highly flexible in that they are not tied to a specific date. Other constraints are highly inflexible, forcing a selected task to start or finish on an exact date. Table 2-2 lists Project's eight constraint types along with their definitions in order from most to least flexible.

Table 2-2 Constraint Types

Constraint	Definition
As Soon As Possible	The As Soon As Possible constraint is the default constraint for a project scheduled from a start date and is assigned to all tasks in the project whether or not a relationship has been assigned. When this constraint is applied, the task will start as soon as possible based on other constraints and relationships within the project schedule.
As Late As Possible	The As Late As Possible constraint is the default constraint for a project scheduled from a finish date. When applied, the task will finish as late as possible based on other constraints and relationships within the project schedule.
Start No Earlier Than	When the Start No Earlier Than constraint is applied, the task will begin on or after a specified date.
Start No Later Than	When the Start No Later Than constraint is applied, the task must begin on or before a specified date.
Finish No Earlier Than	When the Finish No Earlier Than constraint is applied, the task must finish on or after a specified date.
Finish No Later Than	When the Finish No Later Than constraint is applied, the task must finish on or before a specified date.
Must Start On	When the Must Start On constraint is applied, the task must start on a specified date.
Must Finish On	When the Must Finish On constraint is applied, the task must finish on a specified date.

All tasks you enter on your project schedule have the As Soon As Possible constraint assigned by default. In fact, this is the reason all tasks begin on the same day before task relationships have been assigned.

NOTE Project scheduling

Because the project management best practice is to schedule a project from the start date, the assumption is made that all tasks then use the As Soon As Possible constraint. However, if a project has been set to schedule from the project finish date, the default constraint type becomes As Late As Possible.

As you can see in Table 2-2, six of the eight constraints require date-specific information. However, of all of the constraints, using Must Finish On and Must Start On allows for the least amount of flexibility in the project schedule. *As such, you should use these two constraint types sparingly.*

Let's break the eight down into three groups: flexible, inflexible, and somewhat flexible.

The flexible constraints are As Soon As Possible and As Late As Possible. They allow Project to schedule project tasks as soon or as late as the schedule will allow without creating schedule conflicts.

The inflexible constraints are Must Start On and Must Finish On. They are tied to a specific date and, due to their inflexibility, can cause scheduling conflicts or inaccurate task flow. For instance, consider Figure 2-34.

	❶	Task Name	Duration	Nov 11, '07								Nov
				S	M	T	W	T	F	S	S	M
0		**Conf Room Upgrade**	**7 days**									
1		Remove Furniture	2 days									
2		Prep Walls for Painting	2 days									
3		Paint Walls	1 day									
4		Replace Furniture	1 day									

Figure 2-34   Task 3 can start when Task 2 ends

In Figure 2-34 you can see that Tasks 2 and 3 have been linked using a Finish-to-Start relationship. When this relationship is applied along with the default task constraint, Task 3 can begin work as soon as Task 2 is complete (and, as you can see, no lag or lead time has been entered).

However, if we assign the Must Start On task constraint to Task 3 as shown in Figure 2-35, although you might not initially see any difference in the schedule, it can pose a problem. For instance, if a Must Start On constraint is added to Task 3, what will happen if Task 2 finishes a day early? Because we assigned a Must Start On constraint to Task 3, its start date does not change even though Task 2 could possibly take less time. Even though the Must Start On and Must Finish On constraints offer the least scheduling flexibility, sometimes such a constraint is appropriate, such as when entering a task related to a training class that is held on specific dates.

Finally, the somewhat flexible constraints are the remaining four: Start No Earlier Than, Start No Later Than, Finish No Earlier Than, and Finish No Later Than. These constraints offer moderate flexibility in your project schedule while still defining target task start or completion dates. In fact, when you assign a Must Start On or Must Finish On constraint to a task, Project will warn you that you will probably run into conflicts in the future and ask you to consider setting one of these four constraints to allow for a little more schedule "wiggle-room" in your project. Figure 2-36 shows the message you will see.

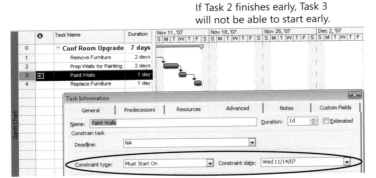

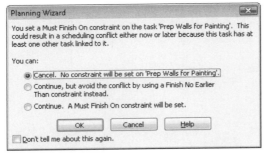

Figure 2-35   Assigning a Must Start On restraint can cause problems, especially if a task ends early

Figure 2-36   Project knows that Must Start On and Must End On constraints are not the best way to plan

---

NOTE   Constraint/relationship conflict

When you modify constraints in your project plan, you always run the risk of creating conflicts between the task you are working with and the overall project plan. If a constraint conflicts with a relationship, the constraint will always take precedence.

Because all tasks have a constraint assigned by default, there really is no need to add or remove a constraint. In this instance we will look only at modifying existing constraints.

To modify a task constraint, follow these steps:

1. Double-click any task to open the Task Information dialog box.
2. Click the Advanced tab.
3. In the Constraint Type drop-down list, select a new constraint. See Figure 2-37.
4. Click OK.

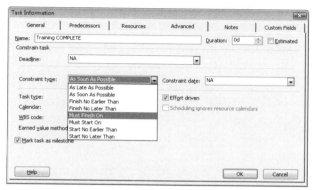

Figure 2-37   Modifying a constraint in the Task Information dialog box

You can also change multiple task constraints. To do this, follow these steps:

1. Select multiple tasks. To select contiguous tasks, hold down the Shift key and select the first and last task in the list. To select noncontiguous tasks, hold down the Ctrl key while selecting each task.

2. Right-click the selected tasks and choose Task Information.

3. In the Constraint Type drop-down list, select a new constraint. See Figure 2-37.

4. Click OK.

When a task's constraint has been modified, a constraint indicator appears in the indicators column next to the affected task. By resting your mouse on top of the constraint indicator, you can view a tooltip that displays both the constraint type and the related date, as shown in Figure 2-38.

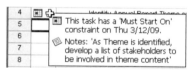

Figure 2-38   The constraint indicator lets you know a constraint has been modified

---

MORE INFO   Constraints

For more information on working with and effectively using constraints in your schedule, see *Microsoft Office Project 2007 Inside Out*, by Teresa S. Stover (Microsoft, 2007).

Quick Check

■ What two constraint types should you avoid and why?

Quick Check Answer

■ You should avoid Must Start On and Must Finish On constraints, if at all possible. These are the two most restrictive restraints and are not flexible when a schedule changes. For instance, if a task is assigned a Must Start On constraint and resources become available for the task to start earlier, that task start date will not automatically update.

Real World

Deanna Reynolds

In the course of completing projects, companies often hire consultants for short-term, temporary assignments to complete highly specialized tasks. The benefit to using a consultant is often obvious—you get a highly skilled worker just when you need one and you do not have to incur any benefit plan costs. However, with consultants often come schedules that vary and that are usually based on other projects of which that consultant is a team member. In this scenario your project plan might indicate, based on task relationships, that a task can be completed on a set date but that your consultant will not be available until two days later. Rather than pushing the start date of the consultant's task out by two days by manually inputting the start date of the task (remember, manually entering a task's start date overrides Project's automatic scheduling feature), you can set either a Start No Earlier Than or a Must Start On constraint on the consultant's task that tells the software that the task in question cannot begin prior to the first date the consultant is available. In some cases this type of scheduling actually builds some slack into your project schedule.

Viewing Constraints

Opening the Task Information dialog box or resting your mouse over individual constraint indicators are both viable ways to view constraints that have been set for individual tasks. Additionally, Project offers a Constraint Date table that allows you to view all project constraints at the same time. Figure 2-39 shows an example.

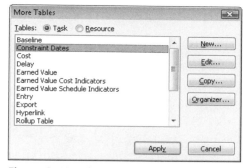

	Duration	Constraint Type	Constraint Date
3	5 days	As Soon As Possible	NA
4	**22 days?**	**As Soon As Possible**	**NA**
5	**4 days**	**As Soon As Possible**	**NA**
6	3 days	Finish No Later Than	Sat 12/29/07
7	2 days	As Soon As Possible	NA
8	1 day	As Soon As Possible	NA
9	1 day	As Soon As Possible	NA
10	**22 days?**	**As Soon As Possible**	**NA**
11	4 days	As Soon As Possible	NA
12	9 days	Start No Earlier Than	Mon 1/8/07
13	2 days	As Soon As Possible	NA
14	1 day?	As Soon As Possible	NA

Figure 2-39   The Constraint Dates table shows all constraints for a project's tasks

To view the Constraint Dates table, complete the following steps:

1. In any open project, choose View, choose Table: *<name of table>*, and then choose More Tables.

2. In the More Tables dialog box, shown in Figure 2-40, select Constraint Dates.

Figure 2-40   Showing the Constraint Dates table

3. Click Apply.

4. To return to Entry table view, from the View menu choose, Table and choose Entry.

NOTE   Change default constraint options

You can change how Project honors task constraints by choosing Tools/Options, and from the Schedule tab, clear Task Will Always Honor Their Constraint Dates.

Setting Task Deadlines

When you simply need to be reminded of a target completion date but do not want these dates to affect the project schedule, a simple solution is to set task deadlines. Task deadlines are target dates you set in the project schedule that do not actually affect the project schedule. This way you can still see reminders of whether your tasks are on schedule, but you do not limit Project's ability to create the project schedule.

Deadlines are displayed on the Gantt Chart as small, downward-pointing arrows at the end of the affected Gantt bar, as shown in Figure 2-41.

Figure 2-41   Task deadlines are displayed as downward arrows

To set a task deadline, follow these steps:

1. Double-click the task to which you are assigning the deadline.
2. In the Task Information dialog box, click the Advanced tab.
3. Enter the deadline date in the Deadline box. See Figure 2-42.

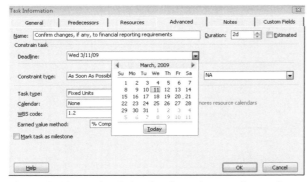

Figure 2-42   In the Calendar drop-down, select a date

4. In the Calendar drop-down list, select a calendar.
5. Click OK.

Resting your mouse on top of that small arrow on a Gantt bar displays a tooltip with the deadline information and, as the project schedule changes, the deadline arrow remains constant at its assigned date. Deadlines can also be seen as a red indicator in the Indicators column.

MORE INFO   Deadlines

For more information on deadlines, refer to the following book: *Microsoft Office Project 2007 Inside Out.*

Using the PERT Chart to Verify Network Completeness

Earlier, this chapter discussed assigning task relationships using the Network Diagram. On the Network Diagram view, each task (and its related information) is represented by a box, or node, and relationship lines are displayed between these nodes. This is shown in Figure 2-43.

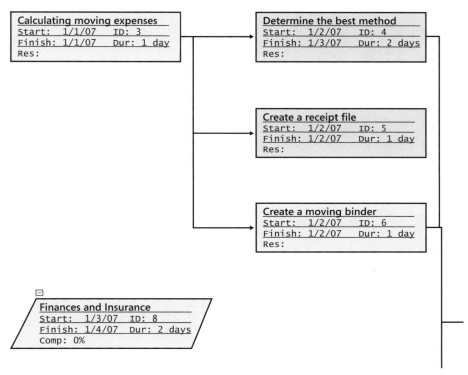

Figure 2-43   Network Diagram view

The Network Diagram is familiar to many project managers. This view is also known as the PERT Chart and displays your project in a flowchart format. As you navigate the Network Diagram, if the zoom level is anything less than 100 percent, by resting your mouse on any node, you can temporarily increase the zoom level of the chosen node for readability.

You can display Network Diagram view from the View Menu, shown in Figure 2-44, as well as from the View bar. From the View menu, choose Network Diagram. From the View Bar (which you can display by choosing View/View Bar), click Network Diagram. In this view you can drag-and-drop task nodes to create task relationships, as explained earlier in this chapter.

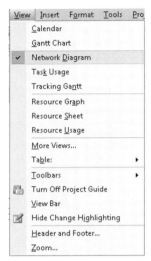

Figure 2-44   Viewing the Network Diagram

NOTE   Task Information dialog box

From the Network Diagram (much like the Gantt Chart), you can access the Task Information dialog box for any task by double-clicking that task's node.

Additionally, each summary task is displayed with a minus (–) or plus (+) symbol near the upper-left corner of the node. Clicking these symbols will collapse or expand the related sub-tasks, allowing you to view only those tasks you need to see at the present moment.

PRACTICE Sequencing Tasks and Creating Task Relationships

In these exercises you will practice what you have learned in this chapter about task relationships, task sequencing, and working with constraints. The first exercise is to select the proper task relationship given a scenario and then apply it, the second exercise is to add both lag and lead time, the third exercise is to apply task restraints, and the fourth exercise is to apply a task deadline and view the deadline in Network Diagram view.

▶ **Exercise 1   Select a Task Relationship and Apply It**

You are in charge of part of a commercial construction and have two tasks that absolutely must finish at the same time. You first need to decide what type of task relationship to apply to which of the two tasks and then input this into Project. You know that in a Finish-to-Finish relationship, the predecessor task and the successor task reach completion at the same time. That is the relationship you will choose. To input this information into Project and complete this exercise, follow these steps:

1. Open a new, blank project.
2. Create Task 1: Install Temporary Water Service.
3. Create Task 2: Install Temporary Electric Service.
4. Set the duration of both tasks to three days.
5. On the Gantt Chart, drag Task 1 to Task 2. This creates a default relationship (Start-to-Finish).
6. Notice the blue arrow linking the tasks in a Finish-to-Start relationship. Double-click this arrow.
7. In the Task Dependency dialog box, select Finish-to-Finish from the Type drop-down list.
8. Click OK.

▶ **Exercise 2   Add Lag and Lead Time**

While creating the schedule for your project, you find out that you will need extra time between two tasks (pouring the concrete foundation and installing column piers). The engineers tell you to calculate about a week for the foundation to cure before you begin installing the piers. To make up for some of this lost time, halfway through the task of installing the building carpet you are going to schedule the task of hanging wallpaper to start instead of waiting for that task to complete. How can you do this in Project?

1. Open a new, blank project.
2. Create two tasks. Name the first Pour Concrete and second Install Piers.
3. Create two additional tasks. Name the first Install Carpet and the second Hang Wallpaper.
4. Set the durations: Pour Concrete 3 days, Install Piers 15 days, Install Carpet 10 days, Hang Wallpaper 8 days.
5. Create Start-to-Finish relationships between the first two tasks and the second two tasks by dragging Task 1 to Task 2 and Task 3 to Task 4 in the Gantt Chart.
6. Double-click Install Piers, and in the Task Information dialog box, click the Predecessors tab.
7. For the task Pour Concrete, change the lag time to seven days. You always enter lag time as a positive number. Click OK.
8. Double-click Hang Wallpaper, the successor task, and in the Task Information dialog box, select the Predecessors tab.
9. For the task Install Carpet, change the lag time to −50%. (Using a negative number in the Lag box configures lead time for the task.) Click OK.

▶ **Exercise 3   Apply a Task Restraint**

In a company project you need to be certain that a task will not start before a specific date. It is okay if it finishes later than this date, but it cannot start before. You need to apply a task constraint. You know that when the Start No Earlier Than constraint is applied, the task will start on or after a specified date. When you apply the Must Start On constraint, the task must start on a specified date. You choose the former.

To complete this exercise and modify a task constraint, complete the following steps:

1. Create a new project using the New Product Launch template located on your computer.
2. Scroll down the Task Name list to task 74: Hire And Train Field Service Personnel.
3. Double-click the task name to open the Task Information dialog box.
4. Click the Advanced tab. In the Constraint Type drop-down list, select Start No Earlier Than.
5. In the Constraint Date drop-down list, select six months from the current date.
6. Click OK.

▶ **Exercise 4   Assign a Task Deadline and View It in Network View**

You know when you would like a specific task to finish, but you are afraid the project will slip and you would like to be able to compare what is really going on with what you would like to actually happen. You want to set a deadline for a task, but you do not want Project to use that deadline to calculate task durations or otherwise change the scope of project. You also want to view your project in Network View after this deadline is applied. To complete this task, follow these steps.

1. Create a new project using the Vendor Request for Proposal Solicitation template located on your computer.
2. Double-click task 21: Finalize Target Companies For RFP.
3. In the Task Information dialog box, click the Advanced tab.
4. In the Deadline drop-down list, select a date that is three months from today's date.
5. Select Standard from the Calendar drop-down list.
6. Click OK. Click the Save button.
7. In the Entry table, select Task 21.
8. From the View menu, choose Network Diagram.
9. In the Network Diagram view, locate Task 21, Finalize Target Companies. It will be selected and will appear in black. Double-click to see the task's Task Information dialog box.

Lesson Summary

■ Creating a relationship between two tasks creates a predecessor task and a successor task. The predecessor task must begin or finish before another task (the successor) can begin or finish.

■ There are four task relationship types. Finish-to-Start is the default and the most commonly used.

- You can define task relationships using the Task Information dialog box and the Predecessors tab. You can also make these changes using the Network Diagram or Gantt Chart view using the Task Dependency dialog box.

- Lag and lead times are both entered in the Task Information dialog box. Lag time is created to put a break between one task and another (like allowing paint to dry before putting in carpet). Lead time is a head start given to a successor task and is often based on the duration of the predecessor task.

- Task constraints are conditions put on the start or finish date of a task. Some constraints are highly flexible while others are highly inflexible.

- Task deadlines are target dates you set for your own use for comparison to the actual project's timeline. Deadlines do not actually affect the project schedule.

- The Network Diagram, or the PERT Chart, displays your project as a flowchart. This lets you view tasks in a different manner, which is sometimes desirable because you can see the "flow" of the project.

Lesson Review

You can use the following questions to test your knowledge of the information in Lesson 2, "Task Relationships." The questions are also available on the companion CD if you prefer to review them in electronic form.

NOTE Answers

Answers to these questions and explanations of why each answer choice is correct or incorrect are located in the "Answers" section at the end of the book.

---

1. You need a task to complete by May 5. You want to apply a constraint to the task, but you want the constraint to be moderately flexible. Which one of the following constraints should you apply to the task and where you should apply it?
   A. Finish No Later Than, applied in the Task Information dialog box
   B. Deadline, applied in the Task Information dialog box
   C. Must Finish On, applied in the Task Information dialog box
   D. Finish-to-Finish, applied in the Task Dependency dialog box

2. You want to be reminded of a task's due date but are reluctant to put an actual finish date on the task. How can you create a reminder for a task's finish date without affecting the scheduling of this task and others?
   A. Apply a flexible constraint to the task.
   B. Apply a moderately flexible constraint to the task.
   C. Delete all constraints applied to the task.
   D. Apply a deadline to the task.

3. Which dependency type should you choose when the predecessor task must finish before the successor task starts?

    A. Finish-to-Start

    B. Finish-to-Finish

    C. Start-to-Start

    D. Start-to-Finish

4. You need to enter, edit, and review tasks and task dependencies in a flowchart view. Which of the following views can you use?

    A. Gantt Chart view

    B. Calendar view

    C. Network Diagram view

    D. Constraint Dates

5. You have two tasks that have a Finish-to-Start relationship. You find out that the successor can actually start before the predecessor finishes. Specifically, the successor can start when the predecessor is three-fourths of the way complete. What do you do to allow for this in Project?

    A. For the successor task, create a lead time of −25%.

    B. For the predecessor task, create a lead time of 25%.

    C. For the successor task, create a lag time of −25%.

    D. For the predecessor task, create a lag time of 25%.

Lesson 3: Estimating and Budgeting Tasks

As thorough a program as Project is, much of estimating lies in your ability to accurately input numbers based on previous project management experience. A common expression in the world of computers is, "Garbage In. Garbage Out." This adage describes exactly what can happen if the numbers you enter into your project schedule aren't realistic, such as those based entirely on guesswork.

In fact, you might notice several questions on the certification exam that rely on your experience as a project manager to determine the common-sense solution to a given scenario. As a result, you will need to be familiar with Project and PMBOK's guidelines for project management.

This lesson considers some options for estimating and budgeting your tasks within both the Project program and the real-life project management world.

After this lesson, you will be able to:
- Estimate task cost.
- Estimate task duration.
- Estimate work.
- Estimate units.
- Create cost and resource budgets.

Estimated lesson time: 150 minutes

Estimating Cost

The benchmark of effective project management is being able to bring a project in within scope, on time, and within budget. This is the well-known triple constraint. A change in one of those variables (scope, time, or budget) will likely cause a change in the other two. Figure 2-45 shows the triple constraint concept.

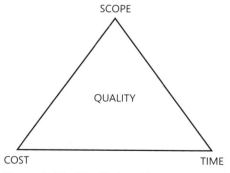

Figure 2-45   The Project Management Triangle

In most cases project costs accumulate from work performed by your project's resources. For instance, the resource, a computer-controlled machine, might work to create metal cutouts. There is a cost associated with both the machine and the metal. In another scenario the resource, a consultant, might work to create a report that offers assistance in creating a product. Using Project, you can set cost estimates for resources or tasks, or both. You already know that tasks are individual work packages defined by a specific duration. Resources are the people, equipment, and material needed to complete individual tasks in your project.

Resource Planning

The majority of the costs associated with your project will more than likely be the result of costs associated with paying for your resources. Because a resource can be a person, a piece of equipment (such as a dump truck), or material (such as nails), these costs may be calculated by the hour, per use, and per unit. Estimating the cost of your project based upon the resources you will be using is called Resource Planning.

When you use the Resource Planning method of cost estimating, your project costs are derived from the values you enter on the Resource Sheet after your resources have been assigned to your project's tasks. (To view the Resource Sheet for a project, choose View/Resource Sheet.) There are three types of resources and, by extension, project costs, that you can create in Project. These are:

- Work
- Material
- Cost

As shown in Figure 2-46, when creating a resource, you have these three options. As resources are created then, you must tell Project what type of resource it is.

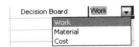

Figure 2-46   Resources can be defined as Work, Material, or Cost

A project's Resource Sheet is shown in Figure 2-47.

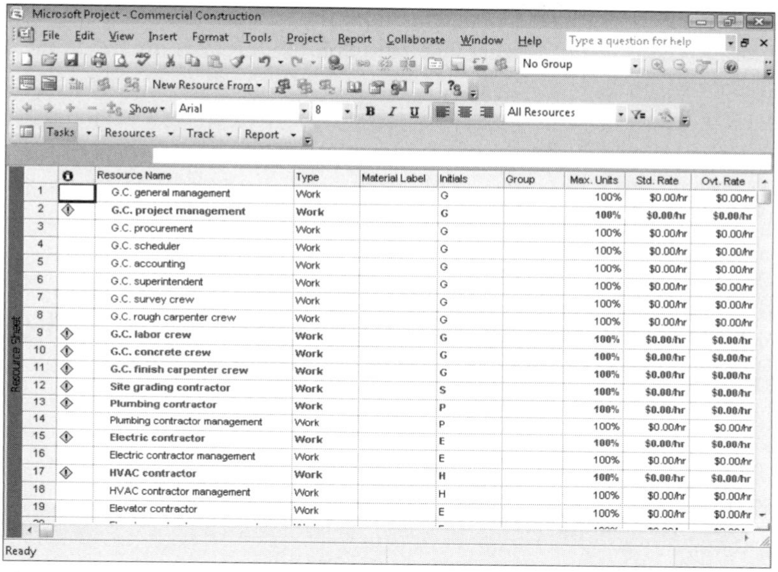

Figure 2-47   A Resource Sheet stores values for work, material, and cost resources within your project file

Work Resources   Work resource types are typically assigned to people or equipment for which you incur charges based upon the amount of time that is worked. For instance, a work resource could be a manager who makes $65,000 a year, a carpenter who charges $65 an hour, or a dump truck that costs $650 a day. After you create work resources in the Resource Sheet, assign their standard (and overtime) working rates, and then assign a resource to a project task, Project multiplies the resource cost rate times the projected work for that task to determine the cost of a task.

MORE INFO   Working with resources

In Lesson 4, "Working with Resources," you will learn about creating resources in, and assigning resources to, your project plan.

Material Resources   Material resources are generally reserved for consumable items or supplies (such as office supplies or construction material), or both, necessary to complete the tasks in your project.

Before you can calculate the cost for material resources, you have to know exactly what you will need to complete the task or project. That means knowing how much paint, shelving, or nails are required, for instance.

NOTE Per-use cost

When you add resources, in addition to standard and overtime rates, you can also enter individual per-use resource costs for both material and work resource types. This per-use cost can be used in place of the standard and overtime rates or in addition to these numbers. In Project the per-use cost accrues for work resources each time the resource is used, such as the cost to set up a crane for a construction project. However, a per-use cost is accrued only once for material resources.

Cost Resources   Cost resources provide a way to track costs that do not depend on:

- The duration of a task, or
- The amount of work needed to complete the task

In other words, a cost resource is a cost associated with the project that doesn't affect the overall project schedule in any way. For instance, a task to meet with the Product Review Team or On-Site Support might require travel to an off-site location. Such travel might incur project-related costs, such as airfare, rental car, hotel, and meal per diem charges.

You can account for these costs in your project by creating a cost resource. Additionally, you can apply any number of cost resources to a task. In fact, you might want to create a cost resource specifically to track airfare and another to track meals because the actual dollar figure of a cost resource can be modified with each task to which it is assigned. Choosing Cost as a resource type is shown in Figure 2-48.

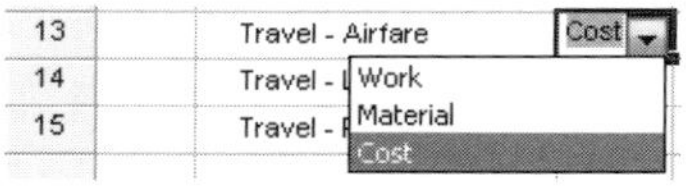

Figure 2-48   Creating cost resources

Exam Tip   Cost resources are a new addition to Project. Previous versions had only two resource types: Material and Work. In order to fully prepare for the exam, be sure you understand the benefit to using the new Cost resource type and in what circumstances you would use this resource type.

MORE INFO   Cost resources

For more information on working with and effectively using cost resources in your project see *Microsoft Office Project 2007 Inside Out*, Teresa S. Stover (Microsoft, 2007).

Historical Information

Another option for estimating cost is to review historical information. As with estimating task durations based on past projects, you can estimate cost the same way. Here are a few instances in which you might use a cost resource in your project plan file:

- If you know from your last project that a flight from Dallas to Seattle costs approximately $800, you can use that information to assign an estimated amount to the cost resource for a similar flight for your project team.

- If you know from recent experience that a dump truck costs $650 a day from a specific vendor, you can use that information to estimate a work resource's cost.

- If you know from experience that a gallon of gas is $3.00 or that paper clips cost about $.03 each, you can use those estimates to figure material costs.

Quick Check

1. Name ways to estimate cost.
2. Name the resource you use to estimate cost for building materials.

Quick Check Answers

1. By calculating work, material, and cost resources, and by accessing historical information.
2. Material.

MORE INFO   Estimating Cost

The Microsoft Web site contains a host of available resources for learning how to work with Project. For information specific to options within the program for estimating cost, visit: *http:// office.microsoft.com/en-us/project/HA102211831033.aspx?pid=CH102202741033.*

Estimating Duration

Time, or duration, is another piece of the triple constraint. The sum total of the duration for all tasks in a project calculates the total duration for the entire project. In other words, add up how long all of the tasks take, taking into consideration what tasks can overlap others, and you will find out how long the project will last. That means you will need to take into account variables such as task dependencies to arrive at an accurate project duration estimate.

In Chapter 1, "Project Initiation," we talked about estimating task duration using the PERT method. Knowing this formula is important to understanding how Project works "behind the scenes." When estimating task duration, you can use a few additional options besides the PERT method that do not necessarily involve Project.

Exam Tip As you will see, much of these task duration estimation techniques fall under the category of "common sense." But do not discount your real-world experience in managing and working on projects. This knowledge will help you as you answer real-world scenario questions on the certification exam.

Historical Information

As previously explained, past projects can help you estimate future task durations. If past project files are available, you can review estimated durations as well as the actual durations of tasks. You can also use this information to see why certain tasks were delayed and why the cost increased (or other factors) and hopefully avoid those problems in the future or add them as defined risks into the new project plan.

We have listed historical information first for a reason. It is better to build on past projects, learn from past mistakes, and use trusted vendors, equipment, and existing information than to reinvent the wheel every time. Accessing recent projects can help you find out how long it takes to perform a task, as well as how much it costs, and whether there were delays or overruns.

Resource Estimates

Use your resources to help you estimate a task's duration. Ask the people who will be performing the work, including team members, team leaders, engineers, and others, how long a specific task takes. You can also refer to a material resource's specification sheet to find out how many items a machine can produce in a day or how deep an auger can drill per hour.

Using your resources to estimate duration can be a very valuable tool. The resource knows better than anyone (or anything) how fast it can work and what it can achieve in a set amount of time. For instance, a maintenance company can tell you exactly how much time will be needed to clean up a job site while a painting contractor can tell you (most likely within a two-hour window) how long it will take to paint a room.

Expert Judgment

If your team includes subject matter experts, they will surely serve as a good resource. You might also want to hire consultants, project and product specialists, and even ask industry groups. You can also find information on the Internet in the form of white papers, blogs, and training.

Experts are a great resource because they know better than anyone how something works or how a specific task needs to be done. For instance, although you might not know how to build a new addition to your warehouse, an expert certainly does. Talking to this expert will help you gain an understanding of what has to be done, when, and why.

You can even access templates that come with Project. Based on the example shown in Figure 2-49, you should consider leaving four days open for obtaining building permits.

	❶	Task Name	Duration	Start	F
0		⊟ **Commercial Construction**	Duration Help on Duration	on 1/1/07	Thu
1		⊟ **Three-story Office Building (7t**	**344 days**	**Mon 1/1/07**	Tht
2		⊟ **General Conditions**	**17 days**	**Mon 1/1/07**	Tue
3		Receive notice to proceed ;	3 days	Mon 1/1/07	Wt
4		Submit bond and insurance	2 days	Thu 1/4/07	I
5		Prepare and submit project	2 days	Mon 1/8/07	Tı
6		Prepare and submit schedu	2 days	Wed 1/10/07	Tht
7		Obtain building permits	4 days	Thu 1/4/07	Tı
8		Submit preliminary shop dra	2 wks	Wed 1/10/07	Tu
9	🖉	Submit monthly requests fo	1 day	Thu 1/4/07	Tl
10		⊟ **Long Lead Procurement**	**70 days**	**Fri 1/5/07**	Tht
11		Submit shop drawings and	2 wks	Fri 1/5/07	Tht
12		Submit shop drawings and	2 wks	Wed 1/24/07	Tı
13		Submit shop drawings and	2 wks	Wed 1/24/07	Tı
14		Submit shop drawings and	2 wks	Wed 1/24/07	Tı
15		Submit shop drawings and	2 wks	Wed 1/24/07	Tı
16		Submit shop drawings and	2 wks	Wed 1/24/07	Tı
17		Detail, fabricate, and delive	12 wks	Fri 1/19/07	Tht
18		⊟ **Mobilize on Site**	**10 days**	**Thu 1/4/07**	Wec

Figure 2-49   Using Project's templates is one way to incorporate expert judgment

Professional, Government, and Industry Standards

Another way to estimate durations is to access information from industries, government requirements, and professional organizations regarding industry standards for tasks in your project. You can use the information to estimate how long a project or task should take by using standard task lists and durations to start.

As an example, certain permits must be obtained before building an extension to a warehouse. These permits take a specific amount of time to apply for and receive. By understanding the government standards for obtaining these permits, you can allow for the necessary time in your project schedule. Figure 2-50 shows some of the final inspections required for a commercial construction project.

137		⊟ **Complete Final Inspections**	**6 days**
138		Complete elevator inspection and certification	3 days
139		Perform architect's inspection	1 day
140		Perform local building agency inspection	1 day
141		Perform fire marshal's inspection	1 day
142		Complete punch list items from all inspections	2 wks
143		Obtain certificate of occupancy	2 days
144		Issue final completion documents including warranties	1 day
145		Issue final request for payment	1 day

Figure 2-50   Be aware of industry and governmental regulations

Exam Tip   Watch for questions that contain information that comes from historical data, resource estimates, expert judgment, or professional, governmental, and industry standards. Although some questions on the certification exam have "red herrings" designed to throw you off with extraneous information, others require that you read it closely to gather all of the data so that you are able to create accurate projections.

Quick Check
- Name some ways to estimate how long a task will take, based on what you learned in this section.

Quick Check Answer
- Historical information such as past projects; resource information such as how long a machine can work; experts' advice; and professional, governmental, and industry standards.

Estimating Work and Units

Task work and units are often misunderstood figures in the project plan. These two figures are tied closely together and with task duration. In fact, these three variables (work, units, and duration) work in a dependant fashion much like the well-known triple constraint (time, scope, cost) previously discussed. A change in one (work, duration, or units) most assuredly guarantees a change in the other two. In order to understand how to estimate work and units, you must first understand what work, units, and duration are.

Work is the amount of effort it takes to complete a task. For instance, one painter is hired to paint a room, and painting the room is his "work." Work is measured in time, such as person-hours or person-days, and is often tied closely to duration, particularly if one person works full time on a task. In this case work equals duration. For example, this work will take one painter eight hours.

Duration is how long a task will take. Continuing with the scenario, it will take the resource—one painter—eight hours to paint the room. If only one resource is used, duration equals work. One painter performing at 100 percent effort equals eight hours to paint a room. (Duration might change as additional resources are added or resources are removed.)

Units are a little trickier. Units describe the ability of a resource to work. Does the resource offer 100 percent or 50 percent? That is, can he or she work an eight-hour day? These are questions you must answer to calculate units. If a painter gives 100 percent to painting a room, that painter will complete the task in eight hours, or one work day. But if the painter can work only four hours each day because of other commitments, he or she works at only 50 percent of capacity. Performing at 50 percent capacity means that it will require a longer duration to complete the eight hours of painting work. Here is another example: if you hire another painter, and each of the two painters gives 100 percent to the task of painting the room, they would probably finish the task in four hours. In this scenario the units for each painter are 100 percent, but the duration decreases to half. We will apply this scenario to the scheduling formula shortly, which will make units clearer.

Real World

Bonnie Biafore

As a project manager, you probably know that resources who work 40 hours a week rarely spend all 40 hours on project work. Company meetings, filling out time sheets, and chatting in the hallway use up working time and reduce productivity. Teams that work in different buildings across a large campus can lose productivity traveling to and fro. If you assign resources at 100 percent in Project, which is the default setting, your resources in the real world would probably have to work a 10-hour day to complete their assignments.

One way to schedule a project taking productivity into account is by shortening the standard work day from eight hours to six hours, for example. Then, assigning a resource at 100 percent represents only six hours of work in one day. This approach makes your schedule more accurate, but it hides the productivity drain.

To schedule a project and show productivity at the same time, reduce the units you use when you assign resources to a task. For example, to assign team members to six hours of work in one eight-hour day, change the resource's units for an assignment to 75 percent. When stakeholders or resource managers ask why you aren't using resources full time, you can ask for help improving productivity.

The Scheduling Formula Terms

If you want to calculate work, duration, or units required for a task, you need to understand the scheduling formula. The formula states that:

Work = Duration*Units

To help understand how these figures relate to each other, you can add the columns for Work and Duration in the Entry table. Figure 2-51 shows an example.

Task Name	Work	Duration
⊟ **Commercial Construction**	**7,322.3 hrs**	**344 days**
⊟ **Three-story Office Building**	**7,322.3 hrs**	**344 days**
⊟ **General Conditions**	**128.27 hrs**	**17 days**
Receive notice to proce	24 hrs	3 days
Submit bond and insura	8 hrs	2 days
Prepare and submit pro	20 hrs	2 days
Prepare and submit sch	17.6 hrs	2 days
Obtain building permits	17.33 hrs	4 days
Submit preliminary shop	41.33 hrs	2 wks

Figure 2-51   Add Work and Duration columns to see that work and duration often go hand in hand

---

MORE INFO   **Adding columns to a table**

For more information on adding columns to a table, see Chapter 4, "Team Collaboration and Multiple Projects."

Using the Scheduling Formula

After you understand this basic formula, you can switch it around to suit any estimate you need to make. In order to do this, you will need to call on your primary school algebra lessons. You might remember that when you hold two values of a three-value equation, you can switch the equation around to determine the missing value. Thus, this formula:

Work = Duration*Units

is the same as:

Duration = Work/Units

Let's work through a couple of examples:

Remember the scenarios earlier in the chapter, regarding a single painter giving 100 percent to the task of painting the room and working for eight hours? Using the formula Duration = Work/Units, you get Duration = 8 hours of work/100% effort, or D = 8/1. Duration is eight hours.

What would happen if we added another painter? How long would the task take? Because Duration = Work/Units, the work required for the task would still be equal to eight hours (it is still going to take eight hours to paint the room) divided by units, which is 200 percent. 200 percent is derived from two painters each giving 100 percent to the task. Duration = 8 hours of work/200% effort (of two painters) is the same as 8/2. 8/2 is 4, or four hours.

MORE INFO   **Changing a percent to a decimal**

To change a percent to a decimal, move the decimal point two places to the left and remove the % sign. 200% is the same as 200.%. Moving the decimal two places to the left and dropping the % sign, 200.% becomes 2.00, or 2.

Exam Tip   When you take the certification exam, you will likely be given paper or a white board and writing implement in order to perform calculation estimates like work or duration for a given scenario. You should also have access to an on-screen calculator. *When you plug the given variables into the Work or Duration formulas, be sure to convert all values to hours.* For instance, your variables might include a duration of one week. When using the formula, one week needs to be entered as 40 hours, assuming the standard working times have not been changed. Then, if necessary, you can convert your answer back to weeks or months based on the possible answers.

Understanding the basic formula is the easy part of work and unit estimation. Now let's take it a step further. To fully understand how to estimate work and units, you will need to be very familiar with Project's three task types:

- Fixed Units
- Fixed Duration
- Fixed Work

By default, each task in Project already holds the Fixed Units task type designation. When you assign a task type to any task, you will be telling Project which variable cannot be changed by the program. Let's look at each of these task types in greater detail using the Work = Duration*Units base formula.

Exam Tip   Unless otherwise specified in the question scenario or a related exhibit, you can safely assume that a task has been assigned a Fixed Units task type and that the task is effort-driven.

Fixed Unit

Because units designate the number of resources working on a task at any one time, logic says that when the units increase the duration should decrease. For instance, consider the following scenario:

Task: Paint Conference Room
Duration: two days
Units: 100 percent
Work: 16 hours

In this task one painter has been assigned to paint a room with a duration of two days. However, Project assumes that two painters will be able to complete the work in half the time, or one day.

Task: Paint Conference Room
Duration: one day
Units: 200 percent
Work: eight hours

In a Fixed Units task, you give Project the option of modifying either duration or work based on the change you make in the project schedule, but not the task units. In the previous example we changed the units to two people (or, 200 percent) allowing Project to make the change to the duration. In the original scenario, what would happen if you modify the work from 16 hours to 8 hours (instead of modifying the units)?

Task: Paint Conference Room
Duration: one day
Units: 100 percent
Work: eight hours

Project will adjust the task's duration (from two days to one day), but not the task's units (because this is a Fixed Units task type). Figure 2-52 shows a task with a Fixed Units task type.

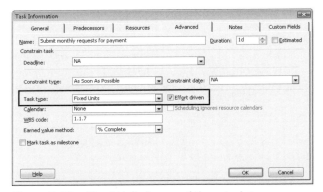

Figure 2-52   Fixed Units is one of three task types

MORE INFO   **Estimating Tasks**

For general information about estimating task durations, read the article here: *http:// office.microsoft.com/en-us/project/HA102171191033.aspx?pid=CH102202741033*. For information about using the Scheduling Formula, read *http://office.microsoft.com/en-ca/project/ HA010199431033.aspx* and work through this 45-minute training video: *http://office.microsoft.com/ training/training.aspx?AssetID=RC010779041033*.

Quick Check

- What is Fixed Units?

Quick Check Answer

- Fixed Units is a task type where the unit value is fixed and cannot be changed by Project when calculating work or duration. If you change the duration of a task, only work is changed. If you change the work applied to a task, only the duration changes.

Fixed Duration

In a Fixed Duration task, you prevent Project from automatically adjusting a task's duration based on changes made to either work or units. Let's use the same scenario as before:

Task: Paint Conference Room
Duration: two days
Units: 100 percent
Work: 16 hours

In this case this task has been assigned the Fixed Duration task type. Now, let's add another full time person to this task and take note of the change:

Task: Paint Conference Room
Duration: two days
Units: 200 percent
Work: 32 hours

Because this task is set to Fixed Duration, we have specified that the task must take a set amount of time, regardless of the number of people working on it. In this case the task will always take two days. If you adjust the units, the work is the only variable left for Project to modify.

Although Fixed Units is the default and offers a great deal of scheduling flexibility, you might need to use Fixed Duration for specific tasks for which additional people do not necessarily add up to faster work. For example, if you have one resource assigned to drive a moving van from Point A to Point B, adding a second person in the van will not allow the first resource to drive any faster. In fact, you could add five resources to drive the van from Point A to Point B, and yet the task will be completed only as quickly as the speed limit will allow. However, if the distance needed to drive is greater than eight hours, then a second driver might allow the task to be completed more quickly because more driving time can be accomplished each work day. Figure 2-53 shows a task with Fixed Duration.

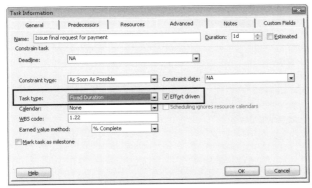

Figure 2-53   Fixed Duration is for a task in which more resources do not necessarily make for a lesser duration

---

Quick Check

■ What is Fixed Duration?

Quick Check Answer

■ Fixed Duration is a task type where duration is fixed. If you change the value for work, units is changed. If you change the value for units, only work is changed. Project does not change duration during calculation.

Fixed Work

Finally, with a Fixed Work task, when you adjust either the duration or units for a task, Project will recalculate the unchanged variable, leaving the Work variable untouched. Let's look at the original scenario again:

Task: Paint Conference Room
Duration: two days
Units: 100 percent
Work: 16 hours

Can you predict what will happen to the task's units if the duration is changed to four days?

Task: Paint Conference Room
Duration: four days
Units: 50 percent
Work: 16 hours

Because Project cannot change the Work for a Fixed Work task, the only other variable that can be modified is the Units. Here, the program needs to take the 16 hours assigned to one resource and spread that time across a four-day duration (instead of a two-day duration). Figure 2-54 shows a task assigned to the Fixed Work designation.

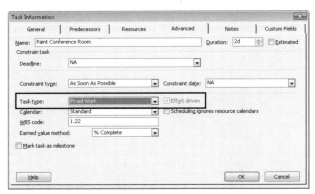

Figure 2-54   Fixed Work is another task type

> ## Quick Check
> - What is Fixed Work?
>
> ## Quick Check Answer
> - Fixed Work is a task type where the work value is fixed. If you change units, only duration is changed. If you change duration, only units are changed. Work is fixed in this task type and is not changed when values change for duration or units.

Effort-Driven Scheduling

The calculations you have seen in the preceding pages all make the assumption that Project is employing effort-driven scheduling to arrive at the changes. It is this effort-driven scheduling that allows Project to make automatic adjustments (and assumptions) to the variables based on the parameters you set by setting the task type.

These automatic adjustments often provide the project manager with an accurate representation of the project's schedule. However, there are times when you would want to disable the effort-driven scheduling feature. For instance, a task that represents a meeting would always have the same duration regardless of the number of people you assign.

You can see a breakdown of adjustments made when effort-driven scheduling is enabled in Table 2-3.

Table 2-3   Task Types and Effort-Driven Scheduling

Task Type	If You Change Units, Project Changes:	If You Change Duration, Project Changes:	If You Change Work, Project Changes:
Fixed Units	Duration	Work	Duration
Fixed Duration	Work	Work	Units
Fixed Work	Duration	Units	Duration

To modify a task's type, follow these steps:

1. Double-click the task to open the Task Information dialog box.
2. In the Advanced tab, in the Task Type drop-down list, make the appropriate selection, as shown in Figure 2-55. Click OK.

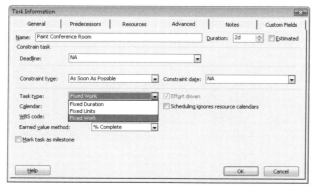

Figure 2-55   Changing the Task Type in the Task Information dialog box

Effort-driven scheduling is active, by default. To disable this feature for any Fixed Units or Fixed Duration task, follow these steps:

1. Double-click the task to open the Task Information dialog box.
2. In the Advanced tab, in the Task Type drop-down list, clear the Effort Driven check box, also shown in Figure 2-55.

Another quick way to work with estimating task work, units, and duration is to use the Task Form in conjunction with the Gantt Chart. This way you can view your original project plan and detailed task information all on the same screen.

You can see this information all on one screen by enabling the split screen view. To view the Gantt Chart and the Task Form on one screen, follow these steps:

1. View the Gantt Chart.
2. From the Window menu, choose Split.
3. Select any task.
4. On the bottom pane, select the Effort-Driven check box to disable this feature for the selected task.
5. Click OK. See Figure 2-56.

Quick Check

■ What is the difference between work and duration?

Quick Check Answer

■ Work is the total scheduled effort for a task, resource, assignment, or project. Work is measured in person-hours. Duration is the amount of time you expect it will take to complete a task.

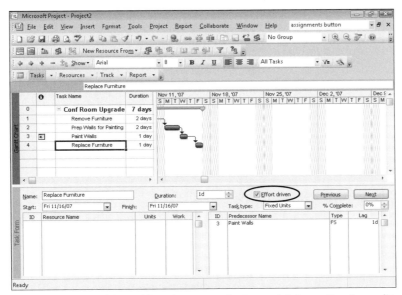

Figure 2-56 Working with task types and other task information in a split screen view using the Task Form and the Gantt Chart

---

NOTE Modifying resource assignments

You have probably noticed that the first time resources are added to a task, no changes are made to the task's duration. You will see the modifications we have outlined in this lesson only when resource assignments are changed after the initial assignments have been made. The next lesson discusses further assigning resources to tasks and modifying resource assignments.

Creating Cost and Resource Budgets

Another method you can use to be sure that your project is coming in within original cost guidelines is to develop a budget in Project. With a budget you can allocate specific dollar amounts to individual project tasks, time periods, and phases or to the entire project. Budget resources do offer a perceived benefit over baseline costs in your project file. When you save a project baseline you have, in effect, the original budget for the project. (With a baseline, you can save exactly what the project looks like today. Then, as the progress of the project begins, you can track the tasks and their progress, allowing you to make a comparison later.) The idea with budget resources is that you can allocate project costs to buckets (accounts) used by your Accounting department.

Creating a budget in Project is a five-step process:

1. Create budget resources.
2. Assign the budget resources you created in the first step to the project summary task. Doing so ensures that your budget is applied to the entire project.

3. Assign values to the budget resources.

4. Align resources to their budget type.

5. Group the resources and view the comparison

MORE INFO   **Creating and assigning resources**

The topics for creating and assigning resources are covered in depth in Lesson 4, "Working with Resources." For more information on creating and assigning resources at the task level, refer to that lesson. In this lesson we are looking only to create and assign estimated budget cost information, which you can then compare to actual project costs as the project progresses.

Step 1: Create Budget Resources

The first step in developing a budget by which you can measure your project cost progress is to create budget-related resources. Much like you create cost resources to track costs associated with the project that do not affect the project schedule, a budget resource is a resource that you assign to the project summary task designed specifically to display the original project budget against actual numbers after the project begins.

You can create several budget resources—each one tracking a different budget line item—such as Travel, Materials, or Overtime. To make it easier for you to recognize, you might even choose to name each budget resource with the word "Budget" as shown in Figure 2-57.

	❶	Resource Name	Type
1	📝	Budget-Materials	Work
2	📝	Budget-Overtime	Work
3	📝	Budget-Travel	Work
4		Cardboard Boxes	Material
5		Content Developer	Work
6		Customer Service Lead	Work
7		Customer Service Team	Work
8		Dump Truck	Work
9		Glossy Paper	Material
10		Logistics	Work
11		Technology Lead	Work
12		Trainer	Work
13		Travel - Airfare	Cost
14		Travel - Lodging	Cost
15		Travel - Per Diem	Cost

Figure 2-57   Name budget resources effectively to make them easier to locate in a full Resource Sheet

Additionally, you will want to define each budget resource as such by opening the Resource Information dialog box. This dialog box is a lot like the Task Information dialog box (in fact, you can open it using the same techniques that you would use to open the Task Information dialog box). Figure 2-58 shows the Resource Information dialog box for the resource Budget-Travel.

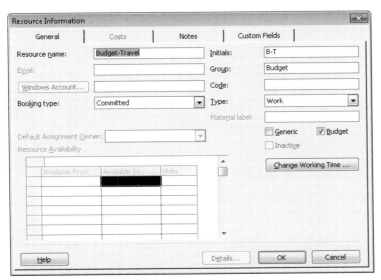

Figure 2-58   The Resource Information dialog box

To specify a budget resource on the Resource Sheet, follow these steps:

1.   View the Resource Sheet.
2.   Create a new resource by typing the name of the resource in the Resource Name field.
3.   Double-click the resource you entered in step 2, and, in the Resource Information dialog box, click the General tab.
4.   Select the Budget check box.
5.   Click OK.

Modifying Multiple Resources   You might recall from the section on working with the Task Information dialog box that you have the option of modifying several tasks at the same time by first selecting the tasks you want to modify and then opening the Task Information dialog box. This can be a quick and easy way to assign the same duration to multiple tasks at one time. Similarly, you can make sweeping changes to multiple resources. However, in this instance you cannot designate multiple resources as budget resources in the Multiple Resource Information dialog box. But there is a workaround. To designate resources as budget resources more quickly, you can insert the Budget column in the Resource Sheet and then follow these steps to change multiple resources:

1.   With the Resource Sheet showing, right-click the column heading to the right of where you want to insert the Budget column.
2.   Choose Insert Column.

3. In the Column Definition dialog box, in the Field Name drop-down list, scroll to select Budget. See Figure 2-59.

Figure 2-59   Add the Budget field to the Resource Sheet view

4. Click OK.

5. For each resource you want to change to a Budget resource, change the No to a Yes. See Figure 2-60.

	ⓘ	Budget	Resource Name	Type
1	📝	Yes	Budget-Materials	Work
2	📝	Yes	Budget-Overtime	Work
3	📝	Yes	Budget-Travel	Work
4		No	Cardboard Boxes	Material
5		No	Content Developer	Work
6		No	Customer Service Lead	Work
7		No	Customer Service Team	Work
8		No	Dump Truck	Work
9		No ▾	Glossy Paper	Material
Yes			Logistics	Work
No			Technology Lead	Work

Figure 2-60   Quickly assigning the "budget" designation to multiple resources displayed on the Resource Sheet

After you have created budget resources, you can choose to display only those resources on the Resource Sheet. This can be helpful if you have several resources and want to focus on only those that have been designated for use with your budget. To filter your Resource Sheet to display only budget resources, follow these steps:

1. With the Resource Sheet open, choose the Project menu.

2. From the Project menu, point to Filtered For: All Resources and choose Budget Resources. See Figure 2-61.

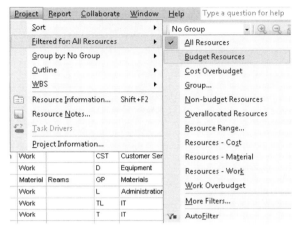

Figure 2-61   Filtering for budget resources only

Step 2: Assign Budget Resources

To make sure the budget resources are allocated to your entire project, you will need to assign them to the project summary task. To achieve this, follow these steps:

1. View the Gantt Chart. If a project summary task is showing, skip to step 5.
2. From the Tools menu, choose Options, and then click the View tab.
3. Select the Show Project Summary Task check box.
4. Click OK.
5. Select the Project Summary Task. (It is Task 0).
6. Choose Tools and then Assign Resources.
7. In the Resource Name column of the Assign Resources dialog box, select the budget resource you created.
8. Click Assign. Notice Project displays a check by the resource name, as shown in Figure 2-62.
9. Click Close.

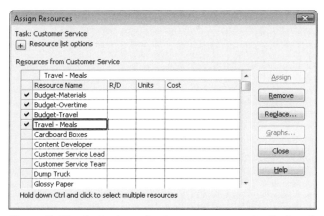

Figure 2-62   Assigning a budget resource to the Project Summary Task

As an aside, you can apply a budget resource filter (much like the one you can use in Resource Sheet view) in Gantt Chart view. To do that, follow these steps:

1. View the Gantt Chart. If a project summary task is showing, skip to step 5.
2. Choose Tools and Assign Resources.
3. In the Assign Resources dialog box, expand Resource List Options.
4. Under Filter By, select the check box. In the drop-down list select Budget Resources. See Figure 2-63.

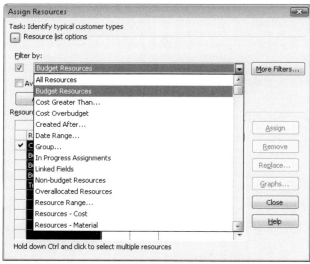

Figure 2-63   Filtering project tasks by budget resources in Gantt Chart view

5. Click Close.

As you work through this process of setting up a project cost budget, remember that you have to work through this process only once for each project. So even though it seems like a lot of leg work initially, the payoff is big as the project progresses and you are easily able to identify where the project schedule is in relation to your initial project budget.

Step 3: Assign Values for the Budget Resources

A budget resource all by itself isn't able to give you any basis of comparison without cost targets. After you have designated the resources for use as budget-related resources and you have assigned those same resources to the project summary task, you can then enter your cost comparison target numbers. To do this, follow these steps:

1. In Gantt Chart view, choose the View menu and Resource Usage.
2. In Resource Usage view, shown in Figure 2-64, you must insert columns for the Budget Work and Budget Cost fields. To do this, follow these steps:

     a. Right-click in the Work column header and choose Insert Column.
     b. In the Column Definition dialog box, in the Field Name drop-down list, select Budget Cost. (Note that you can type **bu** to quickly find the item in the list.)
     c. Click OK.
     d. Repeat this procedure to add Budget Work.

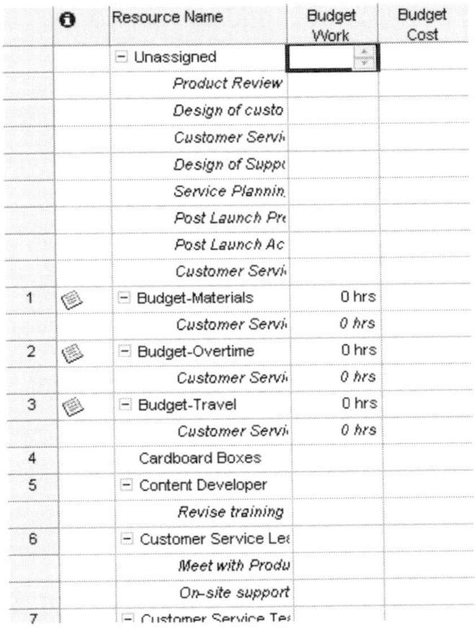

Figure 2-64   Resource Usage View with columns added for Budget Work and Budget Cost

3. On the row representing the project summary task, enter values for the cost and work budgets.

TIP   Budget Work vs. Budget Cost fields

If you are unable to enter a value in the Budget Cost or Budget Work field for a task with a budget resource that is also designated as a cost resource, the value has to be entered in the Budget Cost field, not the Budget Work field. Alternately, for a budget resource that is a work or material resource, you must enter a value in the Budget Work field, not the Budget Cost field.

Step 4: Align Resources to Their Budget Type

Project has several text fields (columns) available that have not yet been designated for any specific use. In this step you will use some of those text fields to create budget resource categories.

You will start by creating the custom text fields that contain words (or phrases) that you can use to identify each budget type. To create a custom field, follow these steps:

1. View the Resource Sheet.
2. Choose Tools, point to Customize, and choose Fields.
3. Under Field, make sure Resource is selected.
4. In the Type drop-down list, verify that Text is selected.
5. In the Custom Fields dialog box, shown in Figure 2-65, locate Text1.
6. Click Rename to display the Rename Field dialog box. This dialog box is also shown in Figure 2-65.

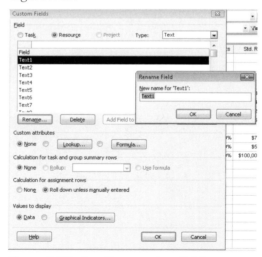

Figure 2-65   Creating a custom field

7. Type a new name for the item and click OK.

8. Under Calculation For Assignment Rows, select Roll Down Unless Manually Entered. (This tells Project that the contents of the Budget Category field should be allocated to assignments in the Task Usage or Resource Usage view unless you manually enter information in an assignment row.)

9. Click OK.

The column(s) you create in this step will be used for grouping and sorting your resource information in the next step. However, before you can start the group, sort, and comparison step, the new column you created needs to be displayed on your Resource Sheet. To display the new, custom column, follow these steps:

1. Right-click the column heading to the right of where you want to insert the new text field and choose Insert Column.

2. In the Column Definition dialog box, in the Field Name drop-down list, select the custom text field you just added.

3. Click OK.

As you enter the text values that you will be using to sort and group your data, remember that these can be anything you choose. However, be careful of misspellings and other typographical errors. The sort and group option is highly specific. If you choose to create a category called "Administration," use only the full term when entering your text in the custom column; variations such as "Admin" and "Adm" can display misleading data.

Step 5: Group the Resources and View the Comparison

Now that your budget categories have been created, you can create a custom group within Project to display budget figures by the line items you have just identified. This is the final step in the budget creation process.

1. Display the Resource Usage view.

2. If they aren't showing, add the Budget Work and Budget Cost columns as described earlier.

3. Choose Project, Group By, and Customize Group By.

4. Under Field Name, in the Group By drop-down list, select the custom text field you added previously. See Figure 2-66.

5. Click OK.

TIP Ungrouping Resource Usage view

You can ungroup the Resource Usage view by choosing Project, Group By, No Group.

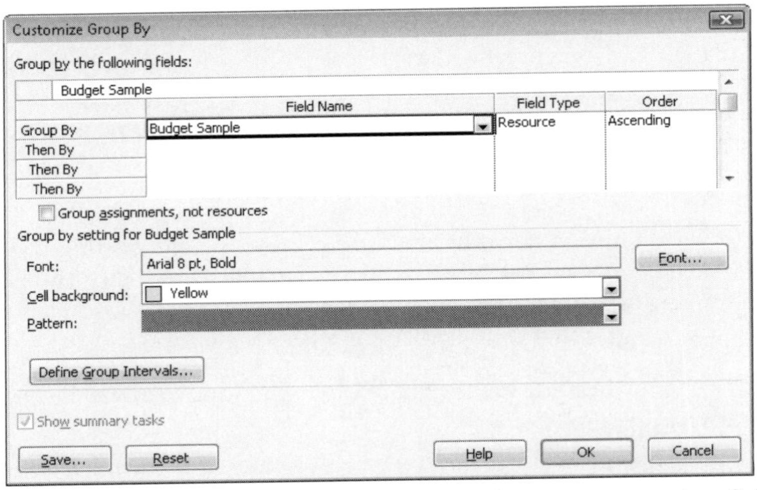

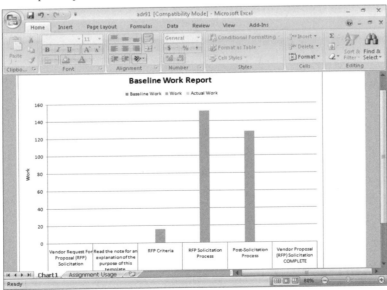

Figure 2-66 Customizing the interface by adding your own custom fields

Another method of viewing your budget is to display the Budget Work Report or Budget Cost Report. To view the Budget Work Report, follow these steps:

1. Choose Report, and then choose Visual Reports.
2. In the Visual Reports – Create Report dialog box, click the All tab.
3. Select the Budget Work Report and click View.
4. The report opens in Microsoft Office Excel, as shown in Figure 2-67.

Figure 2-67 A Baseline Work Report

To view the Budget Cost Report, repeat the steps just presented but select Budget Cost Report in step 3.

Quick Check

- ■ What are the five steps to creating cost budgets?

Quick Check Answers

1. Create budget resources.
2. Assign the budget resources you created in the first step to the project summary task. Doing so ensures that your budget is applied to the entire project.
3. Assign values to the budget resources.
4. Align resources to their budget type.
5. Group the resources and view the comparison

MORE INFO   Viewing project costs

For more information on viewing your project costs, see Chapter 3, "Execute, Monitor, and Control the Project Plan."

MORE INFO   Working with baselines

A baseline lets you compare the state of your project with the original plan. You can have multiple baselines. There is more to baselines than that, however, and the following article offers quite a bit of information: *http://office.microsoft.com/en-us/project/HA101567841033.aspx?pid=CH100666481033*.

PRACTICE **Estimating and Budgeting**

In these practices you will review the concepts learned in this lesson. The first exercise is to estimate task cost. The second exercise is to estimate task duration. The third exercise is to modify a task type. The fourth exercise is to estimate work. The fifth exercise is to create a cost budget.

▶ Exercise 1   Estimate Task Cost

Estimating task costs doesn't have anything to do with inputting data into Project. The process of estimating cost is something you do mentally and later input. To review estimating task costs then, you will need to review what you know by writing it down.

1. Name the three types of project resources that are associated with project cost.
2. Expand on these three resource types by describing what each resource typically represents (goods, people, and so on).

3. Name three tools you can use to assist you in estimating task costs.

   Answers:

   a. Work, Material, and Cost.

   b. Work resources are typically assigned to people or equipment. Material resources are typically applied to material goods. Cost resources are generally applied to items that do not affect the overall schedule of a project, such as meeting with a team or going on a business trip.

   c. Using a past project's data as a baseline, asking an expert for advice, studying industry standards, understanding how long a resource can work and at what capacity.

▶ **Exercise 2   Estimate Task Duration**

You want to estimate how long a task will take to complete. For this task there are three people working full time on the project and there are 24 person-hours needed to complete it. Calculate the duration of the task if the calendar used is the Standard calendar in Project and the work is effort-driven.

1. Because Duration = Work/Units, you know that Duration = 24/Units.

2. Because three people are working on the task at 100 percent each, the Units equal 300 percent.

3. Thus, Duration = 24/300% or 24/3 = 8.

4. This represents eight hours, or one day.

▶ **Exercise 3   Modify Task Type**

A task in your project file needs to be finished in a specific amount of time—four days. One person cannot do the job in four days, so you are going to add more resources to get it done in time. You need to change the task type in Project to reflect this need. To complete this you must modify the task type. Complete the following steps:

1. Open a new, blank project.

2. In the first Task Name field, type **Install Metal Siding**.

3. Under Duration, select 4 days.

4. Double-click the task to open the Task Information dialog box.

5. In the Advanced tab, in the Task Type drop-down list, select Fixed Duration.

6. Click OK.

▶ **Exercise 4   Estimate Work**

You need to calculate how much work will be required to finish a project in five days, using three people. All three people can work on the project for only half of a standard eight-hour day, every day. The task is effort-driven. Calculate the work.

1. Work = Duration*Units

2. Work = 40*Units (40 is the amount of working hours in 5 days. 5*8)

3. Work = 40*150% (Three people*50% each = 150%)
4. Work = 40*1.5
5. Work = 60 hours

This means that it will take 60 person-hours to complete the task. This makes sense if you think about it. If three people work four hours a day, that is 12 person-hours. Multiply 12 person-hours by 5 days, and you get 60 work hours.

▶ **Exercise 5   Create a Cost Budget**

You need to create a cost budget for your team's hotel expenses. You also need to decide on the resource budget type and group and compare the results. To complete this process, complete the following exercise. Note: The purpose of this exercise is to review the steps required to add a budget resource and work with it. In reality, this would be included in an existing project and would not stand alone as it is explained here.

1. Open a new, blank project and choose View and then Resource Sheet.
2. Create the resource Hotel Expenses by typing it in the Resource Name field.
3. Click inside the resource's Type field, and select Cost.
4. Double-click the resource, and in the Resource Information dialog box, click the General tab.
5. Select the Budget check box.
6. Click OK.
7. Choose View and then Gantt Chart.
8. From the Tools menu, choose Options, and then click the View tab.
9. Select the Show Project Summary Task check box.
10. Click OK.
11. Select the Project Summary Task (it is Task 0) by clicking the Task ID field.
12. Choose Tools and Assign Resources.
13. In the Assign Resources dialog box, in the Resource Name drop-down list, verify that Hotel Expenses is selected.
14. Click Assign.
15. Click Close.
16. Click the View menu, choose Resource Usage.
17. In Resource Usage view, insert columns for the Budget Cost and Budget Work fields using the following steps:
    a. Right-click on the Work column, and then choose Insert Column.
    b. In the Column Definition dialog box, in the Field Name drop-down list, select Budget Cost. (Note that you can type **bu** to quickly find the item in the list.)
    c. Click OK.
    d. Repeat this procedure to add Budget Work.

18. If necessary, move the slider so you can view both the Budget Work and Budget Cost columns.

19. To make sure the budget resource is allocated to your entire project, on the row representing the project summary task type **$2000** in the Budget Cost field. Choose View and choose Resource Sheet.

20. Choose Tools, point to Customize, and choose Fields.

21. Under Field, make sure Resource is selected.

22. In the Type drop-down list, verify that Text is selected.

23. In the Custom Fields dialog box, select Text1.

24. Click Rename.

25. Type the name **Expenses** for the item and click OK.

26. Under Calculation For Assignment Rows, select Roll Down Unless Manually Entered. (This tells Project that the contents of the Budget Category field should be allocated to assignments in the Task Usage or Resource Usage views unless you manually enter information in an assignment row.)

27. Click OK.

28. Choose View and then Resource Usage to show the Resource Usage view.

29. Click Project, Group By, and Customize Group By.

30. In the Group By Field under Field Name, select Expenses you added previously.

31. Click OK.

32. Click View and select Resource Sheet.

33. Click Tools, point to Customize, and select Fields.

34. Under Field, make sure Resource is selected.

35. By Type, make sure Text is selected.

36. In the Customize Fields dialog box, locate Text 1.

37. Click Rename.

38. Type a new name for the item and click OK.

39. Under Calculation For Assignment Rows, select Roll Down Unless Manually Entered. (This tells Project that the contents of the Budget Category field should be allocated to assignments in the Task Usage or Resource Usage view unless you manually enter information in an assignment row.)

40. Click OK.

41. Choose View and then Resource Usage to show the Resource Usage view.

42. If they aren't showing, add the Budget Work and Budget Cost columns as explained earlier.

43. Choose Project, Group By, and Customize Group By.

44. Under Field Name, in the Group By drop-down list, select the custom text field Expenses you added previously. Click OK.

Lesson Summary

- To be an effective project manager, you must be able to bring a project in within scope, on time, and within budget. This is the triple constraint. Any change in one of those variables will almost always cause a change in the other two.

- There are three types of resources, and by extension, project costs, that you can create in Office Project 2007. These are: work, material, and cost.

- Being able to estimate cost, duration, work, and units is crucial to applying Project's tools effectively.

- Creating a cost budget is a five-step process that includes creating and assigning budget resources, assigning values to those resources, deciding on each resource's budget type, and grouping and comparing the results.

Lesson Review

You can use the following questions to test your knowledge of the information in Lesson 3, "Estimating and Budgeting Tasks." The questions are also available on the companion CD if you prefer to review them in electronic form.

NOTE Answers

Answers to these questions and explanations of why each answer choice is correct or incorrect are located in the "Answers" section at the end of the book.

---

1. You are creating and leading a new project that you and your company have no experience with. You need a reliable way to calculate costs for tasks in the project. Which of the following offer viable options for obtaining this information? (Choose all that apply.)
   - A. Expert opinions
   - B. Industry standards
   - C. Consultants and other project managers
   - D. Team knowledge and past projects

2. You need to estimate how long a task will take to complete. For this task there are two people working full time on a building project and there are 48 hours of working time needed to complete it. Calculate the duration of the task if the calendar used is the Standard calendar in Project and the work is effort-driven.
   - A. 1 day
   - B. 6 days
   - C. 1.5 days
   - D. 3 days

3. You need to estimate how much work is required for a project. The project specifications are that the work must be completed in four days using a 24-hour schedule, and you have four machines at 50 percent capacity to do it. How much work will be done?

    A. 12 hours

    B. 48 hours

    C. 36 hours

    D. 54 hours

4. You have 40 hours of work to perform and two standard working days to perform it. What unit needs to be applied to the task?

    A. 40 percent

    B. 640 percent

    C. 20 percent

    D. 250 percent

5. Where do you create a budget resource?

    A. Assign Resources dialog box

    B. Resource Sheet and the Resource Information dialog box

    C. Resource Usage sheet

    D. Task Information dialog box in the Resources tab

Lesson 4: Working with Resources

As the project manager, your role is in the project planning and execution, making sure your project meets the triple constraint and comes in on time and within both scope and budget. However, in order to accomplish your project tasks, you will need to assign resources to perform the actual work hours. By definition, these resources are the people, equipment, and material used to complete the project tasks.

As you learn about working with resources in Project, remember that the software can create calculations based only on the data you enter and assumes that your resources are working nonstop during their scheduled time on your project. The program cannot account for work interruptions, long lunch hours, or any other distractions that happen numerous times throughout the work day. For instance, when you schedule your resources to work 100 percent on any given task, Project assumes each resource works eight hours of every day on their assigned tasks. Although this would be an ideal working environment, it simply isn't feasible. When developing your project plans and work hours, you will want to account for this in a way that makes the most sense based on the current project. For some projects it means you schedule six-hour workdays, while on others you might choose to schedule resources at 50 percent (the equivalent to a four-hour workday).

This lesson examines how to add different types of resources to your project plan and assign those resources to specific tasks and customized resource calendars. Additionally, we will spend more time on effort-driven scheduling as we look at managing resources after they have been assigned to tasks.

After this lesson, you will be able to:
- ■ Describe types of project resources.
- ■ Create resource calendars.
- ■ Create project resources.
- ■ Assign resources to project tasks.
- ■ Understand and apply effort-driven scheduling.
- ■ Manage resources.
- ■ Display the resource histogram.

Estimated lesson time: 120 minutes

Adding Resources

Before you can assign any resources to your project tasks, your resources first need to be added to the project plan. As you learned in the previous lesson, there are three types of resources: work, material, and cost. Additionally, you have the option of denoting any resource as budget-related. Sometimes it helps to think of resources as the "nouns" of project management. Your resources are your people and your things that are actually going to get the work done. Resources are particularly helpful in that you can associate costs with them so you can track your total project costs and then compare them to your project budget. If one of your resources is a person, the costs associated with that person might be the salary. If your resource is a consumable item, such as paper, a cost might be whatever price you pay for each ream of paper. If you have a work resource that is a piece of equipment, you might be charged by the hour, by the day, a onetime fee, or any combination of all those. Project can track all those costs associated with your resources.

You add resources to any project plan file from the Resource Sheet view. You can access this view by clicking Resource Sheet in the View bar or by choosing View and then Resource Sheet. The Resource Sheet view mimics a spreadsheet-like or table-like appearance, as shown in Figure 2-68. As such, you can easily navigate it using your Tab, Enter, and arrow keys on the keyboard, much like you can navigate the Entry table in Gantt Chart view.

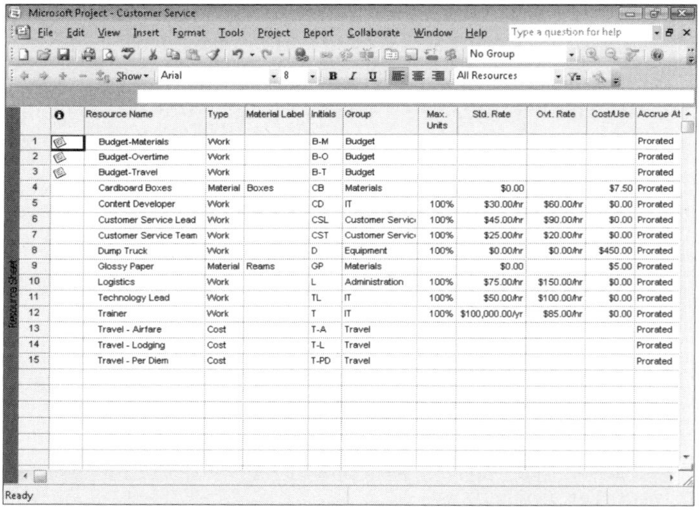

		Resource Name	Type	Material Label	Initials	Group	Max. Units	Std. Rate	Ovt. Rate	Cost/Use	Accrue At
1		Budget-Materials	Work		B-M	Budget					Prorated
2		Budget-Overtime	Work		B-O	Budget					Prorated
3		Budget-Travel	Work		B-T	Budget					Prorated
4		Cardboard Boxes	Material	Boxes	CB	Materials		$0.00		$7.50	Prorated
5		Content Developer	Work		CD	IT	100%	$30.00/hr	$60.00/hr	$0.00	Prorated
6		Customer Service Lead	Work		CSL	Customer Servic	100%	$45.00/hr	$90.00/hr	$0.00	Prorated
7		Customer Service Team	Work		CST	Customer Servic	100%	$25.00/hr	$20.00/hr	$0.00	Prorated
8		Dump Truck	Work		D	Equipment	100%	$0.00/hr	$0.00/hr	$450.00	Prorated
9		Glossy Paper	Material	Reams	GP	Materials		$0.00		$5.00	Prorated
10		Logistics	Work		L	Administration	100%	$75.00/hr	$150.00/hr	$0.00	Prorated
11		Technology Lead	Work		TL	IT	100%	$50.00/hr	$100.00/hr	$0.00	Prorated
12		Trainer	Work		T	IT	100%	$100,000.00/yr	$85.00/hr	$0.00	Prorated
13		Travel - Airfare	Cost		T-A	Travel					Prorated
14		Travel - Lodging	Cost		T-L	Travel					Prorated
15		Travel - Per Diem	Cost		T-PD	Travel					Prorated

Figure 2-68 The Resource Sheet is where you enter resources

NOTE About resource types

There are three resource types: work, material, cost (discussed in more detail in Lesson 3, "Estimating and Budgeting Tasks"). Work resources include people or equipment—anything that might have a time-related rate associated with it. This includes salaried employees who do not receive overtime pay. These employees receive a standard annual salary—they are not hourly employees. Those are still work resources. Project can take their annual rate and break it down to an hourly rate. A material resource is any consumable item, such as concrete, lumber, or printer cartridges. And a cost resource is any resource that has a cost associated with it but does not necessarily affect the scheduling of a project. Examples of such resources include travel, airfare, hotel charges, and meals. Those are all costs that are absorbed into the project schedule but that do not necessarily affect the scheduling of a task. If you were to assign airfare to a task, that does not mean the task is going to get accomplished any faster. It just means that there is a cost associated with airfare for that task.

As you can see, the Resource Sheet contains several columns for storing information about the resources you will be assigning to your project tasks. Table 2-4 explains these columns in detail.

Table 2-4   Resource Sheet Columns

Column	Description
Indicator	When additional information is stored about a resource, such as in the form of a note, an indicator is displayed in this column.
Resource Name	The name by which you will identify the resource. Typically, project managers use both generic resources and actual personnel names. Often, project managers will begin project planning with generic resource names and then switch to specific personnel when they know who they have to work with. On smaller projects, often only specific personnel names are entered, skipping generic resource names altogether.
Type	The resource type (Cost, Material, Work). This is chosen from a drop-down list.
Material Label	The material label is a text-based unit of measurement. If you are tracking a material resource for paper, the material label might be ream. For steel, you could use tons or quite simply whatever it is that makes sense to you within the context of the resource and the project.
Initials	The resource name abbreviation. You will notice as you start to enter your resource name information that the initials will fill in automatically based on the name that you enter in the resource. You can leave it here or you can change it. This is just a text-based field that provides an abbreviation for you.
Group	The high-level group name for the resource. This is a text-based field that can be any name you want, such as employee and consultant resources, or, as shown in Figure 2-68, corporate departments. Some project managers use this field to track external versus internal resources. Other project managers use it to track actual corporate departments. You might see administration, accounting, and human resources in this group field. You just want to stay consistent with whatever groups you choose to go with because you will be able to sort by this field later.
Max. Units	The max units is the highest percentage a resource can be assigned to a task without showing up as overallocated. By default, resources are assigned at the set maximum units percentage. For example, if your resource will be working full-time on any task that you assign that resource to, then the max units should be 100 percent—keeping in mind, however, that 100 percent assumes that your resource is going to work eight hours a day on a task until a task is complete. This field is not available for Cost or Material resource types.
Std. Rate	The rate a resource is paid for regular, nonovertime work. This figure can be entered as an hourly rate or annual salary figure. For instance, you can put $75,000/yr for $75,000 a year. You can also enter it as $75 an hour; that is, the resource's cost. So if you put in an annual rate, Project is going to break that down to hourly and then charge the project schedule accordingly for any work that this resource does on a task the resource is assigned to.

Table 2-4   Resource Sheet Columns

Column	Description
Ovt. Rate	The rate a resource is paid for overtime work. This figure can be entered as an hourly rate or annual salary figure. However, you have to consider using this field only if a resource earns more for overtime than for regular time and if you are actually going to track overtime using Project.
Cost/Use	The costs that are charged each time a resource is used. This field can be used instead of the Standard Rate field if you pay a set fee each time the resource is used or in addition to the Standard and Overtime Rate fields. For instance, a cost per use might be a standard rate, such as $250 to rent a dumpster for a week, along with a standard rate of $450 each time it is emptied.
Accrue At	The accrual options let you choose when regular and overtime costs are paid using the drop-down list to select from Start (at the beginning of the assigned task), Prorated (as the task progresses), and End (at the end of the assigned task). The option you choose determines when the cost is associated with the project or "billed to the project." For instance, if Start is selected, the costs will be billed at the beginning of the task, such as a deposit you pay on rented equipment. If End is selected, the costs will not be billed until the end of the task, such as the cost of a consultant who invoices you after work is complete. And if Prorated is selected, the costs will accrue on a prorated basis as the task is in progress.
Base Calendar	A calendar assigned to the resource using the drop-down list to select from available calendars.
Code	A text-based field where you can store any extra information about a resource.

Real World

Deanna Reynolds and Bonnie Biafore

Let's talk briefly about naming your resources on the Resource Sheet. Often, there is turnover in our businesses. Because of this, it is nice to use the resource title instead of the resource name. This way you can use this Resource Sheet information again from time to time. Additionally, you might have three customer service reps and your customer service manager is going to give you only one for the purposes of this project and you do not know which one you are going to get. By leaving it generic, you are still assigning the work to that particular title but not necessarily to a particular person. This is also helpful because often salary information is private. It is confidential information to which the project manager does not necessarily have access. However, you might have access to the average rate that a customer service rep or that a specific title within your organization might earn. By leaving it generic by title, you can give yourself a ballpark generic figure for the rate and come pretty close to your total project costs.

This scenario definitely promotes an ideal project management world. You might find in your project that generic resources would work on only the tiniest of projects. In this case it's important to assign real people first so you can remember who to call if a task is late. If you have a team and don't know which one you can get, you can create a resource that represents a team and assign the team at the units you need (100 percent of the 300 percent maximum units, for example).

Finally, companies typically use standard burdened rates for their people based on their jobs, not their actual salaries. That's the value that goes in the Standard Rate field. For example, the company takes an engineer with an average salary of $80,000 a year. When you incorporate benefits, the annual cost to the company is around $110,000. In this case the company might set the burdened hourly rate to $75, the annual cost divided by the estimated number of billable hours in a year.

Add Work or Material Resources

To add a new work or material resource to your project file, follow these steps:

1. On the View menu, choose Resource Sheet.
2. In a blank cell in the Resource Name column, type a descriptive name for the resource.
3. Use the Type drop-down list to select Work or Material.
4. Complete the remaining fields that pertain to this resource.

Add Cost Resources

In the past there were only two resources: work and material. Cost resources are new to Project, and, unlike fixed costs, they are created as a type of resource and then assigned to a task. Because cost and material resources do not actually affect the scheduling of a task, you cannot apply a calendar to them. To add a new cost resource to your project file, follow these steps:

1. On the View menu, choose Resource Sheet.
2. In the Resource Name field, type a name for the cost resource (such as **Lodging**).
3. Use the Type drop-down list to select Cost.
4. Complete the remaining fields that pertain to this resource.

You can also enter resource attributes (such as the resource type) using the Resource Information dialog box shown in Figure 2-69. You can open this dialog box by double-clicking any resource.

After the cost resource is created, you can assign the cost resource to a task, and, after the cost resource is assigned to a task, you can enter costs for the resource assignment.

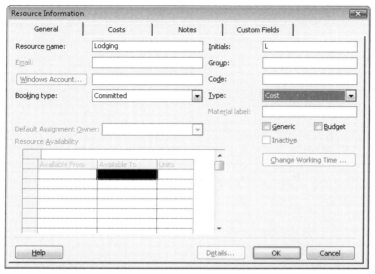

Figure 2-69   The Resource Information dialog box lets you set resource attributes, including the resource type

To assign a cost resource to a task, complete the following steps:

1. Choose View and then Gantt Chart or choose any other task view sheet.
2. Select the task you want to assign the cost resource to.
3. On the Standard toolbar, click the Assign Resources button (it looks like two heads), or use the keyboard shortcut Alt+F10.
4. In the Assign Resources dialog box, shown in Figure 2-70, select the name of the cost resource you want to assign to the task.
5. Select the Cost field for the cost resource and type the cost amount for the resource. See Figure 2-70.
6. Click Assign. Click Close.

When a cost is applied by using a cost resource that is assigned to a task, the amount of the cost resource can vary depending upon how the cost resource is used. A way to think about this concept is that you define a cost resource to represent a type of cost that the project incurs. Then, when you assign the cost resource to a task, you set the value to the specific cost for that task. For example, a task that requires a trip to New York could have a $400 airfare. A task that requires a trip to Singapore could have a $2,000 airfare.

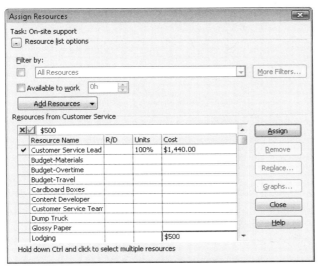

Figure 2-70   Assigning a cost resource to a task

Another example is that, after adding a cost resource for lodging, you might need to make a quick change to the cost applied to reflect planned lodging charges. Because a charge of this type varies according to many factors, a cost resource allows you to add costs specific to an individual task. To do this, follow these steps:

1. Double-click the task the cost resource is associated with.

2. In the Task Information dialog box, shown in Figure 2-71, click the Resources tab. Select the cost resource and modify the amount.

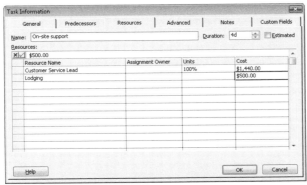

Figure 2-71   Making changes to a cost resource in the Task Information dialog box

3. Click OK.

Quick Check

1. Name the three types of project resources and give an example of each.
2. How do you add work or material resources to your project file? How is adding a cost resource different?

Quick Check Answers

1. Work—a person or a piece of equipment, such as a dump truck. Material—a consumable item, like paper or paint. Cost—something you must pay for that does not affect the project schedule, like travel, meals, and phone charges.
2. Even though you add all resource types to a project file using the Resource Sheet view by typing in the resource name and type, adding a cost resource is different in that you enter associated costs within the task to which the resource has been assigned rather than as a standard, overtime, or cost/use rate on the Resource Sheet.

The Resource Information Dialog Box

Earlier, you saw the Resource Information dialog box as a place in which you can enter and edit resource attributes. The Resource Information dialog box is a lot like the Task Information dialog box, which you open by double-clicking a resource while in Resource Sheet view. Let's look at each of the tabs associated with the Resource Information dialog box.

The General Tab

The Resource Information dialog box provides access to four tabs—all related to specific resource information. The first tab is the General tab, shown in Figure 2-72. Here you have access to information such as the resource name, e-mail address, initials, and group; this is a lot of the same information that you see on the Resource Sheet.

In addition to specific resource availability, the General tab is also where you can change a selected resource's working time. This is a great location (in addition to adding standard working times that might differ from the standard base calendar or from the project calendar) to add personal vacations or holidays that might not be reflected on the project calendar.

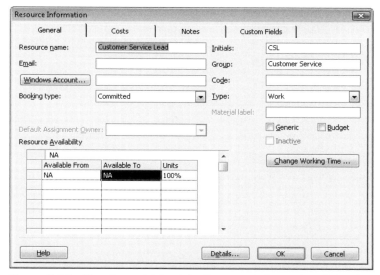

Figure 2-72   The General tab of the Resource Information dialog box

The Costs Tab

In the Costs tab shown in Figure 2-73 you can enter the rates for the selected resource. Here you can enter different rates for the same resource. You will note that this tab has five additional tabs, A, B, C, D and E, to enter a different standard rate, different overtime rate, and a different per-use cost for this individual resource.

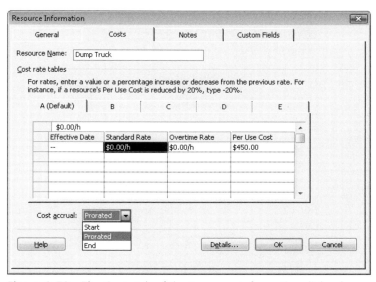

Figure 2-73   The Costs tab of the Resource Information dialog box

The Costs tab is also where you will find the Cost Accrual field. In this field you can choose how you want this resource's costs to accrue: at the start of the task, at the end of the task, or on a prorated basis.

The Notes Tab

The Notes tab, shown in Figure 2-74, is for resource-related information that you want to remember. When you create a note for the resource here in the Resource Information dialog box, you will see the comment indicator display in the Indicator column next to this resource in the Resource Sheet.

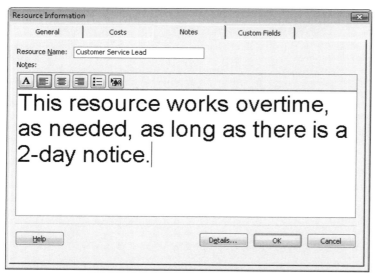

Figure 2-74   The Notes tab of the Resource Information dialog box

The Custom Fields Tab

The last tab in the Resource Information dialog box is the Custom Fields tab, shown in Figure 2-75. You use this tab to access custom fields that you have created. The Custom Fields tab displays custom resource fields that you create in the Custom Fields dialog box.

Quick Check

1. What tab in the Resource Information dialog box would you select to enter different rates for the same resource?
2. Which tab do you use to change a selected resource's working time?

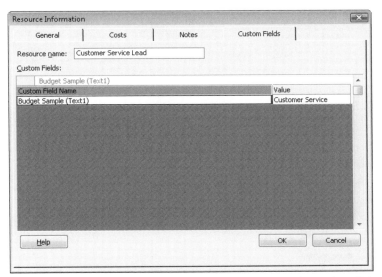

Figure 2-75   The Custom Fields tab of the Resource Information dialog box

Creating Resource Calendars

In Chapter 1 you learned how to create different types of calendars in Project, including calendars that you can apply to the entire project. Additionally, you can apply different, customized calendars to individual tasks and individual resources. In most cases the base calendar is the calendar that describes the standard working times for most resources in your organization. As you know, the base calendar contains standard working times that designate the beginning of the work day at 8:00 A.M., ending at 5 P.M., and allowing employees a one-hour break for lunch. If you want to keep track of a resource's vacation, you can create individual resource calendars copied from the base calendar.

However, not all of your resources will work full time and they do not take a vacation at the same time. In fact, not all of your resources will actually work for your company. In these cases it is a good idea to assign a resource calendar.

Exam Tip   For the purposes of the certification exam, you want to be sure that you clearly understand the differences between a base calendar and a resource calendar. Note that you can apply a resource calendar only to work resources, not to material or cost resources.

When you have an employee who works part-time, (for instance, a four-hour day from 1 P.M. to 5 P.M. or from 8 A.M. to 12 P.M.), this is the perfect time to create a new resource calendar to apply to only that particular resource.

To create a customized calendar for an individual resource, follow these steps:

1. From the Resource Sheet, select a work resource.

2. Choose Tools and then Change Working Time. The Change Working Time dialog box appears, as shown in Figure 2-76.

3. In the For Calendar drop-down list, verify that the work resource to which you want to apply the new calendar is selected. In Figure 2-76 it is G.C. Procurement.

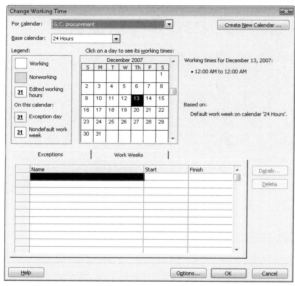

Figure 2-76   The Change Working Time dialog box for a work resource

4. Select a base calendar that is closest to the calendar you would like to create for the resource.

5. Click Create New Calendar to create a copy of the calendar.

6. Select the option Make A Copy Of _____ Calendar, and then name the new calendar appropriately and click OK.

7. Click the Work Weeks tab and click Details.

NOTE **The details for <calendar name> dialog box**

The Options dialog box, shown in Figure 2-77, opens and you configure the following:

   a.   When the week starts

   b.   When the fiscal year starts

   c.   The times the days start and end

   d.   Hours per day, week, and month

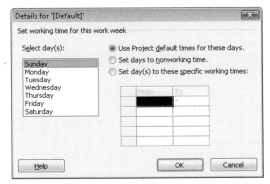

Figure 2-77 Configure your new calendar

  8. To configure the calendar, select Monday, and then select Set Day(s) To These Specific Working Times. (Note that you can also select Set Days To Nonworking Time.)

  9. Using the From and To columns, type the start and end times for this day.

10. Repeat these steps for every day of the week.

11. Click OK. Click OK again to close the Change Working Time dialog box.

To create a recurring exception for the new calendar and resource, follow these steps:

  1. In the Resource Sheet view, select the work resource you used in the previous exercise.

  2. Choose Tools and then Change Working Time. The Change Working Time dialog box appears.

  3. In the For Calendar drop-down list, verify that the new calendar is selected.

  4. In the Exceptions tab, in the Name field, create a new exception by typing a descriptive name. Press Enter.

  5. Choose a start and finish date using the calendars in the Start and Finish columns.

6. With the exception selected, click Details.

7. Select Nonworking or Working Times, depending on what you want to configure.

8. To set working times, type the start and end times for the exception using the From and To fields.

9. Select a recurrence pattern: Daily, Weekly, Monthly, or Yearly, as shown in Figure 2-78.

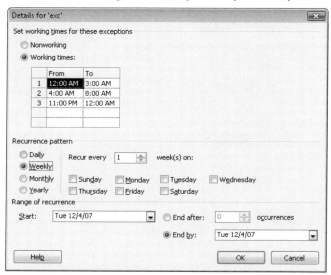

Figure 2-78   Configuring exceptions

10. Configure the recurrence pattern based on the options given. For Daily, you can set how many days to create the exception; for Weekly, which days of the week, and so on.

11. Use the Start and End After or End By drop-down lists to finalize the recurrence.

12. Click OK, and then click OK again.

NOTE   **Resource calendar alternative**

An alternative to creating a resource calendar for a resource who works part-time is to assign the maximum units to a percentage equivalent to the number of hours that resource will work. For instance, a full-time resource working eight hours a day is automatically assigned maximum units of 100 percent. However, if you have a resource who works four hours a day, you can change the max units to 50 percent, as an alternative. That way, Project will simply assign that resource four hours a day to any task in which that resource is assigned.

Typically, at this stage in the project management process the project schedule should not be affected by any new resource calendars that you create because no resources have been assigned to tasks. Remember, the first step is to create the resources. The second step is to assign the resources to the tasks. If, however, you create or customize a resource calendar after resource assignments have been made, you will often notice a change in the project schedule to accommodate new working times.

Quick Check

- When might you assign a resource calendar?

Quick Check Answer

- When the resource does not work full-time, regularly, when the resource is not part of your company, or to track an individual resource's time off. If the resource is not part of your company, you can still use the base calendar if you require that the resource adheres to your company's working schedule.

Applying a Calendar to a Resource

After you have customized resource calendars, you can assign those calendars or other calendars saved within your project file to individual resources directly on the Resource Sheet.

To assign a resource calendar to a resource, complete the following steps:

1. On the View menu, choose Resource Sheet.
2. In the Resource Name field, select the resource to which you want to assign a new calendar.
3. Double-click the resource, and in the Resource Information dialog box, click the General tab.
4. Click Change Working Time, shown in Figure 2-79.

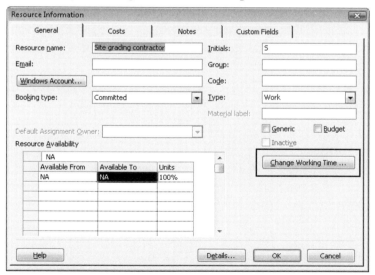

Figure 2-79 Changing a calendar assigned to a resource

5. In the Base Calendar drop-down list, select the new calendar you created.

6. Click OK and OK again.

NOTE   **Assigning the same calendar to multiple resources**

To assign the same calendar to multiple resources on the Resource Sheet, change the calendar of the first resource using the Base Calendar drop-down list, and then, using the mouse or keyboard, select the next several resources that will be using the same calendar. Finally, press Ctrl+D on your keyboard to duplicate the calendar in the first selected resource to the remaining selected resources.

Base Calendars vs. Resource Calendars

The base calendar field on the Resource Sheet displays which calendar is assigned to a particular resource. Chapter 1 covered the different calendars available in Project. They were the project calendar, the resource calendar, the task calendar, and the base calendar. Remember, there are three default calendars that you see with every new project file: Standard, Night Shift, and 24-Hour. You can apply these calendars to a task, a project, or a resource, or all three. Additionally, you can copy any of the three calendars to create your own calendar; again, the calendar you create can be applied to a task, project, or resource. When assigning a calendar to a resource, you can use Standard, 24-Hour, or Night Shift, or from the Resource Sheet you can create another calendar specifically to use with the selected resource or another base calendar that you create.

MORE INFO   **Base calendars**

Base calendars are covered in more detail in Chapter 1. There are three built-in calendars: Standard, 24-Hour, and Night Shift. Additionally, you can create your own.

Quick Check

- What is the difference between a base calendar and a resource calendar?

Quick Check Answer

- A base calendar can serve as the project calendar, the task calendar, or as the basis for a personalized resource calendar. It defines the default working times for the resources in your project. There are three base calendars: Standard, 24-Hour, and Night Shift. A resource calendar is a calendar that defines working and nonworking times and days for a single resource. This calendar applies to a resource, not to an entire project and not to a task.

Assigning Resources

After your resources have been created, you are ready to assign them to the tasks in your project schedule. You will want to assign your resources in the Gantt Chart view. While in Gantt Chart view, you can use the Assign Resources button located on the Standard toolbar. When you click this button, the Assign Resources dialog box opens, as shown in Figure 2-80.

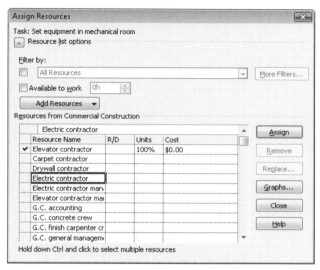

Figure 2-80   The Assign Resources dialog box

In the Assign Resources dialog box you can choose which resources you want to assign to specific tasks within your project. Lesson 3, "Estimating and Budgeting Tasks," when covering estimating work, units, and duration, also briefly discussed effort-driven scheduling. Effort-driven scheduling will be discussed again in this lesson.

The first time that you assign resources to a task, effort-driven scheduling does not come into play. In fact, it has absolutely no bearing on the task duration. The first time you assign your resources to a task your duration remains the same; your work and units remain constant based on the task duration and the max units for the assigned resource. For example, if the resource you assigned has a maximum units of 100 percent, when you assign that resource to a task, the maximum units remain constant at 100 percent (unless you have entered a different value on the Resource Sheet).

The work is automatically calculated based on the duration of the task and the units you assign to the resource in the Resource Sheet. If you assign a customer service representative to a task that currently takes two days and that resource is scheduled at a maximum unit of 100 percent, Project will calculate the work at 16 hours or two 8-hour days (two full days)—unless, of course, that resource has a different calendar assigned and that resource calendar has different working times. However, based on a default generic scenario, remember that Project assumes eight hours a day, five days a week, and maximum units at 100 percent for all resources.

You can assign a resource from the Assign Resources dialog box to a chosen task in Gantt Chart view in several ways:

1. Choose View and then Gantt Chart if you are not already in Gantt Chart view.
2. Select the task to which you want to assign a resource.
3. Click the Assign Resources button on the Standard toolbar or choose Tools and then Assign Resources.
4. In the Assign Resources dialog box, select a resource from the resources list, and click Assign. See Figure 2-81.

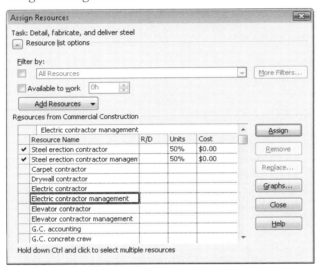

Figure 2-81   Assigning resources to a selected task

5. Click Close.

Assigning a Resource to Work Part-Time

If your resources are assigned maximum units of 100 percent yet on the assigned task you need them to work only part-time, you can modify the maximum units for a resource at the task level without modifying the default maximum units for a given resource.

For instance, if you have a resource with maximum units of 100 percent, you know that Project will assume that resource will work eight hours a day throughout the duration of the task until the task is completed. However, you might have an instance where you need that resource to work only four hours a day just on this specific task, not on other tasks that to which that resource might be assigned. You can do this by adjusting the units at which the resource is assigned to the task.

A better option in this scenario is to modify the maximum units for a resource for a particular task. The easiest way to do that is to open up the Task Form by viewing your project file in a split screen view—that is, to view the Gantt Chart at the top and the Task Form at the bottom.

The bottom pane contains a Units field for each resource assigned to that task. You can modify that Units field to alter the percentage of units that any one resource will work on a selected task.

To modify the units for a selected task using the split screen view, follow these steps:

1. Choose Window and then Split. See Figure 2-82.

Figure 2-82   Split screen view lets you see additional task information, including resources, units, and work

2. Select a task that has resources assigned to it.

3. In the Task Form, select the Units field next to the resource to change. Figure 2-83 shows this option.

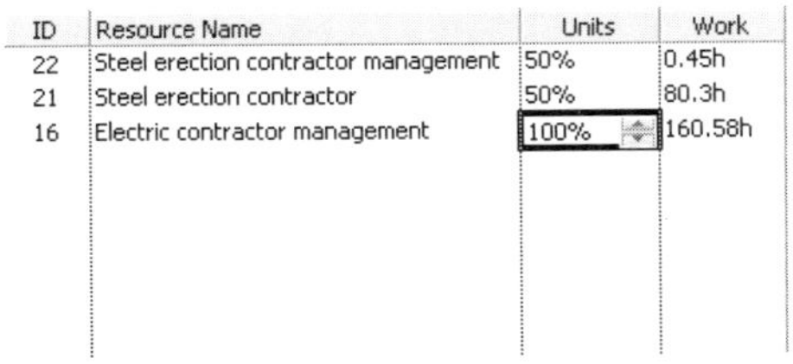

ID	Resource Name	Units	Work
22	Steel erection contractor management	50%	0.45h
21	Steel erection contractor	50%	80.3h
16	Electric contractor management	100%	160.58h

Figure 2-83   Change units applied to a resource

4. Use the spin box or type a number to change the units applied to the resource. Click OK.

Working with Effort-Driven Scheduling

Effort-driven scheduling means that the total work for a task drives the calculations of duration, units, and work for individual assignments. If you add or subtract resources, the total work remains the same, while Project adjusts the task duration or units at which resources are assigned.

On the other hand, if you disable effort-driven scheduling, the total amount of work will change if you add or remove resources, just as the number of person-hours increases as you ask more people to attend a two-hour meeting. Essentially, effort-driven scheduling works hand-in-hand with the task type. We talked about effort-driven scheduling and task types in Lesson 3, "Estimating and Budgeting Tasks," when we covered estimating and budgeting your costs within Project. In that lesson you also had the opportunity to work through some real-world examples. You will do a few more here within the context of actually assigning resources.

NOTE   Learning about effort-driven scheduling

Effort-driven scheduling can be a frustrating part of your work with Project, but it is a worth the extra time you need to devote to fully understand how this feature works. This way you can begin to predict what Project is going to do with your work unit and duration calculations.

Remember, Project does not change anything the first time you assign a resource. Effort-driven scheduling and task types come into play only when you begin modifying original resource assignments. The first time you open the Assign Resources dialog box and assign resources to a task, your duration stays the same, your max units stay at their default setting from the Resource Sheet, and the work is automatically calculated. That is the easy part.

Fixed Units, Fixed Duration, and Fixed Work

The challenging part in understanding effort-driven scheduling arises when you try to predict what is going to happen if you add another resource, if you remove a resource, or if you change the project duration. There are so many variables. But really, you just need to break it down to three. Those three variables are essentially the task types.

The task types are:

- Fixed Duration
- Fixed Units
- Fixed Work

You know that the duration is the length between the start and finish dates for the task. Units are essentially the amount of capacity that any one resource can devote to a task. Work is the amount of time assigned to a task.

Effort-Driven Scheduling Scenarios

Consider a task with a duration of 5 days that has work of 10 hours. That is to say, your resource will be working 2 hours a day for 5 days to arrive at the 10 hours of work.

Now let's apply what we know about effort-driven scheduling. As you know, effort-driven scheduling is enabled by default on all tasks. Additionally, the default task type is Fixed Units. Initially, when you assign a resource to a task, Project applies the maximum units from the Resource Sheet and pulls that entry over to the Entry table (and ultimately to the Task Form).

When you understand the three variables of Fixed Units, Fixed Duration, and Fixed Work, you can then begin to break this down by units, work, and duration.

Making one of those variables "fixed" simply means that Project does not have the ability (or the permission) to modify that one "fixed" variable when a resource assignment changes. However, you always have the ability to modify that variable on a task. For example, on a Fixed Units task you can change the units from 100 percent to 50 percent (or any percentage you choose), but Project will not touch a "fixed" variable during an automatic calculation.

Exam Tip   Consider the following scenario because you might see a similar one on the certification exam. For a task type of Fixed Units, if I change the work, the only variable for Project to change is the duration. In that instance that is the variable that is going to change. On a Fixed Units task where I modify the duration, the work is the variable that is going to change. In many cases, just by breaking it down into those three variables, you can predict which change is going to be made, effectively eliminating one or more incorrect answers on the exam.

Now you know what "fixed" means in terms of this program. In most cases all effort-driven means is "more people equals less duration." Essentially, the more people you assign to a task, the less duration that task should take to complete. Makes sense, in most cases.

Understanding when to use effort-driven scheduling or when to turn it off is critical to getting Project to modify your tasks the way you want when you make changes. However, consider the following scenario.

As a project manager, you have assigned three resources to attend a two-hour project meeting. If you assign three more resources to attend the same meeting, the meeting will still take two hours. In this case, assigning additional resources to a task for a meeting will not necessarily decrease the time associated with completing the task. That is a determination only you as the project manager can make. Project cannot make that determination for you. In this example you would disable effort-driven scheduling because adding additional resources will not make the meeting end any sooner.

Exam Tip   On the certification exam, if you see a question related to what changes will happen in a specific task type scenario (if information is not given to the contrary), you can assume that effort-driven scheduling is enabled and the task type is Fixed Units. Those are the defaults for all tasks. Unless you are told otherwise within the context of the question, you can assume those two factors to be true.

MORE INFO   Task types

For more information on the different task types and whether or not effort-driven scheduling is enabled, see Lesson 3, "Estimating and Budgeting Tasks."

Managing Resources

You already know how to add resources, which was covered in the first topic in this lesson. Now we are moving on to changing, substituting, and removing resource requirements. Additionally, we will look at sorting and filtering options when working specifically with your resources.

To make changes to a resource, the most logical place is on the Resource Sheet. On the Resource Sheet you can either open the Resource Information dialog box (using the steps described earlier) or you can simply type over the text that is there to make a change to an individual resource.

Working with the Resource Sheet is the easy part of working with resources. The bulk of working with resources is probably going to happen on your Entry table in Gantt Chart view using the Assign Resources dialog box. This is where you can make changes to existing resource assignments and remove resource assignments altogether.

To remove resource assignments, follow these steps:

1. Choose View and then Gantt Chart.
2. Select any task and click the Assign Resources button on the Standard toolbar.
3. In the Assign Resources dialog box, select an assigned resource (one with a check mark by it) and click Remove. Figure 2-84 shows an example.

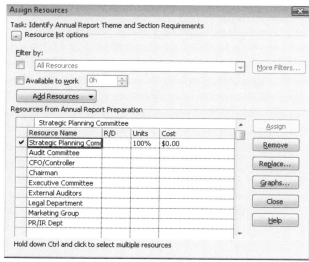

Figure 2-84   Removing an assigned resource

To replace resource assignments, follow these steps:

4. Choose View and then Gantt Chart.
5. Select any task and click the Assign Resources button on the Standard toolbar.

6. In the Assign Resources dialog box, select an assigned resource (one with a check mark by it) and click Replace.

7. In the Replace Resource dialog box, shown in Figure 2-85, select the resource to replace the selected resource.

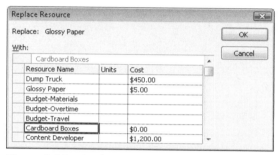

Figure 2-85   Replacing one resource with another

8. Click OK.

As you begin to make changes to your project resource assignments, you might see an exclamation point in the Information field, as shown in Figure 2-86. Click the exclamation point to select from the options shown.

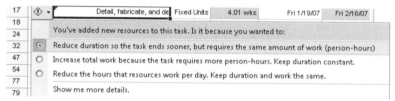

Figure 2-86   Adding resources can lessen a task's duration

The choices shown include the following:

- Reduce Duration So The Task Ends Sooner But Requires The Same Amount Of Work (Person Hours).
- Increase Total Work Because The Task Requires More Person Hours. Keep Duration Constant.
- Reduce The Hours That Resources Work Per Day. Keep Duration And Work The Same.
- Show Me More Details.

You can select any of these to have Project recalculate the task.

Filter Resources

The Assign Resources dialog box contains an option to filter your resources (near the top). In Lesson 3, "Estimating and Budgeting Tasks," we talked briefly about filtering your list based on budget resources and discussed how doing so changes the display of the resources you see in the Assign Resources dialog box. This is incredibly helpful if you have many resources that you need to choose from because the Assign Resources dialog box displays only 9 or 10 resources at one time. The rest are there. You just have to scroll to get to them.

To limit the view to just specific resources, you can use the Filter By drop-down list at the very top of the Assign Resources dialog box. To filter resources, in the Assign Resources dialog box, under Filter By, select the check box and, in the drop-down list, select which resources to show. A similar filter option is also available in the Resource Sheet view. There is also one filter option on the Resource Management toolbar and there is another filter option on the Formatting toolbar.

NOTE   Viewing the Resource Management toolbar

To view the Resource Management toolbar, choose View, Toolbars, and then select Resource Management.

Figure 2-87 shows the filtering option from the Formatting toolbar. To filter using the Formatting toolbar, make sure you're in Resource Sheet view, and then click the down arrow by All Resources. Select the filter to use.

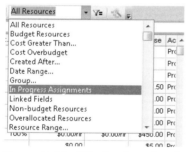

Figure 2-87   Filtering by using the Filter drop-down list on the Formatting toolbar

You can also filter data from the Standard toolbar. To filter resources using the Standard toolbar, make sure you are in Resource Sheet view, in the No Group drop-down list, select Resource Type, Resource Group, Work Vs. Material Resources, or any other option, as shown in Figure 2-88. Resource Type is selected here.

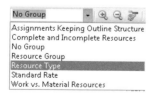

Figure 2-88   Filtering by groups

If you would like to select a specific resource, the Resource Management toolbar has a "Using Resource" filter option. To filter your Gantt Chart tasks to display only those tasks that have a specific assigned resource, follow these steps:

1. Verify that you are in Gantt Chart view.
2. Click All Tasks on the Formatting toolbar and select Using Resource from the drop-down list. See Figure 2-89.

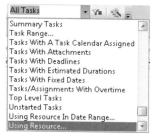

Figure 2-89   Selecting Using Resource from the Formatting toolbar filter options

3. In the Using Resource dialog box, in the Show Tasks Using drop-down list, select the resources for which you want to view the tasks the resource is assigned to.
4. Click OK.

After you have applied a filter, you will need to remove it to bring the display of all available resources back. To view all resources and tasks and remove any applied filter in the Formatting toolbar, using the same tools as before, select the filter you previously applied (perhaps Using Resource) from the Formatting toolbar, as shown in Figure 2-90. Select All Tasks.

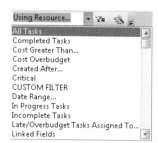

Figure 2-90   Show all tasks and remove the filter

Quick Check

- Name as many views as you can for filtering and viewing resources.

Quick Check Answer

- Assign Resources dialog box, Filter By option. Resource Sheet view, Resource Management toolbar. Resource Sheet view, Standard toolbar.

Displaying the Resource Histogram

When your resources have been assigned to your individual tasks, you will need a way to display the resource assignment information in terms of generic skill or work requirements over time. To do that, you will want to display various views of the resource histogram.

The histogram views simply display your project data with your resource assignment, resource usage, and resource availability shown against a timescale.

Project's Resource Graph view, shown in Figure 2-91, provides just such a view. To access this view, in the Resource Sheet select a resource, and then choose View and Resource Graph.

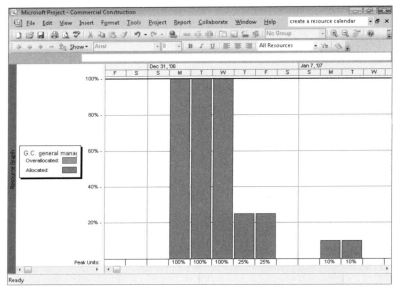

Figure 2-91   Resource Graph view

On the Resource Graph you can see (by resource) the allocated work hours by day and any overallocations or any areas where that resource is scheduled to work. Work that is in excess of the resource's maximum units is displayed in red. Much like the Gantt Chart view, in the Resource Graph you can also modify the timescale at the top. The timescale has three tiers: top, middle, and bottom.

You can modify each of these timescale tiers by double-clicking the timescale that you see in the Resource Graph view. Additionally, you can right-click the timescale and choose Timescale from the shortcut menu to access the same Timescale dialog box. The Timescale dialog box is shown in Figure 2-92. Notice that for each tier you can change the units, label format, tick lines, and more.

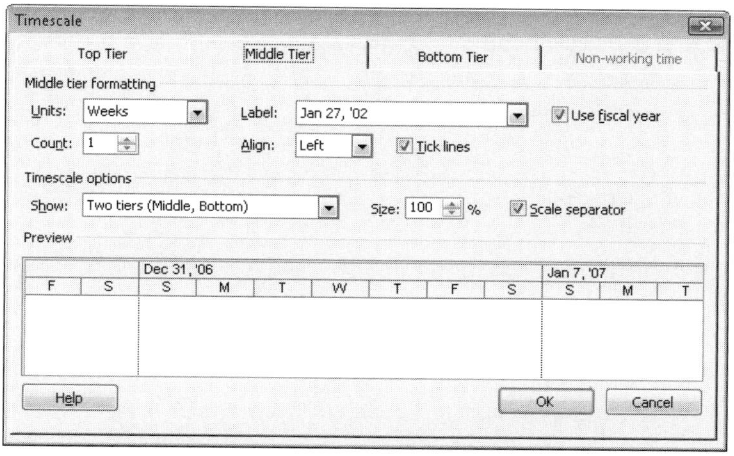

![The Timescale dialog box showing Top Tier, Middle Tier, Bottom Tier, and Non-working time tabs. Middle tier formatting: Units Weeks, Label Jan 27, '02, Use fiscal year checked, Count 1, Align Left, Tick lines checked. Timescale options: Show Two tiers (Middle, Bottom), Size 100%, Scale separator checked. Preview showing Dec 31, '06 and Jan 7, '07 with days.]

Figure 2-92   The Timescale dialog box

When you display the Resource Graph view, it can actually be a little bit overwhelming because it is such a large graph over a large expanse of time and it can be difficult to quickly see which resources are overallocated. A really quick way to get to the first overallocation is to click the Go To Next Overallocation button on the Resource Management toolbar. The Go To Next Overallocation button is called out in Figure 2-93.

Go To Next Overallocation (Alt+F5)

Figure 2-93   The Go To Next Overallocation button

The Resource Graph is probably the most common view used to display the resource histogram information. The Resource Graph is the view that displays resource allocation, cost, and the work over time information—your typical histogram information. However, Project has additional views that you can use to view your resources and your resource information. The most obvious, of course, is the Resource Sheet, which is the view that you use to create and modify your project resources.

For example, the Resource Graph is the best place to review your team and make changes to resource information. It provides the most visual way to see overallocations or resources who have available time.

In addition to the Resource Sheet and the Resource Graph, there is a Resource Allocation view, a Resource Form view, and a Resource Usage view—all displaying different types of resource information. The Resource Allocation view is great for making changes to assignments and seeing the results in your project schedule.

Exam Tip   For purposes of the certification exam, you will want to be very familiar with each of these resource views and the benefits of using each. You might be presented with a question giving you a scenario and asking you which view would show you the most appropriate information based on the question criteria. As such, it is helpful to know what each of these views displays.

The Resource Allocation view, shown in Figure 2-94, is actually a combination view (much like the split screen that you see when you are in Gantt Chart view and you choose Window and then Split to open the Task Form at the bottom). The Resource Allocation view displays the Resource Usage view in the top pane and the Leveling Gantt Chart in the bottom pane.

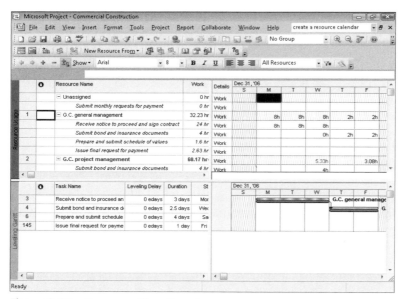

Figure 2-94   Resource Allocation view

The Resource Form, another view shown in Figure 2-95, displays a form for you to enter and edit data about a specific or individual resource.

The Resource Usage view, shown in Figure 2-96, displays a list of your resources showing assignments with the associated cost or work information for each resource over time.

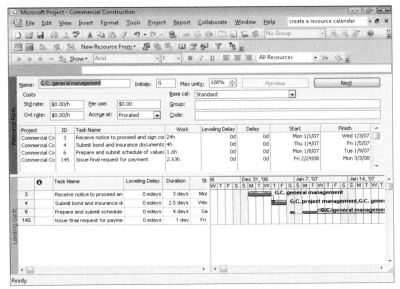

Figure 2-95 Resource Form view

		Resource Name	Work	Details	Dec 31, '06					
					S	M	T	W	T	F
		Unassigned	0 hr	Work						
		Submit monthly requests for payment	0 hr	Work	████					
1		G.C. general management	32.23 hr	Work		8h	8h	8h	2h	2h
		Receive notice to proceed and sign contract	24 hr	Work		8h	8h	8h		
		Submit bond and insurance documents	4 hr	Work				0h	2h	2h
		Prepare and submit schedule of values	1.6 hr	Work						
		Issue final request for payment	2.63 hr	Work						
2		G.C. project management	60.17 hr	Work				5.33h		3.08h
		Submit bond and insurance documents	4 hr	Work				4h		
		Prepare and submit project schedule	4 hr	Work						1.75h
		Prepare and submit schedule of values	16 hr	Work						
		Obtain building permits	1.33 hr	Work				1.33h		
		Submit preliminary shop drawings	1.33 hr	Work						1.33h
		Perform architect's inspection	4 hr	Work						
		Perform local building agency inspection	1.33 hr	Work						
		Perform fire marshal's inspection	4 hr	Work						
		Obtain certificate of occupancy	16 hr	Work						
		Issue final completion documents including	8 hr	Work						
		Issue final request for payment	0.17 hr	Work						
3		G.C. procurement	56 hr	Work				3.5h	12h	12h

Figure 2-96 Resource Usage view

You can access each of these views using the View menu. The View menu offers quick access to the Resource Graph, to the Resource Sheet, and to Resource Usage, as does the View bar. However, to view the Resource Allocation view and the Resource Form view, you will need to choose View and More Views and, from the More Views dialog box, select the appropriate view. See Figure 2-97.

Figure 2-97   The More Views dialog box

Quick Check

■ Which view would you choose to display a list of resources showing allocation, cost, or work information for a resource over a large amount of time?

Quick Check Answer

■ The Resource Usage view.

PRACTICE # Working with Resources

In these practices you will review the concepts learned in this section. The first exercise is to add one work and one material resource to your project using the Resource Sheet. The second exercise is to add a cost resource to a task. The third exercise is to assign a resource to a task. The fourth exercise is to modify the units for a task using split screen view. The fifth exercise is to create a resource calendar for a resource and assign it to that resource. The sixth exercise is to remove and replace resources. The seventh is to filter resources. The eighth is to display a resource histogram.

NOTE   Complete the exercises in order

Complete these exercises in order. The previous exercise must be completed before moving on to the next.

▶ **Exercise 1   Add Work and Material Resources Using the Resource Sheet**

You have been mapping out your Home Move project in Project using the Home Move template. Before the project is complete, you would like to have carpet installed in your new home. You need to add two resources, a carpet contractor and carpet, and assign those resources to a new task, Replace Carpet. To add these resources, create the new task, and assign these resources to the task, complete the following steps:

1. Chose File and New, and then under New Project, click On Computer.
2. In the Templates dialog box, select Project Templates, Home Move, and then click OK.

3. Choose View and then Resource Sheet.
4. In a blank row under Resource Name, type **Carpet Contractor**.
5. Use the Type drop-down list to select Work.
6. For the Carpet Contractor resource, under Std. Rate, type **$30/hr.**
7. Under Resource Name, type **Carpet**.
8. Use the Type drop-down list to select Material.
9. For the Carpet resource, in the Material Label cell, type **Square Yard**.
10. For the Carpet resource, under Std. Rate, type **$25**.
11. Choose File and Save As, and then name the file **Home Move 2**.
12. Choose View and Gantt Chart.
13. Scroll to Task 170.
14. Choose Insert and then New Task.
15. Type **Install Carpet** and give the duration 2 days.
16. With the Install Carpet task selected, click the Assign Resources button on the Standard toolbar.
17. Select Carpet, and then click Assign.
18. In the Assign Resources dialog box, under Units, type **40** for the Carpet resource. Project changes the value to 40 Square Yards and the Cost to $10,000 (40 square yards at $25 per square yard).
19. Select Carpet Contractor and click Assign.
20. Click Close.

▶ **Exercise 2 Add a Cost Resource to a Task**

Your new home is across the country. During the move you will be staying in hotels, eating out, and buying gasoline for the car. You need to add these cost resources to your Home Move project. Continuing from Exercise 1:

1. On the View menu, choose Resource Sheet.
2. In the Resource Name field, type a name for the first cost resource, **Hotels**. Add the other two in the same manner, **Food** and **Gas**. You should have three new resources.
3. Using the Type drop-down list, make the three new resources cost resources.

▶ **Exercise 3 Assign a Resource to a Task**

Continuing from Exercises 1 and 2, you now need to assign your new cost resources to the task Make Any Long Distance Travel Arrangements.

1. Choose View and Gantt Chart.
2. Select the task Make Any Long Distance Travel Arrangements (under Preparing for Moving Day).

3. On the Standard toolbar, click the Assign Resources icon (it looks like two heads), or use the keyboard shortcut Alt+F10.

4. In the Assign Resources dialog box, select Hotels. Click Assign.

5. Assign a cost for Hotels: **$1,000**.

6. Select Food, repeat steps 4 and 5, and again assign a cost of **$1,000**.

7. Select Gas, repeat steps 4 and 5, and assign a cost of **$3500**.

8. Click Close.

▶ **Exercise 4   Modify the Units for a Task Using Split Screen View**

You found out that the carpet contractor can only work half days because he has another job he must finish during the same time he's working on your new home. You need to make the appropriate modifications to your Home Move project. Continuing from Exercises 1, 2, and 3, follow these steps:

1. In Gantt Chart view, select the Install Carpet task. (This should be Task 170.)

2. Choose Window and then Split.

3. In the Task Form, select the Units field next to Carpet Contractor.

4. Use the spin box or type a number to change the units applied to the resource to 50 percent.

5. Click Save.

6. Choose Window and Remove Split.

7. Notice that the duration of the Install Carpet task has changed from two days to four days.

▶ **Exercise 5   Create a Resource Calendar and Assign It to a Resource**

You need to create a schedule for your teenage daughter's task of unpacking her things and getting organized after you get into the new house. You need to create a new work resource called Christina Lee and you want to create a special calendar just for her. Continuing on from previous exercises, follow these steps:

1. From the Resource Sheet (choose View and Resource Sheet to display), create a work resource called Christina Lee Unpacks.

2. Select the resource and choose Tools and Change Working Time.

3. Click the Work Weeks tab and click Details.

4. Select Saturday, and select Set Day(s) To These Specific Working Times.

5. In the Start box, type **10:00 A.M.** for the From time, and set **4:00 P.M.** for the To time. Repeat this for Sunday.

6. Click OK, and then click OK again to close the Change Working Time dialog box.

Later, in Gantt Chart view, you will select the Moving task, click Assign Resources, and add the Christina Lee resource to the task.

▶ **Exercise 6   Remove and Replace Resources**

You have decided you do not want carpet throughout your new home, you want tile. You need to add new resources to replace the old ones. To add new resources and replace old ones using the Home Move template you have been using in previous exercise, follow these steps:

1. Choose View and Gantt Chart.
2. Select the Install Carpet task and click Assign Resources icon on the Standard toolbar.
3. In the Assign Resources dialog box, add two new resources, Tile and Tile Contractor.
4. Double-click the Tile resource, and in the Resource Information dialog box, change the type of resource from Work to Material. Click OK.
5. Select Carpet and click Replace.
6. Select Tile and click OK.
7. Select Carpet Contractor and click Replace.
8. Select Tile Contractor and click OK.
9. Click Close.

▶ **Exercise 7   Filter Resources**

There are many ways to filter resources, and you should be aware of all of them. Using the Resource Sheet view and the Formatting toolbar is quite common. To filter resources in this manner, in this scenario to view only incomplete work in a project, follow these steps:

1. Choose View and Resource Sheet.
2. Choose All Resources on the Resource Management toolbar and scroll to the bottom of the drop-down list.
3. Select Work Incomplete.

▶ **Exercise 8   Display a Resource Histogram**

It is important that you understand the various ways to view resource histograms and what is offered in each view, and there are several. In this exercise you will open the project template Commercial Construction and display a list of all of the resources showing allocation, cost, or work information for each resource over time. To complete this exercise, complete the following steps:

1. Choose File and New, click On Computer, and in the Templates dialog box, click the Project Templates tab.
2. Open the Commercial Construction template.
3. Choose View and Resource Sheet.
4. Select Task 1, G.C. General Management and choose View and then Resource Usage.
5. If necessary, move the slider bar to the right to see the work hours for the resource. Note that you can also insert additional columns to access additional information.

6. Choose View and More Views, and then select Resource Allocation. Click Apply.

7. Resource Allocation view lets you view resource workloads and availability. Resources in red are overallocated, for instance.

Lesson Summary

- Resources are added to a project using Resource Sheet view.
- Effort-driven scheduling means that adding more resources will result in lesser task durations. However, more resources do not always mean less work.
- Calendars can be applied to resources. These calendars are called resource calendars.
- There are many ways to filter resources to make viewing them easier.
- Resource histograms let you see what resources are overallocated or underallocated, among other things.

Lesson Review

You can use the following questions to test your knowledge of the information in Lesson 4, "Working with Resources." The questions are also available on the companion CD if you prefer to review them in electronic form.

NOTE Answers

Answers to these questions and explanations of why each answer choice is correct or incorrect are located in the "Answers" section at the end of the book.

---

1. You need to add a resource to your project that covers flight costs and meals for your sales team. What type of resource do you create in the Resource Sheet?

    A. Travel

    B. Material

    C. Work

    D. Cost

2. You need to display a graph that shows information about your resources over a period of time. You want to be able to change the gridlines on the graph and modify the appearance of individual bars and text. You are specifically interested in resource allocation and cost. What view should you choose?

    A. Gantt Chart view

    B. Task Usage view

    C. Resource Graph view

    D. Calendar view

3. You recently learned that a resource's availability is no longer 100 percent but that the resource can work at 75 percent. You need to change the maximum units assigned to the resource. Where do you make this change? (Choose all that apply.)

    A. In split screen view using the Task Form

    B. In the Resource Information dialog box

    C. In the Assign Resources dialog box for the resource

    D. In the Project Information dialog box

4. You need to add a new resource named Moving Van to your Home Move project. You also need to select a resource type, configure max units, and assign a standard rate and overtime rate for the van. Which of the following describes the proper place to add the resource and its components and also names the correct resource type?

    A. Add the resource in Resource Sheet view and select Material for the resource type.

    B. Add the resource in Resource Sheet view and select Work for the resource type.

    C. Add the resource in the Assign Resources dialog box and select Work for the resource type.

    D. Add the resource in the Gantt Chart view and select Material for the resource type.

5. You want to make an existing cost resource a budget resource. How do you do this? (Choose all that apply.)

    A. Double-click a task to apply the resource to and, in the Task Information dialog box Resources tab, select the Budget check box.

    B. In Resource Usage view, double-click the resource to change and, in the Resource Information dialog box, select the Budget check box in the General tab.

    C. In Resource Graph view, double-click the name of the resource shown and, in the Resource Information dialog box, select the Budget check box in the General tab.

    D. Use Resource Sheet view to add the cost resource and then open the Resource Information dialog box. Select the Budget check box in the General tab.

6. You have a work resource that is an off-site machine and not part of your company. This resource works only on weekends, but works 24 hours each Friday, Saturday, and Sunday when it is not being used by the company's owners. What type of calendar should you apply?

    A. The Standard base calendar

    B. The Night Shift base Calendar

    C. A Resource calendar based on the 24-Hour base calendar and modified.

    D. The 24-Hour base calendar

7. Due to an unexpected change in scope by your stakeholders, you need to change the resources applied to the task of finishing the interior of a new conference room. The two resources currently applied to this task are Wallpaper Hanger and Carpet Contractor. Your stakeholders have decided that although they still want to finish the conference room, they want to lay tile and paint the walls instead. The cost for laying tile is about the same as laying carpet; the cost for painting the walls is about the same as hanging wallpaper. You have created two new resources: Tile Contractor and Painter. What do you do now?

   A. In the Assign Resources dialog box for the task of finishing the interior of the conference room, select the two existing resources (Wallpaper Hanger and Carpet Contractor) and replace them with the new resources (Tile Contractor and Painter).

   B. In the Task Information dialog box's Resources tab for the task of finishing the interior of the conference room, select the two existing resources (Wallpaper Hanger and Carpet Contractor) and replace them with the new resources (Tile Contractor and Painter).

   C. In the Resource Information dialog box's General tab for the two existing resources (Wallpaper Hanger and Carpet Contractor), click Replace to replace the old resources with the new resources (Tile Contractor and Painter).

   D. From the View Bar, select Assign Resources. In the Assign Resources dialog box for the task of finishing the interior of the conference room, select the two existing resources (Wallpaper Hanger and Carpet Contractor) and replace them with the new resources (Tile Contractor and Painter).

8. You have hired two drivers to drive one van cross-country to help in an office move. You have told the drivers they must take no longer than five days to get from point A to point B and they must not drive more than eight hours a day each. Which of the following statements reflect settings you should apply to the task in the Task Information dialog box? (Choose all that apply.)

   A. The task type is Fixed Units.

   B. There is a deadline.

   C. The task is effort-driven.

   D. The calendar choice is None.

9. You know from experience that the machine you use to create the mechanical parts for your project can create 10 per hour and can work 24 hours a day. You just found out that another project requires use of the machine eight hours a day. Knowing this, how much time will it take to create the 640 parts required for your project, if you can use the machine the remaining hours of each day?

   A. 8 days

   B. 2 1/4 days

   C. 6 days

   D. 4 days

10. You need to write a proposal for a grant for your company's Research and Development department. You know from experience that it takes one person four weeks (at 100 percent capacity) to write a good proposal. You need the proposal in one week. What should you do? (Choose all that apply.)

    A. Assign three more people to the task and enable effort-driven scheduling.

    B. Make the task a Fixed Work task.

    C. Assign three more people to the task and disable effort-driven scheduling.

    D. Make the task a Fixed Units task.

Lesson 5: Final Project Planning Steps

At this point your project planning tasks have been entered. You have created your full WBS and applied work breakdown numbers, if applicable. You should have also already created and assigned your resources and developed the majority of your task relationships, setting any task deadlines or constraints of which you are already aware in your project plan file. With all of this information, Project can now calculate an estimated project finish date based on all the information that you have input.

However, more often than not, the finish date created by Project is not always the finish date that your stakeholders are anticipating. This lesson illustrates several things you can do to analyze your project plan, including the project finish date, and then, if necessary, back some tasks up and work with slack and forecasting so that you can change the project finish date. It also examines working with project baselines or saving the initial project plan information, as well as different views that you can use in Project and project reports—both viewing them and printing them.

After this lesson, you will be able to:
- Work with the critical path.
- Analyze task drivers.
- Use slack to reschedule work.
- Understand and create a project baseline.
- View and print basic project reports.

Estimated lesson time: 90 minutes

Working with the Critical Path

As an experienced project manager, you know that the critical path is made up of a series of tasks that must finish on schedule. Any task on the critical path that will affect the project finish date if delayed is called a *critical task*.

Thus far in the project planning process, the most common view has been the Gantt Chart. Using the Gantt Chart Wizard, you can apply formatting to visually see which tasks are on the critical path. However, in Project the critical path is not displayed by default. The critical path is shown in Figure 2-98.

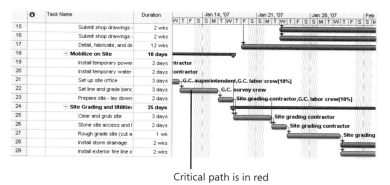

Critical path is in red

Figure 2-98 The critical path is shown in red

Quick Check

- What is the definition of a critical task?

Quick Check Answer

- Any task on the critical path that, if delayed, will affect the project finish date is called a critical task.

Applying the Gantt Chart Wizard to display the critical path is a great way for you to see (in color) exactly which tasks are on the critical path and will affect the project finish date. To display the critical path on the Gantt Chart, follow these steps:

1. Choose View and Gantt Chart.

2. On the Formatting toolbar, locate and click the Gantt Chart Wizard button, which is shown in Figure 2-99. Alternatively, you can choose Format and then Gantt Chart Wizard from the Menu bar.

Figure 2-99 The Gantt Chart Wizard button

3. On the Welcome To The Gantt Chart Wizard page, click Next to begin.

4. On the second page of the wizard, select Critical Path and click Next. See Figure 2-100.

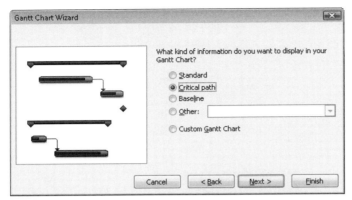

Figure 2-100   Select Critical Path

5. On the third page of the wizard, select Resources And Dates. (Note there are other choices.) See Figure 2-101. Click Next.

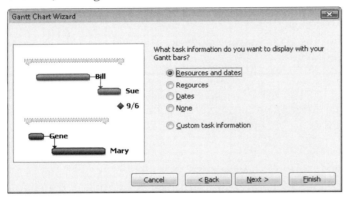

Figure 2-101   Decide what to show on the Gantt Chart

6. On the next wizard page, select Yes to show link lines between dependent tasks. Click Next.

7. Click Format It and then Exit Wizard.

Understanding the Critical Path View

A project's finish date is a function of how long the sum total of the tasks and their relationships will take based on the project's start date.

A couple of things can modify whether or not a task is defined as critical. The first is scheduling resources. If you assign additional resources to a task, the task duration can take less time if effort-driven scheduling is enabled and the task is not of a Fixed Duration task type. A task that takes less time might be pulled off the critical path. Additionally, after a task on the critical path is completed, it is no longer classified as critical because after it is completed it cannot affect the project finish date.

MORE INFO How "critical" is a "critical task"?

In terms of project management, the word "critical," whether we are talking about the critical path or the critical tasks that make up the critical path, really has nothing to do with how important a task is. Instead it is much more a function of whether this task, if delayed or started early, will in some way affect the scheduled project finish date. If a critical task is delayed, the project finish date will be pushed out. If a critical task is started earlier, it either comes off of the critical path or the project finish date finishes sooner. As a result, your project's critical path is fluid. It is going to change throughout the progress of the project as you begin to track when tasks begin and when tasks are completed.

This is important because, as you begin to work with your project, one of the things you can do with the critical path is apply a filter. For example, if you have 100 tasks in your project file and 20 of them are on the critical path, it might be beneficial for you to view only the 20 that are on the critical path just for scheduling purposes. You can modify your view by applying a filter that displays only the tasks on the critical path. To view only tasks on the critical path by applying a filter, follow these steps:

1. Choose Project and then Filtered For.
2. In the Filtered For choices, shown in Figure 2-102, choose Critical.

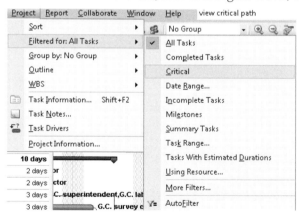

Figure 2-102   Show only critical tasks

MORE INFO Filter for critical tasks

You can also filter tasks from the Formatting toolbar. By default, All Tasks is shown. Select this drop-down list, and then select Critical to display the critical tasks.

> ## Quick Check
> ■ Name two ways you can pull a critical task off the critical path.
>
> ### Quick Check Answer
> ■ If the task is effort-driven, add resources. Complete the task.

One of the things you might notice when you are viewing the critical path is that any task that is on the critical path automatically appears in red while tasks that are not on the critical path appear in blue. Additionally, relationship lines between critical tasks are also red. This is a visual identifier of exactly which tasks affect the scheduling of the project finish date. If you have applied a filter to view only tasks on the critical path, you can remove the filter and view all tasks by following these steps:

1. Choose Project and Filtered For.
2. In the Filtered For choices, select All Tasks. (Additionally, you can select All Tasks from the drop-down list on the Formatting toolbar.)

Analyzing Task Drivers

As you have seen when viewing the critical path, modifying one task can create a domino effect across your other tasks based on relationships, constraints, and a host of other factors. To determine what other factors might affect your task start date, you can use the Task Drivers pane, shown in Figure 2-103.

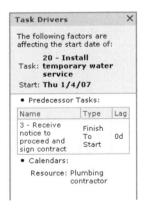

Figure 2-103   Obtain information about task drivers

The Task Drivers pane concisely displays any scheduling factor(s) that affect the selected task. There are several ways to show the Task Drivers task pane:

■ On the Standard toolbar, click the Task Drivers button.

■ Choose Project and then Task Drivers.

- On the Project Guide toolbar, from the Track drop-down list, select See What Is Driving The Start Date Of A Task.

Exam Tip   Although task drivers are not new to Project, the Task Drivers task pane is. This tool is extremely helpful in seeing "at a glance" exactly what factors come into play in terms of scheduling a selected task. Like other new additions to Project (such as Change Highlighting), be sure you understand the purpose of the Task Drivers task pane and the type of information displayed when this task pane is open.

> ## Quick Check
> 1. How can you determine which factors will affect a task's start date?
> 2. Name at least two ways to open this tool.
>
> ### Quick Check Answers
> 1. Open the Task Drivers pane.
> 2. On the Standard toolbar, click the Task Drivers button. Choose Project and then Task Drivers. On the Project Guide toolbar, from the Track drop-down list, select See What Is Driving The Start Date Of A Task.

Table 2-5 describes the type of task driver information this task pane might display. Because this information varies from task to task, you might see one or more of the driver headings shown in Table 2-5.

Table 2-5   Task Driver Pane

Driver/Heading	Description
Actual Start And Assignments	The Actual Start And Assignments information will display if actual start date data has been entered for the selected task.
Leveling Delay	If leveling has been applied to the project in an effort to balance resource workload, the leveling information will be displayed along with the amount of time by which the selected task was delayed in the leveling process.
Constraint Type And Date	When constraints have been applied to a task, those constraints are displayed in the Task Drivers task pane.
Summary Task	When constraints have been applied to a summary task that affects that task's subtasks, the summary task will be listed in the Task Drivers pane when the related subtask is selected.
Predecessor Tasks	In any tasks that have defined relationships (which means that they have been linked), the predecessors, constraint types, and the amount of lag or lead time associated with the selected task will be displayed in the Task Drivers task pane.

Table 2-5   Task Driver Pane

Driver/Heading	Description
Subtasks	When you select a summary task, subtasks and summary tasks that are driving the schedule will be displayed in the Task Drivers task pane.
Calendars	Any calendar that affects the selected task's schedule is displayed as a link in the Task Drivers task pane. To access the Change Working Times dialog box for that calendar, you can click the calendar name in the Task Drivers task pane.

MORE INFO   Task Drivers

For more information on working with Task Drivers, refer to *http://office.microsoft.com/en-us/project /HA101130861033.aspx?pid=CH100666481033*.

Using Slack

In order to fully understand the critical path and working with the critical path, a key term you should be familiar with is "slack." There are two types of slack: free slack and total slack. *Free slack* is specific to the task's relationship with another task. In other words, free slack defines the amount of time that a task can be delayed before it affects or delays another task. *Total slack* is based on the total project—all tasks in the project. Total slack is the amount of time that a task can be delayed before it actually delays the project end date, or the completion of the project. By default, any task that is critical also has zero slack. In other words, any delay in that task will affect a delay in another task and in the project finish date. So a critical task has zero slack.

Exam Tip   For the certification exam, remember that any task that is on the critical path is there if its total slack is zero. If a task is noncritical, that task has some total slack. This means it can be delayed within the slack time without actually affecting the completion date of a project.

For example, Task A might have a relationship with Task B. Task B is the last task in the project. However, there might be two days of play time between the time Task A starts or finishes and the time Task B needs to start or finish. For example, assume that Task A has been assigned a duration of two days and Task B has been assigned a duration of four days. If Task A and Task B were to have a Finish-to-Finish relationship, they need to finish on the same day. In this scenario there is a two-day duration differential between Tasks A and B. Because total slack is the amount of time that a task can be delayed before it delays the completion date of the project, that automatically gives Task A total slack of two days. This means that Task A remains noncritical only until it is delayed more than two days (or more than the total of its total slack time). Just because a task is noncritical today does not mean it is going to be noncritical tomorrow.

Quick Check

- What is the difference between total slack and free slack?

Quick Check Answer

- Free slack defines the amount of time that a task can be delayed before it affects or delays another task. Total slack is the amount of time that a task can be delayed before it delays the project end date.

In fact, you do not even have to display the critical path through the Gantt Chart Wizard in order to see how much slack you have built into your individual tasks in the project. You can view the amount of slack in the Detail Gantt view, shown in Figure 2-104.

Figure 2-104   Slack time shown in the Detail Gantt view

To display the Detail Gantt view, follow these steps:

1. Choose View and then More Views.
2. In the More Views dialog box, select Detail Gantt.
3. Click Apply.

In addition to viewing the slack on the Detail Gantt view, you can also see the actual values for free and total slack in the Schedule table. See Figure 2-105.

	Task Name	Start	Finish	Late Start	Late Finish	Free Slack	Total Slack
27	Rough grad	Thu 1/25/07	Wed 1/31/07	Thu 1/25/07	Wed 1/31/07	0 wks	0 wks
28	Install storr	Thu 2/1/07	Wed 2/14/07	Wed 2/14/07	Tue 2/27/07	1.8 wks	1.8 wks
29	Install exter	Thu 2/1/07	Wed 2/14/07	Thu 2/1/07	Wed 2/14/07	0 wks	0 wks
30	Perform fin	Thu 2/15/07	Wed 2/28/07	Thu 2/15/07	Wed 2/28/07	0 wks	0 wks
31	Erect buildi	Thu 3/1/07	Wed 3/7/07	Thu 3/1/07	Wed 3/7/07	0 wks	0 wks
32	– **Foundations**	**Thu 3/8/07**	**Mon 4/23/07**	**Thu 3/8/07**	**Fri 2/1/08**	**0 days**	**0 days**
33	Excavate f	Thu 3/8/07	Wed 3/21/07	Thu 3/8/07	Wed 3/21/07	0 wks	0 wks
34	Excavate e	Thu 3/8/07	Fri 3/9/07	Wed 1/2/08	Thu 1/3/08	0 days	214 days
35	Form colur	Thu 3/22/07	Tue 3/27/07	Thu 3/22/07	Tue 3/27/07	0 days	0 days
36	Rough-in e	Mon 3/12/07	Thu 3/15/07	Fri 1/4/08	Wed 1/9/08	0 days	214 days
37	Form eleva	Fri 3/16/07	Wed 3/21/07	Thu 1/10/08	Tue 1/15/08	0 days	214 days

Figure 2-105   Free Slack and Total Slack columns on the Schedule table

By default, the Entry table is assigned to the Gantt Chart view; however, you can just as easily assign the Schedule table in its place. All you have to do is choose View, Table, Entry, and then Schedule. Note that this graphic displays the same tasks as shown in the Detail Gantt graphic above to show how the slack in the Slack column matches the slack on the Gantt Chart.

Exam Tip   On the certification exam you might be presented with a graphic of a sample project file. In addition to reading the scenario carefully, check to see if the question is asking whether changes to the project plan file will affect the project finish date. For this type of question, when you see the graphic or the exhibit, make note of the color of the Gantt bars. If they are all blue, you can assume that none are on the critical path. However, if you see red bars, you know that not only are those red bar tasks on the critical path but also the Gantt Chart Wizard has already been applied. So, even though specific information is not given in the scenario, it is going to be up to you to be able to fully comprehend the visual image you have been given and be able to apply what you read and what you see in order to correctly answer the question.

If you get to this point in the project planning process and you realize that all of your tasks are on the critical path, what can you do to pull some of them off the critical path to give yourself some wiggle room within your project plan file? You can start to build in some slack. If everything is on the critical path, there is no slack to begin with.

Build Slack

You can build free and total slack into your project plan in a couple of ways. One of the things you can do to build in some slack is to change the relationship between two tasks. As you look at your project plan file, you might have a Finish-to-Start relationship between two tasks, as shown in Figure 2-106.

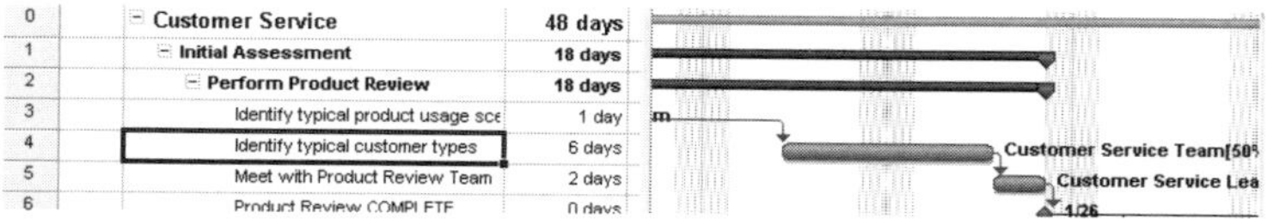

Figure 2-106   Look for Finish-to-Start relationships first

NOTE   Go back to Gantt Chart view

To get back to Gantt Chart view and the Entry table, choose View and then Gantt Chart, and then choose View, Table, and then Entry.

Upon further investigation, you discover that those two tasks could probably be completed at the same time. In this scenario project managers typically try fast-tracking (which is overlapping tasks). Another option is that, instead of using a Finish-to-Start relationship, you can instead assign a Start-to-Start relationship or a Finish-to-Finish relationship—a relationship that would allow those tasks to occur simultaneously, as shown in Figure 2-107.

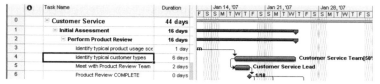

Figure 2-107   Change relationships to lessen project time

If two tasks have the same resources, you might need to do some playing around with the schedule by assigning a different resource to one of the tasks so that those two tasks can happen at the same time.

Another option for building some slack into your project schedule is to actually remove a task or a task requirement. However, use this method only if removing a task requirement will not affect your project scope. Or, if your project scope is affected, be sure to ask the stakeholders for permission before making the modification. You certainly do not want to remove important tasks from your project schedule all in the name of building some slack into the project plan file.

Finally, you can modify Project's default slack option by changing the number associated with slack. Project governs by the rule that marks a task critical if the task has zero slack. But you can change that slack number in the Calculation tab of the Options dialog box, as shown in Figure 2-108. This should be an option only if your company and project stakeholders agree to the change.

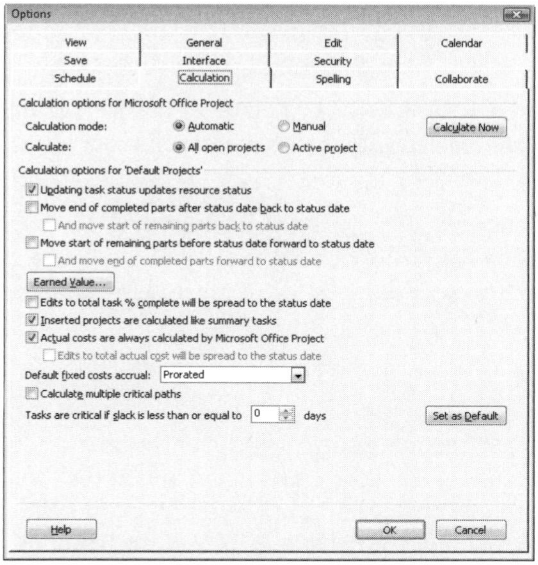

Figure 2-108   Set when tasks are critical

In this way you tell Project that a task is not critical unless it has one day of slack (or a different duration of your choosing). In other words, a task is not critical unless it is going to change the project's end date by one day (or whatever that number is for you). Essentially, you can change the amount of slack required for a task before Project considers it critical. Follow these steps:

1. Choose Tools and then Options.
2. Click the Calculation tab.
3. At the bottom, change the amount of slack required before Project considers the task critical using the spin box.
4. Click OK.

Quick Check

- Name as many ways as you can think of to add slack to a project.

Quick Check Answer

- Change the relationship between two tasks. Assign different resources to a task (or add resources). Remove a task or requirement. Change the number associated with slack to change when tasks become critical.

Summary: Working with Slack

There are two types of slack: free slack and total slack. Free slack is the amount of time you can delay a task before that task will affect or delay another task. Total slack is the amount of time you can delay a task before that task delays the actual project completion date.

A task is on the critical path if its total slack is zero (by default). However, you can use the Options dialog box to change that number to any number that best suits your project planning methods.

Project is constantly recalculating the critical path in the background. Even if you never choose to format the Gantt Chart using the Gantt Chart Wizard, you can also see tasks that have slack in them on the Detail Gantt view and the actual numbers associated with slack in the Schedule table.

Project Baselines

You have reached the end of the project planning stage, tasks have been entered, resources have been assigned, and you have even looked at the critical path and at the available slack. Ideally, you know how much wiggle room you have in your project file. Now is the time when you want to save not just the project plan file, but also a snapshot of where everything sits before the project work actually begins. In Project this is called a "baseline plan."

Create a Baseline

With a baseline, you can save exactly what the project looks like today. Then, as the project progress begins, you can track the tasks and their progress, allowing you to make a comparison later. With this comparison, you can display where the project currently is on top of the project baseline. In this way you can see throughout the duration of the project (and, maybe more important, at the end of the project) how far off you are in the projections that you made during the project planning process. Seeing where your project stands compared to the plan helps you decide what steps to take to get the project back on track. The best thing that we have going for us as project managers is experience and learning lessons from past projects. Baselines allow you to do that not only throughout the duration of the project but also at the end of the project, so that if a similar project comes up later, you have a plan of reference.

In your baseline plan you will store variables such as plan start dates, finish dates, how much you think a task is going to cost, resources, and your resource assignments. Essentially, your entire plan as it stands at the point is saved within the baseline. To save a baseline, follow these steps:

1. Choose Tools, Tracking, and then Set Baseline.
2. In the Set Baseline dialog box, shown in Figure 2-109, accept the defaults and click OK.

Figure 2-109   Create a baseline

You can see the baseline values within another table that has not yet been introduced: the Variance table. Before viewing the Variance table, it is helpful to first display the Task Sheet view. By changing views, you free up your screen real estate to display just a table view.

1. Choose View and then More Views, and in the More Views dialog box, select Task Sheet.
2. Click Apply.
3. Choose View and Table, and then choose Variance. Figure 2-110 shows the Variance table.

When you set the baseline, the dates that are in the Start and Finish fields are copied to fields named "Baseline Start" and "Baseline Finish," and so on, for several fields.

	Task Name	Start	Finish	Baseline Start	Baseline Finish	Start Var.	Finish Var.
0	− Customer Service	Mon 1/1/07	Thu 3/1/07	Mon 1/1/07	Thu 3/1/07	0 days	0 days
1	− Initial Assessment	Wed 1/3/07	Wed 1/24/07	Wed 1/3/07	Wed 1/24/07	0 days	0 days
2	− Perform Product Review	Wed 1/3/07	Wed 1/24/07	Wed 1/3/07	Wed 1/24/07	0 days	0 days
3	Identify typical product	Wed 1/3/07	Wed 1/3/07	Wed 1/3/07	Wed 1/3/07	0 days	0 days
4	Identify typical custome	Wed 1/17/07	Wed 1/24/07	Wed 1/17/07	Wed 1/24/07	0 days	0 days
5	Meet with Product Revi	Wed 1/17/07	Thu 1/18/07	Wed 1/17/07	Thu 1/18/07	0 days	0 days
6	Product Review COMPL	Thu 1/18/07	Thu 1/18/07	Thu 1/18/07	Thu 1/18/07	0 days	0 days
7	− Service Planning	Fri 1/19/07	Fri 2/23/07	Fri 1/19/07	Fri 2/23/07	0 days	0 days
8	− Design Support Service	Fri 1/19/07	Fri 2/23/07	Fri 1/19/07	Fri 2/23/07	0 days	0 days
9	− Design Customer Se	Fri 1/19/07	Tue 1/30/07	Fri 1/19/07	Tue 1/30/07	0 days	0 days
10	Online support	Mon 1/22/07	Thu 1/25/07	Mon 1/22/07	Thu 1/25/07	0 days	0 days
11	Phone support	Fri 1/26/07	Tue 1/30/07	Fri 1/26/07	Tue 1/30/07	0 days	0 days
12	On-site support	Fri 1/19/07	Wed 1/24/07	Fri 1/19/07	Wed 1/24/07	0 days	0 days
13	Design of customer	Tue 1/30/07	Tue 1/30/07	Tue 1/30/07	Tue 1/30/07	0 days	0 days
14	− Develop Levels of Cu	Wed 2/7/07	Fri 2/23/07	Wed 2/7/07	Fri 2/23/07	0 days	0 days
15	Identify types of pro	Wed 2/7/07	Thu 2/8/07	Wed 2/7/07	Thu 2/8/07	0 days	0 days
16	Identify service deli	Tue 2/13/07	Fri 2/16/07	Fri 2/16/07	Fri 2/16/07	0 days	0 days
17	Determine required :	Mon 2/19/07	Fri 2/23/07	Mon 2/19/07	Fri 2/23/07	0 days	0 days
18	Customer Service L	Fri 2/23/07	Fri 2/23/07	Fri 2/23/07	Fri 2/23/07	0 days	0 days

Figure 2-110   The Variance table

About the Variance Table

Typically, when you see the Variance table for the first time, you will not see a lot of changes between the Start and the Finish fields and the Baseline Start and the Baseline Finish fields. If you have not entered any actual data, you will not see any here. If you view the Variance table immediately after setting the baseline, all Project has done at this point is to copy exactly what it sees in the Start and Finish fields and paste that information into the Baseline Start and the Baseline Finish fields. However, when the project begins and the project plan file is updated, you will begin to see variances between the actual Start and Finish fields and the Baseline Start and Baseline Finish fields.

Additional Project Statistics

In addition to the Variance table, you can view other project statistic information (actual versus baseline) in the Project Information dialog box. To see this view, choose Project and Project Information, and then click the Statistics button in the Project Information dialog box. A sample is shown in Figure 2-111.

Project Statistics for 'Customer Service'

	Start	Finish
Current	Mon 1/1/07	Thu 3/1/07
Baseline	Mon 1/1/07	Thu 3/1/07
Actual	NA	NA
Variance	0d	0d

	Duration	Work	Cost
Current	44d	448h	$12,360.00
Baseline	44d	448h	$12,360.00
Actual	0d	0h	$0.00
Remaining	44d	448h	$12,360.00

Percent complete:

Duration: 0%   Work: 0%

Figure 2-111   Statistics for a project

> **Real World**
>
> *Deanna Reynolds*
>
> As your project progresses and you continue to meet with your project stakeholders, you might find (as many project managers do) that stakeholders often forget what they asked for in the beginning. As a project manager, it is a good idea to get a sign-off on the baseline values or where your project stands at the end of the planning phase. That way, if a week (or a month or two months) down the road you go back into a stakeholder meeting and you are asked why the project seems so far off from where it was originally intended, you can show them hard dates and say, "You know what, it is actually only one day off from where we projected it would be," or "Actually, we are two days ahead of where we projected we could be." Often, the hard and fast numbers and dates do a lot more than a simple Gantt Chart view to convince your stakeholders that you are more on track than it appears.

Review Baseline Information

After you set your baseline information, you can review it in many ways: the Schedule table, the Variance table, and the Detail Gantt Chart. You can also apply the Tracking Gantt to see the baseline bars underneath the actual task bars.

NOTE Baseline field data

Typically, you do not modify the date in a baseline field or the data in a baseline field. The data in a baseline field is copied directly from the scheduled values that Project has calculated at the point that you save the baseline. So even though you can edit the baseline data, it is considered project management best practice to leave it at whatever values Project sets when you set the baseline.

If you decide that some of your baseline numbers need to be changed, you should do this by overwriting the existing baseline or by creating a new baseline rather than typing new baseline data directly into the baseline fields (even though you can see them and edit them in a table).

In the Set Baseline dialog box you can set the baseline not just for the entire project but also for selected tasks. The Selected Tasks option is handy when you need to modify baseline information for just a few tasks. It is also handy if, after you have set your initial baseline, you discover that you need to add new tasks to the project plan. If you make large-scale changes as the project progresses—such as adding new tasks or accidentally modifying the baseline information—it is a good idea to set a new baseline for just the affected tasks. To set a baseline for just selected tasks, follow these steps:

1. Choose Tools, choose Tracking, and then choose Set Baseline.
2. In the Set Baseline dialog box, under For:, select Selected Tasks.
3. Click OK.

In addition to the first baseline, you can save up to 10 additional baselines. In any project plan file you can save up to a total of 11 baselines (your original baseline plus 10 more). When you set a baseline, you are saving the duration, the work, and the cost information (typically for the entire project), as well as start and finish information for each task. Because you are saving such a great deal of information, you are significantly increasing the file size of your project file. In fact, the first time that you set a baseline, the file size for your project file can nearly double in size.

MORE INFO   Interim plans

As an alternative to setting baselines, you can also choose to set interim plans, which save only start and finish dates. Interim plans are covered more in depth in Chapter 3.

You can view Gantt bars that reflect each baseline stacked and differentiated on one of your Gantt Chart views using the Multiple Baselines Gantt in Project.

To set and view multiple baselines, follow these steps:

1. Choose Tools, choose Tracking, and then choose Set Baseline.
2. In the Set Baseline dialog box, shown in Figure 2-112, display the Set Baseline drop-down list. Note that in the Set Baseline dialog box you can see each baseline and when it was saved.

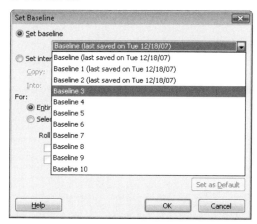

Figure 2-112   Setting multiple baselines

3. Select a free baseline (one without a date associated with it)—in this case Baseline 3.
4. Click OK.
5. Choose View and then More Views.
6. In the More Views dialog box, select Multiple Baselines Gantt.
7. Click Apply. The results are shown in Figure 2-113.

Figure 2-113   Viewing multiple baselines

For long projects, setting baselines is quite beneficial for tracking progress. You may choose to set a baseline every month or every quarter or at the beginning or end of every major phase in your project. This way you can keep tabs on your project, making sure that it is where you thought it would be at this point and, if it is not, making adjustments where necessary.

If you use all your available baselines or you decide that one of your baselines just is not appropriate anymore, you can clear your baselines, effectively removing them from your project plan file. To remove a baseline, follow these steps:

1. Choose Tools and then Tracking.

2. Choose Clear Baseline.

3. In the Clear Baseline dialog box, shown in Figure 2-114, select the baseline plan to remove and click OK.

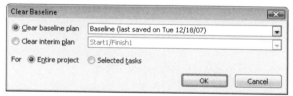

Figure 2-114   Clearing a baseline

Quick Check

- Why are baselines important?

Quick Check Answer

- Baselines contain the planned start and finish dates, durations, costs, and work of tasks and assignments and offer a way to compare where you are now in your project to where you should be or where you want to be.

Project View Options

This chapter has discussed different project views you can use to view the critical path, task drivers, and other project-related information. In order to use the many views to their fullest potential, it is helpful to understand what views are available and how they are created.

As you work with Project, you will find that you probably use a small subset of views the most often (such as the Gantt Chart and Resource Sheet). Those common views were discussed in Chapter 1. At this point you have probably realized that information you enter in one view can be seen across several other views.

As you have seen, some of the views offer more than one component. For example, the Gantt Chart is a combination view that displays both the Entry table and the Gantt Chart, while the Network Diagram view is simply a chart. Combination views are able to display two views at the same time. You can further customize your project views by working with both filters and groups.

MORE INFO   Filters and groups

For more information on working with filters and groups, see Chapter 3.

Overall, the views available in Project can be categorized as either task views, resource views, or assignment views. Each view has been listed in Table 2-6 by category.

Table 2-6   Views by Category

Category	Available Views
Assignment Views	Task Usage Resource Usage
Resource Views	Resource Graph View Resource Sheet Resource Form Resource Name Form
Task Views	Bar Rollup View Detail Gantt View Gantt Chart View Leveling Gantt View Milestone Date Rollup View Milestone Rollup Multiple Baselines View Gantt PA_Expected View Gantt PA_Optimistic Gantt View PA_Pessimistic Tracking Gantt View Descriptive Network Diagram Network View Diagram Network Diagram Relationship View Graph Calendar View PA_PERT Entry Sheet Task Sheet Task Details Form Task Form Task Name Form

To display any view in Project, either choose View and choose an option from the menu, or choose View, and then More Views, select an item in the More Views dialog box, and then click Apply.

NOTE Printing views

You can print each of these views using the Print dialog box. Essentially, if you can display it on your screen, you can send it the printer.

Combination/Split Screen Views   When viewing a combination view, you see one of Project's available views in the top (or left) pane and another in the bottom (or right) pane. For example, when viewing the Gantt Chart, you can choose Window and then Split to display the Task Form on the bottom pane. However, you can customize your combination view to display any other view you deem necessary. To do so, while in a split screen view, right-click the selection bar to the left of the view portion you want to change (as shown in Figure 2-115) and then choose another view using the View menu.

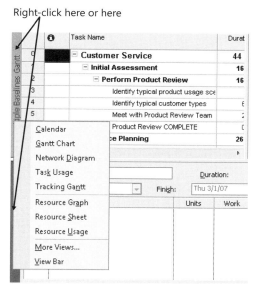

Figure 2-115   Right-click the left edge of any split screen to select a different view

---

MORE INFO Project views

You can read additional information about each of the available project views using the Project Help system. Click inside the "Type a Question for Help" box located in the upper-right corner of your program window. Then type **Views** and press Enter. From the Help system results, click Overview Of Project Views.

Customizing Views with Formatting

Because each of the views within Project can be printed, you might want to engage in a little view formatting before you disseminate this information among your project team. Each view has its own set of formatting characteristics that might include:

- Highlighting milestones
- Changing the color of task bars
- Changing field titles
- Changing field width
- Modifying the timescale
- Modifying the look of nonworking time

The majority of these formatting options can be applied through the use of the Format menu, shown in Figure 2-116.

Figure 2-116 Formatting a view

To customize the formatting for any displayed view, follow these steps:

1. Display the view you want to format from the View menu.
2. Choose Format and then choose the item that matches what you would like to change. You can choose Font, Bar, Timescale, Gridlines, Text Styles, Layout, or other options.
3. Depending on what you select, make choices in the resulting dialog box. Figure 2-117 shows the dialog box for Format/Font.
4. Make changes as desired. Click OK to close open dialog boxes.

MORE INFO Customizing project views

For more information on customizing the content of the Project views, see Chapter 4.

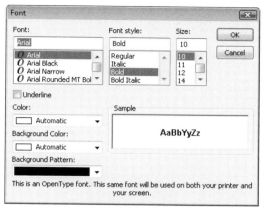

Figure 2-117   The Font dialog box

Project Reports

When you reach the point of having completed the majority of your project planning, it is often helpful to print parts of your project plan. As you saw in the previous lesson, many of the views in Project create nicely formatted printouts.

MORE INFO   **Visual Reports**

New to Project are Visual Reports, which provide a graphical (instead of text-based) representation of your project data. Visual Reports are covered in depth in Chapter 5, "Closing the Project Plan."

In addition to the views, this program offers several predefined text-based reports organized into five categories: Overview, Current Activities, Costs, Assignments, and Workload, as shown in Figure 2-118. You can access these options by choosing Report and then Reports.

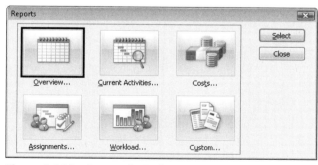

Figure 2-118   Reports in Project

You can also display an abundance of project-related data with just a few clicks. The available reports are many and varied. Some specific reports include:

- Top-Level Tasks
- Critical Tasks
- Should Have Started Tasks
- Who Does What When
- Overallocated Resources

MORE INFO   Available reports

To see all of the reports available in Project, open the Reports dialog box (Report/Reports) and click each of the six text-based report categories. Here you will see each report and can even see a preview.

These are just a few of the more than 20 text reports you can print based on the data you have entered into your project plan file. To print a text report, follow these steps:

1. Choose Report and then Reports.
2. In the Report dialog box, select a report type.
3. Click Select.
4. In the resulting dialog box, select a report type.
5. Click Select.
6. When the report is ready, click Print (or Page Setup). See Figure 2-119.

Figure 2-119   Print a report

MORE INFO   Custom Reports

To learn how to create Custom Reports using the Custom option found in the Reports dialog box, see Chapter 5.

> **Real World**
>
> *Deanna Reynolds*
>
> As a project manager, one of your primary responsibilities is to communicate tasks, assignments, and project progress to your project team members and stakeholders. A common scenario, in fact, is letting your team know when you have them scheduled to work and what they will be doing during that time. In this instance, as long as task assignments have been made, you can print the "Who Does What When" report. This report creates a succinct breakdown, by resource, of what tasks need to be completed, the work hours assigned to each listed task, and the days during the project in which the work will be performed.

PRACTICE Estimating and Budgeting Tasks

In these practices you will review the concepts learned in this section. The first exercise is to display the critical path and then filter tasks so that only critical tasks are showing. The second exercise is to analyze task drivers. The third exercise is to use slack to reschedule work. The fourth exercise is to change the amount of slack a task can have before it becomes critical. The fifth exercise is to create multiple project baselines and view them. The last exercise is to view and print project reports.

▶ **Exercise 1   Display the Critical Path and Filter Critical Tasks**

You need to know how your project is moving forward in terms of the critical path and the progress of your critical tasks. To do this you need to display the critical path and then filter only critical tasks. To complete this exercise, follow these steps:

1. Choose File and then New and click On Computer.
2. In the Templates dialog box, click the Project Templates tab.
3. Select Commercial Construction and click OK.
4. If the project did not open in Gantt Chart view, choose View and Gantt Chart.
5. On the Formatting toolbar, click the Gantt Chart Wizard button.
6. In the Welcome To The Gantt Chart Wizard dialog box, click Next to begin.
7. On the second page of the wizard, select Critical Path and click Next.
8. On the third page of the wizard, select Resources And Dates. Click Next.
9. On the next wizard page, select Yes to show link lines between dependent tasks. Click Next.
10. Click Format It and then Exit Wizard.
11. Choose Project and Filtered For.
12. In the Filtered For choices, select Critical.

▶ **Exercise 2   Analyze Task Drivers**

In your commercial construction project, you need to find out what predecessor tasks are associated with submitting bond and insurance documents. You also need to see what type of relationship it holds, any lag time, and other information. To complete this exercise:

1. Choose File and New, and then click On Computer.
2. In the Templates dialog box, click the Project Templates tab.
3. Select Commercial Construction and click OK.
4. Choose Project and then Task Drivers.
5. Access the required information from the Task Drivers pane.

▶ **Exercise 3   Use Slack to Reschedule Work**

You need to calculate the slack time in your project so you can reschedule work that is likely to fall behind. To complete this exercise you must first find out how much slack time you have and then look for tasks that you can change the relationship for to allow for extra time in the schedule. To complete this exercise, follow these steps:

1. Choose File and New, and then click On Computer.
2. In the Templates dialog box, click the Project Templates tab.
3. Select Home Move and click OK.
4. Choose View and More Views.
5. In the More Views dialog box, select Detail Gantt.
6. Click Apply.
7. Select the first task and click the Scroll To Task button on the Standard toolbar to quickly view the detail Gantt Chart bars.
8. Note the available slack for Task 75: Have Appliances Serviced For Moving, if applicable (three days).
9. Change the relationship between Tasks 158 and 160 to Start-to-Start. Notice how the slack for Task 159 is reduced from two days to one day.
10. Continue modifying task relationships, lag time, lead time, and constraints settings and notice the affect on the selected tasks, surrounding tasks, and the project finish date.

▶ **Exercise 4   Change the Amount of Slack Before a Task Becomes Critical**

You want to change when Project decides a task is critical. The default is 0 days, and you would like to change that to two days. You need to change the amount of slack required for a task before Project considers it critical. To complete this task, follow these steps:

1. In any open project, choose Tools and then Options.
2. Click the Calculation tab.

3. At the bottom, change the amount of slack required before Project considers the task critical from 0 to 2 using the Tasks Are Critical If Slack Is Less Than Or Equal To spin box.

4. Click OK.

▶ **Exercise 5   Create Multiple Project Baselines and View Them**

You want to create a baseline before starting your project, and once a month thereafter. This will allow you to manage the progress of your project and associated tasks. You also need to be able to view these baselines and compare them. To complete this exercise, follow these steps:

1. In any open project, choose Tools, Tracking, and Set Baseline.
2. In the Set Baseline dialog box, click Set Baseline.
3. Accept the defaults and click OK to create one baseline.
4. For the purpose of this exercise, create two more baselines:
    a. Choose Tools, choose Tracking, and then choose Set Baseline.
    b. In the Set Baseline drop-down list, select Baseline 1 and click OK.
    c. Choose Tools, choose Tracking, and then choose Set Baseline.
    d. Under Set Baseline, select Baseline 2 and click OK.
5. Choose View and More Views.
6. In the More Views dialog box, select Multiple Baselines Gantt.
7. Click Apply.
8. Use the scroll bars as needed to view the baselines.

▶ **Exercise 6   View and Print Project Reports**

You need to view both the Gantt Chart and the Task Usage view on the same screen and then you need to create a Project Summary report for your stakeholders. To complete this exercise, follow these steps:

1. In any open project, choose View and Gantt Chart view.
2. Choose Window and then Split. The interface splits into two panes, the Gantt Chart (on the top) and the Task Form (on the bottom).
3. Right-click Task Form on the left side of the bottom pane, and choose Task Usage.
4. Choose Report and then Reports.
5. In the Report dialog box, select Overview, and then click Select.
6. In the Overview Reports dialog box, select Project Summary.
7. Click Select.
8. When the report is ready, click Print.

Lesson Summary

- The critical path is ruled by the critical tasks on it. A task is a critical task if delaying that task will cause a delay in the finish date of the project.
- The Task Drivers pane lets you easily see what governs a task's start date. It might include predecessors, constraints, leveling delays, subtasks, calendars, and more.
- Slack is free time between tasks. Free slack involves the amount of slack between tasks (when one task will delay another), while total slack refers to the slack associated with a task and the project's end date (when one task will delay the entire project).
- The Detail Gantt view lets you view slack in a project, and you can use this information to create more slack if necessary.
- Project baselines give you a starting point to compare project progress.
- There are many types of reports you can view and print, along with multiple views for accessing data the way you need to.

Lesson Review

You can use the following questions to test your knowledge of the information in Lesson 5, "Final Project Planning Steps." The questions are also available on the companion CD if you prefer to review them in electronic form.

NOTE   Answers

Answers to these questions and explanations of why each answer choice is correct or incorrect are located in the "Answers" section at the end of the book.

---

1. You want to add one special task to the Entry table that summarizes the entire project, including duration, work, and costs of all tasks in the project, including the project's timeline from start to finish. What do you need to do?
   A. Show the project summary task.
   B. Show outline numbers.
   C. Outdent each summary task.
   D. Show summary tasks.

2. A task in your project is continually delayed and you need to find out why. You think the delay has to do with a lack of machinery because other tasks are also using the same machines that this task needs to complete. Where can you find out exactly what is causing the delay and whether it has to do with resources or something else, such as constraints, predecessor tasks, or actual start dates?
   A. The Task Information dialog box
   B. The Assignments, Overallocated Resources Report

    C. The Project Information dialog box

    D. The Task Drivers pane

3. You need to find a way to correct a delay in the project and want to adjust the schedule so there is some slack that you can use. You know that the Apply For And Obtain Electrical Permit task (given 1 day) and Apply For And Obtain Water Permit (given 3 days) have both been assigned and have a Start-to-Finish relationship. What can you change about these two tasks to add two days of slack to your project schedule? These two tasks are not effort-driven.

    A. Assign three more people to the task of obtaining the water permit.

    B. Configure the two tasks to have a Finish-to-Finish relationship so that they can finish on the same day.

    C. Delete the task of obtaining the water permit.

    D. Perform automatic resource leveling across the entire project.

4. What should the first baseline you create for a project be based on and when should you create it?

    A. The approved project schedule, which should be created before the project begins

    B. The approved project schedule, one week after the project begins

    C. The project in progress, one month after the project begins

    D. The project in progress, the first time you are aware of a conflict or delay

5. Which of the following are ways to reschedule incomplete work or give tasks that have lapsed or fallen behind more time to complete? (Choose all that apply.)

    A. Build slack in the project schedule.

    B. Remove a task from the project.

    C. Assign additional resources to complete the task more quickly and bring it in on time.

    D. Change the default slack option from 0 to something else, like one day or two.

6. Your stakeholders want you to create and print out three text reports: one that includes only milestones, one that contains top-level tasks, and one that contains only critical tasks. Where in Project can you do this?

    A. Tools/Customize/Forms

    B. File/Print Preview/Page Setup

    C. Report/Reports

    D. View/Report/Reports

Chapter Review

To further practice and reinforce the skills you learned in this chapter, you can perform the following tasks:

- Review the chapter summary.
- Review the list of key terms introduced in this chapter.
- Complete the case scenarios. These scenarios set up real-world situations involving the topics of this chapter and ask you to create a solution.
- Complete the suggested practices.
- Take a practice test.

Chapter Summary

- A project summary task contains an ID number of 0, is not shown by default, and offers general information about the project, including the duration of the project, among other things.
- A work breakdown structure (WBS) is a hierarchical list of summary tasks and subtasks that define the project. You can see the WBS in the Entry table.
- You can customize the WBS by indenting and outdenting tasks, applying WBS outline numbers, defining deliverables, and grouping tasks.
- When creating and modifying tasks, you can enter, delete, or modify, as well as schedule recurring tasks, create milestone tasks, and apply a calendar to a task.
- To estimate tasks you will need to estimate duration, work, cost, and units. You might also need to create cost budgets and use the PERT formula as estimation tools.
- Working with tasks involves setting lead and lag time, setting dependencies, and verifying network completeness.
- Identifying and working with the critical path and critical tasks and working with them to meet a project deadline is important to project management.
- Working with resources, including displaying a resource histogram, setting and budgeting resources, employing resource pools, applying a calendar to a resource, and configuring resource units and assignments is a big part of understanding Project.
- The Scheduling Formula Work = Duration*Units can help you control scheduling behavior when applied to the three task types (Fixed Units, Fixed Work, and Fixed Duration).
- Creating and modifying baselines can help you manage your project, reschedule incomplete work, and maintain control over your project.
- Creating reports and printing them helps keep stakeholders, employees, and managers on track and on task.

Key Terms

Do you know what these key terms mean? You can check your answers by looking up the terms in the glossary at the end of the book.

- baseline plan
- bottom-up planning
- budget resource
- combination view
- constraint
- cost budget
- cost resource
- critical path
- effort-driven scheduling
- Finish-to-Finish (FF) relationship
- Finish-to-Start (FS) relationship
- Fixed Duration
- Fixed Units
- Fixed Work
- free slack
- indent (demote)
- lag time
- lead time
- link
- material resource
- outdent (promote)
- predecessor
- project summary task
- resource
- resource histogram
- Start-to-Finish (SF) relationship
- Start-to-Start (SS) relationship
- successor
- summary task
- task deadline
- task dependency
- Task Form view

- task relationship
- top-down planning
- total slack
- units
- work
- work breakdown structure (WBS)
- work package
- work resource

Case Scenarios

In the following case scenarios, you will apply what you have learned about using Project during the initiation phase of project management including setting up a project and working with both tasks and calendars. You can find answers to these questions in the "Answers" section at the end of this book.

Case Scenario 1: Creating a WBS

You are the project manager for a new marketing campaign. After a long brainstorming session with your project team members, you have developed a list of your initial project tasks, used the top-down method, and defined both summary tasks and subtasks. In fact, these tasks have already been entered into your project file. Answer the following questions:

1. Even though all tasks have been entered and you know, based on your brainstorming session, which tasks are summary tasks and which tasks are subtasks, what can you do within Project to reflect your planned outline?

2. After you have created your project plan outline you can then apply detail level WBS codes. How can you display these WBS codes on your project plan file?

3. Upon further review of your project plan, you realize that you have neglected to add a crucial task. How can you resolve this?

Case Scenario 2: Defining a Project Schedule

You are managing a project that schedules all tasks and resources related to moving your current staff to a new office location within three months. The time frame is short, but you are an experienced project manager with access to your past project management experience and industry experts. Additionally, you have been given full permission to assign company resources as needed in order to bring the project in on time and within scope. Answer the following questions:

1. In consulting with project managers who have been through this type of project before, you learn that you will need to account for time needed for paint to dry, drywall to cure, and other construction elements you had not previously considered. How can you account for this time in your project schedule?

2. Upon further investigation, you realize your project schedule is currently running a couple of days past the move-in date. The project stakeholders have indicated that under no circumstances is the project to be completed late. However, there are two tasks currently scheduled using the default relationship that could run concurrently, as long as they are completed by the same date. What can you do to shorten the length of the project in this instance?

3. Your project plan is now complete and work is set to begin in three days. In keeping with your project management background, you would like to keep a snapshot of the project as it stands at the end of the Planning phase so that you can compare it with the project data as the project progresses and use it for informational purposes on future project. What Project feature can you use to create this snapshot?

Case Scenario 3: Working with Resources

You are planning a new project that oversees a new product your company is planning to develop. The project stakeholders have indicated that you have a strict budget to which the project must adhere and, even though it is anticipated that you will have access to all of the necessary resources, your experience with this company tells you that the available resources can change without warning as company priorities are changed. Answer the following questions:

1. Your resources work in a typical corporate environment. This means that it is highly likely that they will be spread across multiple projects throughout the duration of your project. Rather than create an unrealistic project schedule, how can you tell Project that select resources will be working only part-time?

2. Name views that you can display to better account for when resources have been assigned to work, such as a view that shows the resource histogram.

3. You would like to print a list of tasks for each of your resources to give them an idea not only of what they will be doing on this project, but also when they have been scheduled to work. What can you do to meet this requirement?

Case Scenario 4: Scheduling

You are the project manager for a new marketing campaign. Using Project, you have entered tasks and initial resource assignments into your project file. Answer the following questions:

1. The resource, Marketing Lead, has been assigned to a one-day task (Review Business Model). The assigned resource has asked for a second person to review the business

model simultaneously to be sure nothing is missed. What settings should you apply to the task to effectively apply this additional resource?

2. One of your tasks (Review Service Margins) is currently scheduled to be complete after three full days work by one resource. If a second resource is assigned to this task half-time in an effort to reduce the task's duration, how many hours would each resource be assigned to work?

3. You have just learned that the resource assigned to one of your two-day tasks (Review Marketing Plan For Campaign Budget) has been assigned to work on another project at the same time that your project is occurring. This means that your resource is available to devote only two hours each working day to your project. What value should you change to account for this and what will happen to the task when this value is changed?

Case Scenario 5: Bringing Tasks in On Time

You are managing a project to evaluate your company's current performance evaluation system. As you can imagine, employees depend on performance evaluations being completed promptly. Toward that end, completing several key tasks at specific times is crucial to this project's success. Answer the following questions:

1. A consultant has been hired to help on several aspects of this project related to reviewing the current performance evaluation model and related process. Unfortunately, the consultant is not available to work right away. In fact, he has given you a specific start date. How can you account for the consultant's date of availability at the task level while still allowing for some degree of flexibility in scheduling the project?

2. The company CEO has asked to review and approve the performance plan no later than a specific date. How can you flag that date within the project schedule while still allowing the software to schedule tasks based on calendars, resources, and tasks?

3. As you make changes to one task, you notice that other tasks are affected even though the tasks initially seemed unrelated. What Project feature can you use to see what other project plan elements might affect the scheduling of the selected task?

Suggested Practices

To help you successfully master the exam objectives presented in this chapter, complete the following tasks.

- **Practice 1: Working with a Project Summary Task**   In this practice you will review what a project summary task is and what it offers. You might recall that a project summary task contains an ID number of 0 and that it is not shown by default. If you cannot remember how to show the project summary task or why you would need or want to, open any project, choose Tools and then Options, and click the View tab. Select the Show Project Summary Task check box and then look at what is displayed in your project at Task ID 0.

- **Practice 2: Working with the WBS**   A work breakdown structure (WBS) is a hierarchical list of summary tasks and subtasks that define the project. You should be comfortable with adding tasks, indenting and outdenting tasks, applying WBS outline numbers, defining deliverables, and grouping tasks. To reinforce your knowledge of WBS codes, open the Home Move template, choose Project, choose WBS, and choose Define Code. Create a code for this template.

- **Practice 3: Creating Tasks**   You should be extremely comfortable working with tasks. You need to know how to enter, delete, or modify tasks, as well as how to schedule recurring tasks, create milestone tasks, and apply a calendar to a task.

  To practice adding tasks, open the Home Move template, scroll to Task 172, and click Insert Task. Create a summary task named Four Weeks After The Move. Create subtasks under that task and, using the Indent button on the toolbar, make those tasks subtasks. Create durations and apply resources to the tasks and experiment with Task Information dialog box.

- **Practice 4: Linking Tasks**   After entering tasks, you must be able to set lead and lag time and configure dependencies among tasks. To review this, work through the 45-minute training video "Linking Project Tasks" here: *http://office.microsoft.com/training/training.aspx?AssetID=RC102106881033&pid=CR102140061033.*

- **Practice 5: Estimating Tasks**   To estimate tasks, you will need to estimate duration, work, cost, and units. The Scheduling Formula says Work = Duration*Units. You will also need to create cost budgets and use the PERT formula as estimation tools. Work again through the samples in this chapter, but this time change the numbers given in the examples and recalculate the answers. Take special notice of what happens when a task has a Fixed Duration, Fixed Units, or Fixed Work.

- **Practice 6: Working with Baselines**   A baseline lets you compare the state of your project with the original plan. You can have multiple baselines. Open any project template and practice creating baselines. Change data to see how the baselines you create change.

- **Practice 7: Working with Resources**   Displaying a resource histogram, setting and budgeting resources, employing resource pools, applying a calendar to a resource, and configuring resource units and assignments is a big part of understanding Project. It is important for you to know all you can about resources.

  To reinforce what you've learned in this chapter, in any project choose View, and then choose Resource Sheet. Input various resources that relate to the project. For instance, in the Home Move template you might add resources like Landscaper (a work resource), Sod And Mulch (material resources), and Cookies For Neighbors Who Welcomed Us (a cost resource). With the resources created, add new tasks and assign the new resources to them. For instance, a new task might be Landscape Backyard or Thank the Neighbors.

■ **Practice 8: Creating and Printing Reports**   The best way to review how to create and print reports and become familiar with what reports are available, as well as how they print, is to open each report in Project, view what is there, and print it. Make sure you are aware of all of the available reports.

Take a Practice Test

The practice tests on this book's companion CD offer many options. For example, you can test yourself on just one exam objective, or you can test yourself on all the 70-632 certification exam content. You can set up the test so that it closely simulates the experience of taking a certification exam, or you can set it up in study mode so that you can look at the correct answers and explanations after you answer each question.

MORE INFO   **Practice tests**

For details about all the practice test options available, see the "How to Use the Practice Tests" section in this book's Introduction.

Chapter 3
Execute, Monitor, and Control the Project Plan

At this point in the project management process, the actual project work (completed by your assigned project resources) is underway. Some projects will certainly begin before the Planning phase is complete, but in a best case scenario, your project will follow the designated project management phases of the Project Management Body of Knowledge (PMBOK). During the Execute, Monitor, and Control project phases, you will focus on monitoring your project plan and making course corrections as needed to ensure that milestones are met and deliverables come in on time and within scope and budget.

Experienced project managers know that this phase rarely moves on a straight path. When executing the project plan, monitoring your project progress, and controlling your project plan, you will need to make corrections when things happen that bounce your project off track. Being able to track your project through these twists and turns effectively is the mark of an experienced project manager.

Microsoft Office Project 2007 can assist you (as often as necessary) as you work through change requests by producing status and progress reports and using earned value analysis techniques to track the schedule and cost performance of your project.

Exam objectives in this chapter:
- Enter project information.
- Enter task updates.
- Reschedule incomplete work.
- Track project progress.
- Analyze variance.
- Create, modify, and delete objects.

Lessons in this chapter:

Before You Begin

As you begin this chapter related to the Execution, Monitor, and Control phases of your projects, you will continue to see standard project management terms—many of which might already be familiar. Before you begin, you should:

- Be comfortable creating a work breakdown structure and entering those tasks with their associated relationships and resources into a Project project file
- Understand how Project can assist you during the project Initiation and Planning phases

Lesson 1: Monitoring Project Progress

The real fun in project management starts after you've entered your project tasks and the actual work begins. Unfortunately, some beginner project managers stop here, thinking that their work is complete. After all, the project plan is done—what else is there to do? In reality, there is quite a bit. Just because your project resources know what they are supposed to do and when they are supposed to do it does not mean the project work will be done. And, if it is done, you cannot guarantee it will be done to standards set forth by the project scope or, worse yet, within the project schedule and budget.

If you do not stay on top of your project's performance to ensure that it goes according to schedule or to make adjustments as changes occur, you will quickly lose control of the project and all of its elements. Using Project, you can continuously monitor and update your project plan to reflect the progress you have made. In doing so, you can often see problems as soon as they occur (sometimes ahead of time) and make appropriate adjustments so as not to allow a detrimental domino effect of problems to take hold of your project schedule.

This lesson focuses on techniques and views that you can use in Project to keep tabs on your project's progress.

After this lesson, you will be able to:
- Understand and work with task progress information.
- Work with techniques for tracking and viewing the project schedule, work, cost, units, and scope.
- Update the project.
- Use the Tracking Gantt view.
- Create, modify, and otherwise work with filters.
- Create, modify, and otherwise work with groups.

Estimated lesson time: 135 minutes

Working with Task Progress Information

Abraham Lincoln once asked, "How can you know where you are going if you don't know where you've been?" This is certainly appropriate in the context of tracking your project's progress. Because project plan tasks often depend on other tasks (typically linked by task relationships), a delay in one task can set off a domino effect of delays in your project plan unless you can catch the delay early enough to make an adjustment and brings things back in line.

When it comes to keeping tabs on the completion status of individual tasks in your project, Project offers a couple of options: the Tracking table and the Tracking toolbar. Using these options, you can mark the progress of individual tasks in your project schedule so that you will always know which tasks are complete, which are in progress, and which will start soon.

Exam Tip   Make sure you know what you can track using the Tracking table and Tracking toolbar. You might be asked about these tools on the exam—how to access them and when to use them.

Tracking Table

For complete control over the progress values you enter for your project tasks, you can use Project's Tracking table, shown in Figure 3-1.

	Task Name	Act. Start	Act. Finish	% Comp.	Phys. % Comp.	Act. Dur.
0	− Home Move	Mon 1/1/07	NA	60%	0%	5.7 days
1	+ Five to Eight Weeks Before Moving	Mon 1/1/07	Mon 1/22/07	100%	0%	16 days
41	+ Three to Five Weeks Before Moving	Thu 1/18/07	Tue 2/6/07	100%	0%	14 days
78	− One to Two Weeks Before Moving	Wed 2/7/07	NA	7%	0%	0.74 days
79	+ Household Administration	NA	NA	0%	0%	0 days
101	− Moving	Wed 2/14/07	NA	12%	0%	0.6 days
102	− Movers	Wed 2/14/07	NA	70%	0%	0.7 days
103	Check with mover about moving house plants	Wed 2/14/07	Wed 2/14/07	100%	0%	1 day
104	Obtain moving service contact numbers	Wed 2/14/07	Wed 2/14/07	100%	0%	1 day
105	Acquire labels for boxes	Wed 2/14/07	Wed 2/14/07	100%	0%	1 day
106	Verify that the moving service has your contact numbers	NA	NA	0%	0%	0 days
107	Give moving service written directions to the new location	Wed 2/14/07	NA	50%	0%	0.5 days
108	− Do-It-Yourself	Thu 2/15/07	NA	8%	0%	0.08 days
109	Move possessions to storage facility if necessary	Thu 2/15/07	NA	25%	0%	0.25 days
110	Confirm assistance for moving day	NA	NA	0%	0%	0 days
111	Verify dolly available with truck rental	NA	NA	0%	0%	0 days
112	+ Packing	NA	NA	0%	0%	0 days
122	+ Preparing for Move Day	NA	NA	0%	0%	0 days
130	+ Day of the Move	NA	NA	0%	0%	0 days

Figure 3-1   The Tracking table

As you can see, the Tracking table contains columns related to each task's actual start and finish dates, as well as percent completion figures and actual duration, cost, and work calculations. To view the Tracking table, follow these steps:

1. Choose View.
2. Choose Table.
3. Choose Tracking. See Figure 3-2.

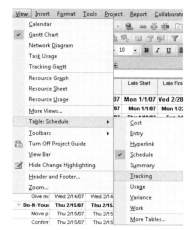

Figure 3-2   Displaying the Tracking table

With the Tracking table displayed, you can enter actual completion figures related to your project tasks. You will learn more about the columns in this table later in this lesson.

MORE INFO   **Updating tasks**

For more information on updating tasks using these and other methods, refer to the following articles located on the Microsoft Web site at: *http://office.microsoft.com/en-us/project/ HA101487641033.aspx?pid=CH100666601033* and *http://office.microsoft.com/en-us/project/ HA102341281033.aspx?pid=CH100666481033*.

Tracking Toolbar

Another option for updating the progress of selected tasks is to use the Tracking toolbar shown in Figure 3-3.

Figure 3-3   The Tracking toolbar

To display the Tracking toolbar, follow these steps:

1. Right-click any toolbar.
2. From the shortcut menu, select Tracking. See Figure 3-4.

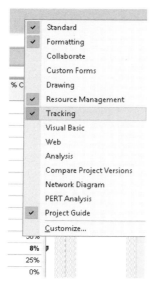

Figure 3-4   Displaying the Tracking toolbar

By default, there are 12 commands on the Tracking toolbar. Each command is described in Table 3-1. The commands listed in the table are in order from left to right on the Tracking toolbar. Rest the mouse on the toolbar buttons to see the command button names. Figure 3-5 shows the first button, Project Statistics, with the command button name displayed.

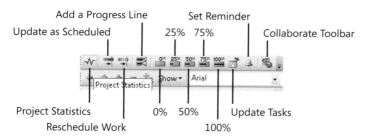

Figure 3-5   Rest the mouse on the buttons to see the button name

Table 3-1   Tracking Toolbar Commands

Command	Description
Project Statistics	Displays the Project Statistics dialog box. In this dialog box you can view a snapshot of your project's current costs and start and finish dates compared with any saved baseline data. Alternatively, you can access this information by viewing the Project Information dialog box (available on the Project menu) and then clicking the Statistics button.

Table 3-1   Tracking Toolbar Commands

Command	Description
Update As Scheduled	For tasks that are exactly on schedule, you can quickly bring them up to an accurate progress status as of the current date by clicking the Update As Scheduled command.
Reschedule Work	The Reschedule Work command automatically reschedules the selected task(s) to the next available date, often the current date.
Add Progress Line	Progress lines visually represent the progress of your project, displayed in the Gantt Chart view. When you click the Add Progress Line button, you will need to click a date in the Gantt Chart to draw a line connecting the progress points of every task in the project. This creates a jagged line on the Gantt Chart. This line points to the left to indicate work that is behind and points to the right to indicate work that is ahead. You can be certain that progress lines are displayed correctly by selecting the Edits To Total Task % Complete Will Be Spread To The Status Date check box located in the Calculation tab in the Options dialog box. This way, when progress lines are displayed, they will reflect the progress of project work on any given date. Additionally, you can customize the appearance of progress lines by right-clicking a displayed progress line and choosing Progress Lines from the shortcut menu to open the Progress Lines dialog box.
0%	Marks the selected task(s) as zero percent complete.
25%	Marks the selected task(s) as 25 percent complete.
50%	Marks the selected task(s) as 50 percent complete.
75%	Marks the selected task(s) as 75 percent complete.
100%	Marks the selected task(s) as 100 percent complete.
Update Tasks	When clicked, displays the Update Tasks dialog box, which allows you to update a wide variety of task progress information.
Set Reminder	When clicked, displays the Set Reminder dialog box, which allows you to create a pop-up reminder to notify you at a designated interval prior to the start or finish of the chosen task(s).
Collaborate Toolbar	Displays the Collaborate toolbar.

Of all of the commands located on the Tracking toolbar, the Update Tasks command offers the most flexibility because it allows you to update a wide variety of task progress information, including percent complete, actual and remaining duration, and actual and finish dates. Figure 3-6 shows this dialog box.

To show the Update Tasks dialog box, select a task and click the Update Tasks button on the Tracking toolbar.

Figure 3-6   The Update Tasks dialog box

NOTE   Use the Task Information dialog box to update task progress

To update the progress of an individual task, you can also double-click the task to open the Task Information dialog box with the information for that task. Then you can fill in the Percent Complete box located in the General tab.

Quick Check

1. Which command on the Tracking toolbar allows you to see the actual and current Start and Finish dates, remaining duration, actual duration, and percent complete for a single selected task?

2. Which command on the Tracking toolbar shows the current, baseline, actual, and variance values for the project?

3. Which command on the Tracking toolbar lets you update tasks that are on schedule?

Quick Check Answers

1. The Update Tasks command.

2. The Project Statistics command.

3. Update As Scheduled.

Tracking the Schedule

Typically, the first place project managers look to determine whether or not their project is progressing as expected is to the project schedule. Often, a delay in the schedule creates a whole host of other project management issues, including increased costs, unavailable resources, and so on.

Using the Project Statistics Dialog Box

The Statistics dialog box, shown in Figure 3-7, provides a snapshot of your entire project, including current, baseline, actual, and variance information.

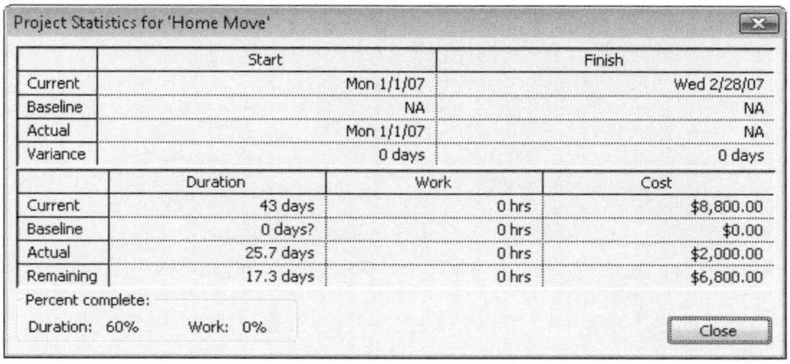

Project Statistics for 'Home Move'			
	Start		Finish
Current		Mon 1/1/07	Wed 2/28/07
Baseline		NA	NA
Actual		Mon 1/1/07	NA
Variance		0 days	0 days

	Duration	Work	Cost
Current	43 days	0 hrs	$8,800.00
Baseline	0 days?	0 hrs	$0.00
Actual	25.7 days	0 hrs	$2,000.00
Remaining	17.3 days	0 hrs	$6,800.00

Percent complete:
Duration: 60%   Work: 0%   [Close]

Figure 3-7 Project Statistics dialog box

To view the Project Statistics dialog box, follow these steps:

1. Choose Project.
2. Choose Project Information.
3. In the Project Information dialog box, click the Statistics button at the bottom.

This dialog box contains a couple of places you can look to quickly determine whether your project is on schedule (providing that you have already saved a baseline). In the upper portion (to the right of Variance and below Finish), make note of the number of days (if any) that your project is off. Additionally, look at the Duration and Work percentage complete numbers displayed in the lower-left corner. Here, if the work complete number is less than the duration of the project that has passed, your project is behind schedule.

MORE INFO **Project baselines**

For more information on setting and working with a project baseline, see Chapter 2, "Project Planning."

Using the Tracking Gantt Chart

The more you work with Project, the more you begin to realize that there are many ways to view your project data. The same is true for viewing your project's progress. However, one view that stands out from the others is the Tracking Gantt Chart, shown in Figure 3-8. Here, you can display a view that compares actual progress to a baseline schedule or cost figure. This way you can immediately identify whether or not your project plan is on schedule.

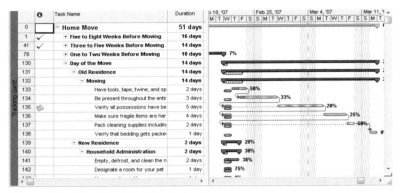

Figure 3-8   The Tracking Gantt chart

To view the Tracking Gantt chart, from the View Bar or the View menu, choose Tracking Gantt.

On the Tracking Gantt chart, you can see a couple of project schedule facts at a glance. First, the project baseline Gantt bars are placed below their corresponding scheduled Gantt bars, which show the current task progress and status. This way you can see exactly where your project is currently tracking in relation to your baseline information. Second, critical tasks are displayed in red, allowing you to see which tasks affect the project finish date and thus are the first tasks to look at if the project is behind schedule.

Other Valuable Tables

There are other tables with fields that display project schedule information. These tables include the Schedule, Summary, and Variance tables. As with other tables, you can choose these using the View menu by choosing Table and then the appropriate table. It's best to choose Task Sheet view first because it switches out of the combination Gantt Chart view into a single view that displays only a table. This allows for more screen real estate with which to display all the columns associated with any table you view.

NOTE   **Using the divider bar**

Some project managers prefer to see both the Gantt Chart and the table at the same time because looking at only table data can make it difficult to quickly spot schedule problems. You can apply any of the tables described here while still in Gantt Chart view. To see the different columns, you can drag the vertical divider to the right, effectively displaying more of the table columns and less of the Gantt timescale.

Schedule Table   The Schedule table, shown in Figure 3-9, includes two columns not seen in Gantt Chart view with the Entry table: Free Slack and Total Slack. These fields display time in your project schedule that you can use when reassigning resources in an effort to shorten the project duration.

Figure 3-9   Schedule table with Free Slack and Total Slack showing

Summary Table   In addition to seeing fields with which you are already familiar (as displayed on the Entry table), the Summary table, shown in Figure 3-10, also shows the percentage complete, cost, and work figures for each listed task.

	Task Name	Duration	Start	Finish	% Comp.	Cost	Work
111	Verify dolly :	1 day	Thu 2/15/07	Thu 2/15/07	0%	$0.00	0 hrs
112	+ Packing	3 days	Fri 2/16/07	Tue 2/20/07	0%	$0.00	0 hrs
122	+ Preparing for	2 days	Mon 2/19/07	Tue 2/20/07	0%	$0.00	0 hrs
130	+ Day of the Move	12.5 days	Wed 2/21/07	Fri 3/9/07	46%	$0.00	128 hrs
153	+ One to Two Weeks /	5 days	Thu 2/22/07	Wed 2/28/07	0%	$0.00	0 hrs
171	Enjoy your new home	0 days	Wed 2/28/07	Wed 2/28/07	0%	$0.00	0 hrs

Figure 3-10   Summary table with % Complete, Cost, and Work showing

Variance Table   In addition to start and finish fields, the Variance table also includes fields for baseline and variance information.

Quick Check

Which table should you use to view and edit the following information?

1. Free Slack and Total Slack
2. Baseline and variance information, as well as start and finish fields
3. Percentage complete, cost, and work figures for each listed task

Quick Check Answers

1. Schedule
2. Variance
3. Summary

MORE INFO   Filters

Filters provide another convenient way to track your project's schedule progress. For more information on filters, see the section later in this chapter entitled "Working with Filters."

Viewing Reports

Many reports also show schedule-related information. Although working with reports in Project is covered in more detail in Chapter 5, "Closing the Project Plan," the following is a list of reports you can view related to your project schedule.

- Unstarted Tasks
- Tasks Starting Soon
- Tasks In Progress
- Completed Tasks
- Should Have Started Tasks
- Slipping Tasks

You can view these reports from the Report menu. Choose Reports, and, in the Reports dialog box, select Current Activities.

Tracking Cost

The success or failure of a project is often determined by whether or not it was completed within budget. As you saw when working with baselines in Chapter 2, you can use your baseline information to compare where you thought your project costs would be with where they actually are. You can also use the budget options available in Project (as shown in Chapter 2) to compare your project costs to budgetary numbers set by your organization. However, if you don't have to compare project costs to specific accounting budget categories, comparing current with baseline is all you need.

The Cost Table

First and foremost, the best place to see your project cost information is in the Cost table, shown in Figure 3-11. In the Cost table you can see data related to fixed costs, total costs, and baseline and variance costs, as well as actual and remaining costs.

To view the Cost table, on the View menu, choose Table, and then choose Cost.

NOTE   **View costs by resource**

The Cost table is ordered by task name by default. You can see a similar Cost table sorted by resources by first displaying the Resource Sheet view (as opposed to the Task Sheet view) and then applying the Cost table.

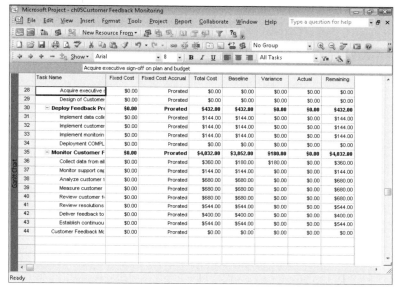

Figure 3-11   The Cost table

View Total Project Costs

In addition to viewing costs by tasks and resources, you can also see total project costs in several areas in Project. This includes summary and detail cost information. Use Table 3-2 as a guide to locating and displaying your costs related to a project.

NOTE   **Show the Project Summary Task**

You can show the project summary task by choosing Tools, choosing Options, and, in the View tab, selecting the Show Project Summary Task check box. While in the Cost table, you can see costs related to the entire project, as well as summary tasks and subtasks.

Table 3-2   Viewing Project Costs

Selected View	Display
Total Project Cost	Displays the Project Statistics dialog box. In this dialog box you can view a snapshot of your project's current costs and start and finish dates compared with any saved baseline data. You can access this information by viewing the Project Information dialog box (Project menu) and then clicking the Statistics button.

Table 3-2 Viewing Project Costs

Selected View	Display
Scheduled, Baseline, Actual, and Remaining Costs	Apply the Cost table.
Total Cost for a Task	View the Resources tab in the Task Information dialog box.
Project Cost Performance	Apply the Earned Value table.

NOTE   Viewing cost detail

You can see cost details in some views by choosing Details on the Format menu and then choosing Costs.

Customize Cost Views

A little used but extremely helpful feature in Project is the customization of the bars shown in Gantt Chart view. For instance, you can display cost information for a selected task next to the related Gantt bar. To do this, follow these steps:

1. Choose View, and then choose Gantt Chart.
2. Right-click a bar inside the Gantt Chart timescale and choose Format Bar.
3. Click the Bar Text tab, and then display the Inside drop-down list from the Inside row, as shown in Figure 3-12.
4. Select Cost from the drop-down list, and then click OK.

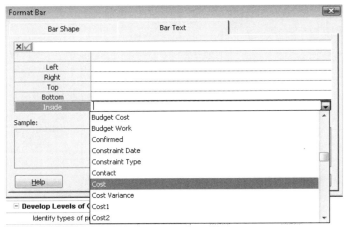

Figure 3-12   Adding Cost to the Gantt Bar

MORE INFO Tracking project costs

For more information on tracking cost in your project, refer to Part Three, "Carrying Out a Project," in the book *On Time! On Track! On Target! Managing Your Projects Successfully with Microsoft Project* by Bonnie Biafore (Microsoft Press, 2006).

Cost Reports

Many reports also show cost-related information. Working with reports in Project is covered in more detail in Chapter 5. The following is a list of reports you can view related to your project costs:

- Cash Flow
- Budget
- Overbudget Tasks
- Overbudget Resources
- Earned Value

To display these reports, follow these steps:

1. Choose Report, and then choose Reports.
2. In the Reports dialog box, select Costs and click Select.
3. Select the desired report from the Cost Reports dialog box and click Select. The available reports are shown in Figure 3-13.

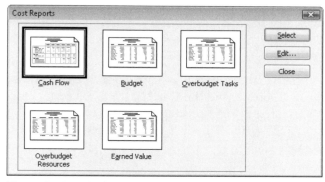

Figure 3-13 Displaying reports

Quick Check

■ Name four ways you can track costs and find out where you need to rein in costs using Project.

Quick Check Answer

1. The Cost and Earned Value tables
2. In various dialog boxes, including the Project Statistics dialog box, the Information dialog box, and the Task Information dialog box
3. By customizing the Cost view in the Gantt Chart
4. Using Cost reports

Tracking Work

In a project the term *work* defines units of time that are required to complete a task. Work can be measured in hours and days much like duration; however, work and duration are not the same. For example, if two resources are assigned to work on one task, the work might be equal to 16 hours while the duration of the task is equal to only 8 hours. Tracking work is helpful both in spotting resources who might need help and because overbudget work often leads to overbudget costs.

Task Usage View

You have already seen the combination view that Project displays when you choose Window and then Split while you are in the Gantt Chart view. This combination displays the Gantt Chart at the top of your screen and the Task Form at the bottom. The Task Form is a good way to see work information for individually selected tasks. Another helpful view when tracking work in a project is Task Usage view, shown in Figure 3-14.

In Task Usage view you can see the resources assigned to each task and the amount of work for each resource within a timescale. And the Task Usage view is customizable to show more than just work for each resource. By right-clicking inside the displayed work area (to the right of the Task Usage view), as shown in Figure 3-15, you can choose to display several additional related sets of information, such as:

■ Work
■ Actual Work
■ Cumulative Work
■ Baseline Work
■ Cost
■ Actual Cost

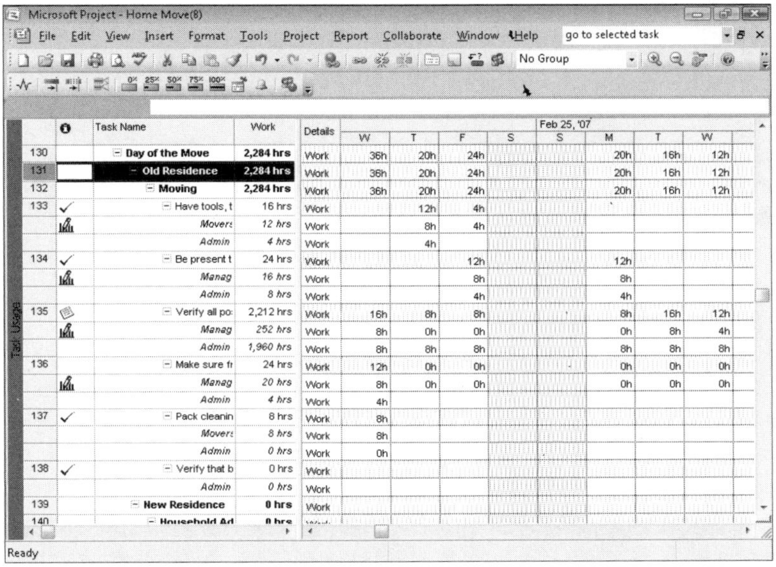

Figure 3-14 Task Usage view

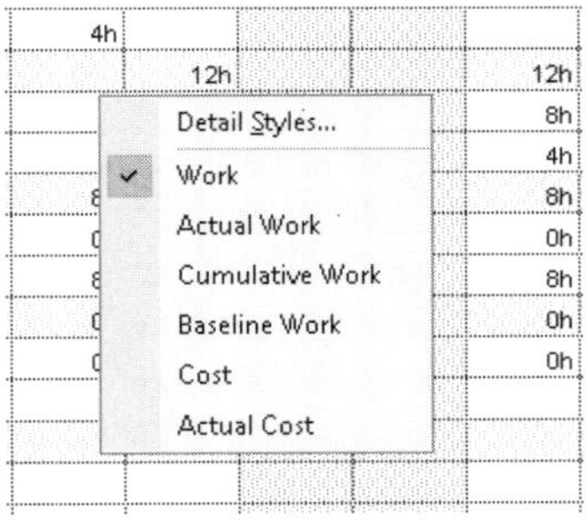

Figure 3-15 Customizing the display of work values in Task Usage view

In Figure 3-16 the Task Usage view has been customized to display both Work and Cost information for the displayed tasks.

To customize Task Usage view, follow these steps:

1. Choose View and choose Task Usage.
2. Right-click inside the work area and choose Work (if it is not already selected).
3. Right-click again inside the work area and choose Cost.
4. Repeat step 3 to select each of the six options. Note that each option adds a row for the corresponding field to the Task Usage timescale.

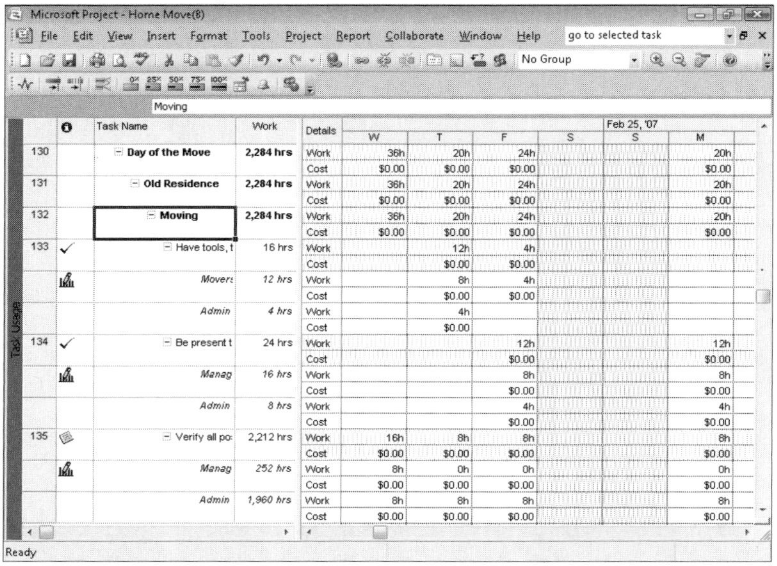

Figure 3-16 Displaying both Cost and Work data in Task Usage view

Resource Usage View

Another great view for tracking work in a project is Resource Usage view. In Resource Usage view you can see the tasks to which each resource is assigned and the amount of work for each assignment in a timescale. However, this view differs from Task Usage view in that the information is grouped by resource instead of by task. Resource Usage view is customizable to show more than just work for each resource. By right-clicking inside the displayed work area, you can choose to display several additional related sets of information, such as:

- Work
- Actual Work
- Cumulative Work
- Overallocation
- Cost
- Remaining Availability

Resource Usage view lists, for each resource, the assigned tasks and the total amount of work that the resource is scheduled to perform on each task, whether per day, week, month, or other time increment. If you are more interested in cost than work, you can use the Resource Usage view to display the cost of a resource's tasks over time, or you can display both cost and work at the same time.

In Figure 3-17, the Resource Usage view has been customized to display Work, Cumulative Work, and Cost information for the displayed resources.

❶	Resource Name	Work	Details	T	W
	Pack cleaning supplies .	0 hrs	Work		
			Cost		
			Cum. Work		
	Verify that bedding gets .	0 hrs	Work		
			Cost		
			Cum. Work		
2	− Manager	288 hrs	Work	0h	0h
			Cost		
			Cum. Work	284h	284h
	Be present throughout th	16 hrs	Work		
			Cost		
			Cum. Work	16h	16h
	Verify all possessions h.	252 hrs	Work		
			Cost		
			Cum. Work	252h	252h
	Make sure fragile items	20 hrs	Work	0h	0h
			Cost		
			Cum. Work	16h	16h

Figure 3-17   Resource Usage view

To customize Resource Usage view, follow these steps:

1. Choose View and choose Resource Usage.
2. Right-click inside the work area and choose Work (if it is not already selected).
3. Right-click again inside the work area and choose Cost. See Figure 3-18.

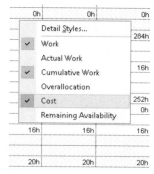

Figure 3-18   Customizing the Resource Usage view

4. Repeat step 3 to select each of the six options. Note what each option offers.

MORE INFO   **Further customizing Task usage view and Resource Usage view**

Task and Resource Usage views, like many views in Project, are customizable in many ways. For instance, when you right-click the work portion of the view, you can choose Detail Styles from the shortcut menu to open the Detail Styles dialog box. Here you can choose from multiple fields to display along with the task information. Additionally, you can format the timescale in much the same way you would format the timescale in another view (such as Gantt Chart view) by right-clicking the timescale and choosing Timescale from the shortcut menu.

Additional Views

In addition to Task Usage view and Resource Usage view, there is also a Work table with fields that display work information. The Work table, shown in Figure 3-19, includes several columns not displayed in Gantt Chart view with the Entry table, including Work, Baseline, Variance, Actual, Remaining, and Percentage of Work Complete for each task.

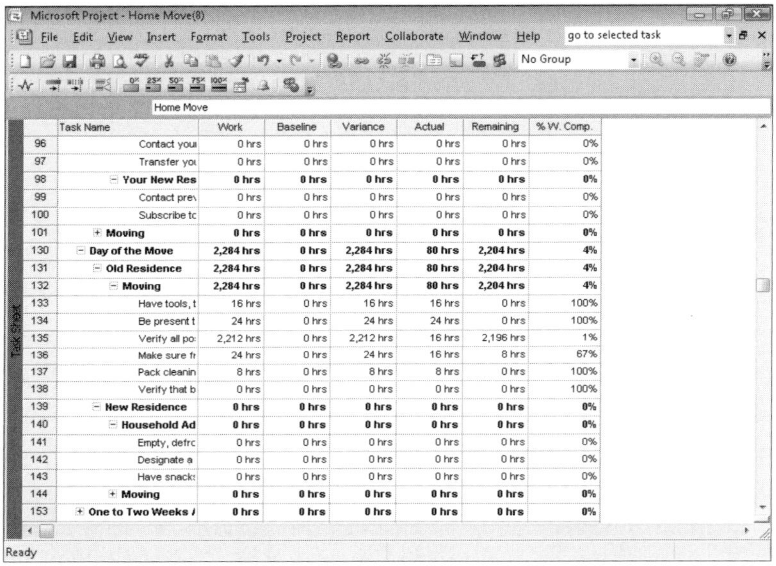

	Task Name	Work	Baseline	Variance	Actual	Remaining	% W. Comp.
96	Contact your	0 hrs	0 hrs	0 hrs	0 hrs	0 hrs	0%
97	Transfer you	0 hrs	0 hrs	0 hrs	0 hrs	0 hrs	0%
98	− Your New Res	0 hrs	0 hrs	0 hrs	0 hrs	0 hrs	0%
99	Contact prev	0 hrs	0 hrs	0 hrs	0 hrs	0 hrs	0%
100	Subscribe tc	0 hrs	0 hrs	0 hrs	0 hrs	0 hrs	0%
101	+ Moving	0 hrs	0 hrs	0 hrs	0 hrs	0 hrs	0%
130	− Day of the Move	2,284 hrs	0 hrs	2,284 hrs	80 hrs	2,204 hrs	4%
131	− Old Residence	2,284 hrs	0 hrs	2,284 hrs	80 hrs	2,204 hrs	4%
132	− Moving	2,284 hrs	0 hrs	2,284 hrs	80 hrs	2,204 hrs	4%
133	Have tools, t	16 hrs	0 hrs	16 hrs	16 hrs	0 hrs	100%
134	Be present t	24 hrs	0 hrs	24 hrs	24 hrs	0 hrs	100%
135	Verify all po:	2,212 hrs	0 hrs	2,212 hrs	16 hrs	2,196 hrs	1%
136	Make sure fr	24 hrs	0 hrs	24 hrs	16 hrs	8 hrs	67%
137	Pack cleanin	8 hrs	0 hrs	8 hrs	8 hrs	0 hrs	100%
138	Verify that b	0 hrs	0 hrs	0 hrs	0 hrs	0 hrs	100%
139	− New Residence	0 hrs	0 hrs	0 hrs	0 hrs	0 hrs	0%
140	− Household Ad	0 hrs	0 hrs	0 hrs	0 hrs	0 hrs	0%
141	Empty, defrc	0 hrs	0 hrs	0 hrs	0 hrs	0 hrs	0%
142	Designate a	0 hrs	0 hrs	0 hrs	0 hrs	0 hrs	0%
143	Have snack:	0 hrs	0 hrs	0 hrs	0 hrs	0 hrs	0%
144	+ Moving	0 hrs	0 hrs	0 hrs	0 hrs	0 hrs	0%
153	+ One to Two Weeks /	0 hrs	0 hrs	0 hrs	0 hrs	0 hrs	0%

Figure 3-19 Task Sheet view, with the Work table applied

To create the view shown in Figure 3-19, from the View menu, choose Move Views, and in the More Views dialog box, select Task Sheet. Then, click Apply.

To view work information by resource, you can apply the same Work table in Resource Sheet view by applying the same steps introduced earlier.

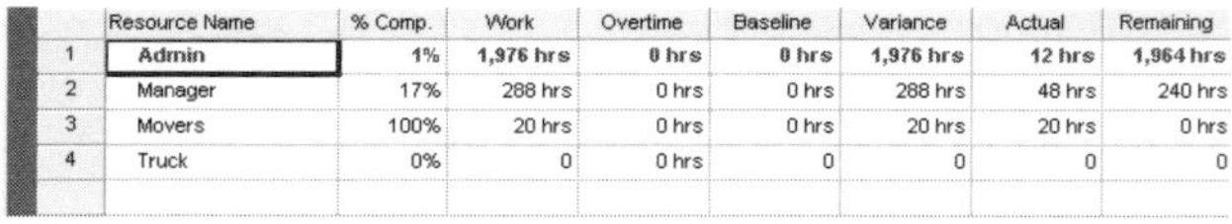

	Resource Name	% Comp.	Work	Overtime	Baseline	Variance	Actual	Remaining
1	Admin	1%	1,976 hrs	0 hrs	0 hrs	1,976 hrs	12 hrs	1,964 hrs
2	Manager	17%	288 hrs	0 hrs	0 hrs	288 hrs	48 hrs	240 hrs
3	Movers	100%	20 hrs	0 hrs	0 hrs	20 hrs	20 hrs	0 hrs
4	Truck	0%	0	0 hrs	0	0	0	0

Figure 3-20 Resource Sheet view, with the Work table applied

A couple of reports also show work-related information. Although working with reports in Project is covered in more detail in Chapter 5, the following is a list of reports related to your project workload that you can view:

- Task Usage
- Resource Usage
- Who Does What When

To create a report, choose Report, choose Reports, and select either Assignments or Workload, shown in Figure 3-21.

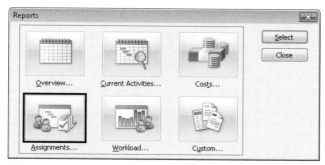

Figure 3-21   Viewing reports for Assignments or Workload

Viewing Units

Units are a little trickier than other data to display in Project but only because there is no Units field that you can add to the tables. You can, of course, view and modify units associated with resources in Resource Sheet view. That is the most common place. However, when you need to work with units specific to an individual task, you can do so in various ways.

Task Information Dialog Box

One way to view units is in the individual task's Task Information dialog box in the Resources tab, shown in Figure 3-22.

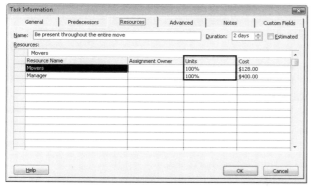

Figure 3-22   Working with units using the Task Information dialog box

Here you can view resource names, assignment owners, units, and costs. Of course, the Task Information dialog box also offers other tabs, where you can obtain additional information.

Task Form View

Another ideal location to view and modify units associated with individual tasks is in Task Form view, shown in Figure 3-23.

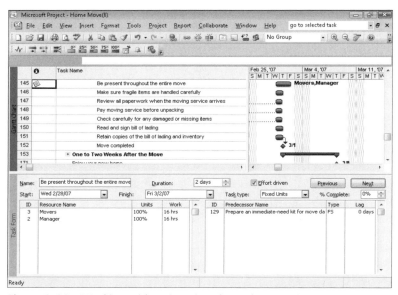

Figure 3-23   Working with units using the Task Form view

To display Task Form view, follow these steps:

- If the View Bar is displayed, turn it off from the View menu to see the blue sidebar and its options. Note that you can also right-click the View bar and choose More Views to perform the same steps.
- Choose View and choose Gantt Chart.
- Choose Window and then Split.
- If Task Form is not showing in the bottom pane, right-click the blue sidebar on the left side of the interface that shows the name of the opened window, choose More Views, and then select the Task Form and click Apply.

Reports

There is also one report that shows unit-related information—the Who Does What report. To show the Who Does What report, follow these steps:

1. In Gantt Chart view, choose Report.
2. Choose Reports, and in the Reports dialog box, select Assignments and click Select.

3. In the Assignment Reports dialog box, select Who Does What.
4. Click Select.

Quick Check

■   What table would you select to see Work, Baseline, Variance, Actual, Remaining, and Percentage of Work Complete for a specific task in a project?

Quick Check Answer

■   The Work table

Tracking Scope

Determining whether or not your project was a success in the end often depends on whether you and your team were able to deliver the project scope. For every project, the project scope can mean something entirely different. And, because the project scope can often expand or shrink throughout the lifetime of the project (typically because of unforeseen circumstances), you will more than likely track your project scope outside of Project in a manner that allows you to document your deliverables. You will often need to include text-based documentation that explains why certain deliverables were not met or justification when a delivered scope does not match the original project scope.

Because scope describes the deliverables and work that comprise a project, it is difficult to pinpoint one report, view, or table in Project that shows the project scope. Instead, in order to analyze scope, you will need to look at several reports, views, and tables.

For example, scope creep is what all project managers work to avoid. In this instance, by diligently watching tasks, deadlines, and start and finish dates, you can see quickly when tasks are beginning or finishing late and get in touch with team members to see if they are doing more work than the scope requires.

Another option for tracking scope is using the Notes available for every task and resource. In this way you can keep reminders handy to document scope changes so you can explain them to anyone who asks or to discuss changes with the assigned resources.

Updating the Project

This lesson has examined many ways to track your project variables. After you understand where to find your project information (such as work and units), you can work through the steps in updating the project.

For example, to indicate progress (or the completion status) on a task, you can use the Tracking toolbar or the Tracking table, or both. The following sections will help you learn how to use the Tracking toolbar, the Tracking table, the Task Information dialog box, and Project Guide's Track task pane to help you monitor and track the progress of your project.

Using the Tracking Toolbar

To use the Tracking toolbar, you must first enable it by choosing View, Toolbars, and Tracking. As noted earlier in Table 3-1, there are 12 buttons on the toolbar: Project Statistics; Update as Scheduled; Reschedule Work; Add Progress Line; 0%, 25%, 50%, 75%, and 100% Complete; Update Tasks; Set Reminder; and Collaborate Toolbar.

Two of the buttons, Update As Scheduled and Reschedule Work, let you bring tasks up to date with a click of a button. Five buttons—0%, 25%, 50%, 75%, and 100% Complete—require you to select a task first and then set its progress by clicking the appropriate button. Other tasks require your input. When you use these commands, Project changes the % Complete to the percentage you choose and updates the work complete to match the duration complete. If the work complete does not match the duration complete, you have to edit the work for the task.

To use the Tracking toolbar to update a task's progress using your own input, complete the following steps:

1. Choose View, Gantt Chart.
2. Verify that the Summary Task is showing on Task 0. If it is not, add it from Tools, Options, and the View tab.
3. Select the Summary Task on ID 0, and, from the Tracking toolbar, click Project Statistics. Note the information available, including start and finish dates, baselines, actual and variance statistics, and data for duration, work, and cost. Click Close.
4. Before adding progress lines, choose Tools and choose Options. In the Options dialog box, click the Calculation tab. Select the Edits To Total Task % Complete Will Be Spread To The Status Date check box.
5. To add a progress line, click the Add Progress Line button on the Tracking toolbar and click inside the Gantt chart to add it.
6. Select a task to modify and click Update Tasks. In the Update Tasks dialog box, shown in Figure 3-24, modify the data required. You can:
   a. Set the percentage of completion
   b. Enter actual and remaining durations
   c. Enter actual start and finish dates
   d. Update information for one task or multiple selected tasks
7. Click Set Reminder to add a reminder for a task.

Figure 3-24   Modify task information in the Update Tasks dialog box

Using the Tracking Table

To use the Tracking table you must first enable it. Choose View, Table and choose Tracking. You will see several columns, including the following:

- **Actual Start**   When you enter start information, Project automatically adjusts the actual start date based on the current date or the scheduled start date. Use the Actual Start field to display, filter, or edit actual start dates for tasks.

- **Actual Finish**   When you enter task information, Project automatically adjusts the actual finish date based on the current date or the scheduled finish date. Use the Actual Finish field to display, filter, or edit actual start dates for tasks. When you specify that a task is 100 percent complete, Project automatically adjusts the actual finish date based on the current status date or the scheduled finish date.

- **% Complete**   When a task is first entered, the percent complete field is 0%. As you enter durations and work, Project calculates the % complete using this formula: Percent Complete = (Actual Duration/Duration)*100. When updating project tasks, you will usually type the value for % Complete, which then calculates Actual Duration. If you enter work, Project calculates the % Work Complete and sets the % Complete to the same value. Use the % Complete field when you want to display, filter, or edit the % Complete data set for a task.

NOTE   % Complete vs. % Work Complete

% Complete specifies the percentage of duration that is complete. % Work Complete specifies the amount of work that's complete, which is actually a better indicator of task progress.

- **Physical % Complete**   Also referred to as Earned Value % Complete, this field is best used when you want to specify the percentage that a task is complete in order to calculate your project's earned value. Unlike the % Complete field, the Physical % Complete field is independent of the total duration or actual duration values used by the % Complete field. Calculated percent complete is never an accurate measure of real work because it represents duration. But Physical % Complete is a field of interest only if you are using Project to look at earned value because you type the % in.

- **Actual Duration** Actual Duration is calculated by multiplying Duration and Percent Complete. If you type a value in the Actual Duration field, Project calculates the following: Remaining Duration = Duration – Actual Duration. Use this field when you want to view, filter, or edit actual durations for tasks.

- **Remaining Duration** This field shows the amount of time required to complete a task that's already been started. Remaining Duration = Duration – Actual Duration.

- **Actual Cost** Actual Cost = (Actual Work*Standard Rate) + (Actual Overtime Work*Overtime Rate) + Resources Per Use Costs + Task Fixed Cost. Use this field to view expenses for a task.

- **Actual Work** When a task is created, actual work hours are 0. As you add percent complete, percent work complete, or actual work information, Project updates the actual work for you. Use the Actual Work field to review, filter, or edit actual work information for a task.

To make changes to any of the data in the Tracking table, input the required information manually. See Figure 3-25.

	Act. Start	Act. Finish	% Comp.	Phys. % Comp.	Act. Dur.	Rem. Dur.	Act. Cost	Act. Work
0	Mon 1/1/07	NA	28%	0%	.46 days	0.04 days	$0.00	80 hrs
1	Mon 1/1/07	Mon 1/22/07	100%	0%	16 days	0 days	$0.00	0 hrs
41	Thu 1/18/07	Tue 2/6/07	100%	0%	14 days	0 days	$0.00	0 hrs
78	Wed 2/7/07	NA	25%	0%	4.8 days	14.7 days	$0.00	0 hrs
79	Wed 2/7/07	NA	69%	0%	4.85 days	2.15 days	$0.00	0 hrs
80	Wed 2/7/07	Thu 2/8/07	85%	0%	2 days	0 days	$0.00	0 hrs
87	Fri 2/9/07	NA	89%	0%	2.67 days	0.33 days	$0.00	0 hrs

Figure 3-25 Using the Tracking table to manually edit task information

Using the Task Information Dialog Box

The Task Information dialog box, available by right-clicking any task and choosing Task Information, also allows you to update task information. In the Resources tab, you can view resource names, assignment owners, units, and costs. Of course, the Task Information dialog box also offers other tabs, where you can obtain additional information. As with other tools, you can input data manually, as desired.

Using the Project Guide's Track Pane

After you have begun to track your task progress, in addition to the views we have already discussed in this lesson, you can use the Project Guide's Track task pane. When you click Track in the Project Guide, you see the Check Progress information shown in Figure 3-26.

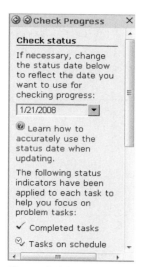

Figure 3-26 Using the Project Guide's Track task pane to edit task information

To access this pane:

1. Choose View and choose Turn On Project Guide. (If Turn On Project Guide is already selected but the Project Guide isn't showing, a quick way to show it again is to choose Turn Off Project Guide and then choose Turn On Project Guide.)

2. Click Track on the Project Guide Toolbar and click Check The Progress Of The Project.

   Choosing Check The Progress Of The Project from the Track drop-down list on the Project Guide toolbar switches your project view to the Tracking Gantt and applies a custom Project Guide table. This view is shown in Figure 3-27. As you can see, the selected task is behind schedule.

	Task Name	Status Indicator	Work	Duration	Start	Finish	2007 8 | 11 | 14 | 17 | 20 | 23 | 2
0	− Home Move	⚲	136 hrs	51 days	Mon 1/1/07	Mon 3/1:	
1	+ Five to Eight Weeks Before Moving	✓	0 hrs	16 days	Mon 1/1/07	Mon 1/2	
41	+ Three to Five Weeks Before Moving	✓	0 hrs	14 days	Thu 1/18/07	Tue 2.	
78	+ One to Two Weeks Before Moving	⚲	0 hrs	10 days	Wed 2/7/07	Tue 2/2	
130	− Day of the Move					Mon 3/1	This task is behind schedule.
131	− Old Residence		136 hrs	14 days	Wed 2/21/07	Mon 3/1	
132	− Moving		136 hrs	14 days	Wed 2/21/07	Mon 3/1	
133	Have tools, tape, twine, and spare b		16 hrs	2 days	Thu 2/22/07	Fri 2/2	50%
134	Be present throughout the entire mo		24 hrs	3 days	Fri 2/23/07	Tue 2/2	33%
135	Verify all possessions have been pa		40 hrs	5 days	Wed 2/21/07	Mon 3	20%

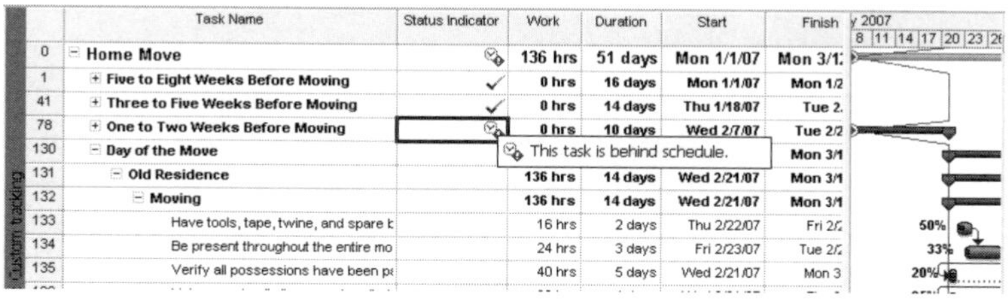

Figure 3-27 By checking the progress of a task you can see when a task is behind schedule

A Status Indicator column has been added with checkmarks to denote completed tasks and other indicators to let you know when specific tasks are behind schedule. From this table you can also see work hours listed for each task. Additional columns available from this custom table are Duration, Start, and Finish. On the right you can see the Tracking Gantt Chart view, complete with progress lines.

Using the Project Guide task pane, you can enter a custom status date to see how your project is faring as of a specific date. In Figure 3-27 the project status date has been set to February 20. However, in Figure 3-28 the status date has been modified to show project status as of February 28. At a glance, you can see the difference in progress lines and status warnings.

Real World

Bonnie Biafore

The way you track project progress typically depends on the information that project customers and stakeholders want to see. Project can handle any level of progress tracking whether you can get by with fast and easy updates or need detailed status. In fact, the information you gather is limited primarily by how much time you have to gather data and enter it into your project plan.

For example, keeping track of the percentage that tasks are complete might be sufficient for a small in-house project. In Project you can use the Tracking toolbar and the Tracking table to update the % Complete field. On the other hand, a large project might have contract terms that require not only percentage complete but also hours worked and hours remaining. The Tracking table includes all the fields you need to provide this level of detail, and the Task Usage or Resource Usage view enables you to enter progress for each resource's assignments.

When you ask for progress from resources, you usually request updates through a specific date, similar to the end date for your organization's timesheets. When you enter progress information through a specific date in Project, it's important to set the status date in Project to that date. That way, Project knows to record actual work before the status date and to schedule remaining work after the status date. In addition, Project uses the status date to calculate earned value fields, such as budgeted cost of work performed (BCWP, also called earned value because it represents the amount of project cost that you've earned by completing work). Finally, Project draws progress lines through the status date to demonstrate visually which tasks are ahead of or behind schedule.

MORE INFO   Applying filters

From the Project Guide task pane you can also modify the view to focus on different information by applying a filter or a group. Applying filters and groups to your project views are covered next.

To check the status of a project, follow these steps:

1. Choose View, and if an option exists for Turn On Project Guide, choose it.

2. On the Project Guide toolbar, in the Track drop-down list, select Check The Progress Of The Project.

3. Type a new status date.

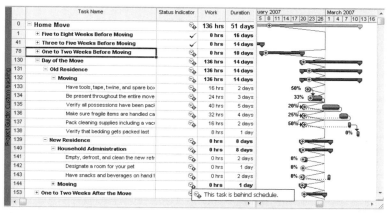

Figure 3-28 Changing the status date often affects multiple tasks

---

MORE INFO **Quickly switch between tables**

Instead of using the View menu to switch between tables, you can use a shortcut menu by right-clicking the empty box to the left of the first column in any displayed table and above the first task ID ("0" if the project summary task is displayed, "1" if it isn't). In the shortcut menu, choose the table you want to display.

Quick Check

- Name four ways to update a project task.

Quick Check Answer

1. Use the Tracking toolbar to
    a. Set the percentage of completion.
    b. Enter actual and remaining durations.
    c. Enter actual start and finish dates.
    d. Update information for one task or multiple selected tasks.
2. Change values in the Tracking table, such as Actual Work and Actual Duration.
3. Use the Task Information dialog box to make changes.
4. Use the Project Guide's Track pane.

Working with Filters

Typically, when you look at a project view, you see all tasks (or resources) associated with the project. You can collapse or expand this view by using the outline that is created when you create your WBS in Project. Applying filters to your view allows you to further refine your project display by hiding tasks (or resources) that do not match your set criteria. This allows you to focus on just the information you need at the moment.

When you apply a filter, you temporarily change the display of project information without making permanent changes to your project information. Project provides several predefined filters from which you can choose, as well as AutoFilters and custom filters.

Predefined Filters

Project offers a couple of ways to access the predefined filters, which include (among several others):

- Completed Tasks
- Critical
- Incomplete Tasks
- Milestones

The first and probably most accessible filter option is located on the Formatting toolbar. Just open the drop-down menu (where All Tasks displays by default, or whatever filter is listed and showing), to view the filtering options. See Figure 3-29 and complete the following steps:

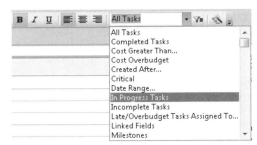

Figure 3-29   Filtering tasks to define a view using the Formatting toolbar

1. Verify that the Formatting toolbar is selected from the View, Toolbars menu.
2. In the drop-down list by All Tasks, (or whatever filter is selected), select the desired filter from the list.

After a filter has been applied, you can display all of your project information by repeating the steps above and choosing All Tasks.

Exam Tip   Selecting a filter does not delete information from your project; it only hides it from your view. Also, when you apply a filter, your data isn't recalculated based on what is filtered out. For example, if you have assigned a one-day task to two resources (each working 8 hours) and then filter for tasks assigned to just one of the resources, the task will be displayed but the work value on the task will show 16 hours, not just the 8 hours assigned to your filtered resource.

You can also access available Project predefined filters by displaying the More Filters dialog box, shown in Figure 3-30.

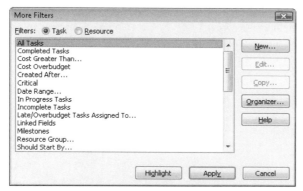

Figure 3-30   Filtering tasks to define a view using the More Filters dialog box

To apply a filter using the More Filters dialog box, follow these steps:

1. Choose Project, choose Filtered For: All Tasks. (All Tasks will be selected if no current filters are already applied.)
2. Choose More Filters.
3. In the More Filters dialog box, select Task or Resource.
4. Select the filter and click Apply.
5. To remove the filter, choose Project, choose Filtered For: <filter> and select All Tasks.

AutoFilters

Project's AutoFilter feature allows you to set criteria based on field (or, column) data. The AutoFilter icon is shown in Figure 3-31.

AutoFilter

Figure 3-31   The AutoFilter icon on the Formatting toolbar

When AutoFilter is enabled, small arrows appear in the column headers for the displayed table, as shown in Figure 3-32.

	🛈	Task Name		Duration		Start		Finish		Predecess		Resource Name	
0		− Home Move		51 days		Mon 1/1/07		Mon 3/12/07					
1	✓	+ Five to Eight Weeks Before M		16 days		Mon 1/1/07		Mon 1/22/07					
41	✓	+ Three to Five Weeks Before I		14 days		Thu 1/18/07		Tue 2/6/07					
78		+ One to Two Weeks Before M		10 days		Wed 2/7/07		Tue 2/20/07					
130		− Day of the Move		14 days		Wed 2/21/07		Mon 3/12/07					

Figure 3-32   AutoFilter offers drop-down lists to allow you to choose your own filters

The Start Header Filter   With AutoFilter, you can quickly filter your project information. For example, using the AutoFilter drop-down list for the Start header, shown in Figure 3-33, you can display tasks starting today, tomorrow, this week, next week, and so on.

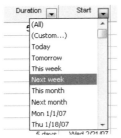

Figure 3-33   Using AutoFilter's Start options

Enable AutoFilter   You can also define filter criteria using multiple fields by setting criteria for each field using the individual AutoFilter arrows.

AutoFilter   You can enable AutoFilter on most tables for tasks or resources, and you can apply an AutoFilter to fields in any sheet view as well.

To enable AutoFilters in your project, follow these steps:

1. Click the AutoFilter button on the Formatting toolbar.
2. Use the AutoFilter arrow drop-down list next to the column heading in the field that contains the information you want to display and then select a value to filter the table. Values will differ based on the filter selected. You might choose days, weeks, today, tomorrow, and so on. The AutoFilter column heading will turn blue.
3. To apply an additional condition based on a value in another field, repeat step 2 in the other field.
4. After an AutoFilter has been applied, you can remove the filter and return all of your project information by choosing Project, Filtered For, and then AutoFilter.

Create a Custom AutoFilter   When the AutoFilter drop-down list is displayed by the various headers, the filter choices will differ greatly based on the field type and the information stored in that field. However, two options are common to every AutoFilter drop-down list: All and Custom. Choosing All removes the filter criteria specific to that field, and choosing Custom allows you to create a custom filter for that field.

With AutoFilter, you can create custom filter criteria with up to two conditions. To create a custom AutoFilter, follow these steps:

1. Click AutoFilter on the Formatting toolbar.
2. Open any AutoFilter drop-down list, and then select Custom.
3. Select the operator you want to use in the first drop-down list. You have several choices available depending on the type of field you've selected:
   a. equals
   b. does not equal
   c. is greater than
   d. is greater than or equal to
   e. is less than
   f. is less than or equal to
   g. is within
   h. is not within
   i. contains
   j. does not contain
   k. contains exactly
4. Select the value by which you want to filter in the second box. Entries will vary depending on the field selected. See Figure 3-34.

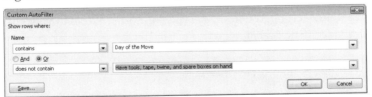

Figure 3-34   Creating a custom AutoFilter

5. Select And or Or and repeat steps 3 and 4 for the second set of boxes.
6. Click Save if you want to save the filter to reuse it later.
7. Name the filter and click OK.
8. Click OK again.

Additional Custom AutoFilter Options   In the previous section you saw what filter options were available for the Task Name field. There are, however, five others. Figure 3-35 shows the options for a custom filter for the Duration field. Note that these all differ a little. For practice, you should enable AutoFilter and go through the options available for each heading in Gantt Chart view.

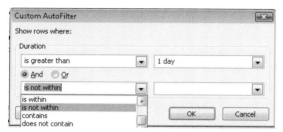

Figure 3-35   Creating a custom AutoFilter for Duration

Figure 3-36 shows the custom AutoFilter options for the Finish field.

Figure 3-36   Creating a custom AutoFilter for Finish

When Other Filters Are Applied   If your view already has a predefined filter applied, the conditions you set for the AutoFilter are applied in addition to those in the current filter. When you save an AutoFilter setting, the filter is saved with other filters in your file and is available only through the More Filters dialog box.

NOTE   **Filters with more than three criteria**

If you need to apply three or more conditions to a field, create a custom task or resource filter.

Using AutoFilter Regularly   If AutoFilter becomes a feature that you use on a regular basis, you can set your Project options to automatically enable AutoFilters for new projects by following these steps:

1.   On the Tools menu, choose Options.

2.   In the General tab, under General options for Office Project, select the Set AutoFilter On For New Projects check box. See Figure 3-37.

Figure 3-37   Making AutoFilter a part of every project

3.   Click OK.

NOTE   AutoFilter—Project vs. Excel

AutoFilter in Project is similar to the AutoFilter feature in Office Excel 2007.

More Custom Filters

In addition to the predefined filters available in Project, you can create your own custom filters. You can do this by creating a new filter from scratch or by simply modifying one of Project's many predefined filters.

Create a Custom Filter Based on a Predefined Filter   To create a custom filter based on a predefined filter, follow these steps:

1.   Choose Project, choose Filtered For, and choose More Filters.
2.   In the More Filters dialog box, select a filter close to the one you want to create.
3.   Click Copy.
4.   Type a descriptive name for the filter.
5.   Click Cut Row to remove a row, click Copy Row to copy a row, click Paste Row to paste a copied row, click Insert Row to insert a row you can define, and click Delete Row to remove a row. Note that you will add and edit criteria here the same way that you earlier

defined criteria using AutoFilter settings. If you aren't sure how to do this, read through the previous section, "Create a Custom AutoFilter."

6. Click OK.

Create a Custom Filter from Scratch   Sometimes you will need to create your own filter with specific criteria. If there is no predefined filter to modify or edit, you have to start from scratch. After you know how to create a filter from scratch, it is easy to copy and modify an existing filter.

To create a custom filter from scratch, follow these steps:

1. Choose Project, choose Filtered For, and choose More Filters.

2. By default, Task is selected as the filter type, so click New because you will be creating a task filter here. (Note that you can also create a resource filter; just click Resource, and then click New.)

3. Type the name of the new filter in the Name box.

4. If you want the filter to appear under Filtered For on the Project menu, select the Show In Menu check box. See Figure 3-38.

Figure 3-38   Creating a custom filter and adding it to the More Filters menu

5. In the And/Or column, do one of the following:
    a. Select And if you want to display rows in your view that meet both conditions.
    b. Select Or if you want to display rows in your view that meet one or both conditions.

6. Click inside the Field Name column and select the field you want to filter.

7. Click inside the Test column and select the operator you want to use to match the value with the selected field.

8. Click inside the Value(s) column and select the values you want to match (or type the value in the box above the table of filter criteria).

9. To add multiple criteria, repeat rows 5–8.

10. If you want the filter to display the summary rows for the filter results, select the Show Related Summary Rows check box. See Figure 3-39.

11. Note that you can also use the Cut Row, Copy Row, Paste Row, Insert Row, and Delete Row buttons as desired.

12. Click OK.

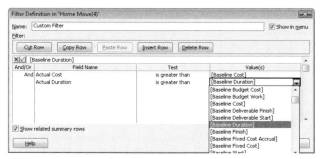

Figure 3-39 Creating a custom filter from scratch

When creating your own custom filter from scratch, note the following limitations:

Filter Rules to Remember   When creating filters, there are a few things to make note of, specifically:

- You cannot apply task filters to resource views.
- You cannot apply resource filters to task views.
- You will not see resource filters in the filter drop-down list when a task view is applied. Additionally, you will not see task filters in the drop-down list when a resource view is applied.
- If three or more criteria are in one group, AND statements are evaluated before OR statements. If multiple groups of expressions exist, the conditions are evaluated in the order in which they are listed.
- Leave a blank line between sets of criteria so these sets are evaluated together and not with other criteria.
- When entering data for the Equals or Does Not Equal criteria, you can use a wildcard character, such as a question mark (?) to find any single character or an asterisk (*) to find any number of characters.
- When you create a filter that uses multiple conditions, each filter condition is evaluated in the order in which they appear in the filter definition. In this way the filter results must pass the first test (or first filter condition) in order to be passed on to the second test, and so on.

Modify an Existing Filter   To modify an existing filter (or a custom filter), follow these steps:

1. On the Project menu, choose Filtered for, and choose More Filters.
2. To define the filter type, select Task or Resource.
3. Select the filter you want to modify and click Edit.

4. Modify the settings for the filter using the controls in the Filter Definition dialog box, as explained in the previous section, "Creating a Custom Filter from Scratch."

5. Click OK.

MORE INFO **Creating filters with multiple conditions**

For more information on creating filters (particularly those using multiple conditions), refer to *Microsoft Office Project 2007 Inside Out* by Teresa S. Stover (Microsoft Press, 2007).

Real World

Deanna Reynolds

As users become more adept at customizing their Project environments, the customized features they develop become more and more difficult to find. The custom filters you create are saved in the predefined filter list (which you can see by opening the More Filters dialog box). An easy way to make your custom filters stand out is to name them using all capital letters. As you can see in the figure below, using all caps helps your custom filters stand out in this long filter list. Another easy method for making your custom filters stand out is to name them with a prefix, such as "A-". This way, custom filters (and other custom elements) are grouped together in a list.

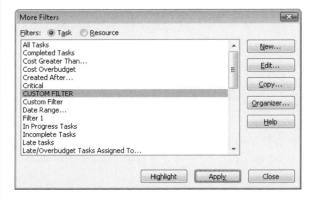

Delete and Copy Filters using Organizer   Sometimes you will need to delete your custom filters (or even copy them to the Global.mpt template so they are available in new projects).

To delete a custom filter, follow these steps:

1. Choose Tools and choose Organizer.

2. Click the Filters tab.

3. Note the filters in the right pane. These are the filters you've created.
4. Select the filter and click Delete to delete it.

In the same Organizer dialog box, you can choose to copy your custom filters to the Global.mpt file. The Global.mpt file contains the basic building blocks available in new blank project files. Therefore, to ensure that your custom filters are available in future projects, you can copy a custom filter to the Global.mpt file by following these steps:

1. Choose Tools and choose Organizer.
2. Click the Filters tab.
3. Note the filters in the right pane. These are the filters you've created.
4. Select the filter and click Copy to copy it to the Global template.

You can also copy your custom filters between two open Project files, effectively allowing you to share your custom filters with other project managers and other project files.

To copy filters between two open projects, follow these steps:

1. Choose Tools and choose Organizer.
2. Click the Filters tab.
3. Note the filters in the right pane. These are the filters you've created.
4. Open a second project to which you want to copy a custom filter.
5. In the Filters Available In drop-down list, on the left side of the dialog box, select the name of the second project.
6. In the filter list on the right side of the dialog box, select the filter you want to copy to the second file.
7. Click Copy.

Quick Check

■ Name as many ways as you can think of to apply a filter to data in Project.

Quick Check Answer

1. Using the filter options on the Standard toolbar
2. Using filters in the More Filters dialog box
3. Selecting a filter from Project/Filtered For menu option
4. Using AutoFilter
5. Creating custom filters from scratch
6. Modifying existing filters
7. Using a filter created in another project

Working with Groups

Like filters, the Grouping feature offers other ways to view your project data. However, although filters hide some data in favor of displaying others, grouping displays all of your project data clustered by chosen group characteristics (such as arranged by duration or start date). Also, much like an organized WBS offers a collapsible and expandable outline format, grouping lets you view collapsed summary information based on groups of tasks, resources, and assignments in your Project tables.

Predefined Groups

The groups you see when you display the Group drop-down list on the Standard toolbar will vary based on whether you are currently viewing your project information by task or resource. Figure 3-40 shows an example of available groups from within a task-based table (such as the Entry table).

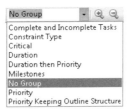

Figure 3-40   Groups available from the Standard toolbar when using a task-based table

When displaying the Group drop-down list from a resource-based table (such as Work), you see a list similar to that shown in Figure 3-41.

Figure 3-41   Groups available from the Standard toolbar when using a resource-based table

Project offers several groups, which include (among several others):

- Complete And Incomplete Tasks
- Critical
- Milestones
- Resource Group
- Work vs. Material Resources

Access Groups Project offers a couple of ways to access predefined groups. The first and probably most accessible group option is located on the Standard toolbar. As shown in Figures 3-40 and 3-41, to select a group, display the Group drop-down list on the Standard toolbar and select a group from the list. You can also access groups from the Project menu by choosing Group By and selecting the desired group.

Sort Data After a group has been applied, your project information is sorted and categorized according to your chosen criteria. In Figure 3-42 you can see a sample project file grouped by duration. You can sort the group values in ascending or descending order. For example, you can sort the group to see 0% complete tasks first or 100% complete tasks first.

	❶	Task Name	Duration	Start	Finish	Predecessors	Resource Names
		⊟ **Duration: 0 days**	**5 days**	**Wed 2/21/07**	**Wed 2/28/07**		
152		Move completed	0 days	Wed 2/21/07	Wed 2/21/07	151	
171		Enjoy your new home	0 days	Wed 2/28/07	Wed 2/28/07	170	
		⊞ **Duration: 1 day**	**50.5 days**	**Mon 1/1/07**	**Mon 3/12/07**		
		⊞ **Duration: 1.5 days**	**1.5 days**	**Thu 2/22/07**	**Fri 2/23/07**		
		⊞ **Duration: 2 days**	**48.5 days**	**Tue 1/2/07**	**Fri 3/9/07**		
		⊟ **Duration: 3 days**	**34 days**	**Fri 1/12/07**	**Wed 2/28/07**		
36	✓	Conduct a sale or donate to charit	3 days	Fri 1/12/07	Tue 1/16/07	31	
40	✓ 📎	Make any long distance travel arra	3 days	Mon 1/15/07	Wed 1/17/07	38	
49	✓ 📎	Schedule disconnection of utilities	3 days	Fri 1/19/07	Tue 1/23/07	47	
51	✓ 📎	Clear up any unpaid taxes or parki	3 days	Fri 1/19/07	Tue 1/23/07	47	
54	✓	Register your children in their new	3 days	Mon 1/22/07	Wed 1/24/07	52	
68	✓	Begin enlisting assistance for mov	3 days	Thu 1/25/07	Mon 1/29/07	65	
88		Fill out mail change of address car	3 days	Fri 2/9/07	Tue 2/13/07	86	
115	📎	Pack items that you do not use reg	3 days	Fri 2/16/07	Tue 2/20/07	111	
135	📎	Verify all possessions have been	3 days	Wed 2/21/07	Wed 2/28/07	129,134	Manager,Admin
		⊟ **Duration: 4 days**	**39.5 days**	**Thu 1/11/07**	**Wed 3/7/07**		

Figure 3-42 The Entry table grouped by duration

Reset a Project View After you have finished viewing your project information in a grouped format, you can reset your project view by displaying the Group drop-down list on the Standard toolbar and choosing No Group.

Use the More Groups Dialog Box You can also access available Project predefined groups by displaying the More Groups dialog box, shown in Figure 3-43.

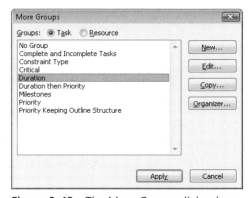

Figure 3-43 The More Groups dialog box

To apply a group using the More Groups dialog box, follow these steps:

1. Choose Project, choose Group By, and choose More Groups.
2. In the More Groups dialog box, select Task or Resource.
3. Select the desired group.
4. Click Apply.

MORE INFO   Available groups

For more information on all of the available groups, type **Available Groups** in the Ask A Question For Help box located in the upper-right corner of the Project window.

Custom Groups

In addition to the predefined groups available in Project, you can create your own custom groups. You do this by creating a new group from scratch or by simply modifying one of Project's many predefined groups (these steps are very similar to those that were described when working with custom filters was discussed).

MORE INFO   Saving custom groups

The custom groups you create are saved in the predefined group list (which you can see by opening the More Groups dialog box). To make custom groups stand out, a good rule to follow is to name them using all capital letters or to use a prefix. Using all caps helps your custom groups stand out.

Create a Custom Group Based on a Predefined Group   To create a custom group based on a predefined group, follow these steps:

1. Choose Project, choose Group By, and choose More Groups.
2. In the More Groups dialog box, select a group close to the one you want to create.
3. Click Copy.
4. Type a descriptive name for the group.
5. Modify the settings for the group using the controls in the Group Definition dialog box, as explained in the next section, "Create a Custom Group from Scratch."
6. Click OK.

Create a Custom Group from Scratch   Sometimes you will need to create your own group with specific criteria. If there is not a predefined group to modify or edit, you have to start from scratch. When you know how to create a group from scratch, it's easy to copy and modify an existing group.

To create a custom task group from scratch, follow these steps:

1. Choose Project, choose Group By, and choose More Groups.

2. By default, Task is selected as the group type, so click New because you will be creating a task group here. (Note that you can also create a resource group; just select the Resource option, and then click New.)

3. Type the name of the new group in the Name box. As you've seen with filters, it's best to name the group with all capital letters or a prefix.

4. If you want the group to appear under Group By on the Project menu, select the Show In Menu check box. See Figure 3-44.

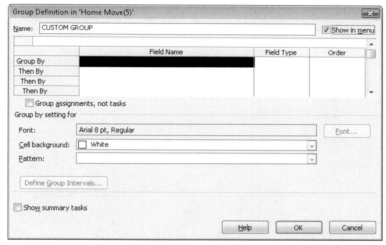

Figure 3-44 Create a custom group and add it to the Group By menu

5. In the Group By row, configure the following three items:
   a. Select a Field Name
   b. Select a Field Type
   c. Select an Order (Ascending or Descending)

6. To add criteria, repeat Step 5.

7. If you want group assignments instead of tasks, select the Group Assignments, Not Tasks check box.

8. Select a font, if desired. This is the font for the summary row. To do this, click Font, make the appropriate choices, and click OK.

9. Select a cell background, if desired. This is the background for the summary row. To do this, in the Cell Background drop-down list, select a color from the list.

10. Select a cell pattern, if desired. To do this, in the Pattern drop-down list, select a pattern from the list.

11. Define group intervals, if desired. To do this, click Define Group Intervals and make the appropriate choices. Click OK. Group interval settings let you further customize the group by letting you define intervals specific to the group. For instance, if you group work performed in hours, you can set the interval for hours to something other than one, like, say, four.

12. Select the Show Summary Tasks check box, if desired.

13. Click OK. Figure 3-45 shows an example of a custom group.

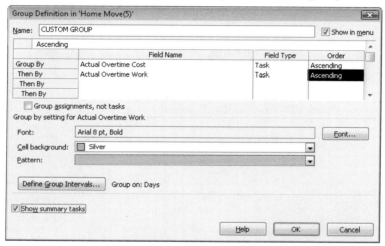

Figure 3-45   Creating a custom group from scratch

Modify an Existing Group   To modify an existing group (or a custom group), follow these steps:

1. Choose the Project menu, choose Group By, and choose More Groups.

2. To define the group type, select Task or Resource.

3. Select the group you want to modify, and click Edit.

4. Modify the settings for the group using the controls in the Group Definition dialog box, as explained in the previous section, "Create a Custom Group from Scratch."

5. Click OK.

Delete and Copy Groups using Organizer   Sometimes you will need to delete your custom groups (or even copy them to the Global.mpt template so they are available in new projects).

To delete a custom group, follow these steps:

1. Choose Tools and choose Organizer.

2. Click the Groups tab.

3. Note the groups in the right pane that are the groups in your file.

4. Select the group to delete and click Delete.

In the same Organizer dialog box, you can choose to copy your custom groups to the Global.mpt file. The Global.mpt contains the basic building blocks available in new blank project files. Therefore, to ensure that your custom groups are available in future projects, you can copy a custom group to the Global.mpt file by following these steps:

1. Choose Tools and choose Organizer.
2. Click the Groups tab.
3. Select the group in the list on the right side of the dialog box and click Copy to copy it to the Global template.

You can also copy your custom groups between two open Project files, effectively allowing you to share your custom groups with other project management and other project files.

To copy groups between two open projects, follow these steps:

1. Choose Tools and choose Organizer.
2. Click the Groups tab.
3. Open a second project to which you want to copy the group.
4. In the Groups Available In drop-down list, select the name of the second project.
5. Select the group in the list on the right side and click Copy. See Figure 3-46.

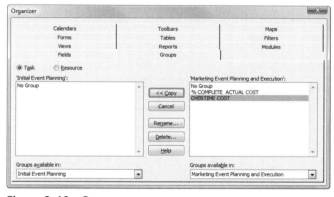

Figure 3-46   Copy a group

Quick Check

■ Name as many ways as you can think of to apply groups to data in Project.

Quick Check Answer

1. Using the Group drop-down list on the Standard toolbar
2. Selecting a group by choosing the Project menu and then Group By

> 3. Using the More Groups dialog box
> 4. Creating custom groups from scratch
> 5. Modifying group filters
> 6. Using a group created in another project

PRACTICE Getting Started with Project

In this practice you will review the main objectives in this lesson. In Exercise 1 you will view and change task progress information, in Exercise 2 you will update a project by rescheduling tasks, in Exercise 3 you will apply and use the Tracking Gantt, and in Exercises 4 and 5 you will work with filters and groups to view data based on criteria.

▶ **Exercise 1   View and Change Task Progress Information**

You can view and change task project information in many ways. There are views, tables, and charts, to name a few. In order to be successful with Project, you need to be aware of what exists and what each view offers. One of the objectives on exam 70-632 is to understand and work with task information, so in this exercise you will review these views, make changes, and make mental notes about (so that you understand) what each view is used for and how it can be used to work with tasks.

To complete this exercise, perform the following steps:

1. Choose File, and then choose Open.
2. Browse to the After The Move project file on the accompanying CD and open it.
3. Choose View, choose Table, and choose Schedule. Note the Free Slack and Total Slack fields for Task 7: Have Pets Licensed. Select the task.
4. Choose View, choose Toolbars, and choose Tracking.
5. On the Tracking toolbar, click 100%. Note the change to Task 7.
6. Choose View, and then choose Task Usage.
7. Right-click in the work area and select Cumulative Work. Repeat to select Cost. Here you can see that Task 7 has a check mark by it, denoting that it is complete.
8. Choose View and choose Tracking Gantt. Note that Task 7 has a check mark by it because it has been completed. Select Task 18: Install Carpet and from the Tracking toolbar click 50%.
9. Choose View, and then choose Gantt Chart.
10. Choose View, Table, and then Entry to display the Entry table.

▶ **Exercise 2   Update a Project**

Some tasks in the After the Move project have gotten off schedule, and work, cost, and units need to be updated. To complete this exercise, perform the following steps:

1. Choose File, and then choose Open. Open the After The Move file on the accompanying CD.
2. If the Tracking toolbar is not currently displayed, choose View, Toolbar, and then Tracking.
3. Select Task 18: Install Carpet and click Update Tasks. In the Update Tasks dialog box, modify the data required. Change the following data to modify the start date and the percentage complete:
    a. Enter an Actual Start date of **Tuesday 1/23/07**.
    b. Set the percentage of completion to 25%.
4. Click OK.
5. Double-click Task 12: Verify That New Schools Have Received Records.
6. In the Task Information dialog box, in the Start drop-down list, change the Start date to January 16, 2007. Click OK. (Here you are rescheduling work.)
7. When prompted, select Move The Task To Start On Tuesday January 16, And Keep The Link.
8. Click OK.

▶ **Exercise 3   Customizing Views**

You need to customize the Resource Usage view so you can see the following information regarding the resources for your project:

- Actual Work
- Cumulative Work
- Overallocation
- Cost

To complete this exercise, perform the following steps:

1. Choose File, choose New, and click On Computer.
2. In the Project Templates tab, select Annual Report Preparation and click OK.
3. Choose View and then Resource Usage.
4. Right-click the work area and select Actual Work.
5. Repeat step 4 to select Cumulative Work, then Overallocation, and then Cost.

▶ **Exercise 4   Work with Filters**

You want to temporarily change the display of project information without making permanent changes to your project information. You do this by applying a filter. However, none of the pre-defined filters offer what you need so you will need to create a custom filter.

To create a custom AutoFilter, follow these steps:

1. Open the After The Move file on the accompanying CD.
2. Click AutoFilter on the Formatting toolbar.
3. Open the AutoFilter drop-down list for the Total Cost column, and then choose Custom.
4. In the first drop-down list, select the Is Less Than operator.
5. In the field to the right, enter **$300**.
6. Select Or and repeat steps 3 and 4 for the second set of boxes. Select the Is Greater Than operator and Baseline Cost.
7. Click OK.

▶ **Exercise 5   Work with Groups**

You want to create a custom group based on a predefined group for a project you are working on.

To create a custom group based on a predefined group, follow these steps:

1. Choose File, choose New, and click On Computer.
2. In the Project Templates tab, select Annual Report Preparation and click OK.
3. Choose Project, choose Group By, and choose More Groups.
4. In the More Groups dialog box, select the Critical group.
5. Click Copy.
6. Name the group Modified Critical.
7. Click the first Then By row and click in the Field Name column. From the drop-down list, choose Deadline.
8. Click OK to group the critical tasks by their deadline date.

Lesson Summary

- The Tracking toolbar offers a summary of tracking tasks you can perform, including viewing project statistics, updating and rescheduling work, adding progress lines, updating tasks, and setting reminders.
- Tables, including Schedule, Summary, Cost, Tracking, Usage, Variance, and Work, offer data in many forms to allow you to see the data you need quickly.
- You can customize many views by right-clicking the work area, filtering data, or creating groups.
- You can track data using the Tracking toolbar, Tracking Gantt, the Task Information dialog box, and the Project Guide's Track task pane.
- Create your own filters and groups to customize your work area and the data shown. Filtering and grouping data changes only the data you see and does not change any project data.

Lesson Review

You can use the following questions to test your knowledge of the information in Lesson 1, "Monitoring Project Progress." The questions are also available on the companion CD if you prefer to review them in electronic form.

NOTE Answers

Answers to these questions and explanations of why each answer choice is correct or incorrect are located in the "Answers" section at the end of the book.

---

1. The time allowed for a task and the time remaining for the task has changed. You need to input that change into your project. Which of the following tables should you use to input this data?

    A. Tracking

    B. Entry

    C. Usage

    D. Variance

2. You need to view the overall progress statistics for a project. Specifically, you want to view a snapshot of your project's current costs and start and finish dates compared with your saved baseline data. Where can you find this data?

    A. Schedule table

    B. Project Information dialog box

    C. Project Statistics dialog box

    D. Task Information dialog box

3. You want to find where the slack is in your project's schedule so that you can reassign tasks and resources that are slipping. What table do you use to locate free and total slack in a project?

    A. Variance table

    B. Project Information dialog box

    C. Schedule table

    D. Resource Sheet

4. You need to quickly see tasks that might be off course and need to be pulled back within the required date range of the project. Which of the following views compares actual progress to a baseline schedule or cost figures, as well as project baseline indicators, and displays critical tasks are displayed in red?

    A. Task Usage

    B. Task Form

    C. Project Information

    D. Tracking Gantt

5. You need to edit the following fields for a task: Work, Actual, Remaining, % Work Complete, and Variance. Which of the following tables offers all of these?

    A. Tracking table

    B. Schedule table

    C. Entry table

    D. Work table

6. You need to view project cost performance, including planned and earned values for tasks. What do you need to do?

    A. Apply the Cost table to Task Sheet view.

    B. Apply the Earned Value table.

    C. View the Task Information dialog box.

    D. Display the Project Statistics dialog box.

7. You want to be able to filter data quickly when using the Entry, Cost, Schedule, Tracking, and Usage tables. How can you achieve this?

    A. Turn on AutoFilter in the Project menu.

    B. Turn on AutoFilter in the View menu.

    C. Create a custom filter for each of these table views.

    D. Open each view, choose Project, choose Filtered By, and choose AutoFilter.

8. You've created your own custom task filter. You want this filter to be available in all other future projects. What tool or set of steps do you perform to achieve this?

    A. When creating the filter, select the Make This A Global Filter check box.

    B. Choose Tools and Options, and, in the Save tab, save the filter to the Global.mpt file.

    C. Choose Tools and Organizer, click the Filters tab and copy the filter to the Global.mpt file.

    D. Each time you open a project, select the custom filter from the Project and Filtered By menus.

9. You need to group data so that you see the duration of each task in a project view. You also need to further define the group by including early finish information. How can you do this?

    A. Copy the predefined Duration filter and add Early Finish to it.

    B. Under Project, choose Group By and select Duration. Click Edit, Copy Group, and add Early Finish.

    C. Copy the predefined Duration group and add Early Finish to it.

    D. Under Project, choose Filter By, and select Duration. Click Edit, Copy Filter, and add Early Finish.

Lesson 2: Implementing Changes

A large part of project management is the project manager's ability to manage change. In the best cases a defined change management process is in place, and more important, followed. In fact, much of the change management process is completed outside of Project. However, when you are ready to implement changes that will affect your project schedule, you can use Project to track your project plan changes.

This lesson looks at the new Change Highlighting feature, as well as techniques for rescheduling incomplete work and splitting a task to account for time when resources are not actively working on their assigned tasks. Then, to see how changes affect your project plan, this lesson discusses setting a project plan status date and setting an interim plan.

After this lesson, you will be able to:
- Using change highlighting for task and schedule analysis.
- Split a task.
- Set a project status date.
- Reschedule tasks and incomplete work.
- Save a project interim plan.

Estimated lesson time: 60 minutes

Using Change Highlighting for Task and Schedule Analysis

As you work with Project, you might wonder why you occasionally see the background color behind your table cells change color (typically, to a light blue). This is a brand-new feature called Change Highlighting.

When this new feature is enabled, you can visually see how any change you make in the project plan affects other project tasks. For example, in the project plan shown in Figure 3-47, you can see that the project currently has a duration of 200 days. Also, Tasks 95, 96, and 97 are all linked in a Finish-to-Start relationship. Next, we will change this data so you can compare the results.

When the task duration for Task 95 is modified, dates related to Tasks 96 and 97 could be affected. When changes to a project plan are highlighted, there is no guessing on your part. Project will tell you through highlighted cells exactly which tasks are affected by any changes you implement. In Figure 3-48 the task duration for Task 95 was modified from one day to three days. Notice the domino effect of changes that occurs in the project plan from this one seemingly insignificant modification.

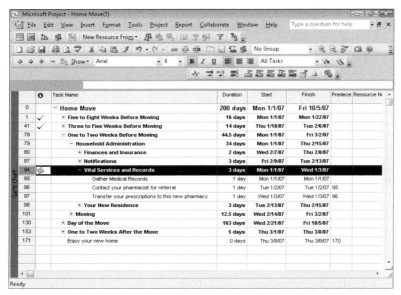

Figure 3-47   Changing duration for a task from one to three days

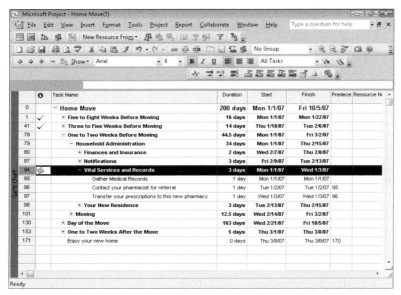

Figure 3-48   With Change Highlighting enabled, you can see how a simple change affects the entire project

Being able to see your changes as they occur without having to continuously scan the project file can be a real time-saver as you analyze your project plan and implement changes.

Even though the Change Highlighting feature presents a nice reminder of the interrelatedness of many tasks in your project, it is only a temporary visual clue. As soon as you save the project file or make another change, the original change highlighting is removed and often replaced with a new set of change data.

If you don't want to see changes appear in blue, you can turn off Change Highlighting altogether. To do that, follow these steps:

1. Choose View.
2. Choose Hide Change Highlighting, as shown in Figure 3-49.

Figure 3-49   Disabling Change Highlighting

And, just as easy as it is to disable, you can bring Change Highlighting back by simply choosing View: Show Change Highlighting from the Menu bar.

NOTE   Interim plans

A second option is to use Project's interim plans feature to save your project file information at a particular point in time. Interim plans store only dates and are discussed in more detail later in this chapter.

Split Tasks

Occasionally, work on a task is interrupted. For instance, what if the assigned resource calls in sick? If another resource is not available to take over during the first person's absence, you might need to interrupt the work on that task until your resource is able to return to work. In cases such as these, you will need to split your task to account for the time between the start and finish of a task in which no work (related to this task) was performed. You do not want to change the finish date, or Project will think the task is taking more time and resources than planned when, in reality, no work is being done on the missed days.

Split a Task

To split a task, follow these steps:

1. From the View menu, choose Gantt Chart.
2. Click Split Task on the Standard toolbar, shown in Figure 3-50, or choose Edit, and then choose Split Task.

Split Task

Figure 3-50   The Split Task icon on the Standard toolbar

3. On the task's Gantt bar, click the area of the bar on the date where you want the split to occur and drag the second part of the bar to the date on which you want work to begin again. When you rest the pointer on the bar, it shows you the date where this split will go. See Figure 3-51.

Figure 3-51   Drag and drop to split a task

4. After dragging and dropping, the task will appear split in the Gantt Chart. See Figure 3-52. This lapse in time is not accounted for in the total task duration. Instead, when a task is split to account for interrupted work, the task's duration remains the same but the task's finish date is modified.

Figure 3-52   A split task has dots to signify that it has been split

Move or Modify a Split Task

After a task is split, you can modify the time between the start and finish dates of the task by moving just a portion of the split task directly on the Gantt Chart. Alternatively, you can move the entire split task (complete with the gaps in the working schedule).

NOTE Dragging to move a split task

If you drag the first portion of a split task, the entire task moves. Alternately, if you drag a portion of a split task and drop it directly next to another portion, it will be incorporated into the other split task portion.

To move (and thus modify) a portion of a split task, follow these steps:

1. Position the mouse pointer over any portion of the split task other than the first portion. The cursor must change to a four-way arrow.

2. Drag the taskbar left to start the selected portion of the split task earlier or drag it right to start it later. Figure 3-53 shows an example of dragging an entire split task.

Figure 3-53   Moving or modifying a split task

NOTE Splitting tasks more than once

You can split a task multiple times. This can be particularly helpful for longer tasks and for those times when you are working in an environment where priorities change daily.

Reunite a Split Task

Split tasks can be reunited as well. To remove a split on a task, drag a portion of the split task on the Gantt bar so that it touches another portion of the split task.

NOTE Quickly reunite portions of a split task

You can quickly remove the split of any task by dragging one portion of a split Gantt bar toward another portion of the same split Gantt bar until both sides are touching. At this point the two portions will reunite.

Quick Check

- Why would you want to split a task? In which view is splitting a task best achieved?

Quick Check Answer

- Splitting a task is best when a task is interrupted or must be completed on non-consecutive days—for instance, if a worker calls in sick and another resource is not available to take over during the first person's absence.

As you make updates to your project tasks, such as tracking task progress and leveling your resources to ensure that no resource is overscheduled, you might see tasks that appear to have been split by someone other than you. That "someone" is usually the Project program.

The software will sometimes split tasks automatically. Although you cannot always predict when a task will split, you can check some of your software defaults to prevent it from happening if this automatic feature interferes with your project management work.

Change Leveling Defaults First, during the leveling process, if splitting tasks is enabled, you might notice that some tasks are split to allow for the even scheduling of your resources. You can check and modify your resource leveling options by opening the Level Resources dialog box. However, disabling this feature can result in very long delays for some tasks when task durations are long.

To enable or disable splits during the leveling process, follow these steps:

1. Choose Tool, and then choose Level Resources.

2. In the Resource Leveling dialog box, shown in Figure 3-54, select or clear the Leveling Can Create Splits In Remaining Work check box. Selecting this option allows splits as a result of leveling; clearing this option prevents splits during resource leveling.

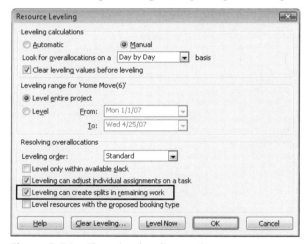

Figure 3-54 Changing leveling options

MORE INFO Resource Leveling

Resource Leveling is covered in greater detail in Chapter 4, "Team Collaboration and Multiple Projects."

Splitting Tasks in Progress   Another time when you might see tasks split are when tasks are in progress. In the Project options, there is an option (enabled by default) that allows the software to reschedule a task's remaining duration when that task slips or is ahead of schedule. Essentially, when this option is enabled, if you mark the progress of a successor task before the predecessor task is completed, the remaining work on a successor task can be shown as a split. However, if this check box is disabled, Project will not split the remaining work of the successor task.

You can disable (or enable) the Split In-Progress Tasks feature by following these steps:

1. Choose Tool, and choose Options.
2. In the Options dialog box, click the Schedule tab.
3. Select or clear the Split In-Progress Tasks check box. See Figure 3-55.

Figure 3-55   Change in-progress split task options

4. Click OK.

Adjust Split Task Features   After a task has been split, you can adjust a couple of the task's features, including the following:

- Task Duration
- Task Gantt Bar Style

To change the total duration of any split task, you simply modify the number located in the Duration column (as you would a task that was not split). Additionally, you do have the option of modifying the duration of just a portion of a split task. To modify the duration of a portion of a split task, complete the following steps:

1. Position the pointer over the end of the split task until the cursor changes to a right-pointed arrow.

2. Drag to the left to shorten the duration of the portion, or drag to the right to lengthen the duration of the portion.

As you have seen, split tasks are shown on the Gantt Chart with dotted lines that connect each split portion. You can modify this appearance by editing the split bar style formatting options. To modify the appearance of a split bar, follow these steps:

1. From the Format menu, choose Bar Styles.

2. In the table, select Split in the Name column.

3. In the Bars tab, outlined in Figure 3-56, under Middle, use the Shape, Pattern, and Color drop-down lists to change the options for the split bar.

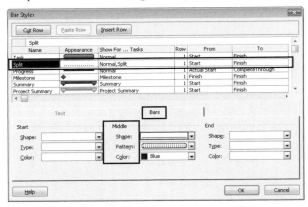

Figure 3-56   Changing formatting options

NOTE   **Customizing bar styles**

As you can see from Figure 3-56, you can modify many of the bar styles shown in Gantt Chart view using the Bar Styles dialog box. Another way to open this same dialog box is through a shortcut menu. To do this, right-click any area of the Gantt Chart (not already occupied by a bar) and choose Bar Styles from the shortcut menu.

Quick Check

- You do not want Project to split tasks automatically. How do you turn this feature off?

Quick Check Answer

- In the Resource Leveling dialog box, clear the Leveling Can Create Splits In Remaining Work check box. Disabling this option prevents splits during resource leveling.

Setting a Project Status Date

By default, the status of your project is always set to the current date. This means that for a status of cost and other project variables as of "today," you do not need to do anything special. However, if you would prefer to view the status of your project as of the last status reporting date, such as the previous Friday (or a date other than the current date), you can modify the project status date. Doing so will adjust the project information to reflect its status as of a specific date. More than this, however, the project status date determines how Project flags your project's tasks in relation to the project schedule.

You modify the project status date in the Project Information dialog box. To see the status of your project based on an earlier or later date, follow these steps:

1. Choose Project, and then choose Project Information.
2. Display the Status Date drop-down list.
3. Use the calendar to select a new status date.
4. Click OK.
5. To return to the current date, repeat steps 1 through 3, and in the calendar, click Today.
6. Click OK. See Figure 3-57.

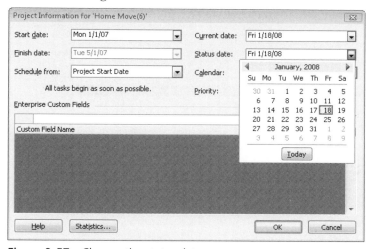

Figure 3-57   Change the status date

Rescheduling Tasks and Incomplete Work

Rescheduling a task is often a necessary step when things are delayed.

During this (and other instances), Project can reschedule any remaining work (based on tasks you select) after a specific date.

To have Project reschedule incomplete work, follow these steps:

1. Select a task to update in the Gantt Chart.
2. Choose Tools, choose Tracking, and choose Update Project.
3. In the Update Project dialog box, select the Reschedule Uncompleted Work To Start After option, and then select a date from the drop-down list. See Figure 3-58.

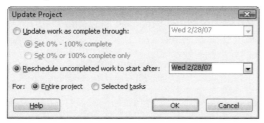

Figure 3-58   Rescheduling incomplete work

4. Click OK.

You can also reschedule work for multiple tasks at the same time. To do this, use the Ctrl key to select noncontiguous tasks or use the Shift key to select contiguous ones. Then select the Update Work As Complete Through option and choose a date from the drop-down list. See Figure 3-59.

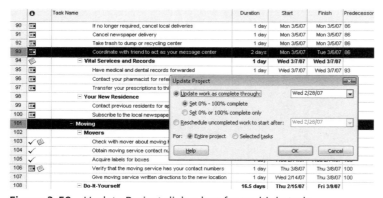

Figure 3-59   Update Project dialog box for multiple tasks

NOTE   **Reschedule Work button**

If your project plan includes a custom status date (a date other than the current date set in the Project Information dialog box), you can use the Reschedule Work button located on the Tracking toolbar. This action reschedules the project's remaining work for the selected task(s) to continue from the project plan's status date.

After this is done, the tasks are split, as shown in Figure 3-60.

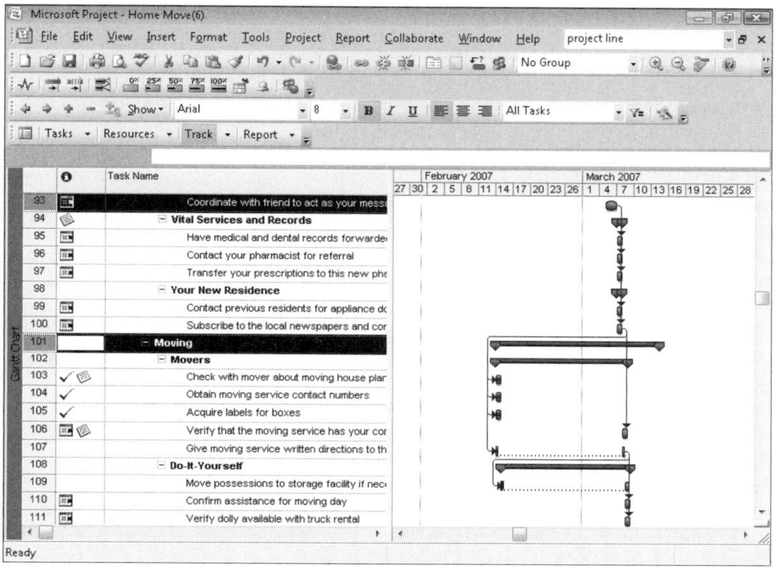

Figure 3-60   Project will split a task if necessary

Real World

Deanna Reynolds and Bonnie Biafore

The reasons for rescheduling a task certainly vary beyond the obvious one of preventing project plan slip. For instance, rescheduling a task might enable the most qualified resources to complete the rescheduled task without working unreasonable hours. And this is just one of many scenarios in which the project manager might find it useful to reschedule tasks and incomplete work. However, using the Update Tasks command is not the way to reschedule a task to use a different resource. In this scenario you would assign that resource and use the resource's calendar to figure out when the task would occur.

Saving and Updating a Project Interim Plan

Saving a project's interim plan is often confused with setting a project baseline. Although there are some similarities between a baseline plan and an interim plan (both allow up to 11 plans, both can be used to document project statistics at the end of a phase or on a specific date, and both save information such as start and finish dates), there is one key difference. *An interim plan saves only the project's start and finish dates.* (You might recall that a baseline plan saves original data related to costs, dates, duration, and work—a feature that can significantly increase your total project file size.)

Save an Interim Plan

One of the benefits of using interim plans is that you can use them to compare your project data against your project baseline data, giving you the ability to assess your project progress in relation to your project plan. Interim plans are not as useful as baselines, but the benefit is that they give you the opportunity to save additional points in time, stored in the Start and Finish fields. To save an interim plan, follow these steps:

1. Choose Tools, and choose Tracking.
2. Choose Set Baseline.
3. As shown in Figure 3-61, select the Set Interim Plan and Entire Project options.

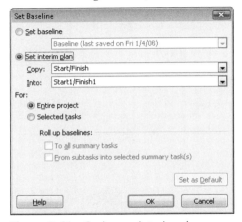

Figure 3-61 Saving an interim plan

4. Click OK.

NOTE Baseline vs. interim

Although baseline plans can significantly increase your project file size, it is nice to have the option of saving smaller bits of project data through the use of interim plans. The key difference between these two plans is that baseline plans store costs, dates, durations, and work. This is very handy when you want to save the result of the planning phase of your project. Baselines also work well for saving your project data at each major planning milestone. Baselines are best saved after your project has actual data. However, to save only task start and finish dates after the project begins, you can use interim plans. Interim plans work well when saved throughout the project, such as on a monthly or quarterly basis. At its core, an interim plan is a scaled-down version of a baseline.

Update an Interim Plan

After an interim plan has been saved, its data is available in the Start and Finish fields. As your project progresses, you can choose to save additional interim plans (up to 10) or you can update an existing interim plan. To update an existing interim plan, follow these steps:

1. Using the Gantt Chart, in the Task Name field, select the tasks that have baseline or interim data that need updating. (If you are updating baseline or interim data for the entire project, skip this step.) You can select up to 10 tasks at one time.
2. Choose Tools, choose Tracking, and then choose Set Baseline.
3. Select Set Interim Plan, shown in Figure 3-62.

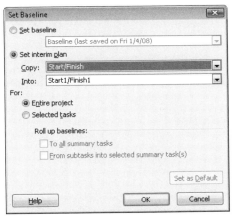

Figure 3-62   Updating an interim plan

4. In the Copy drop-down list, select the data that you are copying.
5. In the Into drop-down list, select the interim plan that you want to update.
6. Under For, do one of the following:
    a. Select the Entire Project option to update the interim data for the entire project.
    b. Select the Selected Tasks option to update the data for only the tasks that you selected in the Gantt Chart view.
7. Under Roll Up Baselines, select how you want the updated baseline data to be rolled up:
    a. Select the To All Summary Tasks check box if you want updated baseline data for the selected tasks to be rolled up to the corresponding summary tasks. Otherwise, baseline data for summary tasks might not accurately reflect subtask baseline data.
    b. Select the From Subtasks Into Selected Summary Task(s) check box if you want baseline data for selected summary tasks to be updated to reflect both the deletions of subtasks and added tasks for which you previously saved baseline values.
    c. Select both check boxes if you want to update both subtasks and their summary tasks.

8. Click OK.

9. Click Yes to overwrite the existing saved data.

Clear an Interim Plan

Finally, to make room for additional interim plans or simply remove previously created interim plans (particularly when working on projects with long durations), follow these steps:

1. If you want to delete the interim plan only for a specific set of tasks, using the Gantt Chart, in the Task Name field, select the tasks that have interim data that needs clearing. (If you are updating baseline or interim data for the entire project, skip this step.) You can select up to 10 tasks at one time.

2. Choose Tools, Tracking, and Clear Baseline.

3. Next to For, do one of the following:

    a. Click Entire Project to delete the interim data for the entire project.

    b. Click Selected Tasks to delete the data for only the tasks that you selected in the Gantt Chart view.

4. In the Clear Baseline dialog box, use the Clear Interim Plan drop-down list to locate the interim plan to clear.

5. Click OK.

PRACTICE Manage a Project in Progress

In these practices you will review what you've learned in this lesson. The first exercise is to enable and use Change Highlighting for task and schedule analysis, the second exercise is to split a task, the third is to reschedule tasks with incomplete work, and the last is to save a project interim plan.

▶ Exercise 1   Change Highlighting

You want to be able to see, through highlighted cells, exactly which tasks are affected by any changes you apply to tasks in your project. You want to verify that Change Highlighting is enabled.

To complete this exercise, perform the following steps:

1. Choose View.

2. If the menu says Hide Change Highlighting, Change Highlighting is already enabled.

3. Open the project template Annual Report Preparation. (Choose File, New, and then click On Computer. Click the Project Templates tab.)

4. Change Task 5 from one day to six days. Note the highlighting.

▶ **Exercise 2   Split a Task**

An employee in charge of a task has had a family emergency. He will be out for an entire week. He has already started a task, no one else can complete it, and you need to split the task in Project.

To complete this exercise, perform the following steps:

1. Create a new project using the project template Annual Report Preparation. (Choose File, New, and click On Computer. Click the Project Templates tab.)
2. Change the number of days for Task 2 from 1 day to 7 days (for the purpose of example only).
3. Click OK if prompted.
4. Click Split Task on the Standard toolbar, or choose Edit, and then choose Split Task.
5. On Task 2's Gantt bar, click the area of the bar on the date where you want the split to occur—in this instance, Saturday 12/30/06. Drag the second part of the bar forward five days.

▶ **Exercise 3   Reschedule Incomplete Work**

You need to reschedule some incomplete work in your project because some tasks are not finished yet.

To complete this exercise, perform the following steps:

1. Create a new project based on the project template Annual Report Preparation. (Choose File, choose New, and click On Computer. Click the Project Templates tab.)
2. Select Task 45: Define PR Messaging About Financial Results in the Entry table.
3. Choose Tools, choose Tracking, and choose Update Tasks. (Alternately, click Update Tasks on the Tracking toolbar.)
4. In the Update Tasks dialog box, change the Remaining Duration field to 4d.
5. Change % Complete to 20%.
6. Click OK.

▶ **Exercise 4   Save and Update a Project Interim Plan**

You need to compare your project dates against your project baseline dates to assess your project schedule progress in relation to your project plan. You also want to update that plan later.

To complete this exercise, perform the following steps:

1. Create a new project based on the project template Annual Report Preparation. (Choose File, choose New, and click On Computer. Click the Project Templates tab.)
2. Choose Tools and choose Tracking.
3. Choose Set Baseline.

4. Select the Set Interim Plan and Entire Project options.
5. Click OK.
    To update the plan, follow these steps:
6. Choose Tools, choose Tracking, and then choose Set Baseline.
7. Select the Set Interim Plan option.
8. In the Copy drop-down list, select the data that you are copying. In this case, Start/Finish.
9. In the Into drop-down list, select the interim plan that you want to update. In this case, select Start1/Finish1.
10. Under For, select Entire Project.
11. Click OK.

Lesson Summary

- The Change Highlighting feature, enabled by default, lets you easily see how the changes you make will affect the project schedule. When changes are saved, the highlighting goes away.
- You can split tasks when a resource cannot complete the task in consecutive days.

  You can view the status of a project based on the current date or on any date you choose.

  You can use interim plans to compare project dates against baseline dates, allowing you to assess your progress in relation to your project plan. Interim plans are stored in the Start and Finish fields.

Lesson Review

You can use the following questions to test your knowledge of the information in Lesson 2, "Implementing Changes." The questions are also available on the companion CD if you prefer to review them in electronic form.

NOTE Answers

Answers to these questions and explanations of why each answer choice is correct or incorrect are located in the "Answers" section at the end of the book.

1. The task of creating metal inlays has been delayed. The machine assigned to the task will be receiving its annual maintenance check over a period of two days during the time it is scheduled to work for you. The machine cannot be used during these days and you do not have another to replace it. Fortunately, the task is not on the critical path. What should you do?

    A. Let Project split the task automatically.

    B. Change the leveling defaults so that Project will not split tasks automatically.

    C. Change the status date of the project.

    D. Split the task and delay it by two days.

2. Every time you make a change to a project, various cells are highlighted. You do not want this to happen. What do you do to disable this feature?

    A. Choose Edit and choose Hide Change Highlighting.

    B. Clear the Show Change Highlighting check box in the Options dialog box.

    C. Choose View and choose Hide Change Highlighting.

    D. Clear the Show Change Highlighting check box in the Project Information dialog box.

3. You want to save a set of task start and finish dates so you can compare these at various intervals of your project. You plan to use this data to monitor project slippage. What do you need to create? (Choose two. Each represents a complete solution.)

    A. Baseline plan

    B. Assignment report

    C. Workload report

    D. Interim plan

Chapter Review

To further practice and reinforce the skills you learned in this chapter, you can perform the following tasks:

- Review the chapter summary.
- Review the list of key terms introduced in this chapter.
- Complete the case scenarios. These scenarios set up real-world situations involving the topics of this chapter and ask you to create a solution.
- Complete the suggested practices.
- Take a practice test.

Chapter Summary

- Use the Tracking table and the Tracking toolbar to keep track of the completion status of individual tasks in your project.
- Use the project schedule to stay on top of project progress, spot problems early, and decide what to do to bring a project back on track. Often, a setback in the schedule creates a snowball effect when it comes to project management issues—specifically increased costs, missed deadlines, and extra work.
- Meticulously watch tasks, deadlines, and start and finish dates. In doing so, you can see quickly when tasks are delayed, and you can make preparations for getting them back on schedule.
- Apply filters and groups to enhance your view of project tasks and data.
- Enable Change Highlighting so you can see how changes you make will affect the project schedule before saving them.
- Split tasks when needed—specifically, when a resource cannot work on them on consecutive days.
- Reschedule tasks and any incomplete work promptly. Rescheduling a task is often necessary to bring a task back on track and to avoid delaying the project further.

Key Terms

Do you know what these key terms mean? You can check your answers by looking up the terms in the glossary at the end of the book.

- AutoFilter
- Change Highlighting
- Cost table

- Earned Value
- filter
- group
- interim plan
- Organizer
- progress line
- project scope
- Resource Usage view
- Schedule table
- split task
- status date
- Summary table
- Task Usage view
- Tracking toolbar
- Variance table
- Work table

Case Scenarios

Case Scenario 1: Monitoring Project Progress

You are a project manager for a company in the midst of a company-wide software roll-out. The scope of this project includes, among many variables, the successful implementation of a company-wide software upgrade. During this roll-out, the stakeholders have made it very clear that company employees should experience zero downtime. To be certain that you bring this project in as expected, you will need to be diligent with task updates and with monitoring the project progress throughout its duration. Answer the following questions:

1. When you reached the end of the project Planning phase, you saved a baseline. This way, you could have a point of reference as the project work began. Now, halfway through the project, you would like to see where the current project is in relation to the previously saved project baseline. How can you see this comparison in Project?

2. One of your project stakeholders has just called and needs to know how far ahead of or how far behind the project schedule you are as of today. Because the stakeholder is on the phone, you would like to deliver the numbers immediately. Where can you go in Project to see this information quickly?

3. Some of your resources are beginning to feel a little overwhelmed with the amount of work to which they have been assigned in the project schedule. What views can you use to see how much work has been assigned to each resource?

Case Scenario 2: Implementing Project Changes

You are managing a project using Project. This project's purpose is to oversee the expansion of your company's employee parking lot. Four weeks into your planned eight-week project schedule, everything seems to be going according to plan. Answer the following questions.

1. One of your resources has just asked for a one-day extension on a critical task. Before you agree to this change, you would like to see how it might affect the project schedule. What can you do?

2. Current weather conditions are threatening a two-day to three-day delay in the paving work. What can you do to save basic project task start and finish dates as of the day before the storm so that you can analyze the variance in the project schedule next week after the storm has passed?

3. Partly through a project task, one of your resources has been pulled off of your project to work on another project for three days. How can you account for this downtime in the project schedule?

Suggested Practices

To help you successfully master the exam objectives presented in this chapter, complete the following tasks. We suggest you work through all of these exercises.

- **Practice 1: Know the Views and Tables**   Open a project and view every table, every view, and every graph available from the View menu. To be successful with Project, you must know what's available and where to find it.

- **Practice 2: Track the Project Schedule, Work, Cost, Units, and Scope**   Work through the practices again, this time inputting your own data. Input data to cause conflicts, and see what happens when you accept the data. Make sure to change scheduling options, work units, the costs of resources, and the scope of the project.

- **Practice 3: Create Your Own Filters and Groups**   Take time to create your own custom filters and groups. Save them. Ask other project managers to share their filters and groups with you, so you can learn from them too.

- **Practice 4: Work with Tasks**   Open a project and practice splitting tasks, modifying split tasks, and reuniting tasks. You will do a lot of this in the real world.

- **Practice 5: Change Project Terms**   Open a project and see what happens when you change the Status Date. Cause tasks to slip and compare interim plans.

Take a Practice Test

The practice tests on this book's companion CD offer many options. For example, you can test yourself on just one exam objective, or you can test yourself on all the 70-632 certification exam content. You can set up the test so that it closely simulates the experience of taking a certification exam, or you can set it up in study mode so that you can look at the correct answers and explanations after you answer each question.

MORE INFO   Practice tests

For details about all the practice test options available, see the "How to Use the Practice Tests" section in this book's Introduction.

Chapter 4
Team Collaboration and Multiple Projects

The work of a project is always completed as a team effort. Even though the project manager is the one tracking the project's progress, it is the collaboration of the team that brings a project in as scheduled. However, the project manager is sometimes the only team member using Microsoft Office Project 2007. Other team members often rely on methods that are more comfortable in their daily working environment, such as Microsoft Excel or Microsoft Access.

Another common scenario is a group of resources in which each one works on several projects. In fact, it is probably fairly rare for any team member to be assigned to only one project at a time. As a result, you will need to "share" your resources with other projects and other project managers.

This chapter breaks away slightly from the flow of the book, which, thus far, has been loosely organized by the project planning phases in the Project Management Body of Knowledge (PMBOK). Instead, the focus here is on ways you use Project to work within your team environment and with multiple projects by sharing your resources. We will also look at customization options available to Project, including program settings and template creation.

Exam objectives in this chapter:
- Set up schedule options.
- Set up calculation options.
- Set up view options.
- Set up general options.
- Set up security options.
- Create and modify a template.
- Import and export data.
- Manage multiple projects.
- Create, modify, and use resource pools.
- Optimize resource utilization.
- Create, modify, and delete objects.

Lessons in this chapter:

Before You Begin

As you read through this chapter, you will continue to see standard project management terms—many of which might already be familiar. Before you begin, you should:

- Be comfortable using the techniques described in Chapter 3, "Execute, Monitor, and Control the Project Plan," related to tracking project progress
- Understand how Project fits into your change management process
- Be comfortable with the differences between setting a baseline and interim plan

Lesson 1: Sharing Data with Other Programs

Project has lots of ways you can work with and display your project data. Even so, there are times when you will need to access other project data not contained within your project file. You might also want to take your project data out of Project and place it into another program (such as Excel) for further analysis and calculation.

This lesson discusses bringing data into Project and ways to take your data out of Project, including saving your project file as an image and as a Web page.

After this lesson, you will be able to:
- Import data from Excel, Access, Outlook, and comma-separated values formats.
- Export data to Excel, Access, Outlook, and comma-separated values formats.
- Take a snapshot of your project plan and save it as an image file.
- Save your project information to a Web page.

Estimated lesson time: 90 minutes

Importing Data

In Project, importing is really just a matter of opening a file native to another file format. Easily importable file formats include project data stored in:

- Excel
- Access
- Outlook
- Comma-separated values (*.csv)

Real World

Deanna Reynolds

The more people you have involved in your project, the more chances there are that everyone is using a different system for storing their project-related information. For instance, Human Resources might have a resource list stored in a proprietary database format while the Accounting department prefers to analyze their information in Excel (because this is a program their staff members use every day). With Project, you can bring all of this data into one project file. In an example like this, have your Human Resource personnel extract the data you need to the comma-separated values (*.csv) format and ask Accounting for a copy of their spreadsheet. Then you can use Project to view all of this data in one format by using the Import Wizard.

You can open any of these file types by choosing File and then Open in an open project file. When you do, Project automatically launches the Import Wizard.

Setting Up Project

When you import and export data using Project, you might find that you are blocked from opening or saving files in legacy formats. To avoid this, follow these steps to change the security settings in Project:

1. Choose Tools, and then choose Options.
2. In the Security tab, select either one of the following options under Legacy Formats:
    a. Prompt When Loading Files With Legacy Or Non Default File Format
    b. Allow Loading Files With Legacy Or Non Default File Formats
3. Click OK.

Supported Import File Types

Project supports the import of multiple types of file formats. Table 4-1 lists these formats.

Table 4-1   Supported Import File Types

File Format	File Name Extension
Project files (1998–2007)	.mpp
Project templates	.mpt
Project databases	.mpd
Project workspaces	.mpw
Project Exchange (for Project 4.0 and 98)	.mpx
Access databases	.mbd
Excel workbooks	.xls
Text files (tab-delimited)	.txt
CSV Text files (comma-delimited)	.csv
XML format files	.xml

Importing from Office Excel

Project information created in Excel transfers easily to Project, providing the file has been saved as an Excel 2003 (or earlier) format. It helps also to follow a field format that is familiar to Project. For example, to import a task list from Excel, you will want to have column headers that match the Entry table, such as:

- ID
- Task Name

- Start
- Finish
- Predecessors

You can see a sample file format for an Excel worksheet in Figure 4-1.

	ID	Name	Duration	Start	Finish	Predecessors	Outline Level
1	ID	Name	Duration	Start	Finish	Predecessors	Outline Level
2	1	Planning and Control	51 days	1/1/2009	3/12/2009		1
3	2	Business plan identifying project opportunity	5 days	1/1/2009	1/5/2009		2
4	3	Define project objective and information needs	5 days	1/8/2009	1/12/2009	3	2
5	4	Identify industry standards for project objectives	5 days	1/15/2009	1/19/2009	4	2
6	5	Develop preliminary conceptual schedule and staffing	5 days	1/22/2009	1/26/2009	4	2
7	6	Initial planning complete	0 days	1/26/2009	1/26/2009	6	2
8	7	Develop appropriation strategy	5 days	2/12/2009	2/16/2009	7	2
9	8	Develop management model and staff plan	10 days	2/19/2009	3/12/2009	7	2

Figure 4-1   Sample file format in Excel for Entry table data

When you follow a familiar format, the data easily falls into place. Another example is a list of resources. Think about the Resource Sheet view and use those same fields in an Excel file. An example is shown in Figure 4-2.

	A	B	C	D	E	F	G
1	ID	Unique_ID	Resource_Name	Initials	Max_Units	Standard_Rate	Overtime_Rate
2	1	1	Product Manager	P	100%	$0.00/hr	$0.00/hr
3	2	2	Data Analyst	D	100%	$0.00/hr	$0.00/hr
4	3	3	Customer Representative	C	100%	$0.00/hr	$0.00/hr
5	4	4	Customer Service Manager	C	100%	$0.00/hr	$0.00/hr

Figure 4-2   Sample file format in Excel for Resource Sheet view

When you are comfortable with the data format in Excel, you are ready to bring that information into your project file. To save the data in Excel and then import the project information into Project, follow these steps:

1. Verify that you have Excel open and the data added.
2. Choose File (or the Microsoft Office button in Excel 2007), and then choose Save As.
3. In the Save As dialog box, browse to a suitable folder to save the file and choose an Excel file format that is compatible with Project. For example, in Excel 2007, you should choose the format Excel 97-2003 Workbook, as shown in Figure 4-3. Depending on who needs access to the data, you might need to save the file in the comma-delimited or tab-delimited format.
4. Click Save.
5. In Project, choose File, and then Open.
6. In the Open dialog box, next to File Name, select Microsoft Excel Workbooks. See Figure 4-4. (Excel 2007 files won't appear in the dialog box.)

Figure 4-3   Saving the Excel file in the Excel 97-2003 Workbook format

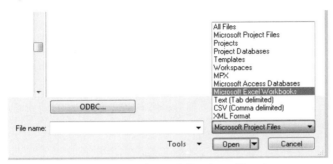

Figure 4-4   Opening a Microsoft Excel workbook

7. Browse to the file saved in Step 3 and click Open.

8. Click Next to start the Import Wizard.

9. When prompted to create a new map or use an existing one, choose New Map, and then click Next. (You'll learn about custom maps later.)

10. You have three options when prompted on how to import the file (Choose Append The Data To The Active Project):

   a. As a New Project

   b. Append The Data To The Active Project

   c. Merge The Data Into The Active Project

NOTE   **The difference between Append and Merge**

"Append" means to add the data to the project, and "merge" means to combine the data. Appended data is tacked on the end of the file; merged data is absorbed. Append data when the imported data is in addition to the existing data in the file; merge data when it is a part of the data in a file.

---

11. Click Next.

12. On the Import Wizard – Map Options page, select only the Tasks check box and the Import Includes Headers check box. See Figure 4-5. Click Next.

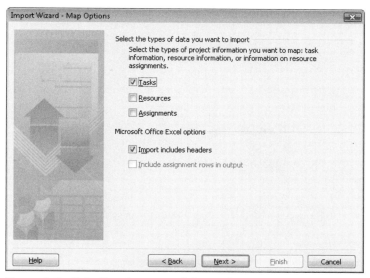

Figure 4-5   Selecting the types of data to import

13. On the Import Wizard – Task Mapping page, in the Source Worksheet Name drop-down list, select the sheet in the Excel workbook that contains the project data. See Figure 4-6.

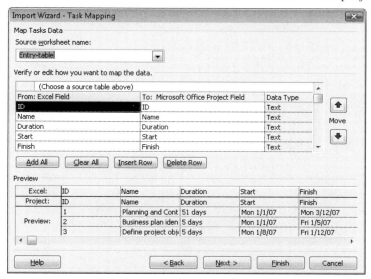

Figure 4-6   Mapping imported data

14. Verify the field mappings in the table and make sure there are no unmapped fields. Click Next.

15. To save the map, click Save Map. In the Save Map dialog box, name the map and click Save.

16. Click Finish.

As you can see, the Import Wizard does a nice job of walking you through each of the steps. Note that there are options to import Tasks, Resources, and Assignments. If you select all three, you'll have to repeat step 13 two more times.

Importing from an Excel Template   When you install Project, you get a bonus Excel 2003 template (if Excel is already installed on your computer). This template has been predefined with the proper import structure. This way you can have your team members complete the template so that you can ensure that the data you receive from others is stored in the proper format.

To use the Office Excel 2003 template using Microsoft Office Excel 2003, follow these steps:

1. Open Excel and choose File, New.

2. In the New Workbook pane, click On My Computer.

3. In the Templates dialog box, click the Slate tab.

4. Select Microsoft Project Task List Import Template. Click OK.

   To use the Office Excel 2003 template in Office Excel 2007:

5. Click the Microsoft Office Button, and then choose New.

6. In the New Workbook dialog box, click Installed Templates.

7. Select Microsoft Project Task List Import Template.

8. Click Create. See Figure 4-7.

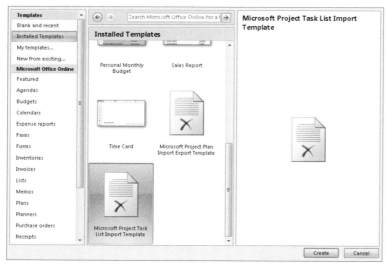

Figure 4-7   Locating the Microsoft Project Task List Import Template

Quick Check

- When creating data in Excel to import to Project, you'll want to use column headers that match the headers in the Entry table. Name the column headers that you think would be good choices for the Entry table. After the data is created, should you save the file as an Excel 2007 file?

Quick Check Answers

1. ID.
2. Task Name.
3. Start.
4. Finish.
5. Predecessors.
6. No, Project does not accept Excel 2007 files.

Importing from Access

When you import data from Access, you need to follow guidelines similar to those you follow when importing from Excel. In particular, the Office Access file should be saved as an Access 2003 (or earlier) format. If you're using Office Access 2007 in conjunction with Project 2007, you should configure the default settings in Access 2007 to automatically save in Access 2002-2003 format. See Figure 4-8.

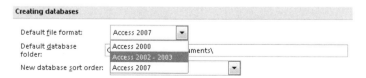

Creating databases

Default file format:	Access 2007
Default database folder:	Access 2000
	Access 2002 - 2003
New database sort order:	Access 2007

Figure 4-8 Saving a database file in Access 2002-2003 format

It helps, also, to follow a field format that is familiar to Project. Figure 4-9 shows an example in Access 2007.

ID	Task Name	Duration	Start	Finish	Predecessors
1	Site Assessment		1/12/2009		
2	Identify potential sites	15	1/29/2009		7
3	Define infrastructure requiremer	15	4/17/2009		21, 11
4	Define utility needs	13	3/22/2009		21, 11
5	Identify project site	8	4/5/2009		21, 11
6	Assess regulatory and environme	16	2/28/2009		21, 11
7	Identify permitting requirement:	3	5/30/2009		15
8	Recommend site	20	6/4/2009		15, 12, 13, 14, 16
9	Site and planning review	5	7/2/2009		17

Figure 4-9 Sample Office Access 2007 file

To save a database in Access 2007, click the Microsoft Office button, point to Save As, and choose Access 2002-2003 Database. See Figure 4-10.

Figure 4-10   Saving the Office Access 2007 file

After you have saved the data format in Access, you are ready to bring that information into your project file. To import the information into Project, follow these steps:

1. In Project, choose File, and then Open.

2. In the Open dialog box, next to File Name, select Microsoft Access Databases.

3. Browse to the file and click Open.

4. Click Next to start the Project Import Wizard.

5. When prompted to create a new map or use an existing one, choose New Map, and then click Next. (You'll learn about custom maps later.)

6. You have three options when prompted on how to import the file (Choose Append The Data To The Active Project):

   a. As a New Project

   b. Append The Data To The Active Project

   c. Merge The Data Into The Active Project

7. Click Next.

8. On the Import Wizard – Map Options page, select the Tasks, Resources, and Assignments check boxes. Click Next.

9. In the Source Database Table Name drop-down list, select the resources or tasks tables you created in the Access file. See Figure 4-11. Click Next.

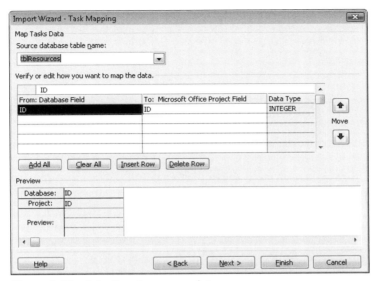

Figure 4-11   Selecting the source data

10. When prompted to map more data, repeat step 9. Click Next.

11. To save the map, click Save Map. In the Save Map dialog box, name the map and click OK.

12. Click Finish.

As you can see, importing from Access is very similar to importing from Excel. In each case you will need to choose the file format and then choose the worksheet (in Excel) or table (in Access) in which the data is located.

Quick Check

- What types of files can be imported into Project? Name as many as you can think of.

Quick Check Answers

1. Project files (1998–2007), templates, databases, and workspaces
2. Project Exchange (for Project 4.0 and 98)
3. Access 2003 or earlier databases
4. Excel 2003 or earlier workbooks
5. Text files (tab-delimited)
6. CSV Text files (comma-delimited)

Exam Tip   Although you don't necessarily have to memorize the file types that can be imported and exported, you do need to understand the procedure for doing so and know that comma-separated value files are a common way to exchange data among programs.

Fields Not Mapped

Sometimes, while importing data from Excel or Access, you'll come across a field that is not mapped. That means that you are importing data that does not have a corresponding column in Project. When this happens, you can select a field for the missing column. (Alternatively, you can delete the related row from the import map. In doing so, the unmapped row will not be imported into Project but will remain in the original data file.) To map data from Excel or Access to a column in Project, open the drop-down list for a field and select the proper column from the list. See Figure 4-12.

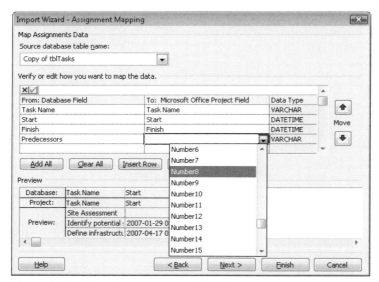

Figure 4-12   Mapping nonmapped fields

You'll learn more about mapping later in this lesson.

Importing from Outlook

Project has a menu option available for importing tasks stored in Outlook. This makes importing from Outlook a little easier than importing from Excel and Access. Figure 4-13 shows the option from the Tools menu.

During the import process, the text of selected tasks within your Outlook 2007 account will be copied into the open Project file beginning at the first blank row in the Entry table.

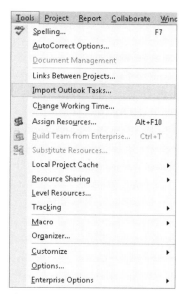

Figure 4-13   Importing data from Outlook

Acquire Tasks in Outlook 2007   Figure 4-14 shows what a list of tasks looks like in Outlook 2007. You can create new tasks in Outlook 2007 by choosing File, New, and then Task if you'd like to create your own for the practice purposes here (just fill in the task information and then click Save & Close).

Figure 4-14   Creating tasks in Outlook 2007

To install the tasks into Outlook from the file on the accompanying CD, complete the following steps:

1. In Outlook 2007, choose File, and then choose Import And Export.
2. In the Import And Export Wizard dialog box, under Choose An Action To Perform, select Import From Another Program Or File. Click Next.
3. In the Import A File dialog box, select Comma Separated Values (Windows). Click Next.
4. Browse to the location of the 04-Import-Outlook file and click Open.
5. Select Replace Duplicates With Items Imported. Click Next.
6. Select Tasks and click Next.
7. Click Finish.
8. To view the tasks, click Go and click Tasks.

Import Tasks from Outlook 2007　After tasks are created in Outlook 2007, you can import them into a Project file. To import tasks from Outlook into an open project file, follow these steps:

1. In Project, choose Tools and choose Import Outlook Tasks.
2. The first time you try to import tasks into Project, you might receive security warnings or notifications, or both. For instance, you might be prompted to specifically allow access to Outlook so that Project can gather the required data. Whether or not you see the notice shown in Figure 4-15 depends on how your security settings are configured. If you receive this message, click Switch when prompted by Project, and then, in Outlook, select the Allow Access For check box, and then click Allow.

Figure 4-15　Allow access if prompted

3. Select the tasks to import, as shown in Figure 4-16.
4. Click OK.

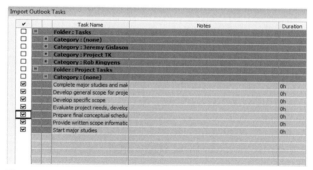

Figure 4-16   Choosing the tasks to import

Quick Check

■ Do you use any kind of import or export wizard when working with Outlook tasks?

Quick Check Answer

■ No. You create tasks in Outlook and import them using the Tools: Import Tasks From Outlook command.

Importing from a Comma-Separated Values File

When the data you need is coming from a source other than Excel, Access, or Outlook, there is still hope. By saving files in either the text (*.txt) or comma-separated values (*.csv) format, data can be brought into Project from these outside sources. Most programs offer a way to save data in one of these two formats, even third-party or company-specific applications. Figure 4-17 shows a text file in Notepad that would serve the purpose well.

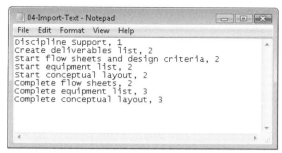

Figure 4-17   A text file that offers the data required, followed by a comma and the outline number

To import data contained in *.txt/*.csv format in Project, follow these steps:

1. Choose File and choose Open.
2. In the Open dialog box, select CSV (Comma Delimited) or Text (Tab Delimited) and browse to the location of the file.
3. Click Open and click Next to start the Import Wizard.
4. Select New Map and click Next.
5. Select Append The Data To The Active Project and click Next.
6. Select the types of data to import (Tasks, Resources, or Assignments) and select the Import Includes Headers check box.
7. Make sure the Text Delimiter is correct, as shown in Figure 4-18.

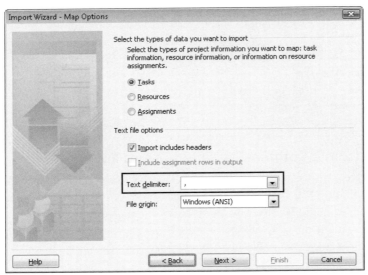

Figure 4-18   Choosing the delimiter used in the file

8. Click Next.
9. If necessary, map unmapped fields by clicking in the field and selecting a Project field from the available drop-down list. Fields in the imported file appear in the left column, and you must pick the corresponding Project field in the right column. You must match the fields during this import process.
10. Click Finish.

Working with Import Maps

When you import data into Project from another program, the Import Wizard refers to an import map. This map contains the instructions for the import, including the data type of the information contained in the original file and whether the information is related to a task, a resource, or an assignment.

If the data you are importing has already been preformatted and you are sure it includes project-specific fields, you can typically bypass the need to create a custom import map or even use one of the predefined maps. Instead, you can choose the template or predefined import map after you have selected a particular file type in the Open dialog box. For example, using the Microsoft Excel Workbooks template ensures that Project will recognize the data contained in the spreadsheet.

However, if you are working to move other data into Project, it might be beneficial to use a predefined import map. You can access a list of these maps through the Import Wizard by choosing "Use Existing Map" on the Import Wizard – Map page. A list of predefined maps is shown in Figure 4-19.

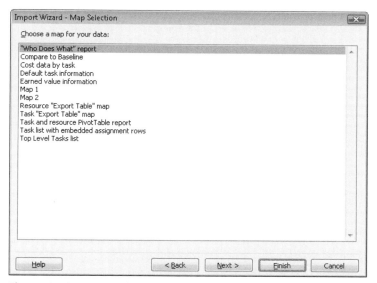

Figure 4-19   During the import process, click Use Existing Map to choose from these options

Exam Tip   You need to know that when importing or exporting data you can create your own mapping options by choosing New Map on the Import Wizard – Map page. When asked on the exam how to import data specific to your project, choose New Map to create a map that suits your company's needs.

Real World

Bonnie Biafore

Sometimes, instead of importing entire tasks, resources, or assignments, you want to import data into the fields for existing elements. For example, you have tasks for your work breakdown structure in a Project file and now want to import the work estimates you received from team members.

To import data into existing tasks, resources, or assignments, you must select the Merge The Data Into The Active Project option in the Import Wizard. You must also tell Project how to match the imported items with the tasks, resources, or assignments already in the file. When you map fields for existing elements in the Import Wizard, Project asks you for a primary key to identify matching records. Choose a field that uniquely identifies the element, such as the WBS code for tasks that you have already defined in both Project and the data file you are importing.

To specify a primary key, on the Import Wizard – Task Mapping page, select the field that represents the unique identifier in the imported data (in the To column). Then, click Set Merge Key. Project inserts MERGE KEY: in front of the field names in both columns.

Using an Existing Map

Using an existing map to import your data is similar to choosing New Map from the Import Wizard. The difference is that the predefined maps already contain instructions for importing data, such as field names and types of data. Examples of existing maps include:

- Compare to Baseline
- Costs Data by Tasks
- Top Level Tasks List

Creating a Custom Import Map

Another option when importing is to create your own custom import maps. In previous examples this was unnecessary because the original information already contained fields that matched fields available in Project. However, there might be times when you have information coming from external sources that simply is not named to correspond to Project field names. In these instances you can create your own import maps and save them for future use.

NOTE Sharing import maps

In addition to saving your custom import maps, you can share them as well. To share a custom import map, use the Organizer (first seen in this book in Chapter 3: Execute, Monitor, and Control the Project Plan). To open the Organizer dialog box, choose Tools and then Organizer. Then click the Maps tab and copy your custom maps from one Project file to another.

To create a custom import map, follow these steps:

1. Choose File and choose Open.
2. In the Open dialog box, for file type, select All Files.
3. Browse to and open the data file you want to import.
4. Click Next to start the Import Wizard.
5. On the Import Wizard – Map page, select New Map and click Next.
6. On the Import Wizard – Import Mode page, select As A New Project and click Next. Note that you can also choose either Append The Data To The Active Project or Merge The Data Into The Active Project. Appending will add the data to the end of the active project, merging will merge the data with data in the active project.
7. On the Import Wizard – Map Options page, select the Tasks and Import Includes Headers check boxes. Click Next. Note that you could also select the Resources or Assignments check boxes, depending on what you wanted to import.
8. Choose the appropriate delimiter, if applicable, and click Next. Note that you can select a comma, Tab, or Space if you've chosen a text file to open.
9. For Map Tasks Data, select Entry-Table, Resource-Sheet, Assignment_Table, Task_Table, or another option. What you see varies depending on the type of data file you're importing, and what part of that file you are importing (tasks, resources, and/or assignments. See Figure 4-20.
10. Map fields that need mapping. In Figure 4-20 we'll map Initials to Assignment Owner, and Material Label to Resource Type.
11. Click Next.
12. When prompted, click Save Map.
13. In the Save Map dialog box, name the map and click Save. See Figure 4-21. You might want to save it using all capital letters or a standard prefix so you can find it easily next time you want to use it.
14. Click Finish.

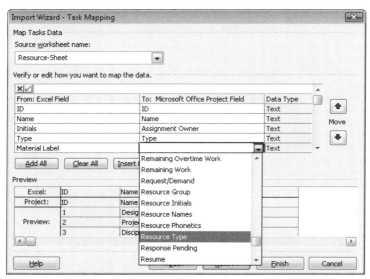

Figure 4-20   Mapping necessary fields

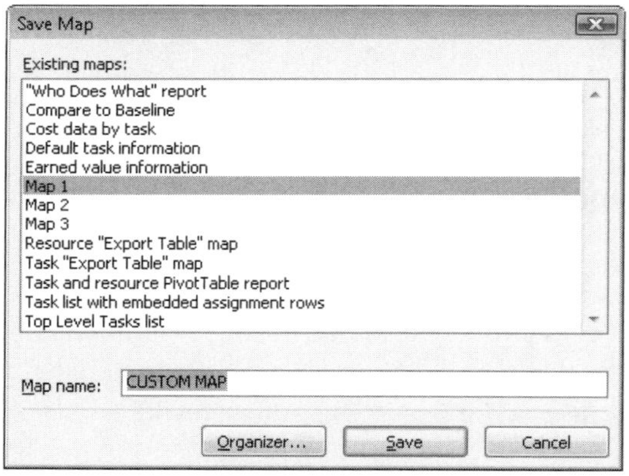

Figure 4-21   Saving a map

The next time you walk through the Import Wizard, any import maps you save will be available when you choose Use Existing Map. You can see an example of a custom map in Figure 4-22.

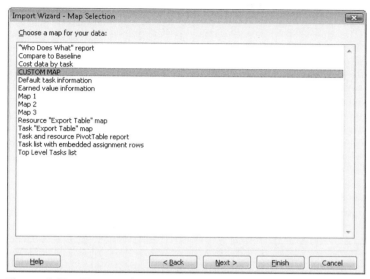

Figure 4-22   The saved custom map is ready for use

Modifying an Import Map

Finally, you can modify your import maps even after they have been created. By following the same set of steps you used to create a custom import map, you can modify any import map. To modify a custom import map, follow these steps:

1.   Open a file and start the Import Wizard.
2.   When prompted, choose Use Existing Map and select the map you want to modify.
3.   Click Next and work through the steps to define the map.
4.   When prompted to save the map, click Save Map.
5.   In the Save Map dialog box, accept the same map name you used before. See Figure 4-23.
6.   Click OK and click Finish.

MORE INFO   **Advanced mapping options**

The Task Mapping dialog box offers a lot of ways to customize a map. For instance, you can use it to add and remove fields, insert and delete rows, base data on a table, and more. For more information, see Chapter 17 in the book *Microsoft Office Project 2007 Inside Out*, by Teresa Stover (Microsoft Press, 2007).

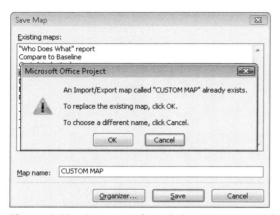

Figure 4-23   Save over the existing map to complete the modification

> ## Quick Check
> - Why would you want to create, modify, and save a custom map?
>
> ## Quick Check Answer
> - You use a custom map to specify names and fields for exporting and importing data from applications like Access and Excel.

Exporting Data

Understanding how to import data into Project makes learning how to export even easier. Exporting is helpful in several project management areas, including to:

- Export project data to team members who do not use (or have a copy of) Project.
- Export project data to Excel to create custom calculations and analyze cost and other project factors.

The act of exporting your project data merely copies the data that currently resides in your project file to another format, such as an Excel workbook or a text (*.txt) or comma-separated values (*.csv) file.

When you export data, Project accesses a set of maps similar to that which you see when importing data. These maps contain the instructions that tell Project how to handle the data it is exporting.

NOTE   **File Linking**

When you import data to or export data from Project, no link remains between the two files.

Supported Import File Types

Project supports the import of multiple types of file formats. Table 4-2 lists these.

Table 4-2   Supported Export File Types

File Format	File Name Extension
Project files (1998–2007)	.mpp
Project templates	.mpt
Excel workbooks	.xls
Excel Pivot tables	.xls
Text files (tab-delimited)	.txt
CSV Text files (comma-delimited)	.csv
XML format files	.xml

Exporting Project Data to Basic Excel Data

To export basic project data into Excel, follow these steps:

1. Open Project, open the appropriate project, choose File, and then choose Save As.
2. In the Save As dialog box, shown in Figure 4-24, select Microsoft Excel Workbook from the Save As Type drop-down list and type a file name. Click Save.

Figure 4-24   Name the file and select Microsoft Excel Workbook as the file type

3. Click Next to start the Export Wizard.
4. Select Project Excel Template when prompted, as shown in Figure 4-25, and click Finish.

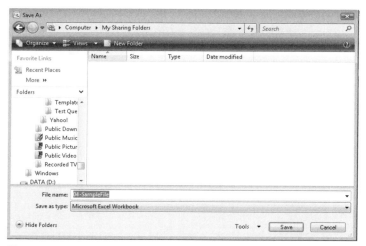

Figure 4-25 Importing basic data using a predefined template

When you export your project data using the Project Excel template, a new workbook is created. After it's opened in Excel, it will contain at least three worksheet tabs, including the following:

- Task_Table
- Resource_Table
- Assignment_Table

Exporting Advanced Project Information

We know from experience that Project contains much more information related to a project than what is exported using the Project Excel template map. For example, cost information is often the data that needs to be shared with project stakeholders. To export other data (such as cost information) to Excel or another file format, such as a text or comma-separated value file, follow these steps:

Open Project, open the appropriate project, choose File, and then choose Save As.

1. In the Save As dialog box, in the Save As Type drop-down list, select Text (Tab Delimited). (Repeat this exercise later with CSV [Comma Delimited]).
2. Name the file and click Save.
3. Click Next to start the Export Wizard.
4. Select Use Existing Map and click Next.
5. On the Export Wizard – Map Selection page, select Cost Data By Task. See Figure 4-26. Click Next.

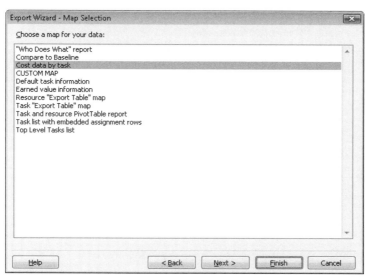

Figure 4-26 Export cost data

6. On the Export Wizard – Map Options page, shown in Figure 4-27, select Tasks. For other mapping tasks, you might choose Resources or Assignments, but for now, we're just exporting task related data. Note you can only choose one per data file.

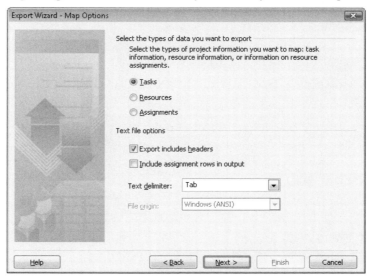

Figure 4-27 Choosing the type of data to export

7. Make sure the Export Includes Headers check box is selected and click Next.

8. On the Export Wizard – Task Mapping page, if there are any nonmapped fields, map them by selecting the appropriate option in the fields' drop-down lists. See Figure 4-28.

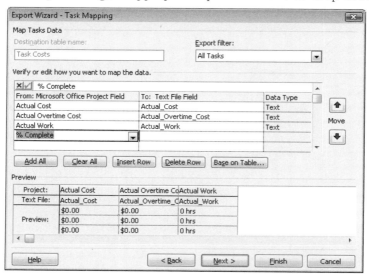

Figure 4-28 Map fields if necessary

MORE INFO **Additional mapping options**

On the Export Wizard – Task Mapping page, you can also:

a. Click Insert Row to add a custom row.

b. Click Delete Row to delete any row.

c. Click Add All to add all fields.

d. Click Clear All to clear all fields.

e. Click the arrows to move selected fields up or down in the list.

f. Use the Export Filter drop-down list to select a filter to export only specific data.

---

9. Click Next and click Save Map if desired.
10. Click Finish.

NOTE **Custom export maps**

Creating custom export maps and working with predefined maps when exporting is identical to performing these same tasks when importing. The only difference is in how you access the Import /Export Wizard. For example, to open the Import Wizard and access the maps, you would choose File and then Open. But to open the Export Wizard and access the same maps, you would choose File and then Save As.

> ## Quick Check
> - What kind of Project file would you choose when creating your own Project Template?
>
> ## Quick Check Answer
> - .mpt

Copy a Picture

Importing and exporting certainly offer great ways to share your data with other project team members. However, one of the downsides to using this method is that the shared information is purely text-based.

Project does offer a few ways to share visual information as well. One of the easiest ways to share a visual image, such as the Gantt Chart, is to take a snapshot of your Project screen using the Copy Picture button located on the Standard toolbar.

Because the Copy Picture button takes a snapshot of your Project screen, you first want to be sure that the information you want to capture is clearly displayed on the screen. This often involves adjusting the zoom level or widening columns.

The Copy Picture command offers more image options than you might initially realize, as shown in Figure 4-29.

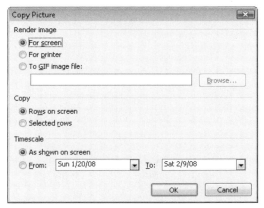

Figure 4-29   The Copy Picture dialog box

At the top of the dialog box, you will first want to choose how you plan to use the image you are copying. To take a snapshot of your current project plan exactly as it appears on the screen and send it to your clipboard, choose For Screen—the first option. If you prefer to take a snapshot based on how the current project plan would print by your computer's default printer (that is, black and white), choose For Printer—the second option. Finally, to save the snapshot as an image that can be used in another location (such as on a Web page), choose To GIF Image File—the third option.

The next set of options allows you to choose whether you want the snapshot to include the rows on the screen (only those rows with data) or just rows that you have previously selected. And just below Copy is a set of Timescale options that allow you to choose to copy exactly what is shown on the screen or just the information between two project dates.

To take a picture of the current view using the Copy Picture button, click the Copy Picture button on the Standard toolbar (see Figure 4-30). If it isn't showing, you will have to click the Toolbar Options down arrow at the end of the Standard toolbar and select Show Buttons On Two Rows. Make the appropriate selections in the dialog box and click OK.

copy picture

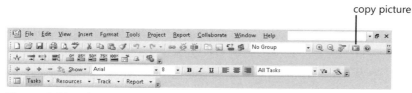

Figure 4-30   The Copy Picture icon looks like a camera

NOTE   Widening columns

The Copy Picture command is slightly finicky in that it will capture only data that is displayed in full on the screen. This means that to capture a column in a table that is displayed, you need to be sure that you can see the right and left edge of the column you want to display before clicking the Copy Picture command.

Because the snapshot is sent directly to your Windows clipboard, you can use that information in a number of ways. This means that you can paste the copied image into a Word document, the Paint program, or PowerPoint.

MORE INFO   Windows Vista

If you're running Project on Windows Vista, you can also use the Snipping Tool. Just click Start, and in the Start Search window, type **Snip**. Under Programs in the results, select Snipping Tool to start this utility. Now simply drag the cursor over the area to copy. It can be a part of a project page, Web page, or anything else you can see on your desktop. You can then e-mail the picture, save it, mark it up, and more from inside the Snipping Tool window.

Saving Project Information as a Web Page

In addition to all of the techniques we have described so far for sharing your project data, if you use Microsoft Office Project Server 2007, you can also save your project information as a Web page. This is probably the most universally accessible technique, combining the best of both worlds—text and visual. However, if you don't have Project Server, you won't be able to access this feature. When you save your project plan task, resource, and assignment information as a Web page, you can then post that information to the Internet or to a company Intranet. You can even choose to e-mail the information to interested team members or stakeholders, or both.

To save your project plan data as a Web page, you must first create an enterprise project. An enterprise project is one that is stored in Project Server. From within an enterprise project, use the File: Publish command to get started and work your way through the wizard. You'll need to start by creating a workspace or subworkspace, selecting the virtual server, and then entering the required information into the Site URL dialog box. After a project is published, you can easily publish updated information using the File: Publish command.

MORE INFO   Publishing projects

For more information on publishing projects, see Chapter 22 of *Microsoft Office Project 2007 Inside Out* (Microsoft Press, 2007).

PRACTICE **Working with Data in Other Applications**

In these exercises you will review the tasks learned in this lesson. In Exercise 1, you'll create data in Excel and then import it into Project, making a mental note that importing data from Access and Outlook is quite similar. In Exercise 2, you'll export data to Access, again taking note that exporting data is a similar process in other applications. In Exercise 3, you'll use the Import From Outlook command to import tasks created there. In Exercise 4, you'll create a custom map, and, in Exercise 5, you'll save a picture of your project using the Copy Picture button on the Standard Toolbar.

▶ **Exercise 1   Import Data from Excel**

To import data from Excel, you must first create and save the data you need to export. Although this data generally comes from resources, in this exercise you'll create some basic data, save it, and then import it into Project. To complete this exercise, perform the following steps:

1. Open Excel 2007, click the Microsoft Office button, choose New, and then Blank Workbook.
2. In field A1, type **ID**, in field B1, type **Task Name**, in field C1, type **Start**, and D1, type **Finish**.
3. In fields A2 through D2, type (again in order) **1**, **Start Project**, **4**.
4. In fields A3 through D3, type (again in order) **2**, **End Project**, **2**.

5. Choose File, and then Save As.

6. In the Save As dialog box, browse to the Desktop, name the file **2010**, and save it as an Excel 97-2003 Workbook.

7. Close Excel 2007 and Open Project.

8. In Project, choose File, and then Open.

9. In the Open dialog box, browse to the Desktop, select Microsoft Excel Workbooks for the file type, select the file named 2010, and click Open.

10. Click Next to start the Import Wizard.

11. Select New Map. Click Next.

12. Select As A New Project. Click Next.

13. Select the Tasks check box. Verify that the Import Includes Headers check box is selected. Click Next.

14. In the Source Worksheet Name drop-down list, select Sheet1.

15. Click Finish.

▶ **Exercise 2   Export Data to Access**

You need to export some basic data from your Customer Feedback Monitoring project to members of your team who do not use Project. They prefer to use Access to organize information. Because Access has the option to open Text files, you've chosen to save your data in that format.

To complete this exercise, perform the following steps:

1. In Project, choose File, choose New, and click On Computer.

2. In the Templates dialog box, in the Project Templates tab, select Customer Feedback Monitoring.

3. Click OK.

4. Choose File and choose Save As.

5. In the Save As dialog box, in the Save As Type drop-down list, select Text (Tab Delimited).

6. Click Save to use the name Customer Feedback Monitoring as the name for the text file.

7. Click Next to start the Export Wizard.

8. Select New Map. Click Next.

9. Select Resources. Verify that the Import Includes Headers check box is selected.

10. In the Text Delimiter drop-down list, select Space. Click Next.

11. In the Resource Mapping dialog box, do the following:

    a. In the first From: Microsoft Office Project Field, select Type. Press the Enter key.

    b. In the second From: Microsoft Office Project Field, select Group By Summary. Press the Enter key.

12. Click Next, and then click Finish.

After you save the exported text file, you can open Access, choose Open As, select Text for file type, browse to this saved file, and open it to see the results.

▶ **Exercise 3   Import Tasks from Outlook**

Some members of your project use Outlook to create project tasks. You don't want to rewrite those tasks and have decided to import them. For the purpose of this lesson, you'll create two tasks in Outlook 2007, save them, and then import them into Project.

To complete this exercise, perform the following steps:

1. Open Outlook 2007, choose File, choose New, and choose Task.
2. In the Task window, for subject type **Test Task 1**. Select Today for the Start Date and Due Date fields.
3. Click Save & Close.
4. Repeat Steps 1, 2, and 3, creating Test Task 2.
5. Open Project.
6. Choose Tools and choose Import Outlook Tasks.
7. If prompted, click Switch or select the Allow Access For check box and specify 5 minutes, or both, to allow Project to access Outlook 2007. Click Allow.
8. In the Import Outlook Tasks dialog box, locate select the Test Task 1 and Test Task 2 check boxes.
9. Click OK. Project imports the Outlook tasks into a Project data file.
10. Leave this file open for Exercise 4.

▶ **Exercise 4   Create a Custom Map**

You have a project for which you want to create a custom map so that you can export its data when necessary. For the purpose of this exercise, you'll use the Annual Report Preparation template in Project. (To review, to open the Annual Report Preparation Template, choose File, choose New, and click On Computer. On the Project Templates tab, select Annual Report Preparation.) To create a custom export map, follow these steps:

1. Choose File and choose Save As.
2. In the Save As dialog box, for Save As Type, select Text (Tab Delimited).
3. Name the file **Project Text Map** and click Save. (You might also need to browse to a location to save the file.)
4. Click Next to start the Export Wizard.
5. Select New Map and click Next.
6. Select Tasks and the Export Includes Headers check box.
7. Choose the Tab text delimiter and click Next.
8. In the From: Microsoft Office Project Field drop-down list, in the first row, select Work. Press the Enter key.

9. Repeat step 9 and select the Duration, Start, Finish, Actual Start, and Actual fields. Finish.

10. Click Next.

11. When prompted, click Save Map.

12. In the Save Map dialog box, name the map **My Project Map 1** and click Save. You might want to save it using all capital letters or a standard prefix so you can find it easily the next time you want to use it.

13. Click Finish.

▶ **Exercise 5   Use the Copy Picture Feature**

You've manipulated the data showing in the Project window to show data you need to share with stakeholders. You simply want to e-mail a picture of your screen to them for review. You need to have Exercise 3 open, or you need to open another project.

To complete this exercise, perform the following steps:

1. On the Standard toolbar, click the Copy Picture button.

2. In the Copy Picture dialog box, select To GIF Image File.

3. Click Browse and browse to the Desktop.

4. Name the file Test. Click OK.

5. For Copy, select Rows On Screen.

6. For Timescale, select As Shown On Screen.

7. Click OK.

8. Locate the file Test on your Desktop.

9. Right-click the file and choose Send To and then Mail Recipient.

10. Click Attach.

11. Fill in the To name in your e-mail, add a message, and click Send.

Lesson Summary

■ With Project, you can import and export data from Excel, Access, and Outlook to share data among team members and stakeholders. If you use Project Server, you can also publish data to a Web page on the Internet or on a company intranet.

■ You can create text files and comma-separated values formats for applications that aren't compatible with other file formats.

■ It is easy to take a snapshot of your project plan and save it as an image file using the Copy Picture command.

Lesson Review

You can use the following questions to test your knowledge of the information in Lesson 1, "Sharing Data with Other Programs." The questions are also available on the companion CD if you prefer to review them in electronic form.

NOTE Answers

Answers to these questions and explanations of why each answer choice is correct or incorrect are located in the "Answers" section at the end of the book.

---

1. You need to import an Excel workbook into Project. What kind of information can you import? (Choose two.)
   A. Tasks
   B. Filters
   C. Costs
   D. Views

2. You want to import data from Outlook, which involves several steps. Which of the following describes these steps? (Choose all that apply.)
   A. Select the tasks to import in the Import Outlook Tasks dialog box.
   B. Work through the Import Wizard.
   C. Choose Tools and choose Import Outlook Tasks.
   D. In the Open dialog box, in the File Type drop-down list, select Microsoft Outlook Tasks.

3. Your stakeholders do not have Project. In fact, they don't have any Office suite applications. You need to send them eight rows of basic task information, including task names and start and finish dates. How can you do this? (Choose all that apply.)
   A. Send the entire project and tell your stakeholders to download the Project Viewer from the Microsoft Web site.
   B. Choose File and Export and send the file to the comma-separated values format.
   C. Save the file as a text file, and then e-mail it to them.
   D. Use the Copy Picture button to take a snapshot of the current display in Project and e-mail them the image.

4. You're exporting data using the Export Wizard, but during the task mapping project, several fields are not mapped. Which of the following answers represents a solution for resolving the unmapped fields? (Choose two.)

    A. In the To field, in the Task Mapping dialog box, select a field from the available drop-down list that can serve as a valid field for the unmapped data.

    B. Select the unmapped field and click Delete Row.

    C. Select the unmapped field and click Add All.

    D. Apply an export filter for the unmapped tasks.

5. The accounting team needs data regarding your project. They use Access 2007. The only information they want is the most current data related to task costs, and there are a large number of them to send. Which one of the following describes a quick-and-easy way to send this data?

    A. Open Resource Sheet view, copy the data desired, choose File, and then Save As, and work through the Export Wizard to send the copied data.

    B. Choose File, and then Export, and send the file in Microsoft Access Database format.

    C. Export the data using the predefined map Cost Data By Task.

    D. Switch to Resource Sheet view, use the Copy Picture button to take a snapshot of your current display in Project, and e-mail them the image.

Lesson 2: Manage Multiple Resources over Multiple Projects

More often than not, resources have more than one set of project duties to work on at any given time. In these situations your resources are probably also working for one or more additional project managers. Project offers the option of creating and sharing a resource pool. With a resource pool, the resources you work with can also be assigned to tasks on other projects with overlapping time frames.

When you (and other project managers) share the same pool of resources, you lessen the risk of overscheduling (or overallocating) your resources, reducing the chance of resource burnout. As a bonus, when your resources are not overallocated, it's more likely that they will be able to complete their assigned work within a given time frame.

After this lesson, you will be able to:
- Describe resource pool considerations.
- Create and share a resource pool.
- Assess resource availability.
- Level resources.

Estimated lesson time: 60 minutes

Resource Pool Considerations

Before you share your resources with other project managers, you will need to create a resource pool. A resource pool, quite simply, is a Project file that contains *only* resource information. You can assign these resources to tasks stored in other Project files. The project files that use a resource pool are called *sharer files*.

Resource pools offer a few advantages to both project managers and project team members:

- With a resource pool, you create one centralized location with current resource information. This way, the resource pool keeps track of all projects to which individual team members have been assigned and helps minimize resource overallocation.

- One well-maintained resource pool eliminates the need for individual project managers to enter resources in each project file. Instead, project managers can create a link from their project file to the project file that contains the resource pool.

- Project managers and stakeholders can view cost and material resource cumulative data across many projects.

Exam Tip   Technically, it isn't necessary to create a resource pool to share resources. In Project, you can share (or borrow) resources from preexisting project plans. Doing so designates the *sharer project* as the *resource pool*. For the purposes of the exam, you need to know that even though sharer projects such as this are less common because you have a reduced ability in monitoring resource allocation information, it is possible. In these instances the resource allocation information is limited to only the plans that are linked to the preexisting project plan.

Introduction to the Organization Breakdown Structure (OBS)   The organizational breakdown structure (OBS) is a project organization framework for identifying accountability, responsibility, management, and approvals of all authorized work scope. Logically, such a structure falls under the realm of resource management because the OBS represents a different level of responsibility within a project or enterprise. The OBS, although referenced as a domain objective for exam 70-632, usually reflects the management structure of an organization, from top-level personnel down through the various levels constituting your business.

Creating a Resource Pool

Creating a resource pool is really no different from creating a regular project file. In fact, in some ways it is easier because no task information needs to be entered. For a quick start, use the keyboard shortcut combination Ctrl+N to create a new, blank project file. Next, view the Resource Sheet and begin entering your list of available resources.

MORE INFO   Creating a resource pool

You can find more information on creating and working with a resource pool in *Microsoft Office Project 2007 Step by Step* by Carl Chatfield and Timothy Johnson (Microsoft Press, 2007), pp. 404–424.

A completed resource sheet is shown in Figure 4-31.

	Resource Name	Type	Material Label	Initials	Max. Units	Std. Rate	Ovt. Rate	Cost/Use	Accrue At
1	Audit Committee	Work		A	100%	$35.00/hr	$75.00/hr	$0.00	Prorated
2	Legal Department	Work		L	100%	$85.00/hr	$150.00/hr	$0.00	Prorated
3	External Auditors	Work		E	100%	$75.00/hr	$150.00/hr	$0.00	Prorated
4	Executive Committee	Work		E	100%	$35.00/hr	$75.00/hr	$0.00	Prorated
5	CFO/Controller	Work		C	100%	$250,000.00/yr	$0.00/hr	$0.00	Prorated
6	Marketing Group	Work		M	100%	$45.00/hr	$90.00/hr	$0.00	Prorated
7	Strategic Planning Committee	Work		S	100%	$0.00/hr	$0.00/hr	$500.00	Prorated
8	PR/IR Dept	Work		P	100%	$35.00/hr	$75.00/hr	$0.00	Prorated
9	Chairman	Work		C	100%	$350,000.00/yr	$0.00/hr	$0.00	Prorated

Figure 4-31   Resource Sheet view and available resources

To create a resource pool like the one in Figure 4-31, follow these steps:

1. In Project, press Ctrl+N to open a new, blank project file.
2. Choose View and choose Resource Sheet.

3. In row 1, type a resource name, resource type, maximum units (in %), standard rate, overtime rates, cost per use values, and other pertinent data.

4. When finished, choose File, choose Save As, and, in the Save As dialog box, type a file name. (Consider naming the file Resource Pool for easier identification.)

5. Browse to the location to save the file and click Save.

Often, you might already have a list of resources in an existing project file. You can easily copy these resources into the new resource pool file. To copy existing resources, follow these steps:

1. Open the file you want to copy the data from.

2. Choose View and choose Resource Sheet.

3. Drag the mouse over the data to copy, right-click the data, and choose Copy Cell. Alternately, select the data using the Ctrl key or Shift key if all of the data listed is not required.

4. In the new project, right-click in Resource Sheet view and choose Paste.

MORE INFO   Creating resources

Creating resources is covered in depth in Chapter 2, "Project Planning."

Quick Check

- Name two ways to add resources to a resource pool.

Quick Check Answer

- You can create a resource pool from scratch by opening a new, blank project and entering the information into the Resource Sheet view manually. Or you can copy and paste resources from an existing project into the Resource Sheet view.

Sharing a Resource Pool

After you have created your resource pool, you can begin sharing the resources you just entered with other project files. However, in doing so, you are given a whole new set of options. This section will discuss the resource pool/sharer file options first and then move on to the steps involved.

When a resource pool is shared, it is important to remember that other project managers are probably linking to and viewing the same information, sometimes simultaneously. As such, you must open the resource pool file as read-only. Opening the file as read-only allows you to view the information, to allow others access to the same pool, and to have resource assignments recorded against the resources in the resource pool. However, if you need to edit the resource information (such as resource billable rates) stored in the resource pool, you will need to open the file as read-write. Opening the file as read-write allows you to make and save changes to the resource pool, but it does not allow the sharer files to update the resource pool.

MORE INFO   Another way to open a resource pool

Another option for opening a resource pool is to open the resource pool and all sharer files as a new master project file. Master project files are covered more comprehensively later in this chapter.

Another option you will see when linking files and working with both resource pools and sharer files is which file you want to take precedence in case of a scheduling conflict. By default, when Project encounters a conflict between the resource pool and the sharer file, the resource pool takes precedence, effectively overwriting the resource information in the sharer file. This is usually preferable because it is beneficial to the management of multiple projects to have one consistent source of information—the resource pool. However, if you are the only person who manages the projects for a team of resources, you can use the resource pool and have the sharer take precedence. That way, you can make resource changes in any project and have those changes populate the resource pool without having to open the resource pool as read-only.

After a resource pool has been created, you can link that pool to an existing project by following these steps:

1. Open the project that will share resources from the resource pool. This will serve as the sharer project. Note the name of the project.

2. Open the project containing the resources that you want to share. This will serve as the resource pool project. Note the name of the project.

3. Choose Window and choose the project that represents the sharer project. Its name will be in the list. In Figure 3-32 the sharer project has been named Sharer Project. (Alternately, you can use the key combination Alt+Tab to switch between the open projects.)

Figure 4-32   Use the Window menu to switch between two open projects

4. In the sharer project, choose Tools, point to Resource Sharing, and then choose Share Resources.

5. In the Share Resources dialog box, shown in Figure 4-33, select Use Resources, and then, in the From drop-down list, select the resource pool project that you opened in step 2.

Figure 4-33 Configuring resource sharing options

6. For On Conflict With Calendar Or Resource Information, select the project file that takes precedence:

   a. Pool Takes Precedence means that resource information in the resource pool project will override any conflicting information from the sharer project. This is the default setting.

   b. Sharer Takes Precedence means that resource information in the sharer project will override any conflicting information from the resource pool project.

7. Click OK.

The resources are now available to use in the active project. If your sharer project already had resources entered, the resources from both of the projects are combined.

Quick Check

1. What is the difference between sharer and resource pool projects?
2. There are two options in the Conflict With Calendar Or Resource Information section. What are they?

Quick Check Answers

1. The project that will share resources from another project is the sharer project. The project that shares its list of resources is the resource pool project.
2. Pool Takes Precedence and Sharer Takes Precedence.

From the resource pool file, you can view which files are linked to the resource pool by following a familiar path: choose Tools, Resource Sharing, and then Share Resources. In the resource pool file, this command opens the Share Resources dialog box, shown in Figure 4-34.

As you can see, in this dialog box you can modify which file takes precedence for each linked sharer file and open any linked sharer file directly from within the open resource pool. When a shared link is selected, you can also choose to remove the link by clicking the Break Link button. You can also discontinue sharing resources from within the sharer file.

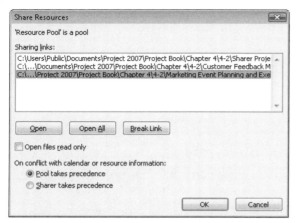

Figure 4-34   Viewing the files linked to the resource pool

To break a link to a resource pool from the resource pool, follow these steps:

1. Open the resource pool file.
2. Choose Tools, choose Resource Sharing, and choose Share Resources.
3. In the Share Resources dialog box, shown earlier in Figure 4-34, select the file to break from.
4. Click Break Link.

To break a link to a resource pool from the sharer file, follow these steps:

1. Open the sharer file.
2. Choose Tools, choose Resource Sharing, and choose Share Resources.
3. In the Share Resources dialog box, shown again in Figure 4-35, under Resources For *<name of project>*, select Use Own Resources.

Figure 4-35   Stop using the resource pool in a sharer file

4. Click OK.

After you have shared (linked) your resource pool, you can assign resources as described in Chapter 2.

> ## Quick Check
> - You have a sharer file and a resource pool file. The sharer file is using resources from the resource pool file. You need to configure the sharer file to use its own resources, not resources from the resource pool. Name two ways to do this.
>
> ## Quick Check Answer
> - From the resource pool file, remove the link by clicking the Break Link button in the Share Resources dialog box. From the sharer file, select Use Own Resources in the Share Resources dialog box.

Assessing Resource Availability

The views for assessing your resource availability when working with a resource pool are the same views you would use when working with resources assigned to an individual project. This is where the various views that present the resource histogram data come into play. These views (which are covered more in-depth in Chapter 2) include the following:

- Resource Graph view
- Resource Sheet view
- Resource Allocation view
- Resource Form view
- Resource Usage view

In fact, you can also use the Resource Management toolbar to view resource overallocations. Overallocated resources are quickly identifiable without filtering because their names are always shown in a red font in the Resource Sheet and Resource Usage views, and these resources have an indicator (shown in the Figure 4-36) in the Indicator field, noting which resources need to be leveled.

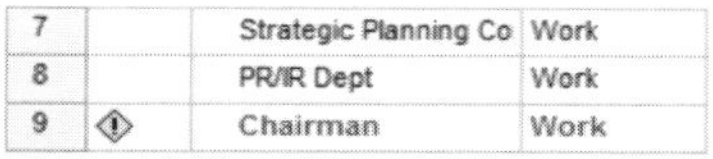

7		Strategic Planning Co	Work
8		PR/IR Dept	Work
9	◈	Chairman	Work

Figure 4-36   Overallocated resources are shown in red with an exclamation point in the Indicators field

Another quick way to view overallocated resources is to use one of Project's predefined filters. For example, you can apply the Overallocated Resources filter to either Resource Sheet view or Resource Usage view to view only those resources that have overallocations. To apply the Overallocated Resources filter, follow these steps:

1. Choose View and choose Resource Sheet (or Resource Usage).
2. On the Formatting toolbar, in the drop-down list for the filter options, shown in Figure 4-37, select Overallocated Resources.

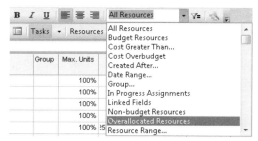

Figure 4-37   Filtering the view by Overallocated resources

3.   To view all resources again, use the drop-down list for the filter options on the Formatting toolbar to select All Resources.

NOTE   **Using task views to display resource overallocation**

Although you can view resource overallocations using a task view, you will not see the same red distinction that you do when using a resource view. From a task view (such as the Gantt Chart), display the Resource Management toolbar to work with resources.

On the flip side, you can also use Project to find resources who have available time or who are underallocated. When you have overallocated resources, looking for underallocated resources is helpful when you want to reassign the extra work to resources with available time. This feature is also useful when you have unassigned tasks and you are looking for someone to do the work. To find underallocated resources, follow these steps:

1.   In any Project file, choose View and choose Resource Usage.

2.   Choose Format, choose Details, and choose Remaining Availability.

3.   In Resource Usage view, in the Rem. Avail. row, review the amount of underallocation. See Figure 4-38.

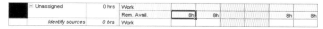

Figure 4-38   Viewing underallocated resources

NOTE   **Use the Resource Graph to show underallocation**

You can also use the Resource Graph to view a bar chart of resource allocation. By reviewing the information one resource at a time, you can quickly see which resources have some time left in their schedule. To do this, from the Resource Graph view, choose Format, Details, and then Work Availability.

If you have applied the formatting details as explained in this lesson, you can revert to the default by altering the settings in the Details option on the Format menu.

Quick Check

- Name as many views as you can for assessing your resource availability when working with a resource pool. There are five. Next, name two that you could use to filter overallocated or underallocated resources.

Quick Check Answers

1. Resource Graph view
2. Resource Sheet view
3. Resource Allocation view
4. Resource Form view
5. Resource Usage view

   Resource Sheet view or Resource Usage view can show overallocated and underallocated resources.

Leveling Resources

When one or more resources are overallocated (whether they are contained within a resource pool or not), you will need to do some fancy project management maneuvering to bring everyone's working hours back in line. Project can level your resources for you by using the resource-leveling feature.

The leveling feature in Project uses techniques such as splitting tasks or adding delay so that your work, generic, or committed resources that were once overallocated are no longer overscheduled. However, because tasks can be delayed or split through the use of leveling, doing so might affect your project's finish date.

NOTE **Leveling work resources**

Project levels only work, generic, and committed resources. This process does not level material, cost, and proposed resources in your project file.

Pre-leveling Tasks

Before you level your project file, it is a good idea to set your task priorities. Chapter 1, "Project Initiation," discussed setting a project's priorities using the 0 to 1000 scale. Overall, when a project's resources are leveled to address overallocation, Project will consider project-level priorities set in the Project Information dialog box over task-level priorities set in the Task Information dialog box when you level resources over several projects.

For example, if you don't want Project to level a specific task, you will want to set that task's priority level to 1000. To modify a task's priority level, follow these steps:

1. Double-click the task you want to modify to open the Task Information dialog box.
2. In the Task Information dialog box, shown in Figure 4-39, set the Priority field to 1000.

Figure 4-39 Changing a task's priority to 1000 to keep it from being leveled

Exam Tip You might see questions related to priority levels and how scheduling of a specific task with a specific priority level might be affected. Be sure you understand task and project priority levels and which takes precedence.

Working with a Resource Pool

When you are working exclusively with a resource pool and you don't want to level the tasks in a sharer file, you will want to set the sharer file's project priority level to 1000. This way, you are defining the priority level for the entire project within the scope of the shared resource pool. For example, if several projects share resources in a resource pool and one project is so important that you do not want its tasks leveled, set that sharer file's priority level to 1000. To modify a project's priority level, follow these steps:

1. Choose Project and choose Project Information.
2. In the Project Information dialog box, shown in Figure 4-40, change the Priority field to 1000.

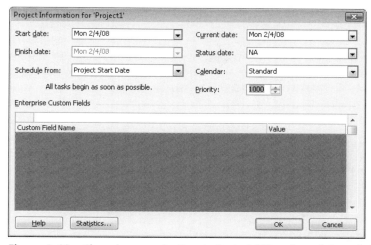

Figure 4-40   Changing a project's priority to 1000 to keep it from being leveled

---

Quick Check

■ How should you configure important tasks (tasks that should take precedence over all others) before you perform resource leveling in your project? Where do you perform this configuration change?

Quick Check Answer

■ Set the tasks' priority to 1000 in the Task Information dialog box.

Performing the Leveling

After your task and project priority levels have been set, you are ready to use Project's resource leveling tool. To level your overallocated resources, follow these steps:

1. On the Tools menu, choose Level Resources.
2. In the Resource Leveling dialog box, shown in Figure 4-41, under Leveling calculations, there are two choices: Automatic and Manual. For this lesson we'll choose Automatic. (If you choose Manual, the dialog box will close and manual leveling will be applied as the desired leveling method.)
    a. Manual leveling occurs only when you click Level Now.
    b. Automatic leveling occurs immediately each time you change a task or resource.

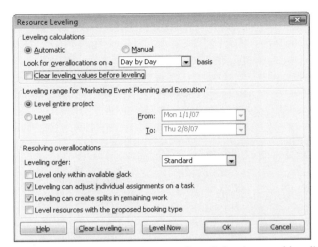

Figure 4-41   The Resource Leveling dialog box and leveling options

---

NOTE   Leveling options

Use automatic leveling when you want to reschedule tasks every time resources have been assigned to work more time than they have available.

---

3. In the Look For Overallocations On A ___ Basis drop-down list, select the desired option. Day By Day is the default.

4. Clear the Clear Leveling Values Before Leveling check box.

MORE INFO   Leveling Options

By clearing the Clear Leveling Values Before Leveling check box, you tell Project to level only the new and unleveled assignments. Leaving this box selected can appreciably slow down your work in the schedule because all tasks are leveled instead of only the ones that actually need leveling.

---

5. Under Leveling Range For, select Level Entire Project or Level. When you choose Level, you set the From and To dates for leveling.

6. In the Leveling Order drop-down list, select the leveling order that you want:

   a. ID Only will level tasks in ascending order based on their *ID numbers (ID number: The number that Project assigns to each task, resource, or assignment as you add them to the project.).*

   b. Standard will look at *predecessor (predecessor: A task that must start or finish before another task can start or finish.)* dependencies, *slack (slack: The amount of time that a task can slip before it affects another task or the project's finish date. Free slack is how much a task can slip before it delays another task. Total slack is how much a task can slip before it delays the project.*), dates, priorities, and constraints (*constraint: A restriction set on the start or finish date of a task. You can specify that a task must start on or finish no later than a particular date. Constraints can be flexible [not tied to a specific date] or inflexible [tied to a specific date].*) to discover whether and how tasks should be leveled. (This is the default.)

    c. Priority, Standard will check task priorities first and only then apply the Standard setting.

7. Under Leveling Order there are four check boxes (select all that apply):

    a. Select the Level Only Within Available Slack check box if you want to prevent the finish date of your project from being delayed due to automatic leveling actions.

MORE INFO **Leveling within available slack**

If you select Level Only Within Available Slack, expect to get error messages stating that Project is unable to level the entire schedule. This happens often because there is generally not enough slack available to reschedule assignments without running out of slack time.

---

    b. Select the Leveling Can Adjust Individual Assignments On A Task check box if you want to let automatic leveling adjust when a resource works on a task independently of other resources that are working on the same task.

    c. Select the Leveling Can Create Splits In Remaining Work check box if you agree to let Project create splits in remaining work.

    d. Select the Level Resources With Proposed Booking Type check box if you want proposed resources to be taken into consideration when leveling.

NOTE **Select the appropriate leveling option**

If you do not select the Leveling Can Create Splits In Remaining Work check box, tasks might be delayed for long periods of time before the assigned resources are available.

---

8. Click Level Now to perform leveling.

9. To clear leveling, before performing any other leveling, open the Resource Leveling dialog box again and click Clear Leveling to clear the results.

10. Click OK.

Exam Tip   You might not see questions related to how to level resources, but you will likely see questions on what happens to the data after leveling it.

Quick Check

■ You want Project to perform automatic leveling. Which option should you clear to level only new and unleveled assignments versus all the assignments in the project?

Quick Check Answer

■ Clear the Clear Leveling Values Before Leveling check box.

Assignment Contouring

Presenting a slightly different option for rescheduling your resources from leveling is assignment contouring. *Assignment contouring* is a method by which you can adjust the number of hours in a day that a resource is assigned to work. Essentially, with assignment contouring, you have more flexibility in scheduling your resources on overlapping tasks without running the risk of entering into an overallocation situation.

The types of contouring available within Project are listed in Table 4-3.

Table 4-3   Available Assignment Contours

Contour	Description
Flat	The default scheduling contour and the setting that evenly allocates the number of work hours across a set duration.
Back Loaded	Assigns more hours to each day from the start to the finish of a task.
Front Loaded	Assigns fewer hours to each day from the start to the finish of a task.
Double Peak	Increases the hours scheduled per day from the start to the end of the task, excluding the first day the task is scheduled. Includes a peak near the beginning and the end of the task.
Early Peak	Increases the hours scheduled per day from the start to the end of the task, excluding the first day the task is scheduled. Includes a peak near the beginning of the task and then decreases the hours scheduled per day until the end of the task.
Late Peak	Increases the hours scheduled per day from the finish to the start of the task, excluding the last day the task is scheduled.
Bell	Often causing a task's duration to double, this contour schedules work to peak in the middle.
Turtle	Working just like the Bell contour, this contour schedules work to peak in the middle. However, more full-time work days are scheduled to minimize the impact on the schedule duration.

You manage assignment contours in the Assignment Information dialog box, shown in Figure 4-42, which you can access from either Task Usage or Resource Usage view.

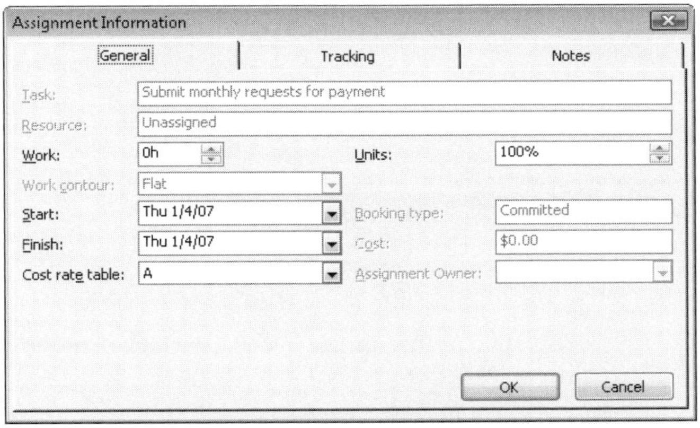

Figure 4-42   The Assignment Information dialog box

Exam Tip   You might see one or two questions on the exam related to contour leveling types. The questions might ask what type to use in a specific circumstance, such as "Which contour should you select if you want to increase the hours scheduled per day from the start to the end of the task to make sure you meet the project's deadlines?" In this example you would choose "Front Loaded."

NOTE **Opening the Assigning Information dialog box**

To open the Assignment Information dialog box from either the Task Usage or Resource Usage view, you must double-click a resource that has an assignment. If you double-click a resource that does not have an assignment, you will open the Task Information dialog box. To see which resources have assignments, add the Assignment column to the view.

To view the Assignment Information dialog box, follow these steps:

1. Choose View and choose either Task Usage or Resource Usage.
2. Double-click an assignment row to view the Assignment Information dialog box. In the Task Usage view, assignments appear in additional rows below each task. In the Resource Usage view, resource assignments appear below each resource. Figure 4-43 shows an example of an assignment row in Task Usage view. Note also that the Assignment column has been added next to the Task Name column.

	❶	Task Name	Assignment	Work	Duration	Start	Finish
0	📝	− Annual Report Prep:	No	628 hrs	2.5 days?	Mon 1/1/07	Wed 2/28/07
1		− Perform Initial Plann	No	48 hrs	6 days?	Mon 1/1/07	Mon 1/8/07
2		− Review project file/	No	8 hrs	1 day?	Mon 1/1/07	Mon 1/1/07
		Strategic Plar.	Yes	8 hrs		Mon 1/1/07	Mon 1/1/07
3		− Confirm changes, if	No	8 hrs	1 day?	Tue 1/2/07	Tue 1/2/07
		CFO/Controlk	Yes	8 hrs		Tue 1/2/07	Tue 1/2/07
4	📝	+ Identify Annual Rep	No	8 hrs	1 day?	Wed 1/3/07	Wed 1/3/07
5		− Confirm other secti(	No	8 hrs	1 day?	Thu 1/4/07	Thu 1/4/07
		Strategic Plar.	Yes	8 hrs		Thu 1/4/07	Thu 1/4/07
6		− Confirm SEC filing a	No	8 hrs	1 day?	Fri 1/5/07	Fri 1/5/07
		CFO/Controlk	Yes	8 hrs		Fri 1/5/07	Fri 1/5/07
7		− Selection of Interna	No	8 hrs	1 day?	Mon 1/8/07	Mon 1/8/07
		Audit Commit	Yes	8 hrs		Mon 1/8/07	Mon 1/8/07

Figure 4-43 An assignment row is shown below a task in Task Usage view.

3. In the General tab, select the desired setting in the Work Contour drop-down list. See Figure 4-44.

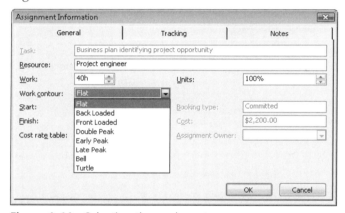

Figure 4-44 Selecting the work contour

4. Click OK.

PRACTICE Resource Pools, Resource Leveling, and Assignment Contouring

In these practices you will review what you've learned in this lesson. The first exercise is to create and share a resource pool. The second exercise is to link a resource pool to an existing project. The third exercise is to break a link with a resource pool. The fourth exercise is to level resources manually and automatically. The fifth exercise is to apply assignment contouring.

NOTE Perform exercises in order

You must perform these exercises in order because each exercise builds on the previous one.

▶ **Exercise 1   Create and Share a Resource Pool**

Several projects in your company use the same resources. You want to make sure everyone draws resources from the same pool to avoid resource conflicts among projects and project managers. You want to create a resource pool, and you'll start by copying resources from another project. After the resource pool is created, you want to share it.

To complete this exercise, follow these steps:

1. In Project, press Ctrl+N to open a new, blank project file.
2. Choose View and choose Resource Sheet.
3. Choose File, choose New, and, in the New Project pane, click On Computer.
4. In the Templates dialog box, in the Project Templates tab, select the Customer Feedback Monitoring template.
5. Click OK.
6. In the Customer Feedback Monitoring project, choose View and choose Resource Sheet.
7. Drag the mouse over the rows and columns for resource IDs 1 through 4. With all of the data selected, right-click and choose Copy Resource.
8. Minimize the Customer Feedback Monitoring file and maximize the new project file you created in steps 1 and 2.
9. Right-click inside the Resource Sheet and choose Paste. All the resources you copied will be pasted to the new file.
10. Choose File and choose Save As. Name the file **RESOURCE POOL** and click Save.
11. Leave the RESOURCE POOL file open to complete the remaining exercises in this lesson.
12. Close and do not save changes to the Customer Feedback Monitoring project.

▶ **Exercise 2   Link to a Resource Pool and Create a Task to Use a Resource Pool Resource**

You want to link the resource pool you created in Exercise 1 to a new project and then create a task that uses a resource from the pool. To complete this exercise, follow these steps:

1. Open a new, blank project by choosing File, then New, and then clicking Blank Project.
2. Choose File and Save As and name the file **Sharer**.
    (The Resource Pool file should still be open.)
3. Choose Tools, point to Resource Sharing, and then choose Share Resources.
4. In the Share Resources dialog box, select Use Resources, and then, in the From drop-down list, select RESOURCE POOL.
5. Under On Conflict With Calendar Or Resource Information, select Pool Takes Precedence.
6. Click OK.
7. Under Task Name, in the first available cell, type Review Contract.
8. Double-click the task to open the Task Information dialog box.
9. Click the Resources tab.

10. Click inside the first cell under Resource Name, and from the drop-down list, choose Customer Service Manager.
11. Click the Units field, and from the drop-down list, choose 100%.
12. Click OK.
13. Leave all files open and save them.

▶ **Exercise 3   Break a Link with a Resource Pool**

To break a link to a resource pool from the resource pool, follow these steps:

1. In the RESOURCE POOL file, choose Tools, choose Resource Sharing, and choose Share Resources.
2. In the Share Resources dialog box, select the Sharer file.
3. Click Break Link.
4. Close all files without saving changes.

▶ **Exercise 4   Level Resources Manually and Automatically**

You've made changes to your project and have noticed that many of your resources are now overallocated. As a result, you will need to level your project resources. Then you want to configure Project to level resources automatically in the future. To complete this exercise, follow these steps:

1. Open the Sample Office Move file.
2. View the Gantt chart to see that the current project duration is 169 days in duration.
3. View the Resource Sheet. Note the overallocated resources.
4. Select the Movers resource. You are going to use Project to level this resource manually.
5. Open the Tools menu and choose Level Resources.
6. In the Resource Leveling dialog box, select Manual.
7. Under Leveling Range, select Level Entire Project.
8. Click Level Now.
9. In the Level Now dialog box, choose Selected Resources, and then click OK.
10. View the Gantt chart to see that the current project duration has been extended to 169.5 days. By extending the project an extra four hours, the Movers resource is no longer overallocated.
11. Choose the Tools menu and choose Level Resources.
12. In the Resource Leveling dialog box, select Automatic.
13. Under Leveling Range For, select Level.
14. In the From box, enter **01/01/09**.
15. In the To box, enter **04/20/09**.
16. In the Leveling Order drop-down list, select Standard. Selecting Standard tells Project to first examine *predecessor (predecessor: A task that must start or finish before another task can*

start or finish.) dependencies, *slack (slack: The amount of time that a task can slip before it affects another task or the project's finish date. Free slack is how much a task can slip before it delays another task. Total slack is how much a task can slip before it delays the project.*), dates, priorities, and constraints (*constraint: A restriction set on the start or finish date of a task. You can specify that a task must start on or finish no later than a particular date. Constraints can be flexible [not tied to a specific date] or inflexible [tied to a specific date].*) to decide whether and how tasks should be leveled. (This is the default setting.)

17. Under Leveling Order, there are four choices:

    a. Level Only Within Available Slack

    b. Leveling Can Adjust Individual Assignments On A Task

    c. Leveling Can Create Splits In Remaining Work

    d. Level Resources With The Proposed Booking Type

    e. Select the check boxes for Leveling Can Adjust Individual Assignments On A Task and Leveling Can Create Splits In Remaining Work. If necessary, clear the remaining check boxes.

18. Click Level Now to perform leveling.

19. In the Level Now dialog box, verify that Entire Pool is selected and click OK. At this point, only two resources are still overallocated: the Office Manager and the Network Support Manager.

20. Leave the Sample Office Move project file open to complete Exercise 5.

▶ **Exercise 5   Apply Assignment Contouring**

You need to deal with what you think will soon become overallocated resources and have decided to apply assignment contouring. Specifically, you want to increase the hours scheduled per day so that a peak occurs near the beginning and near the end of the project. To complete this exercise, follow these steps:

1. Using the Sample Office Move file from the previous exercise, choose View and choose Resource Usage.

MORE INFO   Bold vs. italic

Assignments appear in italics, and tasks and resources appear in regular bold font.

---

2. Locate the Office Manager. This resource is displayed in red because this resource is still overallocated.

3. Using the Resource Management toolbar, click the Go To Next Overallocation button to highlight the first occurrence at which the Office Manager has been overscheduled. (You might find that you need to scroll the calendar to the right in order to find the first occurrence where the Office Manager is overallocated.)

4. In reviewing the Office Manager's assignments, you can see that on June 1, 2009, this resource is assigned to work 16 hours. You can modify these hours by using work contouring. Double-click the Obtain Estimates From Signage Companies task that has been assigned to the Office Manager.

5. In the Work Contour drop-down list, select Late Peak.

6. Click OK.

7. The Office Manager's working hours have now been reduced to 12 hours for this overallocated day. Double-click the Assign Office Space task that has been assigned to the Office Manager.

8. In the Work Contour drop-down list, select Bell.

9. Click OK. This resolves the overallocation on June 1, 2009. However, additional overallocations were created later in that same week. At this point, you could consider creating a split task, assigning additional resources to the affected task, extending the task's duration, or asking the Office Manager to work overtime.

10. Close the Sample Office Move project without saving your changes.

Lesson Review

You can use the following questions to test your knowledge of the information in Lesson 2, "Manage Multiple Resources over Multiple Projects." The questions are also available on the companion CD if you prefer to review them in electronic form.

NOTE   Answers

Answers to these questions and explanations of why each answer choice is correct or incorrect are located in the "Answers" section at the end of the book.

---

1. Which of the following are reasons for creating a resource pool? (Choose all that apply.)
   A. To create a centralized location with current resource information that all project managers can access and use
   B. To allow project managers to claim their resources so that no one else can use them at the time they need them
   C. So that project managers and stakeholders can view cost and material resource data whenever they want
   D. To help minimize resource overallocation

2. When creating a resource pool, where must you input resource data?
   A. Summary table
   B. Gantt Chart view
   C. Project Information dialog box
   D. The resource pool file

3. You want to create a logical framework for identification of accountability, responsibility, management, and approvals of all authorized work scope. What do you need to create?

    A. A work breakdown structure

    B. A summary task

    C. An organization breakdown structure

    D. An enterprise resource list

4. When Project automatically levels resources, you want to be sure that any conflicts that arise between the sharer file and the resource pool are always resolved in the same way. Specifically, you want the resource pool to always win any conflict. What setting do you need to enable to configure this?

    A. Sharer Takes Precedence

    B. Use Resources

    C. Priority, Standard

    D. Pool Takes Precedence

5. You do not want Project to automatically level resources. You want to perform any leveling manually. You've configured this in the Resource Leveling dialog box. How do you now manually level resources each time you need to? (Choose all that apply.)

    A. Click the Level Now button on the Standard toolbar.

    B. Choose Project and choose Level Now.

    C. Click Level Now in the Resource Leveling dialog box.

    D. Choose Tools, Level Resources, and Level Now.

6. You want to apply assignment contouring to tasks in your project. Which contouring method increases the hours scheduled per day from the finish to the start of the task?

    A. Back loaded

    B. Front loaded

    C. Early peak

    D. Turtle

7. You need to know what resources aren't being used to their potential. How can you find out which resources are underallocated? (Choose two. Each represents part of the answer.)

    A. Choose Format, choose Details, and choose Remaining Availability.

    B. View the project's Resource Usage view.

    C. Choose Project, choose Filter, and in the More Filters dialog box, select Underallocation.

    D. Note the amount of underallocation in the Rem. Avail. row.

Lesson 3: Manage Multiple Projects

As you have seen, importing and exporting are handy features when working with people who do not have access to (or who do not understand) Project. These methods enable you to share data between the project file and other, easily accessible file types, such as Excel, Word, Outlook, and Access. Sharing data is extremely important in keeping team members and project stakeholders apprised of project status and variables. Another way of keeping team members apprised is by assigning someone to manage specific phases of a project. Using Project, team members can each track an assigned project phase. Doing so enables the project manager (and other involved management personnel) to create a master project that updates when the smaller project phases are updated. For business continuity and ease of use, you can also create custom project templates for use on future projects. You already know that Project comes loaded with several predefined templates. However, you can create your own templates for your use or to share with others.

This lesson discusses working with master projects and cross-project links, as well as creating and modifying custom project templates.

After this lesson, you will be able to:
- Create a master project.
- Create cross-project links.
- Create and modify Project templates.

Estimated lesson time: 45 minutes

Creating a Master Project

Soon after you begin managing your first project, you learn that project management can be challenging. Even more of a challenge is managing one very large project or lots of smaller projects. Implementing master projects in Project can ease some of the burden.

Master projects are individual project files that contain other separate inserted project files. These inserted project files are called *subprojects*. This means that you can use one master project to view several small subprojects all on one screen. Each of the subprojects can be managed separately, either by you or by another project manager.

What's more, when subprojects are grouped into one master project, your filters, views, and reports will reflect the data from all projects combined. This allows you to see the "big picture" of your project management responsibilities in one place.

Create a Master Project

Creating a master project is not too difficult. To create a master project, follow these steps:

1. Open the project that you want to become a master project.
2. Choose View and choose Gantt Chart.
3. In the Task Name field, click the row below where you want to insert the project. You can insert a project anywhere in the outline.
4. Choose Insert and choose Project.
5. In the Insert Project dialog box, browse to the project to insert, select it, and click Insert.
6. There are additional options when inserting projects:
   - ❏ To insert multiple projects, hold down Ctrl and click the projects in the order that you want to insert them.
   - ❏ To insert a project and to make the inserted project read-only, click the down arrow on the Insert button, and then choose Insert Read-Only. See Figure 4-45.
   - ❏ If you do not want the subproject to be automatically updated with changes from the original project or if you don't want to show changes from the subproject in the original project, clear the Link To Project check box. See Figure 4-45.

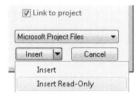

Figure 4-45   Insert a file as read-only or linked, or both

Add the Project Field

After you combine multiple projects into one master project plan file, you will quickly see how easily you can use the project filters, groups, and views with which you are already accustomed to working with in this "larger" project plan file. However, you can sometimes get "lost" trying to figure out which tasks belong to which inserted project. One way around this is to add the Project field as a column in your table. In Figure 4-46, you can see that the Project field has been inserted just before the Task Name field in the Entry table.

	Project	Task Name
0	**Annual Report Preparation**	⁻ **Annual Report Preparation**
1	**Annual Report Preparation**	⁻ **Customer Feedback Monitoring**
1	**Customer Feedback Monitoring**	⁻ **Develop Customer Feedback Collection**
2	**Customer Feedback Monitoring**	+ **Define sources of customer feedbac**
6	Customer Feedback Monitoring	Determine Data Collection Methods
7	**Customer Feedback Monitoring**	+ **Determine Data Analysis Methods**
12	Customer Feedback Monitoring	Design of Feedback Collection and Analys
13	**Customer Feedback Monitoring**	+ **Design Customer Issue Response Pı**
20	**Customer Feedback Monitoring**	+ **Design Customer Feedback Monitoring**
2	**Annual Report Preparation**	+ **Marketing Event Planning and Execuı**
3	**Annual Report Preparation**	+ **Perform Initial Planning**
12	**Annual Report Preparation**	⁻ **Design Annual Report**
13	**Annual Report Preparation**	⁻ **04-SampleFile**
1	**04-SampleFile**	+ **Planning and Control**
14	**Annual Report Preparation**	+ **Sharer Project**
15	Annual Report Preparation	Assign resources to preliminary design
16	Annual Report Preparation	Develop preliminary design and information re
17	**Annual Report Preparation**	+ **Evaluate/Confirm Report Distribution Me**
22	Annual Report Preparation	Plan/confirm production schedule
23	Annual Report Preparation	Annual Report Design Complete

Figure 4-46   Viewing projects for tasks using the Project column

To insert the Project field into any table, follow these steps:

1. In the master project, select the Task Name column by right-clicking the header for the column. (Alternatively, you can right-click on any column to insert the Project field to the left of that column.)

2. Choose Insert Column.

3. In the Column Definition dialog box, in the Field Name drop-down list, select Project.

4. Select how you would like to align the data. The defaults are shown in Figure 4-47. The column will appear to the left of the Task Name column (or whatever column you selected in step 1).

Figure 4-47   Add the Project column to show what projects are assigned to what tasks

5. Click OK.

Access Project Information

Even after a subproject has been added to a master project plan file, the subproject file can be individually updated by either you or someone else with access to the subproject file. As long as the subproject is continually saved in the original save location, the link between the subproject and the master project will remain in effect. With this link, any changes made to and saved within the subproject will be readily apparent in the master project file. Similarly, changes made to a subproject from within the master project file will be reflected in the subproject when it is opened individually. In fact, from within the master project plan file, you can access the Inserted Project Information dialog box for the subproject by following these steps:

1. Double-click the Task Name field for the subproject.
2. In the Inserted Project Information dialog box, shown in Figure 4-48, click the Advanced tab.

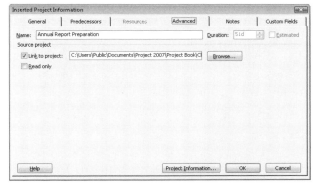

Figure 4-48   Accessing project information for the subproject

3. To view the project information, click Project Information.

Remove a Subproject Link

Interestingly enough, the Inserted Project Information dialog box is also the place you would go to remove a link between a subproject and a master project. When you remove a link to a subproject from a master project using the Inserted Project Information dialog box (otherwise known as the Task Information dialog box), the subproject information remains in the master project file—only the link between the two files is removed. To remove this link, follow these steps:

1. Double-click the Task Name field for the subproject.
2. In the Inserted Project Information dialog box, shown in Figure 4-48, click the Advanced tab.
3. Clear the Link To Project check box, shown in Figure 4-49.
4. Click OK.
5. If prompted to save either file, click Yes.

Figure 4-49   Remove the link to a project

MORE INFO   **Master project plans**

Master project plans are also known as consolidated projects. Also, subprojects are also known as inserted projects. For more information on working with master projects (consolidated projects), type **Create Master Project** in the Ask A Question For Help box located in the upper-right corner of your Project window.

Remove a Subproject

To remove a subproject and its tasks from a master project plan, all you need to do is delete the subproject's summary task by following these steps:

1. Open the master project that contains the subproject to delete.
2. Right-click the subproject to delete.
3. From the shortcut menu, choose Delete Task. See Figure 4-50.

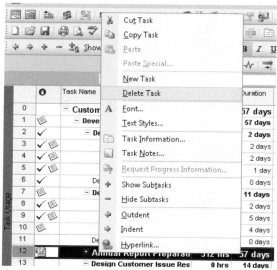

Figure 4-50   Deleting a subproject

4. When prompted, as shown in Figure 4-50, select Continue.

5. Click OK.

6. If prompted to save the file, click Yes.

Master Projects and Resource Pools

Subprojects that contain a link to a resource pool work fine within a master project plan file. However, the first time you expand the inserted project's tasks (by clicking the plus sign [+] displayed to the left of the inserted project's task name in the master project file), you might be presented with a choice. See Figure 4-51.

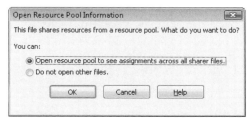

Figure 4-51 Opening sharer files

In the Open Resource Pool Information dialog box, you can choose to open the linked resource pool so that you can view the assignments that have been made across all of the sharer files or select the option to not open any other files. Either way, you will still be able to review the task information for the subproject.

Quick Check

For each of the following statements, decide whether it is true or false:

1. Master projects contain inserted project files.
2. The projects inserted into a master project are called subprojects.
3. You can keep any inserted project from being updated by clearing the Link To Project check box.
4. Removing a link to a subproject and removing the subproject by deleting its associated summary task are the same thing.

Quick Check Answers

1. True.
2. True.
3. True.
4. False. Removing a link leaves the subproject in the master project but does not allow it to be updated when the master project is. Deleting the subproject removes it completely.

Creating Cross-Project Links

At first, you might wonder why you would ever need to create a cross-project link. After all, with resource pools and master projects, this topic seems to be fairly well covered. However, there is another option for creating relationships between the data contained in two or more project files and, in particular, their tasks. That is where cross-project linking comes in. Cross-project links are useful when two or more projects have only a few tasks that affect one another. For example, a milestone within a development project might trigger a task in an advertising campaign project.

Typically, when you create a cross-project link, you are linking between a primary (or source) project task and a secondary (or destination) project task. With this technique, when the information is changed in the primary (or source) project file, the information in the secondary (or destination) project will automatically update as well.

Create a Cross-Project Link

It is a simple matter of using the Copy and Paste Special commands to create a cross-project link. To create a cross-project link between two tasks, follow these steps:

1. Open the project containing the source information you want to link. Select the data by dragging the mouse or using the Ctrl or Shift keys.
2. Right-click the selected information and choose Copy Task (or Copy Cell).
3. Open the project where you will paste the information.
4. In the newly opened project (step 3), from the View menu, choose the task view in which you want to paste the information.
5. Right-click the task that should be positioned below the tasks you want to paste. Select New Task to insert a blank task. You must insert a blank task because the Paste Special overwrites the row you select.
6. Select the row where you want to paste the information by dragging the mouse over the view.
7. Right-click the area and choose Paste Special.
8. In the Paste Special dialog box, select Paste Link. See Figure 4-52.
9. Click OK.

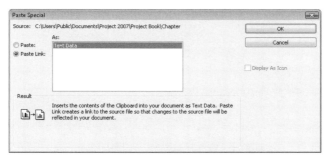

Figure 4-52 Paste the selected text data as a link

Create a Cross-Project Link for Task Dependencies

When you use the method described above, you create a cross-project link that allows multiple files to update with just one change to the source. Another method of cross-project linking is associated with task dependencies. For example, you might create a cross-project link using task dependencies when the start or finish of a task in your current project depends on the start or finish of a task being tracked in a separate project file.

MORE INFO **Task dependencies**

Task dependencies are covered in detail in Chapter 2.

In this instance it is the dependency that you are focusing on, not the text of the task. Creating a cross-project link of this type often requires the addition of a ghost task to your project plan file. A *ghost task* acts as a placeholder in your project plan file and links to tasks outside the project in which it is held.

Exam Tip Make sure you know what cross-project linked tasks look like because you will likely be given a question that involves a graphic with cross-linked projects.

To create a cross-project link associated with task dependencies, follow these steps:

1. Open the master file that contains the cross-project links. If prompted, select Open Resource Pool To See Assignments Across All Sharer Files.
2. Open the second project file that contains the tasks you want to link. Note that both projects must be open to link tasks between them.
3. Choose Window and choose Arrange All. You should now be able to see both projects. See Figure 4-53.

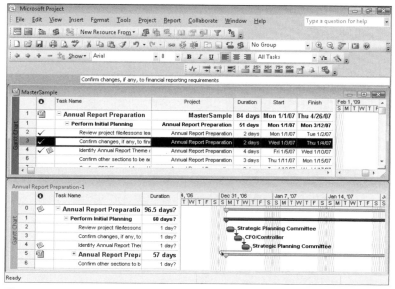

Figure 4-53 Arrange the two open projects

4. Double-click the task that will act as the external task or external predecessor.

5. In the Task Information dialog box, click the Predecessors tab.

6. In the ID column, type the name of the master project followed by the Task ID number of the external predecessor followed by a backslash.

7. Click OK (see Figure 4-54).

2	✓	Review project file/lessons learned from last	2 days	Mon 1/1/07	Tue 1/2/07	
3	✓	Confirm changes, if any, to financial reporting	2 days	Wed 1/3/07	Thu 1/4/07	2
4	✓	Identify Annual Report Theme and Section Re	4 days	Fri 1/5/07	Wed 1/10/07	3
5	✓	Determine appropriate data analysis method	1 day	Wed 1/3/07	Wed 1/3/07	
6		Confirm other sections to be added or remove	3 days	Thu 1/11/07	Mon 1/15/07	4,C:\Users\Public
7		Confirm SEC filing and Annual Report Checkpo	2 days	Tue 1/16/07	Wed 1/17/07	6
8		Selection of Internal Auditors	5 days	Thu 1/18/07	Wed 1/24/07	7

Figure 4-54 Linked tasks are dimmed in the task list

8. Click OK.

MORE INFO Creating cross-project links

For more information on creating cross-project links, see *Microsoft Office Project 2007 Step by Step*, pp. 429-432.

When files are linked with external task dependencies, each time an update is made and the linked file is reopened, you will be prompted to update the cross-project links with a dialog box similar to that shown in Figure 4-55.

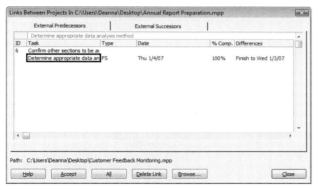

Figure 4-55   Update linked data

When you see this dialog box, you will need to select any listed updates on both the External Predecessors tab and the External Successors tab by selecting the updates and clicking either the Accept or Delete Link button, depending on your current project management needs. When you are finished, you can click the Close button to close the Links Between Projects In *<file name>* dialog box.

If this dialog box becomes bothersome or you would simply prefer to not see it, you can suppress its view in the Project Options dialog box. The Options dialog box, with the View tab selected, is shown in Figure 4-56.

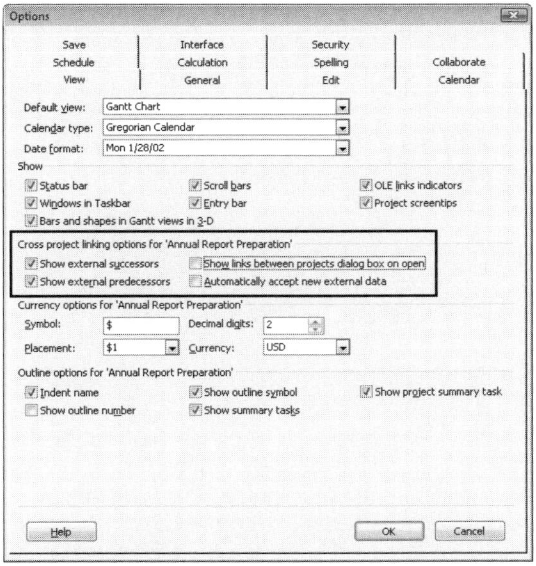

Figure 4-56   Clearing the Show Links Between Projects Dialog Box On Open option

When you are using the Options dialog box, you can choose to display external successors and predecessors related to cross-project links, display the Links dialog box, or automatically accept all external links without a prompt.

> ## Quick Check
> - When is it a good idea to use cross-project links? What do cross-project links do or achieve for you and your project?
>
> ## Quick Check Answer
> - If your project has a specific task that depends on another specific task in a separate project, you can apply cross-project links to tie the tasks to each other. What this offers you is information. For instance, if a task in another project that your task depends on runs late, your own project's task will reflect the change.

Creating New Project Templates

The more projects you manage, the more steps you might find yourself repeating. For instance, you might create the same filter for displaying in-progress tasks or create the same custom table. In these cases you can create a custom project template—much like the predefined templates that are available in Project.

Creating custom templates can save you a lot of time during the project planning phase and, when sharing with coworkers and other project managers, can help to ensure consistency across company-wide projects.

A template is a project file that has already been created and that contains existing project information that you can use to help you start a project more quickly. Each template can contain tasks, milestones, task durations, and task dependencies, among other things, such as custom project items and resources.

Project template files are saved with an .mpt file extension and typically are saved in the Microsoft Office Templates folder. By saving your templates in this location, they will be easily accessible when you choose to view new templates located on your computer.

NOTE Custom templates vs. Global.mpt

The custom templates you create should not be confused with Project's Global.mpt file. The Global.mpt file is a general project template that contains default settings that all new blank projects are based on. You can save custom filters, tables, and other project elements to the Globat.mpt file through the Organizer. Doing so makes these custom elements available when you create a new, blank project. Custom templates, on the other hand, although they can contain all of these custom elements, often also contain task and resource data.

Before saving a project plan file as a template, you should remove any confidential or identifying data from the template file that you might not want distributed if you were to share your template with other project managers. Some key places to review within your project file before saving it include the following:

- **Task and Resource Notes**   Are there any notes you have added that will not apply to future projects?
- **Constraints**   Set everything back to the most flexible scheduling constraints—as soon as possible or as late as possible—to remove project-specific dates.
- **Resource Sheet**   Do you want to keep billing rate information with the template? When you choose to save a file as a template, you will be given the option to remove confidential cost data for resources.

After the confidential or proprietary data has been removed from the project file, you are ready to save it as a template. You can save any project file as a template. To save a project file as a template, follow these steps:

1. Open the project file you want to use as a template.
2. Choose File and choose Save As.
3. In the Save As Type drop-down list, select Template.
4. Browse to a location to save the file.
5. In the File Name text box, type a name for the file, and then click Save.
6. In the Save As Template dialog box, shown in Figure 4-57, select the check boxes for items you do not want to be saved as part of the template.

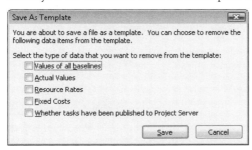

Figure 4-57   Select the check boxes for the items you do not want to save to the template

7. Click Save.

After your template has been saved, open the New Templates dialog box to verify that the custom template you just created is listed (or to begin a new project based on the template you created). To open the Templates dialog box, choose File, New, and click On Computer. See Figure 4-58.

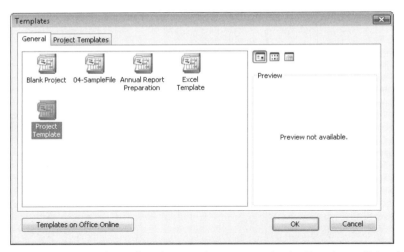

Figure 4-58   Verifying that the template appears in the Templates dialog box

Modifying an Existing Project Template

Opening any template from New Templates dialog box (by choosing New: File: On Computer) creates a new project file based on the template, but does not open the original template file. This is a huge safety net and, in general, one of the biggest benefits in working with templates. Because a new project file based on the template is created, you significantly lessen the risk of overwriting the original file.

When you do want to make changes to the original file, you will need to either directly open the template file using the Open command or open a copy of the template using the New command and overwriting it using Save As.

To open a template file for modification, follow these steps:

1. Choose File and choose Open.
2. In the Open dialog box, browse to the *<the hard disk drive letter>*:\Program Files> Microsoft Office\Templates\1033 folder.
3. In the templates list, select the template you want to open. See Figure 4-59.
4. Click Open to open the template in Project.

NOTE Tips for using Windows Vista

In Windows Vista, you can locate the Templates folder by clicking Start, and in the Start Search window, typing **1033**.

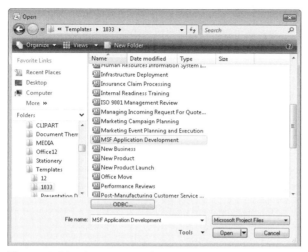

Figure 4-59   Open a template

To overwrite an existing template file, follow these steps:

1. With the template open, make the desired changes.
2. Choose File and Save As, and then choose Template.
3. Choose the same file name and click Save to overwrite the existing file.

Exam Tip   Make sure you know the difference between copying, modifying, and creating a template from scratch, including what file type you use to save it.

PRACTICE **Master Projects, Subprojects, Cross-Linked Projects, and Templates**

In these practices you will review what you've learned in this lesson. The first exercise is to create a master project and insert a subproject. The second exercise is to unlink a subproject and delete a subproject. Exercise 3 is to create a cross-project link between two projects and create linked tasks. Exercise 4 is to create your own template.

NOTE   Complete exercises in order

Do all of these exercises in the order they are presented. Each depends on the prior exercise for successful completion.

▶ **Exercise 1   Create a Master Project**

You want to create a project that you can use to view and manage several smaller subprojects all on one screen.

To complete this exercise, perform the following steps:

1. Create a new, blank project file.
2. Click inside the first blank task name cell to position the cursor.
3. Choose Insert and choose Project.
4. In the Insert Project dialog box, browse to the project Annual Report Preparation, located on the accompanying CD, and click Insert.
5. Click inside the next blank task name cell and choose Insert and then Project.
6. In the Insert Project dialog box, browse to the project Customer Feedback Monitoring, located on the accompanying CD, and click Insert.
7. Click inside the next blank task name cell and choose Insert and then Project.
8. In the Insert Project dialog box, browse to the project Marketing Event Planning and Execution, located on the accompanying CD, and click Insert.
9. Expand each of the subprojects to see all tasks related to each subproject. When prompted, select Open Resource Pool To See Assignments Across All Sharer Files. Click OK. Project opens the file that contains the resource pool for this project.
10. Save this file as My Master Project. When prompted, click Yes To All to save changes to the new project file and all inserted subprojects. When prompted, click OK to save the resource pool file as well.

▶ **Exercise 2   Unlink or Delete a Subproject**

You want to unlink one subproject in your master project while retaining the listed tasks and delete another subproject and its tasks from the master project file. To complete this exercise, perform the following steps:

1. If necessary, open the My Master Project file you created in the previous exercise. (You will also find a copy of this file on the accompanying CD.)
2. Double-click the Customer Feedback Monitoring summary task.
3. In the Inserted Project Information dialog box, click the Advanced tab.
4. Clear the Link To Project check box.
5. Click OK.
6. When prompted to save the Customer Feedback Monitoring file, click Yes.
7. When prompted to update the resource pool, click OK. The tasks associated with the Customer Feedback Monitoring file are still listed in the master project file; however, the link between these tasks and the original inserted project has been broken.

8. Click in the left-most box for task 33, Marketing Event Planning and Execution. This is the task ID field. The entire row should be highlighted.

9. Right-click the task and choose Delete Task.

10. When prompted, select Continue. Delete 'Marketing Event Planning And Execution' And Its Subtasks.

11. Click OK. The Marketing Event Planning And Execution project and all related tasks are removed from the master project file. If Project displays a message stating that the selected item has some actual values, click Yes to continue with deleting this task.

12. Save this file as Edited Master Project. When prompted, click Yes To All to save changes to the new project file and all insert subprojects.

13. When prompted, click OK to update to the Resource Pool.

14. Close the Edited Master Project file and the Resource Pool file.

▶ Exercise 3   **Create a Cross Link**

You want to create a cross link between two tasks stored in different project files. To complete this exercise, perform the following steps:

1. From the accompanying CD, open the 2009 Annual Report Preparation file and the 2010 Annual Report Preparation files. When prompted, click OK to open the resource pool associated with these files.

2. In the 2009 Annual Report Preparation file, select Task 33: Theme Production Complete. You want to select the entire row for this task.

3. Right-click the selected task and choose Copy Task.

4. Display the 2010 Annual Report Preparation file.

5. Select Task 1 in the 2010 Annual Report Preparation file. You want to select the entire row for this task.

6. Right-click and choose Paste Special.

7. In the Paste Special dialog box, select Paste Link.

8. Click OK. The two tasks are now linked.

9. Save both files.

10. In the 2010 Annual Report Preparation file, double-click Task 1: Theme Production Complete. Note that Project takes Task 33 in the 2009 Annual Report Preparation file.

11. Close all open files.

▶ Exercise 4   **Create Your Own Template**

You've been starting and completing projects for some time now and want to create a template file for future projects based on what you know you will need. As part of the template creation process, you want to remove any data that you know you won't need in future projects.

To complete this exercise, perform the following steps:

1. Open the MasterSample2 file on the accompanying CD. You are going to use this file to create a template that you can use to create other projects.
2. Double-click task 1: Marketing Event Planning And Execution and click the Notes tab.
3. Select the text in the Notes text box and delete it. Click OK.
4. Double-click task 3: Define And Plan The Event and click the Advanced tab.
5. Change the Constraint Type from Must Start On to As Soon As Possible. Click OK.
6. Choose View and choose Resource Sheet. Delete any confidential pay rate information.
7. Choose View and choose Gantt Chart.
8. Change the relationship between tasks 4 and 5 to the default Finish-to-Start relationship. (Open the Task Information dialog box for task 5 and click the Predecessors tab.) Click OK to close the Task Information dialog box.
9. Choose File and choose Save As.
10. In the Save As Type drop-down list, select Template.
11. Browse to a location to save the file. It is recommended you use the default save location so that your new template will appear with others in the Templates dialog box in Project.
12. In the File Name text box, type **Initial Event Planning**.
13. Click Save.
14. In the Save As Template dialog box, select the check boxes for items you do not want to save as part of the template.
15. Click Save.

Lesson Summary

- Master projects are project files that contain other project files. These inserted project files are called subprojects.
- You use a master project to view and manage multiple projects at once. Filters and views show information for all projects in the master project.
- You can reconfigure a master file quickly by unlinking projects or deleting them altogether.
- When applying a cross-project link, you are linking project tasks where one task depends on another. This way, when information changes in the predecessor project file, the information in the secondary (or destination) project will automatically update as well.
- Templates can be created and modified to serve as a starting point for future projects.

Lesson Review

You can use the following questions to test your knowledge of the information in Lesson 3, "Manage Multiple Projects." The questions are also available on the companion CD if you prefer to review them in electronic form.

NOTE Answers

Answers to these questions and explanations of why each answer choice is correct or incorrect are located in the "Answers" section at the end of the book.

---

1. You are creating a template for future projects, but you do not want your new template to include information you've amassed regarding the current costs for dump trucks, concrete, and other material resources because you are sure this information will change. What is the fastest way to configure your new template so that it does not include this information?

   A. When saving the project as a template, clear the Fixed Costs check box in the Save As Template dialog box.

   B. When saving the file as a template, clear the Resource Rates check box before saving the file.

   C. In the open project, from Resource Sheet view, change rates for all resources to $0.00.

   D. When saving the project as a template, select the Resource Rates check box in the Save As Template dialog box.

2. How do you modify an original Microsoft Project template (not a template that you create)?

   A. In Project, open the template using File: New: On Computer, make changes as desired, and then save the template in the default location offered in the Save As dialog box.

   B. In Project, open the template using File, New, On Computer, make changes as desired, and then save the template in the default location offered in the Save As dialog box. When prompted, click Save The File As A Template.

   C. In Project, browse to <*hard disk drive letter*>:\Program Data\Microsoft\MicrosoftOffice \Templates. Open the template, make changes as desired, and then save the template in the default location offered in the Save As dialog box.

   D. In Project, browse to <*hard disk drive letter*>:\Program Files\MicrosoftOffice \Templates\1033. Open the template, make changes as desired, and then save the template in the default location offered in the Save As dialog box.

3. You are creating a cross link for task dependencies among tasks. Both the source and secondary files are open. You have opened the Task Information dialog box for the external task to link. What do you do now?

    A. In the Predecessors tab, in the ID column, type the name of the master project, followed by the Task ID number of the external predecessor, followed by a backslash.

    B. Copy the information to cross link from the source project and paste it into the master project.

    C. Select the Link To Project check box.

    D. In the Resources tab, type the name of the master project in the first available Resource Name field.

4. Which of the following represents part of the process required to create a master project? (Choose all that apply.)

    A. Create at least one cross-project link between a master project task and a secondary project task.

    B. Insert a subproject using the Insert: Project command.

    C. Save the master project.

    D. View the master project file using the Gantt Chart.

5. You need to create a cross-project link between two projects. You've copied the task data you want to link. What do you do now? (Choose two.)

    A. In the Paste Special dialog box, select Paste Link.

    B. Drag the mouse over the area to paste the data in the secondary project, right-click, and choose Paste Special.

    C. Open the Task Information dialog box.

    D. In the Predecessors tab of the Task Information dialog box, in the ID column, type the name of the master project, followed by the Task ID number of the external predecessor, followed by a backslash.

Lesson 4: Project Customization

A big part of getting Project to perform the way you need it to based on the types of projects you manage and your company specifications lies in customizing the program's default settings. Those customization settings are the subject of this lesson.

One thing you have seen throughout this book are areas of customization specific to viewing your project plan data, such as creating custom filters and custom groups. This lesson takes that type of customization a step further and examines more Project objects that you can customize.

> **After this lesson, you will be able to:**
> - Set up schedule options.
> - Set up calculation options.
> - Set up view options.
> - Set up general options.
> - Set up security options.
> - Customize tables.
> - Customize the view.
> - Customize formulas.
> - Customize the Project display.
>
> **Estimated lesson time: 165 minutes**

Set Up Schedule Options

In the Options dialog box (Tools, Options), you can use the Schedule tab to set your preferences for how Project schedules your project tasks. Specifically, you can set global scheduling options for the program, as well as scheduling options for only the open project. In this tab you can also use a series of check boxes to set your preferred options when working with new tasks, task dependencies, in-progress tasks, constraints, and estimated durations. Near the top of the Schedule tab you can set global scheduling options for the Project program, including the following:

- **Show Scheduling Messages**   To stop the display of messages about schedule inconsistencies, clear this check box. This check box is selected by default.
- **Show Assignment Units As A**   Choose to display resource assignment units within project views as either a percentage or a decimal. By default, Project displays resource assignment units as a percentage.

MORE INFO   Scheduling

For more information about how scheduling works in Project, visit the Microsoft Project help page "How Scheduling Works In Project" at *http://office.microsoft.com/en-us/project /HA102130271033.aspx?pid=CH100666481033*.

Just below the global scheduling options are a set of options specific to the project that is currently open (the local project):

- **New Tasks**   By default, when you enter new tasks into a project file, the start date is set to the start date of the project. This is usually what you want because the task links that you add are typically what determine the start date. Using the New Tasks drop-down list on the Schedule tab, you can set new tasks to start on the current date instead of the project start date. However, when you set new tasks to start on the current date, rather than assigning the As Soon As Possible constraint, new tasks will be set with a Start No Earlier Than constraint (or Start No Later Than constraint if the project is scheduling from the finish date).
- **Duration Is Entered In**   Using days, minutes, hours, weeks, or months, you can set the default time unit for the Duration field. By default, this option is set to Days. If you modify this option midway through a project, current duration units will not change.
- **Work Is Entered In**   Using days, minutes, hours, weeks, or months, you can set the default time unit for the Work field. By default, this option is set to Hours.
- **Default Task Type**   By default, new tasks are assigned the Fixed Units task type. Using this option, you can modify this setting to assign new tasks to any one of the three available task types, Fixed Units, Fixed Work, and Fixed Duration.

Exam Tip   Memorize the names of the options and what each does in the lower portion of the Schedule tab, listed next. You'll probably be asked which option to select in a particular circumstance.

The lower portion of the Schedule tab contains a series of check boxes (each selected by default) relative to the local project, including the following:

- **New Tasks Are Effort Driven**   When this option is selected, new tasks are scheduled with the effort-driven designation.
- **Autolink Inserted Or Moved Tasks**   When this option is selected, Project links a task you insert to its predecessor and successor.
- **Split In-progress Tasks**   When this option is selected, if a task slips (or the work on successor task is marked complete before the work on the predecessor task), Project will reschedule remaining duration and work, often resulting in a split task.

- **Tasks Will Always Honor Their Constraint Dates**   When you use both task dependencies and constraints, the status of this check box will determine which should take precedence in the event of a conflict. Tasks with constraint dates will use task dependencies to determine their start and finish dates instead of constraint dates. If selected, tasks obey the applied date constraint even if it means not following the task dependency—for example, having a successor task start before the finish of its finish-to-start predecessor task.

- **Show That Tasks Have Estimated Durations**   When this option is selected, tasks with estimated durations are displayed with a question mark (?) in the Duration field.

- **New Tasks Have Estimated Durations**   When this option is selected, all new tasks are entered with an estimated duration.

MORE INFO   Understanding options in the Schedule tab

With the Schedule tab selected in the Options dialog box, click Help. The associated help files offer valuable information on each of the options listed here.

Near the bottom of the Schedule tab lies the Set As Default button, also shown in Figure 4-59. Many of the settings located in the Schedule tab apply only to the local project (with the exception of the two global settings near the top). To apply the local settings you customize to new projects, click the Set As Default button.

Exam Tip   The Set As Default button appears near the bottom of many of the tabs located in the Options dialog box. In each case the Set As Default button allows you to apply the customized local project settings to new projects.

Quick Check

- By default, which of the following options are selected in Project and must be manually cleared if the option is not desired?
  - ❑ New Tasks Are Effort Driven
  - ❑ Autolink Inserted Or Moved Tasks
  - ❑ Split In-Progress Tasks
  - ❑ Tasks Will Always Honor Their Constraint Dates
  - ❑ Show That Tasks Have Estimated Durations
  - ❑ New Tasks Have Estimated Durations

Quick Check Answer

- All of these are selected by default. (For the exam, make sure you know what each does.)

Set Up Calculation Options

In the Options dialog box (Tools, Options), you can use the Calculation tab, shown in Figure 4-60, to set your preferences for how Project calculates dates and costs for your projects.

Figure 4-60   The Calculation tab

Specifically, you can set calculation options for the program, as well as calculation options localized to the open project. In this tab you can also use a series of check boxes to set your preferred options when working with task status updates, the calculation of inserted projects, whether or not actual costs are calculated by Project, and the default fixed cost accrual.

Near the top of the Calculation tab you can set global scheduling options for the Project program, including the following:

- **Calculation Mode**   Choosing Automatic specifies that a project's variables should be calculated automatically (as soon as a change is made). When set to Manual, you will be forced to click the Calculate Now button (also shown in Figure 4-60) to recalculate your project. A couple of shortcut keys are tied to manual calculation. To recalculate all open projects, press F9. To recalculate just the active project, press Shift+F9.

- **Calculate**   When set to All Open Projects, Project recalculates all open projects when either an automatic or manual calculation is performed. Alternatively, when set to Active Project, Project recalculates only the current project when either an automatic or manual calculation is performed.

Just below the global calculation options is a set of options specific to the project that is currently open (the local project):

- **Updating Task Status Updates Resource Status** When selected, this feature automatically updates your project's actual and remaining work and cost whenever a task's percent complete, actual duration, or remaining duration is updated. This is in effect only for task updates less than 100 percent complete. When a task reaches completion, all assignment work is also marked complete.

- **Move End Of Completed Parts After Status Date Back To Status Date** This option relates directly to tasks that have been scheduled to start after the project's set status date but instead started early. When this option is selected, a task's completion portion moves back to finish at the status date. The default status of this check box is cleared, which means that the completion portion of the task is set to finish as previously scheduled.

- **Move Start Of Remaining Parts Before Status Date Forward To Status Date** This option relates directly to tasks that have been scheduled to start before the project's set status date but instead started late. When it's selected, a task's remaining portion moves forward to start of the status date. The default status of this check box is cleared, which means that the remaining portion of the task is set to start as previously scheduled.

MORE INFO Understanding options in the Calculation tab

With the Calculation tab selected in the Options dialog box, click Help. The associated help files offer valuable information on each of the options listed here.

The series of check boxes available in the Calculation tab is separated in the middle, with the addition of an Earned Value button:

Earned Value is often misunderstood. Simply put, Earned Value is the cost of work performed up to the status date or current date—that is, the project value earned by completing the work performed so far. To calculate this measurement, Earned Value analysis uses your original schedule and cost estimates that have been saved with a baseline and your actual work to date to show whether the actual costs incurred are on budget and the actual schedule is going according to plan. By clicking the Earned Value button, you open the Earned Value dialog box, shown in Figure 4-61.

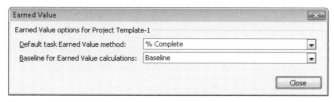

Figure 4-61 The Earned Value dialog box

In this dialog box you can choose between % Complete and Physical % Complete for the default task Earned Value method and which baselines (of 11) you want to use to make Earned Value comparisons.

Below the Earned Value button is another series of check boxes related to project costs, including:

- **Edits To Total Task % Complete Will Be Spread To The Status Date**   When this option is cleared (its default status), actual cost edits are accrued at the end of the actual task duration. When it's selected, changes to total actual cost are evenly distributed across the schedule to the status date.

- **Inserted Projects Are Calculated Like Summary Tasks**   Selected by default, this option displays and calculates inserted projects as though they were summary tasks. That is, if the inserted project as a whole is not on the critical path, the critical path tasks within the inserted project do not appear as critical tasks in the master project. This creates a single critical path calculation in the master project plan file.

- **Actual Costs Are Always Calculated By Microsoft Office Project**   In its default status, when selected, this option does not allow the entering of any additional actual costs until after the task has been marked as 100 percent complete.

- **Default Fixed Costs Accrual**   By default, fixed costs are accrued on a prorated basis. Using the Default Fixed Costs Accrual drop-down list, you can set how Project accrues fixed costs for new tasks, including accruing costs at the start or end of a task.

The final two options in the Calculation tab relate to critical path default settings:

- **Calculate Multiple Critical Paths**   By default, Project sets the project finish date as the late finish date for tasks that do not have successors or constraints. However, when this option is selected, the late finish date for these tasks becomes their early finish date, thus making the task critical.

- **Tasks Are Critical If Slack Is Less Than Or Equal To __ Days**   You can modify Project's default slack option by changing the number associated with slack. Project governs by the rule that marks a task as critical if the task has zero slack.

Quick Check

- What does calculation mode do when it is set to automatic? What is the difference between automatic and manual?

Quick Check Answer

- Automatic calculation makes sure that the project's variables are calculated automatically and as soon as a change is made. When the mode is set to manual, you have to click the Calculate Now button each time you want to recalculate your project.

Set Up View Options

In the Options dialog box (Tools, Options), you can use the View tab, shown in Figure 4-62, to set your preferences for how Project displays your project information.

Figure 4-62   The View tab

Specifically, you can change the default view that you see when you create a new project, as well as which screen elements, external links, currency, and outline information are displayed.

Near the top of the View tab, you can set global view options for the Project program:

- **Default View**   By default, Project displays the Gantt Chart at startup as the default view. You can modify this default view to any of the available project views, such as the Network Diagram.

- **Calendar Type**   With three calendar choices, you can specify the default calendar type for your projects. The default calendar type is the Gregorian calendar.
- **Date Format**   Several available options are listed in the Date Format drop-down list that are available for setting the default format for displaying dates in all project files. The default format is <*day of week*> mm/dd/yy, where *day of week* is Monday, Tuesday, and so on. For example, you might see a date of Mon 10/17/08 in Project.

Below the initial view settings are a series of check boxes under the heading "Show." You can use these options to enable or disable specific Project interface elements:

- Status Bar
- Windows In Taskbar
- Bars And Shapes In Gantt Views In 3-D
- Scroll Bars
- Entry Bar
- OLE Links Indicators
- Project Screentips

The View tab contains a short section of options that you can use when working with task dependencies between the current project and other projects (cross-project linking):

- **Show External Successors**   By default, external successors are shown in the current project. To hide their display, clear this check box.
- **Show External Predecessors**   By default, external predecessors are shown in the current project. To hide their display, clear this check box.
- **Show Links Between Projects Dialog Box On Open**   By default, the Show Links Between Projects Dialog Box On Open (shown in figure) opens this dialog box when you open a project with links to other projects. To hide this dialog box, clear this check box.
- **Automatically Accept New External Data**   When the Show Links Between Projects Dialog Box On Open check box is cleared, this option becomes active. When selected, Project accepts and automatically updates changes to task dependencies between projects.

MORE INFO   **Understanding options in the View tab**

With the View tab selected in the Options dialog box, click Help. The associated help files offer valuable information on each of the options listed here.

The next set of options in the View tab is available for modifying the currency options for the local project are the following:

- **Symbol**   Next to Symbol, select a type of currency from the Currency drop-down list. When you do so, Project automatically inserts the symbol for the currency type you selected. Alternatively, you could type your preferred currency symbol.

- **Placement**   Use the Placement drop-down list to specify where the currency symbol is placed in relation to the number.

- **Decimal Digits**   In the Decimal Digits box, type or select the number of digits that appear after the decimal point in currency.

- **Currency**   Use the Currency drop-down list to specify the default currency type for the local (or active) project.

The final options listed in the View tab relate to how you want Project to handle outlining options for the local project:

NOTE   Outline options

The outline options explained here are the most common because they are the ones you see when you open the Options dialog box from Gantt Chart view. However, the outline options you see might differ based on your current project view.

- **Indent Name**   When this option is selected, subtasks are indented in the Task Name column.

- **Show Outline Number**   When this option is selected, outline numbers are displayed next to each task name.

- **Show Outline Symbol**   In Project, outline symbols such as the plus (+) and minus (−) sign are shown next to summary tasks and subtasks. Clearing this option hides the outline symbol display.

- **Show Summary Tasks**   Summary tasks are typically displayed with their subtasks. When this option is cleared, the summary task is hidden. However, all tasks that are not summary tasks are still visible.

- **Show Project Summary Task**   Enabling this option displays a project summary task at ID "0."

Exam Tip   Although you probably won't be asked to name a specific option in the previous list, you will be asked where to make changes in Project. Usually, this will come in a scenario form, such as "You can't see the outline numbers in your Project. What do you need to enable?"

> ### Quick Check
> - What are the three global view options for Office 2007 and what does each offer?
>
> ### Quick Check Answer
> - Default view displays the Gantt Chart at startup as the default view. Calendar type view offers three calendar choices, and you can specify the default calendar type for your projects. Date format offers several options for setting the default format for displaying dates in project files.

Set Up General Options

In the Options dialog box (Tools, Options), you can use the General tab, shown in Figure 4-63, to set your preferences for the general configuration of Project.

Figure 4-63   The General tab

Specifically, you can set general options globally for Project, for the Planning Wizards, and for general option local to the current project.

Near the top of the General tab you can set general options for the Project program:

- **Set Autofilter On For New Projects**   To have AutoFilter displayed automatically when you create a new project, select this check box.
- **Prompt For Project Info For New Projects**   When this option is selected, users will see the Project Information dialog box when a new project is created.

■ **Open Last File On Startup**   When you are using the same project file every time you open Project, you can select this check box to have the program automatically open the last file on which you were working.

■ **Recently Used File List __ Entries**   By default, the number of recently used files shown at the bottom of the File menu is four. You can modify this setting to any number between zero and nine.

■ **User Name**   Enter a user name that identifies the author of your project files.

■ **Undo Levels**   In Project, you can set the number of undo levels to 99, although the default number is 20.

■ **Service Options**   Using the Service Options button, you can modify the customer feedback and document management options. You use the customer feedback options to specify whether you want to participate in the Microsoft Customer Experience Improvement Program to help Microsoft identify problems or new features needed in Project. You use the document management options to configure Project to work with data files on a SharePoint Web site or a workspace. The Service Options dialog box is shown in Figure 4-64.

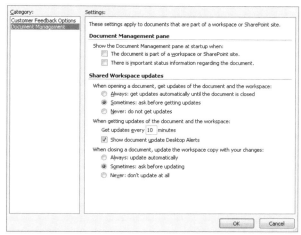

Figure 4-64   Service Options dialog box

Planning Wizard

Near the center of the General tab you can specify how you want the Planning Wizard to interact with your project files. The settings you apply to the Planning Wizard are global. As such, these settings are applied to all project files.

Using the Planning Wizard   As you work with Project, you will see the Planning Wizard dialog boxes pop up from time to time. The role of the Planning Wizard is to guide you when you are scheduling tasks and to warn you about conflicts and errors, as well as to offer possible shortcuts. For example, a common Planning Wizard dialog box is seen when entering durations. If you enter the same duration in three consecutive tasks, you will see the dialog box shown in Figure 4-65.

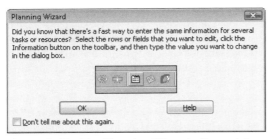

Figure 4-65   The Planning Wizard offers advice

This Planning Wizard dialog box offers a quick shortcut tip that might save you time in entering future durations. Another common Planning Wizard dialog box is seen when tasks are moved or rescheduled and a resource assignment conflict arises or when scheduling uses inflexible constraints. With the Planning Wizard enabled in the General tab of the Options dialog box, you can be sure you will see these helpful hints when warranted.

By default, all of the Planning Wizards are set to display when needed. These settings can be customized as follows:

- **Advice From Planning Wizard**   This first box activates the remaining three Planning Wizard check boxes. To disable all dialog boxes associated with the Planning Wizard, clear this check box. To disable only certain Planning Wizard elements, leave this check box selected and customize the setting using the lower check boxes.
    - **Advice About Using Microsoft Office Project** – When selected, the Planning Wizard displays shortcuts for working with Project.
    - **Advice About Scheduling** – When selected, the Planning Wizard displays scheduling clarification messages.
    - **Advice About Errors** – When selected, the Planning Wizard displays error messages.

Exam Tip   On the exam you might encounter a scenario in which a user wants to see errors related to scheduling but not to errors and how to use Project. You need to know that you can disable all but what the user wants to see without disabling the Planning Wizard completely.

Resource and Task Options

Near the bottom of the General tab you can set new resource and task options for the local (open) project file:

- **Automatically Add New Resources And Tasks**   When this option is selected (it is selected by default), this setting allows Project to automatically add resources that are new to a file's resource sheet or a linked resource pool. When this check box is cleared, Project displays a dialog box notification to let you know that a new resource or task has been created when you make a new assignment.
- **Default Standard Rate**   The amount next to this option sets the standard pay rate for new resources (typically seen in Resource Sheet view).
- **Default Overtime Rate**   The amount next to this option sets the overtime pay rate for new resources (typically seen in Resource Sheet view).

MORE INFO   Understanding the options in the General tab

With the General tab selected in the Options dialog box, click Help. The associated help files offer valuable information on each of the options listed here.

> ## Quick Check
>
> - You want to configure the General options to change how Project looks and what it offers at startup. Specifically, you want AutoFilter to be on automatically and open the last file you were working on when you last closed Project. What other options can you configure in the General tab?
>
> ## Quick Check Answer
>
> - Several other options are available in the General tab. You can:
>   - ❑ Prompt for project information regarding new projects.
>   - ❑ Change the number of entries listed in the recently used file list.
>   - ❑ Type a user name to identify the author of your project files.
>   - ❑ Change the number of Undo levels.
>   - ❑ Change service options to modify the customer feedback.
>   - ❑ Enable or disable the Planning Wizard.
>   - ❑ Automatically add new resources and tasks.
>   - ❑ Change the default standard and overtime rates.

Set Up Security Options

In the Options dialog box (Tools, Options), you can use the Security tab, shown in Figure 4-66, to set your preferences for the security configuration of Project and the local project file.

Specifically, you can set security options to remove all personal information from the local project file, adjust the default macro security level, and work with legacy formats.

Figure 4-66   The Security tab

Privacy Options

Near the top of the Security tab you can specify that personal information be removed from the file when the file is saved. By selecting the Remove Information From File Properties On Save check box, when the file is saved, Project removes the data stored in the Author, Manager, Company, and Last Saved By fields found in the Properties dialog box (File, Properties). The Properties dialog box is shown in Figure 4-67.

Figure 4-67   The File Properties dialog box

When you select this check box, only the four fields listed above are removed from the project file. Other confidential information might still remain. Also, this setting is applied only to the local project and is not a global Project setting.

Macro Security

Just below the option to remove information from the project file property fields is a Macro Security button for designating macro security options. When you click it, the Security dialog box, shown in Figure 4-68, is displayed.

Figure 4-68   The Security dialog box for macro settings

In the Security dialog box, you can set the security level for filtering projects that contain macros. The default security setting is High. This means that only macros that come from a trusted source will be allowed to run. You can view your trusted sources by clicking the Trusted Publishers tab. By default, all installed add-ins and template files are automatically trusted and will be allowed to run while any unsigned macros are automatically disabled.

Exam Tip   You need to know that the default setting for macro security is high. You might encounter a question that asks why a macro can't run and what needs to be done to allow it to.

MORE INFO   **Understanding the options in the Security tab**

With the Security tab selected in the Options dialog box, click Help. The associated help files offer valuable information on each of the options listed here.

Quick Check

■ You've set privacy options so that that personal information is removed from the file when the file is saved. Is it safe to share the file or might other personal information still be included in the project?

Quick Check Answer

■ The data removed prior to a save includes the Author, Manager, Company, and Last Save By fields found in the Properties dialog box (File, Properties). However, only the four fields listed above are removed. Other confidential information might still remain.

Customizing Tables

Project has a table for just about every type of data you might want to display related to your project plan. But if you find yourself switching back and forth between two or more tables, consider creating a custom table that contains just the fields you need all in one place. In addition, if you don't see the fields you need when creating a custom table, you can create them in the Custom Fields dialog box.

Create a New Table

When you create a new table, you only need to know what fields you would like to see in the final result. In fact, if one of Project's existing tables provides a close match, instead of creating a new table from scratch, you can make a copy of an existing table and make modifications to the copy (much like copying a project calendar and creating your own).

The steps for table creation are essentially the same whether you use a blank table or an existing table as your starting point. To create a custom table, follow these steps:

1. Choose View and choose Table. Choose More Tables.
2. Select Task or Resource for the table type.
3. To create a new table, click New; to copy and edit an existing table, select the table most like the one you want to create and click Copy.

   If this is your first time creating a table, select an existing table.
4. Name the table. See Figure 4-69. Consider using all capital letters or a standard prefix for easy identification.
5. Select the Show In Menu check box if you want the table to appear in the Table menu.
6. To delete a row, select it and click Cut Row.
7. To copy a row, select it and click Copy Row.

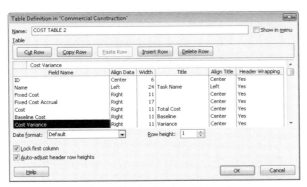

Figure 4-69   The Table Definition dialog box

8. To insert a row, in the Field Name list, select the field underneath the place you want the new row to be inserted and click Insert Row.

9. Use the drop-down list to select the field to add to the custom table. See Figure 4-70.

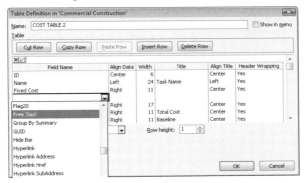

Figure 4-70   Inserting a row

10. To delete a row, select it and click Delete Row.

11. If desired, change Row Height from 1 to another option.

12. If desired, change Date Format from Default to another option.

13. If desired, clear the Lock First Column or Auto-Adjust Header check boxes, or both.

14. Click OK.

As you can see, when you create a custom table, you have full control over which fields will be displayed. And although Project has a wealth of fields (displayed as columns in a table) to choose from, you also have the option of creating a custom column (field) if you do not see what you want in the drop-down lists.

Create Custom Columns and Fields

With custom columns you have full control over what information you want to display in your tables. You might have seen what is shown in Figure 4-71 while working through the steps in this book—options for Text 1, Text 2, and so on, all of which you can customize to suit your project's specific needs.

Creating a custom field involves slightly more than merely placing a title at the top of a column. Project fields can contain all types of data. As such, you will need to specify the purpose of newly created fields in the Custom Fields dialog box. For example, a field can contain text and formulas, or it can look up a value in another field. To create a custom field, follow these steps:

1. Choose Tools, choose Customize, and choose Fields.

2. Select Task or Resource, depending on the type of field you want to create.

3. In the Type drop-down list, shown in Figure 4-71, select the type of field you want to create. Notice that there are several field types for Task, including Cost, Date, Duration, Finish, Flag, Number, Outline Code, Start, and Text.

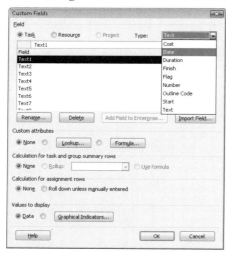

Figure 4-71   Creating a custom field

4. Select an available field and click Rename.

5. In the Rename Field dialog box, type a name for the new field. Consider using all capital letters to distinguish your fields from Project's or use a distinguishing symbol (like a # sign).

NOTE Importing a custom field

You can also click Import Field and, in the Import Custom Field dialog box, select the project to import the field from, and then select the field type and name.

---

6. Under Custom Attributes:
   a. Select None if you do not want to use a lookup table to specify field values or use a formula to calculate a field's value.
   b. Select Lookup if you want to build a list of values that you can choose from to enter a value in the field. If you select this, you'll need to click the Lookup button to open the Edit Lookup Table dialog box. You use this dialog box to specify values for this field.
   c. Select Formula if you want to apply a formula for calculating the contents of the field. If you select this option, you'll need to click the Formula button to define or import a formula.
7. Under Calculation For Task And Group Summary Rows:
   a. Select None if you don't want to define a rollup function or a formula for calculating the values for a summary task or a group summary row.
   b. Select Rollup if you want to specify that the values of this custom field should be rolled up to summary rows. In the Rollup box, select the method you want to use to roll up the data to the task and group summary rows of this field. To learn more about Rollup Options, click the Help button. Options vary depending on the field selected.
   c. Select Use Formula if you want to use the selected formula to calculate a rollup value for the task and group summary rows—for example, if you create a custom field to show the largest variance for any task in a group.
8. Under Calculation For Assignment Rows:
   a. Select None if the task in this field is not to be distributed across assignments.
   b. Select Roll Down Unless Manually Entered if the field contents are to be distributed across assignments.
9. Under Values To Display:
   a. Select Data to display actual data in the field.
   b. Select Graphical Indicators to specify criteria associated with the field that are like stoplights that show whether a task is ahead of, behind, or on schedule, and to define the indicators you want to use.
10. Click Help for more information about these field options.
11. Click OK.

Real World

Bonnie Biafore

Sometimes a different kind of rollup calculation can come in handy. For example, suppose you want to see the highest task cost within each summary task so that you can see which tasks provide the most opportunity to cut costs. Project rolls up values for built-in fields by totaling the values in all the subtasks. You can't choose a different rollup calculation, such as Average, Maximum, or Minimum.

The workaround to this problem is a custom field that points to the built-in field you want. For example, use the task field Cost1 and set it up with a formula that makes it equal to the field Cost. Then, choose Maximum as the rollup calculation. This way, the Cost1 values for lowest-level tasks equal the Cost values for those tasks. However, the Cost1 value for a summary task equals the largest cost for a single task below the summary task.

Add Custom Fields as Columns

You can add custom fields to custom tables and existing tables. You can also add a custom field directly to any table you are currently viewing by following these steps:

1. In any view or sheet with columns, right-click any column head.
2. Choose Insert Column.
3. In the Column Definition dialog box, shown in Figure 4-72, use the Field Name drop-down list to select the custom column you created.

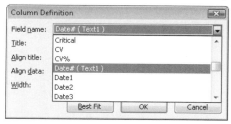

Figure 4-72   Inserting a custom column

4. Click OK.

Share a Custom Table

Just as you shared custom filters and groups earlier, so can you share custom fields and custom tables. To do this, copy the custom field or the custom table to the Global.mpt file using the Organizer. To share a custom table, complete the following steps:

1. Open the project that contains the custom table.
2. Choose Tools and choose Organizer. The Organizer automatically assumes that you want to copy custom tables or fields to the Global.mpt file.
3. Click the Tables tab.
4. Select Task or Resource, depending on what type of table you want to copy.
5. Select the custom table in the right pane and click Copy. See Figure 4-73.

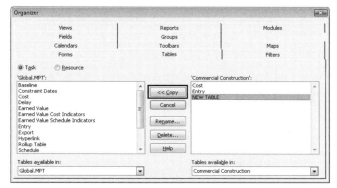

Figure 4-73   Copying a custom table to the Global.mpt template

6. Close the Organizer.

   To share a custom field, follow these steps:

7. Open the project that contains the custom field.
8. Choose Tools and choose Organizer.
9. Click the Fields tab.
10. Select Task or Resource, depending on what type of field you want to copy.
11. Select the custom field in the right pane and click Copy. See Figure 4-74.

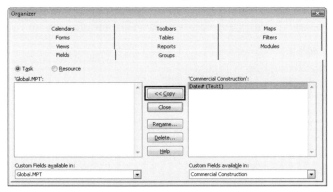

Figure 4-74   Copying a custom field to the Global.mpt template

12. Close the Organizer.

Quick Check

■ You created a new table, but you can't find it anywhere. You are sure you saved the table, but it's not in the More Tables list. What did you do wrong?

Quick Check Answer

■ You need to select the Show In Menu check box if you want the table to appear in the Table menu.

Creating Formulas

Aside from "regular" fields such as those that are text-based and date-based, you can opt to display the results of a formula in a custom field. You enter formulas using the Edit Formula dialog box, shown in Figure 4-75.

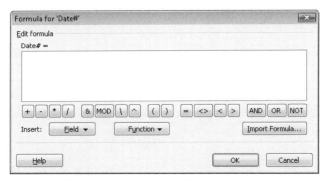

Figure 4-75   Creating a custom formula

If you are already familiar with the formula syntax employed by Excel or Access, you can type your desired formula directly in the Formula dialog box. Alternatively, you can use the available calculation buttons, which include mathematical operators and options for inserting fields and functions.

To display the Formula dialog box, follow these steps:

1. Choose Tools, choose Customize, and choose Fields.
2. Click the Formula button.

When you have displayed the Formula dialog box, use Table 4-4 to understand the meaning of each of the available calculation buttons. Figure 4-76 calls out each of these items.

addition, subtraction, multiplication,
division, string concatenation, modulus

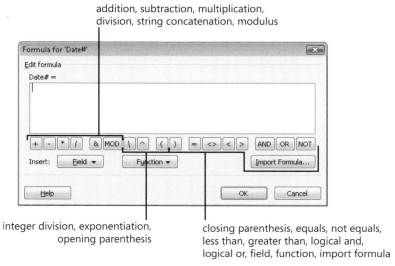

integer division, exponentiation,
opening parenthesis

closing parenthesis, equals, not equals,
less than, greater than, logical and,
logical or, field, function, import formula

Figure 4-76   Create a formula

Table 4-4   Formula Dialog Box Options

Command Button	Description
Addition	Adds two values.
Subtraction	Subtracts two values.
Multiplication	Multiplies two values.
Division	Divides two values.
String Concatenation	Combines two strings. For example, [firstname] & ' ' & [lastname] will be displayed as "firstname lastname." Notice that to insert a space between two strings, you must use ' ' between the strings.
Modulus	Displays the resulting remainder after dividing two integers.
Integer Division	Displays the whole integer result of dividing two integers, ignoring any remainder.
Exponentiation	Indicates that you want to raise a value to the power specified.
Opening Parenthesis	When combined with Closing Parenthesis, this helps define the order of operations in a formula.
Closing Parenthesis	When combined with Opening Parenthesis, this helps define the order of operations in a formula.
Equals	Indicates that the left side of an equation should match the right side of an equation.

Table 4-4   Formula Dialog Box Options

Command Button	Description
Not Equals	Indicates that the left side of an equation should not match the right side of an equation.
Less Than	Indicates that the left side of an equation should be less than the right side of an equation.
Greater Than	Indicates that the left side of an equation should be greater than the right side of an equation.
Logical AND	Compares two expressions. If both are true, the result is "True." However, if either is false, the result is "False."
Logical OR	Compares two expressions. If either is true, the result is "True."
Logical NOT	Negates the logical value of the expression it precedes, making a true expression False or a false expression True.
Field	Inserts a project field into a formula.
Function	Inserts a function into a formula, then replaces the argument place-holders with actual values or expressions.
Import Formula	Imports a formula from another project or another field in this project.

Exam Tip   Some test takers get one or two questions regarding formulas, but most do not. Just to be safe, make sure you know where and when to create a formula, but don't focus too much on how to create it.

If you opt to use a formula in a custom field, in addition to creating the formula using the commands described in Table 4-4, you also need to indicate that you will be using the custom formula by following these steps:

1. Choose Tools, choose Customize, and choose Fields.
2. Select Task or Resource, depending on the type of field you want to create.
3. In the Type drop-down list, select the type of field you want to create. Notice there are several for Task, including Cost, Date, Duration, Finish, Flag, Number, Outline Code, Start, and Text.
4. Select the Formula option button. The dialog box shown in Figure 4-77 appears. Click OK.
5. Click Formula.
6. In the Formula dialog box, create or import the formula. Click OK.
7. Click OK.

Figure 4-77   Formula disclaimer

Quick Check

You are creating three formulas for use in three custom project fields. You want the formulas to do the following:

1. Combine two sets of text data, lastname and SSN.
2. Cube a number in a data field.
3. Display the remainder after dividing two integers.

What command button in the Formula dialog box should you use in each instance?

Quick Check Answers

1. String Concatenation
2. Exponentiation
3. Modulus

Customizing Views

Just like tables, Project also has a view for just about every type of data you might want to display related to your project plan. But that does not mean that you will not have a need to display your data in a way not being offered. In this case you can create a new view.

Project has two types of views: Single and Combination. A *single view* displays one chart, one sheet, or one form on the screen. A *combination view* displays any two single views on one screen (with one view at the top and another view at the bottom). This means that you can create a combination view that consists of two of Project's predefined views, two of your custom single views, or one single and one combination view. And, just like tables, if one of Project's existing views provides a close match, instead of creating a new view from scratch, you can make a copy of an existing view and make modifications to the copy.

Creating a Single View

You create custom views using the More Views dialog box, shown in Figure 4-78. This is the same dialog box you open to select from the many predefined views.

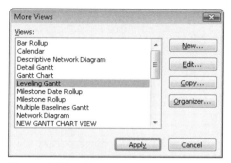

Figure 4-78   Use More Views to create a custom view

To create a custom single view, follow these steps:

1. Choose View, and then choose More Views.

2. To create a new view from scratch, click New. If you click New, you are prompted to select either Single View or Combination View. Select Single View, and then click OK. If you choose to edit an existing view, select the view closest to the one you want and click Copy.

3. In the View Definition dialog box, shown in Figure 4-79, name the new view. You might want to name the view with all capital letters or a standard prefix so that it's easily distinguishable from predefined views.

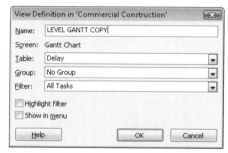

Figure 4-79   Configuring the new view definitions

4. For Table, select the table you want to see by default in this view.

5. For Group, select the group you want to see by default in this view.

6. For Filter, select the filter you want to apply to this view.

7. If desired, select the Highlight Filter check box.

8. To show the new view in the View list, select the Show In Menu check box.

9. Click OK. Click Close.

Creating a Combination View

Combination views display two single views—either views that are predefined or custom single views. To create a combination view, follow these steps:

1. Choose View, choose More Views.
2. Click New.
3. In the Define New View dialog box, shown in Figure 4-80, select Combination View and click OK.

Figure 4-80   Creating a combination view

4. In the View Definition dialog box, shown in Figure 4-81, name the new view. You might want to name the view with all capital letters so that it's easily distinguishable from predefined views.

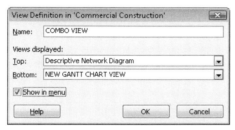

Figure 4-81   Defining the combination view

5. For Top, select the view you want to see by default in this view.
6. For Bottom, select the option you want to see by default in this view.
7. To show the new view in the View list, select the Show In Menu check box.
8. Click OK. Click Close.

Exam Tip   You will likely see a question regarding creating a combination view. Remember, combination views have a top and a bottom option, and single views have Table, Group, and Filter options. Also, don't be fooled by choices that suggest that you format the bar charts in the Gantt Chart. That will not work.

Sharing a View

Just like filters, groups, tables, and fields, you copy views to the global template so the view is available in future projects. To share a custom view, complete the following steps:

1. Open the project that contains the custom view.
2. Choose Tools and choose Organizer.
3. Click the Views tab.
4. Select the custom view in the right pane and click Copy. See Figure 4-82.

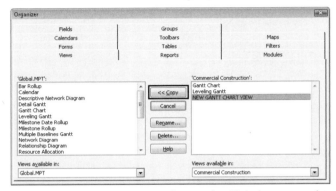

Figure 4-82   Copy a custom view to the Global.mpt template

5. Close the Organizer.

Quick Check

■   What type of view should you create if you want to view two single views on one screen (with one view at the top and another view at the bottom)—specifically, Task Usage on top and Resource Sheet on bottom?

Quick Check Answer

■   Combination view

Customizing the Display

All throughout this training kit, you have seen several ways of customizing your Project display, including:

■   Creating a work breakdown structure.
■   Displaying outline numbers.

- Modifying default currency settings.
- Adding a project summary task.
- Setting the default duration type.
- Creating custom tables, fields, views, and formulas.

In addition to these methods, there are a few additional ways you can customize your Project display. This lesson explores these additional ways.

Change Column Title Text

Using the Column Definition dialog box, shown in Figure 4-83, you can modify column titles that appear for each displayed field in a table (seen in a view like Gantt Chart view or Task Sheet view) to any text that is more meaningful to your project. You can open this dialog box by double-clicking any column header.

Figure 4-83 Changing column data

To make a change to a column header, follow these steps:

1. In any sheet view, double-click the column heading whose text you want to change.
2. In the Column Definition dialog box, shown in Figure 4-83, type a new column heading in the Title field.
3. In the Align Title drop-down list, select the alignment you want to use for the title (Left, Center, or Right).
4. In the Align Data drop-down list, select the alignment you want to use for the text in the column itself.
5. In the Width box, type or select the width you want the column to be or click Best Fit to automatically adjust the column width to fit the longest information in any cell.
6. If you don't want the text to wrap in the column heading, clear the Header Text Wrapping check box.

As you can see, the Column Definition dialog box also has options for adjusting the column width, wrapping long text titles, and aligning both the field data and the column data.

Specify Default Font and Patterns

Using the Text Styles dialog box, shown in Figure 4-84, you can adjust how Project displays specific project items, such as critical tasks or milestones.

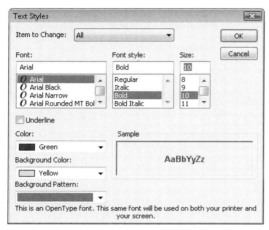

Figure 4-84   Changing formatting styles

To use the Text Styles dialog box to modify the display of project data, follow these steps:

1. Choose Format and choose Text Styles.
2. In the Item To Change drop-down list, select All. Note that you can also select from a number of other options, including, but not limited to, Row & Column Titles, Critical Tasks, External Tasks, Highlighted Tasks, and Marked Tasks.
3. Select the font, font style, and font size in their respective boxes.
4. Select the Underline check box to underline text.
5. In the Color drop-down list, select the color that you want to use.
6. To change the background color of the cell, in the Background Color drop-down list, select a color.
7. To change the background pattern of the cell, in the Background Pattern drop-down list, select a pattern.

NOTE   Formatting Gantt bars

You can change how bars appear in the Gantt Chart from Format: Layout. Options include rounding edges, showing bar splits, and changing the date format, among others.

Show the Standard and Formatting Toolbars on One or Two Rows

Project has not taken advantage of the Ribbon that is found in programs like Word 2007 and Excel 2007; the quick commands are located on the Standard and Formatting toolbars. Typically, these two toolbars are displayed as two separate rows. However, in the interest of designating more of your screen to your project plan, you can switch the display of the Standard and Formatting toolbars to one row by following these steps:

1. Right-click any toolbar and choose Customize. See Figure 4-85.

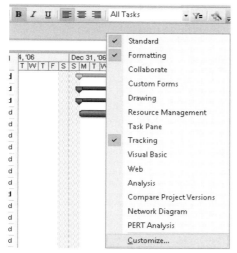

Figure 4-85   Customizing the toolbars

2. In the Options tab, under Personalized Menus And Toolbars, clear the Show Standard And Formatting Toolbars On Two Rows check box. See Figure 4-86.

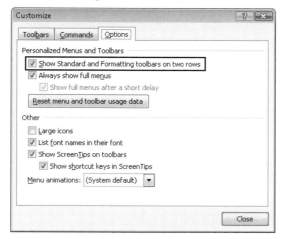

Figure 4-86   Configuring toolbars

3. Click Close.

Customizing Menus and Toolbars and Creating Custom Toolbars

You can further customize how Project's interface appears by rearranging the commands on menus and toolbars and by creating your own custom toolbars.

Rearrange Menu Commands   Along the same lines as modifying the display of the Standard and Formatting toolbars, you can also rearrange and change toolbar buttons using the Rearrange Commands dialog box, shown in Figure 4-87.

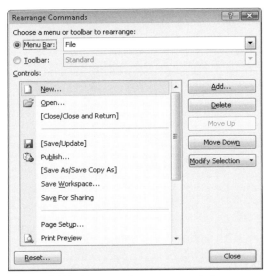

Figure 4-87   Rearranging commands for a menu or toolbar

To rearrange commands on a predefined Project menu, follow these steps:

1. Right-click any toolbar and choose Customize.
2. Click the Commands tab.
3. Click Rearrange Commands.
4. Select Menu Bar, and, in the drop-down list, select the menu whose commands you want to rearrange.
5. Select any item in the Controls list and click Add, Delete, Move Up, or Move Down to change the location of the command.
6. In the Modify Selection drop-down list, select an option to reset the data for a selected command and change the command to Text Only, Image And Text, Assign Macro, or something else. See Figure 4-88.
7. Click Close.

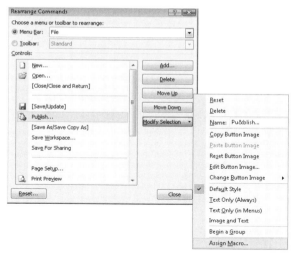

Figure 4-88   Editing commands on a menu

Rearrange Toolbar Commands

1. You can also rearrange commands on a toolbar. To rearrange commands on a predefined Project toolbar, follow these steps:

2. Right-click any toolbar and choose Customize.

3. Click the Commands tab.

4. Click Rearrange Commands.

5. Select Toolbar, and, in the drop-down list, select the toolbar whose commands you want to rearrange. In Figure 4-89, the Formatting toolbar is selected.

6. Select any item in the Controls list (such as Font) and click Add, Delete, Move Up, or Move Down to change the location of the command.

7. Use the Modify Selection drop-down list to reset the data for a selected command, change the command to Text Only, Image And Text, Assign Macro, or something else.

8. Click Close.

Exam Tip   Although you might not be asked how to change a font or font size for a header, you might be asked how, why, or when to create a custom toolbar.

Figure 4-89   Editing commands on a toolbar

Create a Custom Toolbar   Create your own toolbar to make accessible the tools and commands you use most often. To create a custom toolbar, complete the following steps:

1. Right-click any toolbar and choose Customize.

2. Click the Toolbars tab and click New.

3. In the New Toolbar dialog box, type a name for the new toolbar, and then click OK. Consider using all capital letters so it can be easily located. See Figure 4-90.

Figure 4-90   Creating a custom toolbar

4. Click the Commands tab and click Rearrange Commands.

5. Select the Toolbar option and locate the new toolbar in the drop-down list. See Figure 4-91.

6. Click Add to open the Add Command dialog box, also shown in Figure 4-91.

7. Select a category in the Categories list that contains the item you'd like to add to your toolbar.

8. Locate a command in the Commands list to add and click Add.

9. Repeat steps 6 and 7 until you have added all the buttons and menus that you want, click Close, and click Close again.

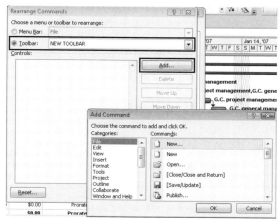

Figure 4-91   Personalizing your toolbar

PRACTICE **Create Custom Elements**

In these practices you will review what you've learned in this lesson. The first exercise is to configure various options in the Options dialog box. The second exercise is to create a custom table. The third exercise is to create a custom field. The fourth exercise is to create a formula. The fifth exercise is to create a combination view. The sixth exercise is to customize the Project interface by altering default text and colors. The final exercise is to create a custom toolbar.

▶ **Exercise 1   Use the Options Dialog Box to Customize Project**

Each time you start a new project, you find yourself customizing Project the same way every time. You'd like to change several settings in the Options dialog box so that your preferences will be saved for future projects.

To complete this exercise, perform the following steps:

1. Open Project and choose Tools and then Options.
2. In the View tab, in the Default View drop-down list, select Calendar. (Don't worry—at the end of this exercise, you'll click Cancel so no changes will be applied to your version of Project.)
3. Under Currency Options, change the Decimal Digits from 2 to 0.
4. Click the General tab.
5. Select the Set AutoFilter On For New Projects and Open Last File On Startup check boxes.
6. Change Recently Used File List to 9.
7. Change Default Overtime Rate to \$20/h. Click Set As Default.
8. Click the Schedule tab.
9. Clear the New Tasks Are Effort-Driven check box.

10. Clear the Split In-Progress Tasks check box.
11. Click Set As Default.
12. Click the Calculation tab.
13. Change the Calculation Mode to Manual.
14. Click Set As Default.
15. Click the Security tab.
16. Select the Remove Information From File Properties On Save check box.
17. Click the View tab and clear the Status Bar and Entry Bar check boxes.
18. Click Cancel. You do not want to apply these changes to your version of Project.

▶ **Exercise 2   Create a Custom Table**

You find that you are creating the same table again and again in various projects, and you would like to create a custom table that you can ultimately save and use it for future projects.

To complete this exercise, perform the following steps:

1. Choose View and choose Table. Select More Tables.
2. Choose Task for the table type. In this exercise you will create a task table.
3. Select the Summary table in the More Tables list. Click Copy.
4. Name the table **COST TABLE 2**.
5. Select the Show In Menu check box if you want the table to appear in the Table menu.
6. Select Cost and click Cut Row.
7. Select ID and click Insert Row.
8. Use the drop-down list in the blank row and select Actual Cost.
9. To delete a row, select the row and click Delete Row.

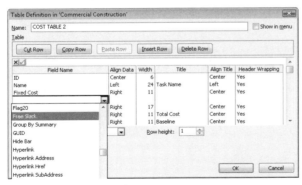

10. Change Row Height from 1 to 2.
11. Click OK.

▶ **Exercise 3   Create a Custom Field**

You want to create a custom field for use in the custom tables you create. To create a custom field, follow these steps:

1. Choose Tools, choose Customize, and choose Fields.
2. Select Resource to create a new resource field.
3. In the Type drop-down list, shown in Figure 4-71, select Text.
4. Select Text 4 and click Rename.
5. Name the new resource field **Publisher Name**, and then click OK.
6. Accept the defaults for the new text field.
7. Click OK.

▶ **Exercise 4   Create a Formula**

You want to create a new field named Cost and apply a formula to it. To complete this exercise, follow these steps:

1. Choose Tools, choose Customize, and choose Fields.
2. Select Task.
3. In the Type drop-down list, shown in Figure 4-71, select Cost.
4. Click Rename and name the field **COST FORMULA**. Click OK.
5. Select the Formula option. Click OK.
6. Click Formula.
7. In the Formula dialog box, do the following:
   a. In the Field drop-down list, select Cost, and then select Overtime Cost.
   b. Click /.
   c. In the Field drop-down list, select Cost, and then select Actual Cost.
8. Click OK, and then click OK again.
9. To avoid making changes to your project, click Cancel.

▶ **Exercise 5   Create a Combination View and Save It to the Global.mpt Template**

You want to create a custom view and share it with others who use the same Global.mpt template that you do. Doing so will greatly reduce confusion related to your project by making the items you need available quickly and intuitively. (Note that adding a custom view to the Global.mpt template is similar to sharing filters, groups, fields, and tables, and, as such, the same techniques can be applied in those circumstances.)

1. Choose View, choose More Views.
2. Click New.
3. In the Define New View dialog box, select Combination View and click OK.
4. In the View Definition dialog box, name the new view **SHARED VIEW**.

5. For Top, select Calendar.
6. For Bottom, select Task Sheet.
7. Select the Show In Menu check box.
8. Click OK. Click Close.

To copy the custom view to the Global.mpt template:

1. Choose Tools and choose Organizer.
2. Click the Views tab.
3. Select SHARED VIEW in the right pane and click Copy.
4. Close the Organizer.

▶ **Exercise 6 Customize the Interface**

You'd like to change the font, color, and shading of portions of the Project interface. To do this, you need to change the display options.

To complete this exercise, perform the following steps:

1. In Gantt Chart view, double-click the Task Name header.
2. Change Align Title to Center.
3. Change Align Data to Center.
4. Change the width to 36.
5. Select the Header Text Wrapping check box.
6. Click OK.
7. Choose Format and choose Text Styles.
8. In the Item To Change drop-down list, select Critical Tasks.
9. For Font, select Calibri.
10. For Font Style, select Bold.
11. For Size, select 18.
12. For Color, select Yellow.
13. For Background Color, select the second option (Red).
14. Click OK. (You'll see the changes after inputting data.)

▶ **Exercise 7 Create a Custom Toolbar**

You want to create a toolbar that contains the tools you most often use. To complete this exercise, follow these steps:

1. Right-click any toolbar and choose Customize.
2. Click the Toolbars tab and click New.
3. In the New Toolbar dialog box, name the toolbar **MY TOOLBAR**. Click OK.
4. Click the Commands tab and click Rearrange Commands.

5. Select Toolbar and, from the drop-down list, choose MY TOOLBAR.
6. Click Add.
7. Under Categories, select Project.
8. Under Commands, select Project Information.
9. Click OK.
10. Repeat steps 7, 8, and 9 using the following selections:
    a. View; Reports
    b. Tools; Macros
    c. Tracking; Reschedule Work
11. Click OK, click Close, and click Close again.

Lesson Summary

- You can change schedule, calculation, view, general, and security settings in the Options dialog box.
- Customized tables and fields let you customize Project to suit any project.
- You can create or import formulas to calculate data in a field or table.
- You can customize the Project display with custom toolbars and menus so you can access data quickly.

Lesson Review

You can use the following questions to test your knowledge of the information in Lesson 4, "Project Customization." The questions are also available on the companion CD if you prefer to review them in electronic form.

NOTE Answers

Answers to these questions and explanations of why each answer choice is correct or incorrect are located in the "Answers" section at the end of the book.

1. You need to make changes to how Project works with tasks. Specifically, you want Project's default settings to configure all new tasks so that they are not effort-driven. Also, you do not want Project to add estimated durations to new tasks you create. Where in the Options dialog box can you make this change?
    A. Schedule tab
    B. General tab
    C. Collaborate tab
    D. Calculation tab

2. You want to configure Project so that it will link tasks when you cut, move, or insert them for Finish-to-Start task relationships. You want Project to create task dependencies for you in these instances, too. What do you need to configure in the Schedule tab of the Options dialog box?

   A. Select the New Tasks Are Effort-Driven check box.

   B. In the New Tasks drop-down list, select Start On Project Start Date.

   C. Select the Autolink Inserted Or Moved Tasks check box.

   D. Clear the Tasks Will Always Honor Their Constraint Dates check box.

3. You want to set up the Earned Value setting so that Physical % Complete is the calculation method. You also want to use the most current baseline for value comparisons. Which steps should you follow to do this? (Choose all that apply.)

   A. Select the Calculation tab.

   B. Click Earned Value and make the desired changes.

   C. Enable Edits To Total Task % Complete Will Be Spread To The Status Date.

   D. Open the Options dialog box.

4. What feature, when enabled, automatically updates your project's actual and remaining work and cost whenever a task's percent complete, actual duration, or remaining duration is updated?

   A. Edits To Total Task % Complete Will Be Spread To The Status Date

   B. Move Start Of Remaining Parts Before Status Date Forward To Status Date

   C. Updating Task Status Updates Resource Status

   D. Move End Of Completed Parts After Status Date Back To Status Date

5. You want to display the project-level summary task. Where do you enable this?

   A. Options dialog box, View tab

   B. Project Information dialog box

   C. Options dialog box, General tab

   D. The Organizer dialog box

6. You are working on a project for a company overseas and need to change the currency settings for the current project to match their monetary system. How do you do this?

   A. Make the changes using the Options dialog box, the Calculation tab, and the Currency Options settings.

   B. Make the changes in the Properties dialog box for the project.

   C. Make the changes in the Project Information dialog box.

   D. Make the changes using the Options dialog box, the View tab, and the Currency Options settings.

7. You've made a lot of changes to a project and have not saved them. You did this to find out what would happen if those changes were created and applied and have decided not to apply them. Now you want to undo the last 30 of the 50 changes you made. Unfortunately, you can only undo the last What can you do to ensure that you won't encounter this problem again? (Choose all that apply.)

   A. Create a copy of the project so that changes you apply won't be saved to the original.

   B. Save your workspace before making any changes and revert to it when applicable.

   C. Change the number of undo levels to 99.

   D. Create and save a baseline and revert to it when applicable.

8. Every person who works on your latest project will receive the same standard and overtime rates. You want to set these rates as the default for your project. How and where do you make the change? (Choose all that apply. Each answer represents part of the solution.)

   A. Make the changes in the Options dialog box and the Calculation tab.

   B. Make the changes in the Options dialog box and the General tab.

   C. In the Options dialog box and the Schedule tab, select the New Tasks Are Effort Driven check box.

   D. Click Set As Default.

9. You want Project to alert you each time a new resource or task is created when you make a new assignment. What can you do to make this happen?

   A. Select the Show External Successors and Show External Predecessors check boxes in the Options dialog box.

   B. Clear the Automatically Accept New External Data check box.

   C. Change the Calculation mode to Manual.

   D. Clear the Automatically Add New Resources And Tasks check box in the Options dialog box.

10. You don't like getting advice on Project or scheduling from the Planning Wizard, but you do appreciate the helpful information about the errors that appear. How can you configure the Planning Wizard in the Options dialog box so that you receive messages only about errors and nothing else? (Choose all that apply.)

    A. Clear the Advice From Planning Wizard check box.

    B. Clear the Advice About Scheduling check box.

    C. Select the Advice About Errors check box.

    D. Clear the Advice About Using Microsoft Office Project check box.

11. You want to be able to open legacy formats of files in Project. Right now, you can't open any at all. Which options in the Options dialog box can you use in Project to allow you to use legacy-formatted files? (Choose all that apply.)

    A. Select the Legacy Formats option Prompt When Loading Files With Legacy Or Non Default File Format.

    B. Select the Legacy Formats option Allow Loading Files With Legacy Or Non Default File Formats.

    C. Select Prompt For Project Info For New Projects.

    D. Clear the option Do Not Open/Save Files With Legacy Or Non Default File Formats In Project.

12. Your boss is on his way to your office and will be there in 10 minutes. He wants to see specific data on the same screen; he's not interested in a printout or having to wade through views. Specifically, he wants to compare the Calendar view and the Tracking Gantt. How can you achieve this? (Choose two. Each answer represents a complete solution.)

    A. Create a new single view. For Screen, select Calendar. For Group, select Complete And Incomplete tasks.

    B. While in Calendar view, select Window: Split. Right-click the default Task Form view bar in the bottom pane and select Tracking Gantt.

    C. In the More Views dialog box, select Calendar and click Edit. Add the Tracking Gantt to the view using the View Definition dialog box.

    D. Create a combination view using the Calendar as the top view and the Tracking Gantt as the bottom view.

13. Your business uses company-specific field names for resources to track resource information. These text fields have already been created and are in use in a coworker's project. You need to add these custom fields to your current project file and rename one of these resource fields in the current project. How do you import custom fields and change a custom field's name in the current project? (Choose three. Each answer represents part of the solution.)

    A. Choose Tools, Customize, Fields. In the Custom Fields dialog box, select Resource. In the Custom Fields dialog box, select the field to rename, and then click Rename.

    B. Open both the current project file and the file that contains the custom resource fields you want to add to your file.

    C. Use the Import wizard to import the data contained in your coworker's project file.

    D. Within the Organizer window, copy the custom resource fields contained in your coworker's file to your current project.

14. You need to apply a formula to a field in your project. The formula has already been created in another project called Calculation Project 4. What do you need to do to import the formula? (Choose two. Each answer represents a part of the solution.)

    A. In the Custom Fields dialog box, click Formula, and then Import Formula.

    B. In the Organizer, in the Fields tab, select the formula and click Copy.

    C. Open the Project file that contains the formula.

    D. Choose Insert: Project and insert the Project file that contains the formula.

15. Team members who created the task and resource data for an upcoming project did not use the heading Actual Cost when they created the tasks and their associated resources in Excel. Instead, they used the term OurCost. Because this is a short project, you don't want to worry about mapping fields when importing and exporting. You do want to change the default heading for Actual Cost to OurCost to avoid confusion as data is passed back and forth among the teams. Where can you rename the Actual Cost field?

    A. In the Column Definition dialog box for Actual Cost

    B. In the Custom Fields dialog box, under the Cost choices

    C. In the Font dialog box

    D. In the Text Styles dialog box

16. You want to format the Bar Shape and Bar Text for all of the applicable screens in your project. However, when you display the Format menu, the Bar option is dimmed. Why?

    A. In the Project Properties dialog box, under the Custom tab, custom settings have been configured.

    B. Change Highlighting is turned off.

    C. In the Options dialog box, from the View tab, Bars And Shapes In Gantt Views In 3-D is disabled.

    D. You are in a view that does not offer a bar chart.

17. The date format in the Gantt Chart is month/day, but the tasks in this project are extremely time sensitive. You want to change the default date format to show the month/day/year, followed by the current time. Where do you make this change?

    A. File, Layout

    B. In the Options dialog box, in the View tab

    C. Format, Bar Styles

    D. Format, Gridlines

Chapter Review

To further practice and reinforce the skills you learned in this chapter, you can perform the following tasks:

- Review the chapter summary.
- Review the list of key terms introduced in this chapter.
- Complete the case scenarios. These scenarios set up real-world situations involving the topics of this chapter and ask you to create a solution.
- Complete the suggested practices.
- Take a practice test.

Chapter Summary

- You can share data in many ways. You can import and export data to and from Excel, Access, and Outlook and create comma-separated values formats as well as text files. You can also publish data to an intranet or the Internet.
- When you (and other project managers) share a resource pool, you lessen the risk of overscheduling (or overallocating) your resources, as long as you use the pool to even out assignments. The pool makes it easier to do this.
- You can use Project's manual and automatic leveling features to resolve resource leveling problems, such as overallocation and underallocation.
- Importing and exporting allow you to work with people who do not have access to (or do not understand) Project. You can share data between Excel, Word, Outlook, and Access, or any program that can create or read comma- or text-delimited files.
- Master projects are project files that contain inserted project files. These are the subprojects.
- A cross-project link lets you configure a link between a primary (or source) project task and a secondary (or destination) project task. With this set up, as information is changed in the primary (or source) project file, the information in the secondary (or destination) project will automatically update as well.
- Templates, including default templates that ship with Project and those you create based on existing templates or from scratch, let you start new projects more easily because they include data, tasks, or settings that you'll need in the new project.
- Customizing Project's default settings allows you to tweak the program interface, calculation options, scheduling options, and more to suit your needs for both the current project and future ones.

Key Terms

Do you know what these key terms mean? You can check your answers by looking up the terms in the glossary at the end of the book.

- assignment contouring
- AutoLink
- exporting
- field
- ghost task
- importing
- import/export map
- leveling
- master project
- organizational breakdown structure (OBS)
- overallocation
- resource pool
- sharer file
- single view
- subproject
- underallocation

Case Scenarios

In the following case scenarios, you will apply what you have learned about using Project in this chapter. You can find answers to these questions in the "Answers" section at the end of this book.

Case Scenario 1: Sharing Project Data

You are starting a project using Project. You have just held your first project meeting with the team members and have learned that, due to their expertise, many of them have been through several similar tasks before and have a good idea of the tasks that need to be completed and how long each task will task. This is great news, but none of your team members have experience with Project. Answer the following questions:

1. You would like to take advantage of the experience that your project team members bring to the project. In particular, you would like to gather information from the Accounting department. Much of this department's information is stored in Excel. How can you use this information in your new project plan file?

2. Human Resources has offered a list of employees and their billable rates to help populate your resource list. The data is currently stored in a proprietary software program. How can you use this information without retyping everything?

3. You have been able to gather information from several sources to launch the tracking of this project. And you can foresee gathering similar information for future projects. What steps can you take now to save yourself a little bit of time during the import process in the future?

Case Scenario 2: Sharing Resources

You are managing a project using Project. This new project is just one of many your company is tracking. As a result, your project team is shared among several other projects. Answer the following questions:

1. You have been given strict instructions that your project needs to come in on time. However, your resources are all working on other projects that are running concurrently with your project. What option is available within Project that allows you to see the workload of your resources on other projects as well as your own?

2. One of the benefits to using a resource pool is that you can see how your resources are allocated across all projects that share the resource pool. You are concerned about an overallocation for one of your resources because when you view the Resource Sheet, that resource is displayed with a red font. Name another view that shows resource overallocation.

3. In reviewing your project plan, you realize that one of your resources is overallocated. Which feature can you use to resolve an overallocation, understanding that using it could mean the delay or splitting of any affected tasks?

Case Scenario 3: Working with a Master Project

You are managing a large project using Project. At the end of the planning phase, you determine that this project will have three major components, each built at the same time. Because the work to be completed in each phase is highly specialized, you have enlisted the help of experts in each area to manage the phase tasks. Answer the following questions:

1. What method can you use that allows each of the experts to keep track of their tasks while still being able to maintain easy access to monitoring and reporting data for all projects, making changes as you deem necessary?

2. Some tasks in Phase 3 rely on the completion of tasks in Phase 2 before they can begin. What can you do to set up this type of dependency between the two phases if each phase is stored in a separate project file?

3. You have already created a master project plan file and inserted the necessary sub-projects. At the completion of Phase 1, it is no longer necessary to maintain the link between the subproject and the master project, although you would like to keep a list of the completed tasks in the master project file. How can you accomplish this?

Case Scenario 4: Customizing Project

You have been using Project for a few months. At this point you have a few sets of data that often pertain to your projects but that do not seem to have a related field for storage. Also, you seem to favor the same three tables for displaying your table data. Answer the following questions:

1. Currently, you are storing a few sets of data that don't have related project fields in Excel. It is becoming cumbersome to go back and forth between these two programs. Instead, you would like to store this customized information in your project file. How can you accomplish this?

2. You are often switching between the Entry, Cost, and Schedule tables to see updates to one or two columns in each table. How can you make this task easier?

3. The field headers displayed in the Entry Table (such as Task Name) are simply not descriptive enough for the people who will be updating the current project plan. What can you do to incorporate industry-specific terminology into the field header text?

Suggested Practices

To help you successfully master the exam objectives presented in this chapter, complete the following tasks. We suggest you work through all of these exercises.

- **Practice 1: Import and Export** Import and export data into Project from Outlook, Excel, and Access, and understand options for saving as text files and similar options. It's important that you be able to share your data with others in any format they need.

- **Practice 2: Publish a Project to the Web** Find someone who has a Project Server. Create an enterprise project or download a template online and go through the steps to save the project to the Internet or to a company intranet.

- **Practice 3: Resource Pools** Learn as much as you can about resource pools. Although you'll likely see only a handful of questions on the test about them, in the real world you'll probably access resource pools frequently. Consider visiting a company that uses a resource pool or skim though a larger Project book, such as *Microsoft Office Project 2007 Inside Out* (Microsoft Press, 2007).

- **Practice 4: Linking Project Tasks** Visit *www.microsoft.com/en-us/training* and search for "Linking Project Tasks." View the 45-minute training video on linking tasks in Project.

■ **Practice 5: Work with Templates**   Practice creating templates, and then sharing them using the Organizer. Try to create a template that suits your work needs, including display options, security options, and calculation options.

■ **Practice 6: Learn About Leveling**   The best way to learn more about leveling is to create a project with a dozen or so tasks, with resources, durations, and dependencies. Change the data associated with these tasks and watch what happens after leveling.

■ **Practice 7: Incorporate Word and PowerPoint**   Learn how to present your project in Microsoft Word, PowerPoint, or Visio at *www.microsoft.com/en-us/training*. Search for "Present Your Project."

Take a Practice Test

The practice tests on this book's companion CD offer many options. For example, you can test yourself on just one exam objective, or you can test yourself on all the 70-632 certification exam content. You can set up the test so that it closely simulates the experience of taking a certification exam, or you can set it up in study mode so that you can look at the correct answers and explanations after you answer each question.

MORE INFO   **Practice tests**

For details about all the practice test options available, see the "How to Use the Practice Tests" section in this book's Introduction.

Chapter 5
Closing the Project

Closing the project is a time for celebration. Typically, the bulk of the work is complete and many of your team members have already moved on to their next projects. Hopefully, you have made it successfully through the entire project, and, by adhering to the project management principles in the Project Management Body of Knowledge (PMBOK) and fully utilizing Microsoft Office Project 2007 to track your project's progress, you have easily navigated any roadblocks that cropped up. However, just because the project's tasks have been completed does not mean you have closed the project.

Only a couple of tasks are left for you, the project manager, to complete as you formally close your project. In addition to capturing lessons learned from the project, you will probably want to prepare some reports for yourself and for the project stakeholders.

This chapter looks at ways you can capture lessons learned, analyze project variance, create an Earned Value report, manage by exception using filters, and work with Project's Reports and Visual Reports features.

Exam objectives in this chapter:
- Track project progress.
- Analyze variance.
- Create reports.

Lessons in this chapter:

Before You Begin

As you read through this chapter, you will continue to see standard project management terms—many of which might already be familiar. Before you begin, you should:

- Have a good understanding of how to use Project to plan, track, and manage your project
- Have an idea of the types of data you would like to extract from a project plan to capture lessons learned upon closing the project

Lesson 1: Reporting

Project reporting is a technique used throughout the project—not just at the end. For example, predefined reports include summaries of tasks to which resources have been assigned and an update on tasks currently on the critical path. But you can use several reports when formally closing the project plan as well.

Additionally, Project offers a new Visual Reports feature that helps you present the project data in a vibrant way and even use that data for analysis by exporting it to Microsoft Excel 2007 and Microsoft Visio.

In this lesson you will learn how to preview and print basic reports and how to create visual reports, including an Earned Value report. This lesson will also revisit the subject of filters as it looks at managing by exception.

> **After this lesson, you will be able to:**
> - Capture lessons learned.
> - Create visual reports.
> - Create an Earned Value report.
> - Manage by exception using filters.
>
> **Estimated lesson time: 45 minutes**

Capturing Lessons Learned

Even though projects vary depending on the task at hand, you can still learn lessons from one project to carry over to the next. Throughout the project, and especially at the end, you will want to gather and document anything that worked well (or not so well) so that future project managers (and you) can learn from your experiences. Doing so provides a nice opportunity to formally close the project, giving team members an opportunity to evaluate their job performances before moving on. A couple of key questions you can ask yourself and others involved are:

- What did we do right?
- What did we do wrong?
- What do we need to improve?

MORE INFO   PMBOK'S Closing phase

For more information on the Closing phase of a project, refer to PMBOK's guidelines. You can also review the following article available from Microsoft Office Online: *http://office.microsoft.com/en-us/project/HA011277661033.aspx*.

Some of this information comes verbally or in writing from your project team. But some of this information can be acquired from Project's reporting feature.

Creating a Basic Report

The previous chapter, "Team Collaboration and Multiple Projects," referred to several available basic reports that you can use to communicate the project status to those involved. These reports are available in a task, resource, or crosstab format. You can access the Reports dialog box, shown in Figure 5-1, by choosing Report and then Reports from the Menu bar.

Figure 5-1   The Reports dialog box

To print a basic report, follow these steps:

1. Choose Report, and then choose Reports.
2. Select your desired report category and click Select.
3. Select a report in the *<Category of* Report> Reports dialog box and click Select. Project displays a preview of the report.
4. In the window containing the preview of the report, click Print to print the report. Figure 5-2 shows a sample Who Does What report (prior to any work being done).

Who Does What as of Wed 2/4/09
Customer Feedback Monitoring

ID	ⓘ	Resource Name	Work
1		Audit Committee	0 hrs
2		Legal Department	0 hrs
3		External Auditors	0 hrs
4		Executive Committee	0 hrs
5		CFO/Controller	0 hrs
6		Marketing Group	0 hrs
7		Strategic Planning Committee	0 hrs
8		PR/IR Dept	0 hrs
9		Chairman	0 hrs

Figure 5-2   A sample report

5. To change the appearance of any report prior to printing it, click Page Setup, make the necessary changes, and then click Print Preview to see them.

6. Click Print.

If you encounter the error message shown in Figure 5-3, you have created a custom report or defined criteria for the report for fields or cells that do not have any printable data. If you see this message, click OK and set new report parameters.

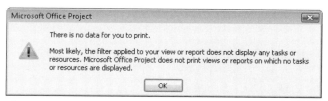

Figure 5-3   The error shown when Project has no data to display in a report

---

Exam Tip   Open each report and see what it offers. You might be asked on the exam which report would work best in a given situation. For instance, what report would best show tasks that have yet to be started? (Choose the Current Activity: Unstarted Tasks report.)

Creating Visual Reports

New to Project, the Visual Reports feature displays your project data in a PivotTable format. *PivotTables* provide an interactive summary representation of your data. PivotTables, along with PivotCharts, are great ways for summarizing data on the fly, allowing you to break down your data in different ways.

The beauty of Project's visual reports is that they are displayed in either Excel 2003 (or later) or Visio Professional 2007 formats. These display formats allow you to work with your project data and customize it to display just the information you need.

You can access the Visual Reports – Create Report dialog box, shown in Figure 5-4, by choosing Report and then Visual Reports from the Menu bar.

Visual reports offer a great deal of flexibility. You can choose to view report templates available for either Excel 2003 (or later) or Visio Professional 2007, or both. Note that you that you can't display these reports unless you have Excel, Visio, or both, installed on your computer. For example, if you try to select only Visio in the Visual Reports – Create Report dialog box, you won't see any reports listed if you don't have Visio installed on the computer. In Excel 2003 (or later), these visual reports are displayed in the form of PivotTables or PivotCharts. A sample PivotChart is shown in Figure 5-5.

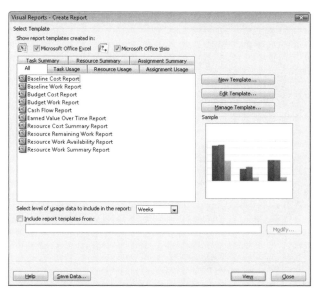

Figure 5-4   The Visual Reports dialog box

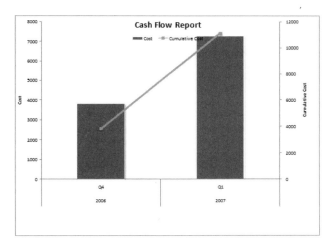

Figure 5-5   A sample PivotChart

In Visio Professional 2007 these visual reports are displayed in the form of PivotDiagrams. A sample PivotDiagram is shown in Figure 5-6.

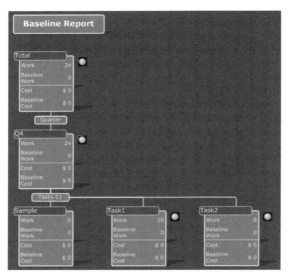

Figure 5-6   A sample PivotDiagram

Regardless of which program you choose to view your visual reports, each view allows you to customize what project information you see while viewing the report—this represents on-the-fly analysis at its best because visual reports offer a dynamic interface and a vibrant data display that are not available with basic reports.

To create a visual report, follow these steps:

1. Choose Report, and choose Visual Reports.
2. Click the All tab, and select the report that you want to create.
3. Select Years, Quarters, Months, Weeks, or Days from the Select Level Of Usage Data To Include In The Report drop-down list.
4. Click View to generate the report and open it in Excel or Visio.

If the report that you want to create is not listed in the All tab in step 2 but is stored on your computer or a network drive, select the Include Report Templates From check box, and then click Modify to browse to the location that contains your report. When you locate the report, select it and click OK.

MORE INFO   **Working with PivotTables and PivotCharts**

For more information on working with PivotTables and PivotCharts, refer to the following article at Microsoft Office Online: *http://office.microsoft.com/en-us/excel/ HP101773841033.aspx?pid=CH101768451033*.

> **Quick Check**
>
> - What would you use to create a basic report that contains information about tasks that are in progress?
>
> **Quick Check Answer**
>
> - Report, Reports, Current Activities.

Creating an Earned Value Report

Earned value analysis is a way of evaluating project schedule and cost performance using monetary measures. When applied, earned value measures the actual amount of work accomplished, regardless of the effort expended or the time elapsed. As such, it is a valuable method for measuring project performance because you can see how much you have planned to spend versus what you have spent, as well as how much work you expected to be complete compared to what is actually complete.

You've learned about the earned value concept and looked at a few of the earned value fields already. When you need to create a report based on this data, there are three earned value task tables in Project, as shown in Figure 5-7, and one resource earned value table.

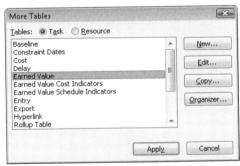

Figure 5-7   Displaying an earned value table

MORE INFO   **Using earned value to track your project's progress**

For more information about using earned value to track your project's progress, refer to the following article available on Microsoft Office Online: *http://office.microsoft.com/en-us/project/ HA101567921033.aspx?pid=CH100666601033*.

To calculate and review earned value in various ways using Project, you will first want to define your preferred Earned Value options. To define these options, follow these steps:

1. Choose Tools, choose Options, and then click the Calculation tab.
2. Click Earned Value to display the Earned Value dialog box. See Figure 5-8.

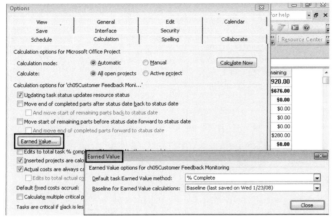

Figure 5-8   Obtaining earned value information

3. In the Default Task Earned Value Method drop-down list, select the calculation method that you want Project to use when it calculates the Budgeted Cost of Work Performed (BCWP). You can select from % Complete and Physical % Complete.
4. In the Baseline For Earned Value Calculations drop-down list, select the baseline that you want Project to use when it calculates the earned value totals.
5. Click Close. Click OK.
6. Choose View, and choose More Views.
7. In the More Views dialog box, select Task Sheet, and then click Apply.
8. Choose View, choose Table, and then choose More Tables.
9. In the Tables list, select Earned Value, Earned Value Cost Indicators, or Earned Value Schedule Indicators, and then click Apply.
10. To see a breakdown of the earned value of tasks by period, choose View, and choose Task Usage.

In addition to the earned value tables, you can also use Project's reporting feature to display earned value data. Located under the Costs category in the Reports dialog box (choose Report and then Reports), you can view the Earned Value report, shown in Figure 5-9.

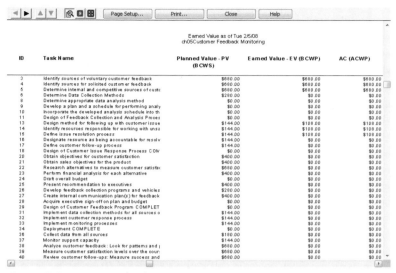

Figure 5-9 An Earned Value report

To view the Earned Value basic report, follow these steps:

1. Choose Report and choose Reports.
2. Select the Costs category and click Select.
3. Select the Earned Value report and click Select. See Figure 5-10.

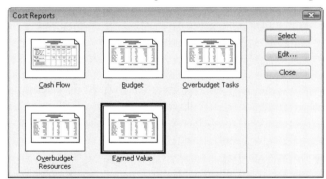

Figure 5-10 Creating an Earned Value cost report

The Earned Value report is a basic Project report. You can also view the Earned Value Over Time visual report to see earned value information in a chart format, as shown in Figure 5-11.

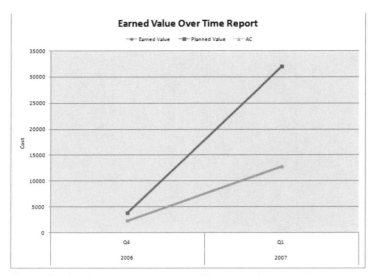

Figure 5-11 An Earned Value Over Time visual report

To display the Earned Value Over Time visual report, complete the following steps:

1. Choose Report, and choose Visual Reports.
2. In the Visual Reports dialog box, in the All tab, select Earned Value Over Time report.
3. Click View.

Exam Tip   Be careful when answering questions about reports on the exam. If you see words like "dynamic" or "vibrant" when describing a desired report, the question is most likely looking for a "visual report."

As you can see in Figure 5-11, the Earned Value Over Time report displays a graph in Excel that plots the actual cost of work performed, the budgeted cost of work scheduled, and the budgeted cost of work performed over time (earned value).

Using the status date to plot earned value   Rather than using the current date as your earned value calculation, modify the status date in the Project Information dialog box (Project menu) to enter a date to use as a status date for earned value calculations.

Quick Check

■ Describe what earned value analysis is and what it offers in Project.

Quick Check Answer

■ Earned value analysis evaluates schedule and cost performance and presents that performance in terms of monetary value.

Manage by Exception Using Filters

In every project you will most likely have some experienced resources and others who are inexperienced and need more supervision. If this is the case, you might opt to forego micro-managing in place of the management by exception approach. In other words, you would allow your team members to complete their assignments, intervening only when the project plan seems to be off-track or the work of the resources is not meeting the scope standards.

Just as you use filters to view specific project data in the Project program, you can use the same filters to modify what information is displayed in your reports. In this way you can print a customized report without having to create a new report from scratch.

To modify a predefined report to filter out unnecessary project data, select any report (such as the To-Do List), and then click Edit. Clicking Edit will bring up the dialog box associated with this report. If you've chosen to edit the To-Do List, for example, the Task Report dialog box opens. This is shown in Figure 5-12. From here, use the Filter drop-down list to choose a filter to apply to the selected report, again, shown in Figure 5-12.

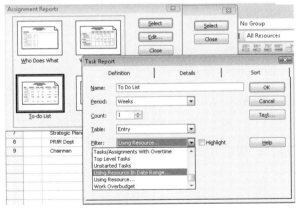

Figure 5-12   Task Report dialog box

You won't always see the Task Report dialog box, however. For example, if you edit the Task Usage report, the Crosstab Report dialog box opens. You can filter data there. If you edit the Overallocated Resources report, the Resource Report dialog box opens. In this case you can filter data there.

If you often find yourself using the same filter on the same report, consider creating a custom report. Creating custom reports is covered in the next lesson.

PRACTICE Using Basic and Visual Reports

In these practices you will review how to use the Reports menu options to create basic and visual reports. In Exercise 1 you will create and print a basic report. In Exercise 2 you'll create and print an Earned Value visual report. In Exercise 3 you will apply a filter to a report in order to view only desired data.

▶ **Exercise 1   Create and Print a Basic Report**

You are working on a project for a new construction site and need to print the critical tasks for the project for your stakeholders.

To complete this exercise, perform the following steps:

1. Choose File, choose New, and click On Computer.
2. In the Templates dialog box, click the Project Templates tab.
3. Double-click the Commercial Construction report.
4. From the Report menu, choose Reports.
5. Select Overview, and then click Select.
6. In the Overview Reports dialog box, select Critical Tasks.
7. Click Select.
8. Click Print.

▶ **Exercise 2   Create and Print an Earned Value Visual Report**

You need to print a report that plots actual cost of work performed, planned value, and earned value for your project. This needs to represent the data over time.

To complete this exercise, perform the following steps:

1. Choose File, choose Open, and browse to the Practice Files folder on the accompanying CD.
2. Open the ch05Customer Feedback Monitoring project.
3. From the Report menu, choose Visual Reports.
4. In the All tab, select Earned Value Over Time report.

5. In the Select Level Of Usage Data To Include In This Report drop-down list, select Weeks.

6. Click View.

7. Choose File and then Print to print the report.

▶ **Exercise 3   Apply a Filter to a Report**

You want to print a report for task usage, but you want to view and print only critical tasks.

To complete this exercise, perform the following steps:

1. Choose File, choose New, and click On Computer.

2. In the Templates dialog box, click the Project Templates tab.

3. Double-click the Commercial Construction report.

4. From the Report menu, choose Reports.

5. Select Workload, and click Select.

6. Select Task Usage, and click Edit.

7. In the Filter drop-down list, select Critical.

8. Click OK, and then click Select to display the filtered report.

9. Click once in the report to zoom in on the data.

10. Click Print.

Lesson Summary

- Basic and visual reports let you review your project's progress by reporting on various data in it, such as current activities, costs, assignments, workload, budget, and more.

- An Earned Value report plots actual cost of work performed, planned value, and earned value for your project and displays that data over time.

- Filtering data prior to printing it can provide just the desired data in a report.

Lesson Review

You can use the following questions to test your knowledge of the information in Lesson 1, "Reporting." The questions are also available on the companion CD if you prefer to review them in electronic form.

NOTE   Answers

Answers to these questions and explanations of why each answer choice is correct or incorrect are located in the "Answers" section at the end of the book.

1. You've just finished a lengthy and important project and are starting the formal closure process. You have determined that the stakeholders are pleased with the outcome and that the goals of the project were met. Now you want to capture data that can help you and your team learn from the mistakes made in this project so you won't repeat them. What can you create to get this data? (Choose two.)

   A. Basic and visual reports in Project

   B. Reports that are filtered to include only specific data

   C. A project template that is saved to the Templates folder

   D. The Overbudget visual report

2. How do you create an Earned Value report? (Choose two. Each answer represents part of the solution.)

   A. In the All tab, select Earned Value Over Time report.

   B. Open the Basic Reports dialog box.

   C. Open the Visual Reports dialog box.

   D. From the Overview options, select Earned Value Over Time report.

3. You want to view and print a basic report about current activities in your project, but you want to view tasks in progress only for a specific range of dates. How can you create such a report?

   A. Use AutoFilter to filter the data you want on the screen, and then choose File, Print.

   B. Create a basic Current Activity report and filter the data prior to printing.

   C. Create a visual Task Summary report and filter the data prior to printing.

   D. Switch to Task Usage view, select the desired data, and print the data using File, Print.

4. You just finished a project and want to review the data so that you can to learn what you can improve on next time. You'd like to create a vibrant, colorful report in bar graph form that contains information on the budgeted work for the project. What type of report should you create in Project?

   A. Basic report

   B. Excel report

   C. Microsoft PowerPoint report

   D. Visual report

Lesson 2: Custom Reports

There is no doubt that Project comes loaded with enough predefined reports to extract much of the information you need from your project file. However, when you reach a more advanced level of working with your projects in this program, you might develop the need to create your own reports—ones that are specific to your project and to your work as a project manager. That is where creating custom reports comes in.

In this lesson you will learn how to create a custom report in Project, as well as how to modify a custom report and set print options for a custom report.

After this lesson, you will be able to:
- ■ Create custom reports.
- ■ Modify a custom report.
- ■ Set custom report print options.

Estimated lesson time: 45 minutes

Creating Custom Project Reports

Even though Project has more than 25 predefined basic reports (and visual reports), you have the option of creating a custom basic report based on your individual project needs. Custom reports can be summarized by:

- ■ Task
- ■ Resource
- ■ Calendar
- ■ Crosstab

You create custom reports in the Custom Reports dialog box, shown in Figure 5-13. Custom is one of the six categories you see when you open the Reports dialog box (Report menu).

Figure 5-13   The Custom Reports dialog box

There are many ways to create reports. These are defined in the next several sections.

Create a Custom Report by Editing an Existing Report

One way to create a report is to use a report that is already available in Project and then rename and edit it. You can create new custom Task, Resource, Monthly Calendar, or Crosstab reports. To create a custom Task report based on an existing Project report, follow these steps:

1. Choose Report, and choose Reports.
2. Select Custom, and then click Select.
3. To create a task report, click New in the Custom Reports dialog box, select Task, and then click OK.
4. In the resulting dialog box, type a name for the report in the Name box. Figure 5-14 shows the dialog box that opens when Task is selected. (Clicking Resource in step 3 will open the Resource Report dialog box; clicking Monthly Calendar will open the Monthly Calendar Report Definition dialog box; clicking Crosstab will open the Crosstab Report dialog box.)

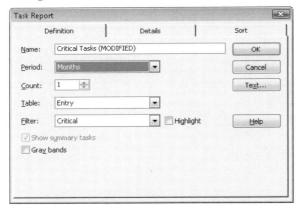

Figure 5-14   Editing an existing report using the Task Report dialog box

5. In the Period drop-down list, select the time period that you want to display.
6. In the Count text box, type the number of time periods you want to report. (The Count box is unavailable if you select Entire Project from the Period drop-down list.)
7. In the Table drop-down list, select the table that you want to display.
8. In the Filter drop-down list, select the filter that you want to apply.
9. If desired, select the Highlight check box to show the filtered tasks with different formatting.
10. If desired, select the Show Summary Tasks check box to include summary tasks in the report.
11. If desired, select the Gray Bands check box to display the report with gray divider lines in the formatting.

12. If desired, sort the task or resource data in a report. To do so, click the Sort tab, select the field that you want to sort on in the Sort By drop-down list, and then select Ascending or Descending.

13. To sort by the second or third sort criteria, select the field that you want in the appropriate Then By drop-down list, and then select Ascending or Descending. See Figure 5-15.

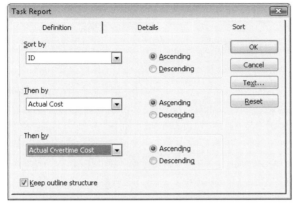

Figure 5-15   Sort data if desired

14. Click OK.

15. Note that the edited report is now available in the Custom Reports dialog box. Click Select to view the report.

Create a New Custom Resource Report

You can also create a new report from scratch. These reports can be Task reports, Resource reports, Monthly Calendar reports, or Crosstab reports. Additionally, you can apply options like showing summary tasks, highlighting filtered data, and applying gray bands to specific data. To create a new Resource report (creating a new Task report is similar), complete the following steps:

1. Choose Report, and choose Reports.

2. Select Custom, and then click Select. Click New to create a new report from scratch.

3. In the Define New Report dialog box, select Resource. (Note that Task is also an option and is similar to creating a Resource report.) See Figure 5-16. Click OK.

4. In the Resource Report dialog box, in the Definition tab, type a name for the report in the Name box.

5. In the Period drop-down list, select the time period that you want to display.

6. In the Count drop-down list, select the number of time periods you want to report. (The Count box is unavailable if you select Entire Project.)

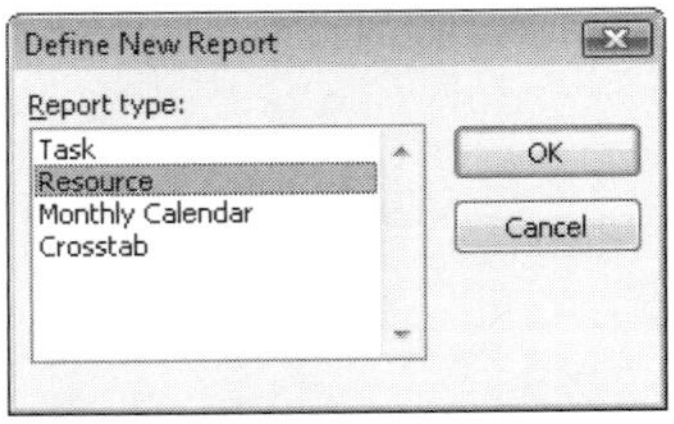

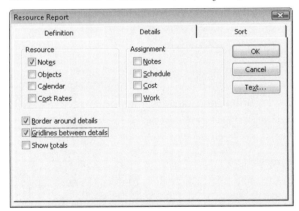

Figure 5-16 Defining your new report

7. In the Table drop-down list, select the table that you want to display.

8. In the Filter drop-down list, select the filter that you want to apply.

9. Select the Highlight check box to show the filtered tasks with different formatting.

10. Select the Show Summary Tasks check box to include summary tasks in the report.

11. Select the Gray Bands check box to display the report with gray divider lines in the formatting.

12. Click the Sort tab, select the field that you want to sort by in the Sort By drop-down list, and then select Ascending or Descending.

13. To sort by the second or third sort criteria, select the field that you want in the appropriate Then By drop-down list, and then select Ascending or Descending.

14. Click the Details tab to view details regarding the new report. Note that you can select various check boxes to include notes, objects, and other data by selecting it. See Figure 5-17.

Figure 5-17 Customizing the report

15. Click Text to display the Text Styles dialog box.

16. In the Item To Change drop-down list, select an item.

17. Under Font, select a font for this item. Under Font Style, select a style for the item. Under Size, select a size for the item.

18. Select the Underline check box to underline the data.

19. Select a choice for Color, Background Color, and Background Pattern. Click OK.

20. Repeat steps 16 through 20 for any other item to format.

21. Click OK.

22. Note that the edited report is now available in the Custom Reports dialog box.

Create a Custom Calendar Report

It is also possible to create a monthly calendar report. This report can contain filters to filter tasks, work, and other data; a calendar; and labels with ID, Name, and Duration, among others. To create a custom calendar report, follow these steps:

1. Choose Report, and choose Reports.

2. Select Custom, and then click Select.

3. Click New, select Monthly Calendar, and then click OK. (To edit a monthly calendar report, click its name in the Reports box, and then click Edit.)

4. In the Monthly Calendar Report Definition dialog box, type a name for the report. See Figure 5-18.

Figure 5-18   Create a calendar report

5. Select the calendar that you want to use from the Calendar drop-down list.

6. Select the Gray Nonworking Days check box to show nonworking days in gray.

7. Select the Solid Bar Breaks check box to show a solid line at the end of a bar when a task continues into the next week.

8. Select the Print Gray Bands check box to show a gray divider line between the dates that separate task information that doesn't fit on the calendar.

9. Select Bars, Lines, or Start/Finish dates to format how tasks are shown in a monthly calendar report.

10. Select or clear the ID, Name, and Duration check boxes to format task labels in a monthly calendar report.

11. Click OK.

Create a Crosstab Report

Although you are probably already familiar with task, resource, and calendar reports because those are some of the most commonly used reports, crosstabs have not yet been introduced in this training kit. A crosstab report customizes the information that it displays based on a specified period of time. A sample crosstab report is shown in Figure 5-19.

Report 4 as of Mon 2/11/08
Customer Feedback Monitoring

	12/31	1/7	1/14	1/21	1/28
Audit Committee					
Legal Department					
External Auditors		32 hrs	84 hrs	80 hrs	
Executive Committee		32 hrs	84 hrs	80 hrs	
CFO/Controller		32 hrs	84 hrs	80 hrs	
Marketing Group					
Strategic Planning Committee					
PR/IR Dept					
Chairman		32 hrs	84 hrs	80 hrs	

Figure 5-19   A sample crosstab report

To create a custom crosstab report, follow these steps:

1. Choose Report, and choose Reports.
2. Select Custom, and then click Select.
3. Click New, select Crosstab, and then click OK. (To edit a crosstab report, select its name in the Custom Reports dialog box, and then click Edit.)
4. In the Definition tab, type a name for the report in the Name box.
5. In the Crosstab section, select the time period that you want to display. See Figure 5-20.

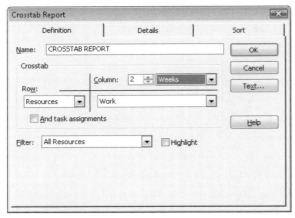

Figure 5-20   Creating a crosstab report

6. Select whether to display tasks or resources from the Row drop-down list.

7. Select the task or resource field that you want to appear in the crosstab report from the field drop-down list. (This is the unlabeled drop-down list displayed to the right of the Row drop-down list.)

8. Select either the And Resource Assignments or the And Task Assignments check box to include assignments with tasks or resources. These check boxes appear only when Resources are selected to show in the Row box or when Tasks are selected to show in the Row box.

9. Select a filter to display from the Filter drop-down list.

10. Select the Highlight check box to show the filtered items with different formatting.

11. In the Details tab, select the format that you want from the Date Format drop-down list.

12. To include zero values, select the Show Zero Values check box.

13. In the Sort tab, select the field that you want to sort by in the Sort By drop-down list, and then select Ascending or Descending.

14. To sort by the second or third sort criteria, select the field that you want in the appropriate Then By drop-down list, and then select Ascending or Descending.

15. Click OK.

Quick Check

- You need to create custom reports for three people in your company. The first custom report needs to display the requested data based on a specified period of time. The second person needs to view data that has been filtered to show only nonbudget resources. The third person needs a report that shows tasks drawn on a calendar instead of a Gantt Chart or other view and that shows the data over a period of months. What type of report should you create for each?

Quick Check Answer

- Create a crosstab report for the first person. Create a new custom filtered resource report for the second person. Create a calendar report for the third person.

Modifying a Custom Report

You can modify both custom reports and predefined reports using the Custom Reports dialog box. In addition to using the New button to create a new custom report, you can use the Edit button to edit any selected report. As explained in the first section of this lesson, to modify a custom report, select the report, click Edit, and then edit the report as desired.

Also, in the Custom Reports dialog box you can use the Copy button to make a copy of an existing report. In this way you can copy all the existing settings, making minor changes where necessary and saving those changes as a new report. This dialog box also contains an Organizer button for accessing the Organizer, where you can copy your custom creations from the current project into the Global.mpt file or other open project files, allowing you to share your custom projects with others. This training kit has discussed the Organizer in regard to several topics, including:

- Filters
- Groups
- Templates

As an added note, you can apply a method to naming your custom reports similar to that mentioned when creating other custom items within Project. Like filters, the custom reports you create are saved within the predefined basic report list. An easy way to make your custom reports stand out is to name them using all capital letters or to use a standard prefix. As you can see in Figure 5-21, using all capital letters helps a custom report stand out from this long report list.

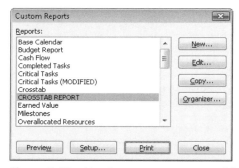

Figure 5-21   Naming a custom report with all capital letters to make it easier to locate

You can easily delete custom reports when they are no longer needed, just like filters and groups, using the Organizer dialog box. To delete a custom report, follow these steps:

1. Choose Tools, and choose Organizer.
2. In the Reports tab, select the custom report to delete. See Figure 5-22.
3. Click Delete and then Yes to confirm the deletion.

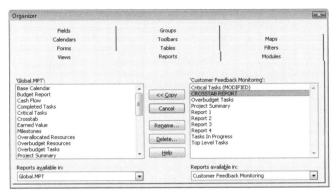

Figure 5-22   Deleting a custom report

Setting Custom Report Print Options

Printing reports is often more involved than choosing File and Print from the Menu bar, although many project views can be printed using this simplified method. If you need to print only what you see on your screen, this method might be all you need. When you choose Print from the File menu, you will see the Print dialog box, shown in Figure 5-23.

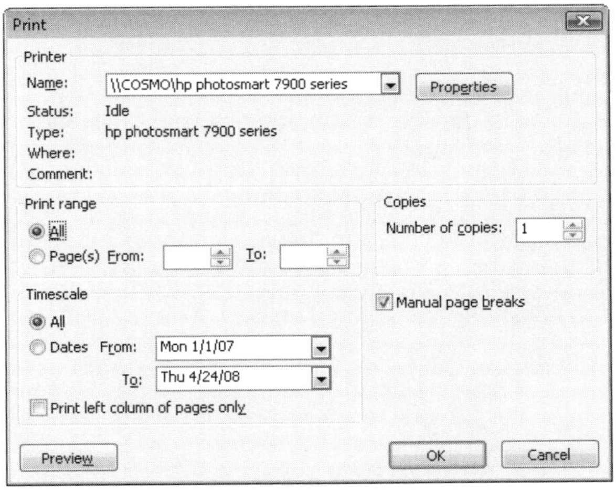

Figure 5-23   The Print dialog box

In the Print dialog box you can set your print range, project plan timescale, and the number of copies. This works fine for basic print jobs. But when working with reports, you might want to access additional options. These options are found in the Page Setup dialog box, shown in Figure 5-24. You can access this dialog box by choosing File and then Page Setup.

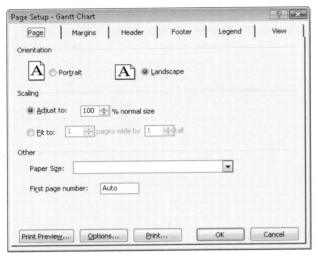

Figure 5-24 The Page Setup dialog box

To view the Page Setup dialog box for a report listed under one of the five main basic report categories, follow these steps:

1. Choose Report, and choose Reports.
2. Select any report category and click Select.
3. Select any report and click Select.
4. Click Page Setup. (If you selected a custom report, in the Custom Reports dialog box select the report and click Setup.)

Whether it's a custom report or a basic report, Project opens the Page Setup dialog box with six tabs. The first four tabs (Page, Margins, Header, and Footer) are the most commonly used with reports. Legend and View are available when printing a project view, such as the Gantt Chart view, but are not available when printing reports. The Page Setup dialog box tabs are:

- Page
- Margins
- Header
- Footer
- Legend
- View

Page Tab

In the Page tab, shown in Figure 5-24, you can specify page options for the report (or current view), including page orientation, page scaling, and paper size.

Near the top of the dialog box, under Orientation, you can specify whether the report should print Portrait (vertically) or Landscape (horizontally).

In the middle of the dialog box, under Scaling, you can reduce the zoom level of the selected report to allow for more data on a printed page. Next to Adjust To, you can reduce or enlarge the printed project data based on the percentage you enter. Alternatively, use the Fit To option to define the number of pages wide and tall that a report would ideally fit into.

At the bottom of the Page tab, you can specify the size of the paper on which you will be printing, as well as the number of the first page related to printed page numbers.

Five command buttons are located at the bottom of the dialog box that are available from every tab in the Page Setup dialog box. Table 5-1 explains their purposes.

Table 5-1   Page Setup Dialog Box Command Buttons

Command	Description
Print Preview	Opens the Print Preview window and displays the report as it would appear when printed.
Options	Opens the Printer Properties dialog box, allowing you to modify your specific printer settings but not the printer itself (to change the printer, you will need to open the Print dialog box [File menu]).
Print	Opens the Print dialog box, which you can use to send the selected report to the printer.
OK	Accepts the page setup changes you have made and closes the Page Setup dialog box.
Cancel	Discards the page setup changes you have made and closes the Page Setup dialog box.

Margins Tab

The Margins tab, shown in Figure 5-25, in the Page Setup dialog box is specifically for working with page margins related to the report (or current view). In this tab you can set your top, bottom, left, and right margins and designate the addition of a border around the printed pages.

The bulk of this tab is taken up by page margin settings. Using the spin boxes, you can increase or decrease the displayed margins. Near the bottom of the Margins tab, using the options, you can choose to display a border around every page or accept the default setting of printing your report without borders. Even though the Outer Pages option is visible (but dimmed), this option is available only when printing Network Diagram view.

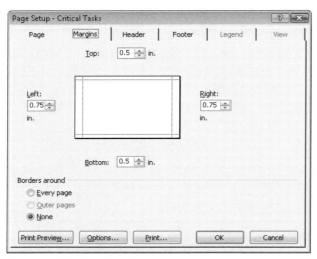

Figure 5-25   The Margins tab

Header and Footer Tabs

Although they are two separate tabs, the Header tab, shown in Figure 5-26, and the Footer tab, shown in Figure 5-27, contain similar options.

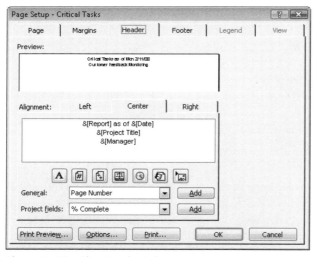

Figure 5-26   The Header tab

In these two tabs you can specify the exact information that should appear on the top (header) and bottom (footer) of each printed page, including text, automatically generated page numbers, dates, and times.

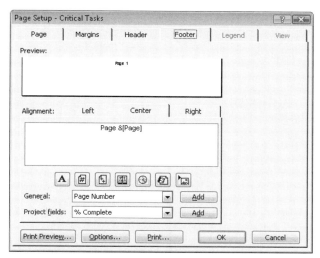

Figure 5-27 The Footer tab

The top portion of the Header and Footer tabs is devoted to a live preview of how the header or footer looks with each change you make.

In the center of these tabs is an Alignment section. The Alignment section is divided into three tabs organized by their position on the page. The Left tab displays information that appears aligned with the left margin, while the Right tab displays information that appears aligned with the right margin. And the Center tab displays information that will appear centered on the page between the left and right margins.

Just below the Alignment tabs is a set of toolbar buttons that you can use to format the text you add and include elements that are automatically generated from your project file. These toolbar buttons are explained in Table 5-2. Figure 5-28 shows what commands go with what buttons.

Table 5-2 Header and Footer Tab Command Buttons

Command	Description
Font	Opens the Font dialog box. From this dialog box, you can change the font, font size, color, and text style of the selected text.
Page Number	Inserts page numbers in the header or footer when the report is printed.
Total Pages	Inserts the total number of pages in the printed view or report and adjusts the page numbers automatically when the report is printed.
Date	Inserts the date the report is printed into the header or footer.
Time	Inserts the time the report is printed into the header or footer.
File Name	Inserts the file name of the active project into the header or footer.

Table 5-2   **Header and Footer Tab Command Buttons**

Command	Description
Picture	Opens the Insert Picture dialog box, which you can use to select an image to insert into the header or footer. Many project managers use this feature to insert a company logo into a printed report page.

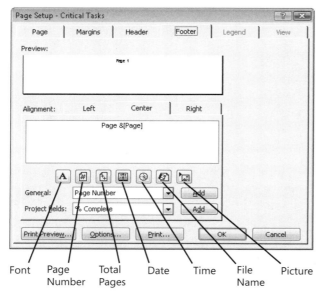

Font   Page   Total   Date   Time   File   Picture
        Number Pages   Name

Figure 5-28   Alignment buttons

Exam Tip   Although you probably won't be asked how to print a file on the exam or how to con-figure the Page Setup options, you might be asked if it is possible to print a report with headers, footers, pictures, dates, and times. The answer to those questions would be yes, by configuring options in the Page Setup dialog box.

PRACTICE Working with Custom Reports

In these exercises you will review what you've learned in this lesson. The first exercise is to create your own custom report. The second exercise is to modify a custom report. The third exercise is to set custom report print options.

▶ **Exercise 1   Create a Custom Report**

You need to create a custom report that includes filtered information regarding the tasks assigned to your project. You want the report to cover a period of three weeks, you want to view cost for the resources, and you want to filter the resources to show only material resources.

To complete this exercise, perform the following steps:

1. Choose File, choose Open, and browse to the 05Customer Feedback Monitoring file on the accompanying CD.
2. Choose Report, and choose Reports.
3. Select Custom, and click Select.
4. In the Custom Reports dialog box, click New.
5. In the Define New Report dialog box, select Task. Click OK.
6. In the Definition tab, type **Monthly Milestones** for the name.
7. For Period, select Months.
8. For Count, select 2. (This will show two weeks of data.)
9. For Table, select Entry.
10. For Filter, select Milestones.
11. Select the Highlight check box.
12. Click OK.
13. Click Preview to view the report.

▶ **Exercise 2   Modify a Custom Report**

You want to modify the report you created in Exercise 1. Specifically, you want to change the name and add details.

To complete this exercise, perform the following steps:

1. Using the ch05Customer Feedback Monitoring file you opened in Exercise 1, choose Report and choose Reports.
2. Select Custom. Click Select.
3. Select the Monthly Milestones report.
4. Click Edit.
5. In the Definitions tab, type a new name, **MOVING DETAILS**.
6. In the Details tab, under Task, select the Notes check box.
7. Under Assignment, select Cost.
8. Click OK.
9. Click Preview.

▶ **Exercise 3   Configure Custom Print Options**

You need to print a custom report and apply custom print settings. Specifically, you want to adjust the scaling to 75 percent, print in Portrait view, configure 1-inch margins, and create a header.

To complete this exercise, perform the following steps:

1. Choose File, choose New, and click On Computer.
2. In the Project Templates tab, select Home Move, and then click OK.
3. Choose Report, and choose Reports.
4. Select Custom, and click Select.
5. In the Custom Reports dialog box, select Task.
6. Click Setup.
7. In the Page tab, for Orientation, select Portrait.
8. For Scaling, select 75%.
9. In the Margins tab, change the Top, Left, Bottom, and Right options to 1.00.
10. In the Header tab, click the Insert Page Number button and the Insert Current Time button.
11. Click OK.
12. Click Preview to see the report.

Lesson Summary

- Custom reports let you create several types of reports, including Task, Resource, Calendar, and Crosstab.
- With custom reports, you can configure what data to show by using the Filter options.
- Custom reports allow configuration of time periods, what tables to use, details, and sorting data by groups.

Lesson Review

You can use the following questions to test your knowledge of the information in Lesson 2, "Custom Reports." The questions are also available on the companion CD if you prefer to review them in electronic form.

NOTE   Answers

Answers to these questions and explanations of why each answer choice is correct or incorrect are located in the "Answers" section at the end of the book.

1. You need to create a custom report that contains resource data. You need to be able to set the period of time for the report in weeks. You also need to specify that the report only offers information on resources and includes their assignments. What type of report would you choose?

    A. A visual report

    B. A basic resource category report

    C. A custom monthly calendar report

    D. A custom crosstab report

2. You need to create and print a report that includes information regarding your project's resource usage over the past two months. You also want to include in the printout the schedule and calendar, and you'd like to add a border around the details added. Finally, you need to sort the data before it's printed. In what one place can you make all of these changes?

    A. In the Page Setup dialog box

    B. In the Visual Reports dialog box

    C. In the Print dialog box

    D. In the Resource Report dialog box

Chapter Review

To further practice and reinforce the skills you learned in this chapter, you can perform the following tasks:

- Review the chapter summary.
- Review the list of key terms introduced in this chapter.
- Complete the case scenarios. These scenarios set up real-world situations involving the topics of this chapter and ask you to create a solution.
- Complete the suggested practices.
- Take a practice test.

Chapter Summary

- Reports provide a unique way to review how well a project worked, what went wrong, and what succeeded.
- Basic and visual reports offer ready-made configurations for reports you'll need most often.
- Custom reports let you control what data is offered in the report.
- Printing reports allows you to easily share data with stakeholders, team members, and supervisors.

Key Terms

Do you know what these key terms mean? You can check your answers by looking up the terms in the glossary at the end of the book.

- PivotChart
- PivotDiagram
- PivotTable
- report
- visual report

Case Scenarios

In the following case scenarios, you will apply what you have learned about using Project in this chapter. You can find answers to these questions in the "Answers" section at the end of this book.

Case Scenario 1: Displaying Views and Reports

You are managing a project using Project. You have been diligent about entering all project data and updates and feel confident that your project file is an accurate representation of your project's progress as of the current date. Answer the following questions:

1. Throughout the project you have maintained a high-level approach and have refrained from micromanaging your resources. That approach has worked so far. However, you are a little concerned that the project might be heading in the direction of costing more than the original budgeted cost of work performed. Rather than look at every task, you would like to see a report of tasks with a cost variance of more than $500. How can you accomplish this view?

2. One of the project stakeholders has asked to see a detailed list of the project's resources and the work they have been assigned, completed, and are currently working on. You sent the original Who Does What report, which seemed to provide the information, but you have just learned that the stakeholder would prefer the report in a format that allows her to make adjustments to the working time and analyze the changes in a visual format. How can you send her this information?

Case Scenario 2: Working with Custom Tables and Reports

You are managing a project using Project. You have come to rely heavily on Project for managing your project and have already created several custom tables and views to better analyze your project data. Answer the following questions:

1. Word has spread among other project managers that you have several custom elements that might be beneficial to their work with Project. In a roundabout way, a few of them have asked you to share your secrets. You tell them that there are no custom templates, but only custom tables, views, and reports. How can you share this information?

2. You have created so many custom reports while using Project that a few of them are simply no longer needed. How can you delete these reports?

3. Your supervisor has asked you to add the company logo to each page of a printed report. How can you accomplish this?

Suggested Practices

To help you successfully master the exam objectives presented in this chapter, complete the following tasks. We suggest you work through all of these exercises.

- **Practice 1: View Basic Reports**   Open any project in progress and choose Report, Reports. Open each report once, taking note of what each report offers. Make sure you understand the differences among similar reports, such as Task Usage and Resource Usage.

- **Practice 2: View Visual Reports**   Open any project in progress and choose Report, Visual Reports. Open each report once, taking note of what each report offers. Make sure you understand the differences among similar reports, such as Budget Cost Report and Budget Work Report.
- **Practice 3: Create a Custom Report**   Open any project in progress and choose Report, and then Reports. Click Custom. Select a report to edit. Create as many custom reports as you have time to, paying careful attention to what options are available for each report and how those options change depending on the report selected
- **Practice 4: Print a Report**   Open any project in progress and, using what you've learned in Practices 1, 2, and 3, print at least two reports. You need to be aware of what these reports look like when they come from the printer so that you can know what your supervisor and stakeholders will see when you print them.

Take a Practice Test

The practice tests on this book's companion CD offer many options. For example, you can test yourself on just one exam objective, or you can test yourself on all the 70-632 certification exam content. You can set up the test so that it closely simulates the experience of taking a certification exam, or you can set it up in study mode so that you can look at the correct answers and explanations after you answer each question.

MORE INFO   **Practice tests**

For details about all the practice test options available, see the "How to Use the Practice Tests" section in this book's Introduction.

Answers

Chapter 1: Lesson Review Answers

Lesson 1

1. **Correct Answers: A and D**

   A. **Correct:** By default, Project Guide is not enabled. You can enable it manually from the View menu by choosing Turn On Project Guide.

   B. **Incorrect:** Changing the view has no effect on whether or not the Project Guide is showing. If the view is changed, space will be made available for the Project Guide task pane.

   C. **Incorrect:** Turn On Project Guide is not a valid option from the Insert menu.

   D. **Correct:** By default, Project Guide is not enabled. You can enable it manually in the Tools, Options dialog box.

2. **Correct Answers: B and C**

   A. **Incorrect:** Because the question clearly states that this is the first time his company will be involved in a tradeshow, there is no existing tradeshow project to refer to or build from.

   B. **Correct:** The template Tradeshow Planning, Execution, and Wrap-Up, which is available from the Project Templates choices, would make a great start for his project and includes the tasks mentioned in the question.

   C. **Correct:** One of the choices in the New Project window under Templates is Templates On Office Online. Clicking this button opens your Web browser to the Web page *http://office.microsoft.com*, where you can search for the template you want.

   D. **Incorrect:** Initiating a project and selecting a start date will not help John input tasks or assign resources and therefore is not a viable answer because, as the question stated, John does not want to have to input common tasks.

3. **Correct Answer: A**

   A. **Correct:** This choice represents the correct sequence of events you must follow to access the desired template.

   B. **Incorrect:** You cannot specify a template choice anywhere but from the File, New, option. There is no link in the Project Guide task pane to select a template.

   C. **Incorrect:** The Project Information dialog box offers a place to input a start date and a finish date and to assign how to schedule the project (from the start date or the finish date). There is no option to select a template here.

    D. **Incorrect:** You cannot import a template after creating a new, blank project. You must select the template to define the project as a first step.

4. **Correct Answer: D**

    A. **Incorrect:** Templates from Office Online already have information in them, including tasks, resources, and assignments.

    B. **Incorrect:** Templates from existing projects already have information in them, including tasks, resources, and assignments.

    C. **Incorrect:** Templates from the Project Templates tab in the Templates dialog box already have information in them, including tasks, resources, and assignments.

    D. **Correct:** In order to have complete control over a project, you must start with a blank project. All other project types have tasks, resources, and assignments already input.

5. **Correct Answer: D**

    A. **Incorrect:** Because a Gantt Chart prints primarily the way it looks on the screen, configuring the timescale in days makes the problem worse, not better, by taking up more screen real estate.

    B. **Incorrect:** Because a Gantt Chart prints primarily the way it looks on the screen, configuring the timescale in years might make the view too small to be legible, depending on the length of the project.

    C. **Incorrect:** Although the ability to make a Gantt Chart fit on one page is available, it is not the default setting. By default, you generally print what you can see in the Gantt Chart on the screen.

    D. **Correct:** To make sure an entire month fits in the viewing area of the Gantt Chart, you must adjust the zoom level. To print only one month, in the Timescale options in the Print dialog box, select the dates to print. All printers have an option to print in Landscape view.

6. **Correct Answer: A**

    A. **Correct:** In the Print dialog box you have many options, including adjusting the percentage level or making the data fit to a single printed page.

    B. **Incorrect:** Unlike the Gantt Chart print setup, modifying the zoom level on the Network Diagram has no bearing on the size at which the diagram will print.

    C. **Incorrect:** To modify the printed size of a Network Diagram, you'll need to change your print settings in the Page Setup dialog box, not the Project Information dialog box.

    D. **Incorrect:** Turning off the Project Guide task pane has no bearing on what prints at the printer.

Lesson 2

1. **Correct Answer: C**

    A. **Incorrect:** The Standard calendar in Project uses a 40-hour work week where an employee works 8:00 A.M.–5:00 P.M. with a one-hour lunch. One week does not equal seven working days. Seven work days is one work week and two days.

    B. **Incorrect:** You cannot right-click the Gantt Chart to add a new task. It is not an option.

    C. **Correct:** The Entry Table is the quickest way to input a task and set a duration. The duration of seven days is the correct duration because the standard calendar offers a five-day work week.

    D. **Incorrect:** Although using the Entry Table to input a task is correct, the Standard calendar in Project uses a 40-hour work week where an employee works 8:00 A.M.– 5:00 P.M. with a one-hour lunch. One week does not equal seven work days. Seven work days is one work week and two days.

2. **Correct Answers: A, C, and D**

    A. **Correct:** Double-clicking any task in the Entry Table opens the Task Information dialog box, where all of the desired changes can be made.

    B. **Incorrect:** Double-clicking a task bar in the Gantt Chart opens the Format Bar dialog box, not the Task Information dialog box.

    C. **Correct:** Right-clicking a task in the Entry Table does offer Task Information in the drop-down list. Selecting it opens the Task Information dialog box, where all of the desired changes can be made.

    D. **Correct:** Shift+F2 is a valid key combination for opening the Task Information dialog box, where all of the desired changes can be made.

3. **Correct Answers: A, B, and D**

    A. **Correct:** It is possible to change the duration of a task from any tab in the Task Information dialog box, and you can change the calendar only from the Advanced tab.

    B. **Correct:** Because it is possible to change the duration of a task from any tab in the Task Information dialog box and you can change the calendar only from the Advanced tab, this answer is correct.

    C. **Incorrect:** You can change the calendar only from the Advanced tab.

    D. **Correct:** Because it is possible to change the duration of a task from any tab in the Task Information dialog box and you can change the calendar only from the Advanced tab, this answer is correct.

4. **Correct Answer: D**

   A. **Incorrect:** The Task Information dialog box does not offer a place to configure a task to recur.

   B. **Incorrect:** You cannot open the Recurring Task Information dialog box by right-clicking a task in the Entry Table.

   C. **Incorrect:** The Project Information dialog box does not offer a place to configure a task to recur.

   D. **Correct:** You create a new recurring task from the Insert menu by clicking Recurring Task. This opens the Recurring Task Information dialog box, where you can input the task information desired.

5. **Correct Answers: C and D**

   A. **Incorrect:** Simply naming the task a milestone will not make it a milestone.

   B. **Incorrect:** No such option exists when right-clicking a task icon in the Gantt Chart. You must set the duration of a task to zero for it to be a milestone.

   C. **Correct:** The option to Mark Task As Milestone is a valid way to configure a task as a milestone using the Task Information dialog box.

   D. **Correct:** You must set the duration of a task to zero days for it to be a milestone.

6. **Correct Answer: A**

   A. **Correct:** The formula for estimating a tasks duration is ((Optimistic + Pessimistic + (4*Expected))/6. Using the formula correctly gives the correct answer of 18.5 days.

   B. **Incorrect:** You arrived at this answer by assuming that the expected number of days was also the calculated duration, which it is not.

   C. **Incorrect:** You arrived at this answer because you switched the Optimistic and Expected numbers in the equation.

   D. **Incorrect:** You arrived at this answer because you switched the Pessimistic and Expected numbers in the equation.

7. **Correct Answer: C**

   A. **Incorrect:** The Expected Gantt shows a Gantt Chart for a task whose duration has already been calculated.

   B. **Incorrect:** You can't calculate the PERT before you've entered the data in the PERT Entry Form.

   C. **Correct:** The first thing you must do is input the data into the PERT Entry Form.

   D. **Incorrect:** The PERT Entry Sheet displays the PERT Entry Sheet table with columns for Task Name, Duration, Optimistic Duration, Expected Duration, and Pessimistic Duration.

Lesson 3

1. **Correct Answers: A and B**

   A. **Correct:** If you click Tools and then choose Options, the Options dialog box appears, in which you can make these changes, as well as days per month, when the week starts, and when the fiscal year starts.

   B. **Correct:** If you click Tools and choose Change Working Time, and then Options, the Options dialog box appears, in which you can make these changes as wells as days per month, when the week starts, and when the fiscal year starts.

   C. **Incorrect:** The Project Information dialog box offers only a place to select a calendar, not to change the hours worked and similar options.

   D. **Incorrect:** The Task Information dialog box offers only a place to select a calendar, not to change the hours worked and similar options.

2. **Correct Answer: C**

   A. **Incorrect:** Project does not come with a calendar named Alternate.

   B. **Incorrect:** Although you can start a project with a template from an online source, you are unlikely to find a project that comes with its own calendar, especially one that meets your needs.

   C. **Correct:** Creating a new calendar from scratch will allow you to input your own precise hours, work weeks, and other criteria to meet your project's specific needs.

   D. **Incorrect:** First, you cannot use the Project Information dialog box to change the Standard calendar's hours and times. Second, you would have to change the Standard calendar drastically to meet this project's needs.

3. **Correct Answer: B**

   A. **Incorrect:** Although you can modify the 24-Hour calendar here, it would be quicker to modify the Night Shift calendar's hours.

   B. **Correct:** You can copy a calendar and modify an existing calendar in the Change Working Time dialog box.

   C. **Incorrect:** Although you can modify the Standard calendar here, it would be quicker to modify the Night Shift calendar's hours.

   D. **Incorrect:** You can copy, rename, and delete calendars only in the Organizer dialog box. You cannot modify them there.

4. **Correct Answers: A and B**

   A. **Correct:** Modifying the calendar and then applying it to a task using the Task Information dialog box is a valid option.

   B. **Correct:** Applying a calendar to a task using the Task Information dialog box and then modifying the calendar is a valid option.

C. **Incorrect:** Although you can modify the calendar in the Working Times dialog box, applying it in the Project Information dialog box will apply it to the entire project, not one task.

D. **Incorrect:** Although you can modify the calendar in the Working Times dialog box, applying it in the Project Information dialog box will apply it to the entire project, not one task.

Chapter 1: Case Scenario Answers

Case Scenario 1: Managing a Software Roll-out Project

1. When creating a new project file, you can access the option to create a new project file from an existing project file. This way you'll have access to both tasks and resources that worked successfully in similar projects.

2. The Gantt Chart view is the obvious choice when someone asks to see a timeline of the project schedule and would be a correct answer in this situation. However, keep in mind that the Network Diagram also works well when communicating the project schedule using a flowchart appearance.

3. Because the weekly meetings are entirely related to this project, you can create a recurring task with a duration equal to the length of the meeting. This way the project schedule takes into account the time the key resources are involved in the meeting.

Case Scenario 2: Scheduling a Project

1. Company-wide nonworking days such as holidays are prime examples of exceptions to be added to the base project calendar. These exceptions are defined in the Change Working Time dialog box accessed by choosing Tools/Change Working Time from the Menu bar.

2. Creating a recurring exception in the Change Working Time dialog box would allow you to set four working hours for every Friday throughout the duration of your project.

3. Assign the 24-Hour calendar to the one task that requires around-the-clock work to allow for 24-hour scheduling only for the duration of the selected task, allowing the project to return to the base calendar scheduling for the remaining project tasks.

Case Scenario 3: Task Durations

1. (6 hours [Optimistic] + 14 hours [Pessimistic] + (7 hours [Expected]*4)/6) = 8 hours = 1 day.

2. Zero days—this is an example of a milestone. Milestones can be defined in Project with a duration of zero (0) days.

3. (5 days [Optimistic] + 20 days [Pessimistic] + (10 days [Expected]*4)/6) = 10.83 days.

Chapter 2: Lesson Review Answers

Lesson 1

1. **Correct Answer: C**

   A. **Incorrect:** You cannot create a task in the Zero Task ID field of the Entry table. You must create that task by selecting the Show Project Summary Task check box in the Options dialog box.

   B. **Incorrect:** It is not possible to outdent a summary task. These tasks are already at the left edge of the outline, which is the highest level.

   C. **Correct:** Choosing Tools and then Options displays the View tab in the Options dialog box. In the View tab you can select the Show Project Summary Task check box and the Show Outline Number check box to enable outline numbering.

   D. **Incorrect:** In the WBS Code Definition For *<Project Name>* dialog box you can indeed create a code mask. However, this is not the default WBS outline code. You cannot use the Project Information dialog box to select the Show Project Summary Task check box.

2. **Correct Answers: A, B, and D**

   A. **Correct:** Choices for outlines include Numbers (Ordered), Uppercase Letters (Ordered), Lowercase Letters (Ordered), and Characters (Unordered). Additionally, each section can have up to 10 letters or characters.

   B. **Correct:** Choices for outlines include Numbers (Ordered), Uppercase Letters (Ordered), Lowercase Letters (Ordered), and Characters (Unordered). Additionally, each section can have up to 10 letters or characters.

   C. **Incorrect:** Keystrokes, such as Tab, are not acceptable codes for a WBS.

   D. **Correct:** Choices for outlines include Numbers (Ordered), Uppercase Letters (Ordered), Lowercase Letters (Ordered), and Characters (Unordered). Additionally, each section can have up to 10 letters or characters.

3. **Correct Answers: A, B, and C**

   A. **Correct:** Edit and Indent is a valid option for indenting a task to make it a subtask.

   B. **Correct:** Clicking the Indent icon on the Formatting toolbar is a valid option for indenting a task to make it a subtask.

   C. **Correct:** This key combination is a valid option for indenting a task to make it a subtask.

   D. **Incorrect:** There is no option in the right-click options for indenting a task.

4. **Correct Answer: A**

   A. **Correct:** In the top-down method, you identify the major phases of a project before defining the tasks. This is a best practice method.

    B. **Incorrect:** Although this is also an acceptable method of project planning, in the bottom-up method you list the tasks first and then define the major phases.

    C. **Incorrect:** There is no such thing as the top-up method.

    D. **Incorrect:** There is no such thing as the bottom-down method.

5. **Correct Answers: A and D**

    A. **Correct:** You can use a template and modify its WBS to suit your own needs.

    B. **Incorrect:** This is not a valid option from the Insert menu.

    C. **Incorrect:** When you choose to show the outline number, Project displays an outline number next to each task name. You can use this number as the basis for your WBS, but it is not how you create the WBS.

    D. **Correct:** You can use a blank project and input all tasks yourself and then define them as summary and subtasks.

6. **Correct Answer: C**

    A. **Incorrect:** Tasks are deliverable units of work.

    B. **Incorrect:** A code mask for a WBS outline is only a set of numbers, letters, and characters that define the actual outline.

    C. **Correct:** Summary tasks define phases of a project. Because a list of summary tasks does not include a complete list of the tasks to be performed, it is just what the boss needs to see.

    D. **Incorrect:** The project summary task is a one-row summary of the entire project and does not include summary tasks associated with project phases.

7. **Correct Answer: D**

    A. **Incorrect:** Outdent and Indent are used to modify the WBS to change a summary task to a subtask and vice versa. You want to change how you view the tasks, not their position in the WBS hierarchy.

    B. **Incorrect:** Showing and hiding assignments is irrelevant here. The subject is talking about tasks, not assignments.

    C. **Incorrect:** Linking and unlinking tasks requires you to select the tasks to link or unlink. You do not want to make any changes to the tasks here; you only want to view or hide them.

    D. **Correct:** Showing and hiding subtasks allows you to view subtask information quickly.

Lesson 2

1. **Correct Answer: A**

    A. **Correct:** Finish No Later Than is a task constraint and is more flexible than Must Finish On. Task constraints are applied using the Task Information dialog box.

    B. **Incorrect:** Setting a deadline for a task has no affect on the project calendar.

    C. **Incorrect:** Must Finish On is task constraint, but it is inflexible. It is, however, applied in the Task Information dialog box.

    D. **Incorrect:** Finish-to-Finish is a task dependency, not a constraint, although it is applied in the Task Dependency dialog box.

2. **Correct Answer: D**

    A. **Incorrect:** Flexible constraints include As Soon As Possible and As Late As Possible. These constraints will be taken into account as the project progresses, and changes will be made to due dates of tasks as tasks complete.

    B. **Incorrect:** Moderately flexible constraints include Start No Earlier Than, Start No Later Than, Finish No Earlier Than, and Finish No Later Than. These constraints will be taken into account as the project progresses, and changes will be made to due dates of tasks as tasks complete.

    C. **Incorrect:** Every task has a constraint, and a constraint cannot be deleted.

    D. **Correct:** A deadline, configured in the Task Information dialog box in the Advanced tab, lets you set a reminder for a task instead of a set finish date.

3. **Correct Answer: A**

    A. **Correct:** In a Finish-to-Start dependency, as soon as the predecessor task finishes, the successor task can start.

    B. **Incorrect:** In a Finish-to-Finish dependency, as soon as the predecessor task finishes, the successor task can finish.

    C. **Incorrect:** In a Start-to-Start dependency, as soon as the predecessor task starts the successor task can start.

    D. **Incorrect:** In a Start-to-Finish dependency, as soon as the predecessor task starts the successor task can finish. This is rarely used.

4. **Correct Answer: C**

    A. **Incorrect:** Gantt Chart view offers the Entry table and a Gantt Chart, which is a bar chart.

    B. **Incorrect:** Calendar view lets you view task and durations for a specific week or range of weeks. It does not offer this information in a flowchart.

    C. **Correct:** Network Diagram view is the only view with a flowchart.

    D. **Incorrect:** Constraint Dates is a view much like the Gantt Chart view, with information about constraint types and due dates.

5. **Correct Answer: A**

    A. **Correct:** To add this information to Project 2007, you need to add a negative value to the successor task, in this case −25%.

    B. **Incorrect:** Lead time is always a negative number.

C. **Incorrect:** You always apply lead time to the successor task. Lead time is the amount of time a successor task can start prior to the predecessor task finishing. Lag time represents a delay and not a head start.

D. **Incorrect:** To note a head start, you use lead time, as well as a negative number.

Lesson 3

1. **Correct Answers: A, B, and C**

   A. **Correct:** Getting an expert opinion on how much a specific task will cost is a good way to obtain reliable information.

   B. **Correct:** Understanding how long it will take to apply for permits and obtain inspections and what the industry standards are for installing specialty items like Ethernet wiring, computerized machinery, and electrical wiring will help you further define the task and its associated costs.

   C. **Correct:** Consultants can help you define your project and its costs, as can experienced project managers. Finding someone who has worked through the process before is certainly a good resource.

   D. **Incorrect:** Because your company has never created or worked on a project like this one, it is unlikely that your team members or any past projects will offer much viable information up front.

2. **Correct Answer: D**

   A. **Incorrect:** Duration = Work/Units. Work is 48 hours and units equals 200 percent. Duration = 48/2 = 24 hours. 24 hours on a 24-hour calendar would be one day. However, on a standard calendar 24 hours = 3 days.

   B. **Incorrect:** This answer is acquired if the units is set at 100 percent and not at the required 200 percent. Remember, two people are working full time on the task.

   C. **Incorrect:** If you changed 48 hours to 6 days, and input 6 for Work, you would get the answer 1.5 days. Work needs to be calculated in hours for this scenario.

   D. **Correct:** Duration = Work/Units. Work is 48 hours and units equals 200 percent. Duration = 48/2 = 24 hours. On a standard calendar, 24 hours = 3 days.

3. **Correct Answer: B**

   A. **Incorrect:** You would arrive at this answer only if you mixed up the variables in the formula Work = Duration/Units and instead used Work = Units/Duration. The answer of 1/2 day would equal 12 hours on a 24-hour calendar.

   B. **Correct:** Using the formula Work = Duration/Units and knowing that the duration is 4 days on a 24-hour schedule and that units = 200% (four machines at 50% capacity), the formula reads W=4/200%=4/2=2. 2 days is 48 hours on a 24-hour calendar.

C. **Incorrect:** This answer is not mathematically attainable using the formula and is an incorrect guess.

D. **Incorrect:** This answer is not mathematically attainable using the formula and is an incorrect guess.

4. **Correct Answer: D**

A. **Incorrect:** You'll get this answer if you switch the variables in the equation from the correct order of Duration = Work/Units to Duration to an incorrect representation of the formula Duration = Units/Work.

B. **Incorrect:** Switch the variables in Duration = Work/Units to Work = Units / Duration, change the result to a percentage, and you will get this answer.

C. **Incorrect:** Use the formula Duration = Work/Units and forget to change the duration from 2 days to 16 hours, and you will get this answer.

D. **Correct:** Duration = Work/Units. Duration is 16 hours (2 standard 8-hour working days), and Work is 40 hours. So 16 = 40/Units. When you solve for units, you get 2.5. Changing this to a percent, units = 250%. (There are many ways to solve for units, but one is to restate the formula so that Units = 40/16.)

5. **Correct Answer: B**

A. **Incorrect:** The Assign Resources dialog box is where you assign budget resources, not create them.

B. **Correct:** Budget resources are added to a project using the Resource Sheet, and you define the resource as a budget resource in the Resource Information dialog box.

C. **Incorrect:** The Resource Usage sheet is where you assign values to budget resources.

D. **Incorrect:** The Resources tab of the Task Information dialog box is for assigning the task to other resources, not creating resources.

Lesson 4

1. **Correct Answer: D**

A. **Incorrect:** Travel is not a valid resource. The three types of resources are material, work, and cost.

B. **Incorrect:** Material resources are for consumable items like paint, carpet, concrete, and paper.

C. **Incorrect:** Work resources are often machines or people. Dump trucks and employees fall into this category.

D. **Correct:** Cost resources cover expenses that do not affect the project in terms of material or work. Generally, travel, meals, hotels, and similar items are included here.

2. **Correct Answer: C**

   A. **Incorrect:** In Gantt Chart view, although you can change the appearance of individual bars or text, you cannot view the allocation of resources over time.

   B. **Incorrect:** Task Usage view shows information about tasks, not resources.

   C. **Correct:** Resource Graph view meets all the criteria in the question.

   D. **Incorrect:** This view shows the project in terms of a monthly calendar and focuses on tasks, not resources.

3. **Correct Answers: A, B, and C**

   A. **Correct:** The Task Form in split screen view offers a place to change units for a resource.

   B. **Correct:** The Resource Information dialog box offers a place to set dates, rates, per-use cost, and resource units.

   C. **Correct:** The Assign Resources dialog box offers a place to change max units for a resource.

   D. **Incorrect:** The Project Information dialog box is where you can change the start and finish dates for a project, choose how to schedule the project, and select a calendar, among other things. It does not offer a place to manage resources for the project.

4. **Correct Answer: B**

   A. **Incorrect:** Although the Resource Sheet view is the correct place to add the resource, the resource type is Work, not Material. Materials are consumable items and a moving van is not consumable.

   B. **Correct:** The Resource Sheet view is the correct place to add the resource and the resource type Work. Work resources perform tasks, such as vans, painters, employees, and consultants.

   C. **Incorrect:** Although you can perform many tasks on resources using the Assign Resources dialog box, including assigning, removing, and replacing resources, you cannot add resources here. Work is the correct resource type, however.

   D. **Incorrect:** You cannot add resources in Gantt Chart view, only tasks. Additionally, the resource type is Work, not Material.

5. **Correct Answers: B, C, and D**

   A. **Incorrect:** Although following this series of steps does take you to a list of resources, you cannot make the resource a budget resource in the Task Information dialog box.

   B. **Correct:** This is a viable way to open a resource's Resource Information dialog box, and in this box is the option to make the resource a budget resource.

   C. **Correct:** This is a viable way to open a resource's Resource Information dialog box, and in this box is the option to make the resource a budget resource.

    D. **Correct:** This is a viable way to open a resource's Resource Information dialog box, and in this box is the option to make the resource a budget resource.

6. **Correct Answer: C**

    A. **Incorrect:** The Standard base calendar is for resources that work from 8 A.M. to 5 P.M. and five days a week.

    B. **Incorrect:** For single off-site resources with odd working hours, a resource calendar is a best practice. The Night Shift calendar will not offer the required hours or times for work.

    C. **Correct:** Resource calendars should be created and applied to single resources that require their own working times and schedules.

    D. **Incorrect:** The 24-Hour base calendar does not match the resources working times or days and would need to be modified. Creating a resource calendar is best.

7. **Correct Answer: A**

    A. **Correct:** To replace one resource with another, select the task and open the Assign Resources dialog box.

    B. **Incorrect:** The only place where you can replace one resource with another is the Assign Resources dialog box. It is not an option in the Task Information dialog box.

    C. **Incorrect:** The only place where you can replace one resource with another is the Assign Resources dialog box. It is not an option in the Resource Information dialog box.

    D. **Incorrect:** Although you do make this change in the Assign Resources dialog box, there is no option to access it from the View Bar.

8. **Correct Answers: B, C, and D**

    A. **Incorrect:** Because the drivers have only five days to achieve their goal, the task is of a fixed duration, not of fixed units.

    B. **Correct:** Because the drivers must arrive by a certain day, there is a deadline.

    C. **Correct:** Because each driver will have to drive 8 hours a day, totaling 16 hours each day of travel time, the task is effort-driven.

    D. **Correct:** No calendar needs to be applied because the task must be started and completed based on the dates set for the task.

9. **Correct Answer: D**

    A. **Incorrect:** You arrived at this number if you incorrectly assumed the machine worked on your project 8 hours a day, instead of 16. At 8 hours a day, the machine would create 80 units, and 640/80 = 8.

    B. **Incorrect:** You arrived at this number if you incorrectly assumed the machine worked on your project 24 hours a day instead of 16. At 24 hours a day, the machine would create 240 units, and 640/240 = 4 1/4.

    C. **Incorrect:** Six days is simply an educated guess. The machine can create 10 parts per hour and you have the machine for 16 hours a day, which means that the machine can create 160 in one day. 640/160 = 4, or 4 days.

    D. **Correct:** The machine can create 10 parts per hour, and you have the machine for 16 hours a day, which means that the machine can create 160 in one day. 640/160 = 4, or 4 days.

10. **Correct Answers: A and B**

    A. **Correct:** Adding three more people to the task will reduce the task's length greatly. If all are working at 100 percent and if one person can do a job in four weeks, then four people can do the same job in one week.

    B. **Correct:** A fixed-work task means that if Project must do recalculation and if you revise units, then duration is recalculated.

    C. **Incorrect:** You must enable effort-driven scheduling to tell Project that more resources means less duration.

    D. **Incorrect:** A fixed-units task means that if you revise duration, work is recalculated. If you revise units, duration is recalculated. And if you revise work, duration is recalculated. You do not want any of these scenarios here. You want to keep the amount of units steady at 100 percent for each resource.

Lesson 5

1. **Correct Answer: A**

    A. **Correct:** The project summary task has a task ID of 0 and must be enabled to be shown on the Entry table. The project Summary task meets all the criteria in the scenario.

    B. **Incorrect:** Outline numbers are a hierarchical structure that you use for organizing tasks in the Entry table, not for summarizing the project.

    C. **Incorrect:** Summary tasks are outdented as far as they can be. If you could outdent them, they would still not become project summary tasks.

    D. **Incorrect:** Summary tasks and project summary tasks are two different things. Summary tasks are listed in the WBS along with their associated subtasks. A project summary task has an ID of 0 and is listed only once.

2. **Correct Answer: D**

    A. **Incorrect:** The Task Information dialog box offers the start and finish dates, predecessors, resources, and other information, but it does not offer information on what might be affecting the start date of a task.

    B. **Incorrect:** This is a printable report that lists overallocated resources. It will not detail the information required in the scenario.

    C. **Incorrect:** The Project Information dialog box provides information such as start and finish dates, how the project is scheduled, and which calendar is used. It does not offer information about single tasks.

    D. **Correct:** The Task Drivers pane provides information on scheduling factors for the task selected. Using the Task Drivers pane you can find out what is causing a specific task's delay.

3. **Correct Answer: B**

    A. **Incorrect:** Because the tasks are not effort-driven, adding additional resources will not make the process complete any more quickly.

    B. **Correct:** In this scenario there is a two-day duration differential between the tasks. Changing the relationship gives the first task total slack of two days. This means that Task A remains noncritical only until it is delayed more than two days (or more than the total of its total slack time).

    C. **Incorrect:** Obtaining the water permit is an important task in the project and cannot be removed or deleted.

    D. **Incorrect:** Automatically leveling resources does not give you any control over the task duration or resource assignments.

4. **Correct Answer: A**

    A. **Correct:** The first baseline you create should be of the approved project schedule prior to the project start date. This is the only time the original plan and the current plan will be the same.

    B. **Incorrect:** The first baseline should be a snapshot of the approved project plan prior to the project starting. However, additional baselines might be collected weekly.

    C. **Incorrect:** The first baseline should be a snapshot of the approved project plan prior to the project starting. However, interim baselines might be collected once a month.

    D. **Incorrect:** The first baseline should be an approved project plan prior to the project starting. You should take this snapshot prior to any tasks being done.

5. **Correct Answers: A, C, and D**

    A. **Correct:** Finding and adding slack to the project schedule can give tasks that are falling behind more time to complete.

    B. **Incorrect:** You cannot remove tasks from a project because those tasks are part of making the project work.

    C. **Correct:** Assigning more resources to an effort-driven task will cause the task to end more quickly, freeing time in the project schedule.

    D. **Correct:** Changing the default slack time from 0 to something else will cause some tasks to change from critical to noncritical immediately.

6. **Correct Answer: C**
    A. **Incorrect:** This option lets you create customized forms, not create and print reports.
    B. **Incorrect:** Page Setup lets you configure printer settings, not create reports.
    C. **Correct:** The Report/Reports option allows you to choose from various reports, including Top-Level Tasks, Critical Tasks, and Milestones, and print them.
    D. **Incorrect:** There is no option on the View menu for Report.

Chapter 2: Case Scenario Answers

Case Scenario 1: Creating a WBS

1. To denote tasks as subtasks, you will need to highlight (select) those tasks and click the Indent button. Summary tasks are created automatically when subtasks have been demoted.
2. Select the Show Outline Number in the View tab of the Options dialog box.
3. Use the Insert key on the keyboard to insert a blank row to add the forgotten task. Then use the Indent and Outdent buttons to properly place the task in the existing WBS.

Case Scenario 2: Defining a Project Schedule

1. Although inserting tasks to account for the extra time is a viable option, the best practice in Project is to add lag time to any task that requires some time before the next task in the project schedule can begin.
2. Modify the relationship between the two tasks from Finish-to-Start to Finish-to-Finish.
3. You can create a project baseline to store the project data as it stands before project work begins. You can even choose to store up to 10 additional baselines for the current project to provide snapshots of the project each week, each month, or at the end of each major phase.

Case Scenario 3: Working with Resources

1. You actually have a couple of options to indicate part-time work (even though the resources are full-time employees). Because you are not currently using a resource pool, you can set the working time on the resource calendars for selected resources to encompass the total hours each day that you anticipate that person will be available to devote to your project. Alternatively, you can modify the Max Units fields for selected resources to a percentage less than 100.

2. The closest view to the resource histogram in Project is the Resource Graph. Additional resource views that might be helpful in this case are the Resource Allocation, Resource Form, and Resource Usage views.

3. Use Project's reporting feature to print the "Who Does What When" report for your project's resources.

Case Scenario 4: Scheduling

1. Because the default settings are in effect, adding an additional resource would decrease the duration of the one-day task to four hours. For this question, the second person would actually be doubling the time it takes to complete this task. Because the review can happen simultaneously, you need to change the task type to Fixed Duration and disable effort-driven scheduling.

2. Assuming that the default task type and effort-driven scheduling settings are applied, adding a half-time resource to this task creates working time for the full-time resource of 16 hours and working time for the half time resource of 8 hours. This also decreases the duration to two days.

3. Because this resource is unable to devote more than two hours each working day, the resource's working units have decreased from 50 percent to 25 percent. Decreasing the work units in this scenario (assuming the task type is set to the default—Fixed Units) forces Project to increase the task duration to four days.

Case Scenario 5: Bringing Tasks in On Time

1. On any task in which the consultant is an assigned resource, create a Start No Earlier Than constraint associated with the first day the consultant is available. Additionally, add a text reminder in the Notes tab to remind you (and others viewing the project file) which tasks assigned to the consultant might not start as soon as possible. Another option is to set up the consultant's resource calendar so that the start date is the consultant's first working day.

2. You can create a task related to the CEO's review and approval of the performance plan. Then assign a task deadline. This way, Project can still schedule based on other factors, and if the task deadline passes before the task occurs, you will receive a reminder from the program.

3. You can use the Task Drivers task pane to see elements of the project plan file that are related to the selected task.

Chapter 3: Lesson Review Answers

Lesson 1

1. **Correct Answer: A**
    A. **Correct:** The Tracking table shows the actual start and finish dates and actual duration, among other things. It also offers various ways to change the information.
    B. **Incorrect:** The Entry table shows the duration, start and finish dates, predecessors, and resource names. It does not offer a place to change the time remaining for a task.
    C. **Incorrect:** The Usage table shows task usage data, including work, duration, start, and finish. It does not offer a place to change the time remaining for a task.
    D. **Incorrect:** The Variance table shows start and finish dates along with baselines and variance data. It does not offer a place to change the time remaining for a task.

2. **Correct Answer: C**
    A. **Incorrect:** The Schedule table shows start and finish dates, late start and late finish dates, and free and total slack. It does not offer a snapshot of your project's current costs and start and finish dates compared with your saved baseline data.
    B. **Incorrect:** The Project Information dialog box shows the current date, start and finish dates, the calendar used, and similar data. It does not offer a snapshot of your project's current costs and start and finish dates compared with your saved baseline data.
    C. **Correct:** The Project Statistics dialog box, available from the Tracking toolbar, offers this information.
    D. **Incorrect:** The Task Information dialog box shows data for specific tasks, not an entire project.

3. **Correct Answer: C**
    A. **Incorrect:** The Variance table shows start and finish dates, along with baselines and variance data. It does not show free and total slack.
    B. **Incorrect:** The Project Information dialog box shows the current date, start and finish dates, the calendar used, and similar data. It does not offer free and total slack information.
    C. **Correct:** The Schedule table shows start and finish dates, late start and late finish dates, and free and total slack.
    D. **Incorrect:** The Resource Sheet is a view that offers information about resources, including maximum units, standard rates, overtime rates, and similar data.

4. **Correct Answer: D**

    A. **Incorrect:** The Task Usage view shows information about the work that needs to be done, along with the duration, start dates, finish dates, and a timeline. It does not offer a visual representation of project baseline indicators, such as critical tasks.

    B. **Incorrect:** The Task Form view shows information about resources, units, and work for a project, along with the predecessors and start and finish dates. It does not offer a visual representation of project baseline indicators, such as critical tasks.

    C. **Incorrect:** The Project Information dialog box shows the current date, start and finish dates, the calendar used, and similar data. It does not offer any visual representation of the project.

    D. **Correct:** The Tracking Gantt offers all of this and more, allowing you to immediately identify whether or not your project plan is on schedule and within scope.

5. **Correct Answer: D**

    A. **Incorrect:** The Tracking table shows the actual start and finish dates and actual duration, among other things. It also offers various ways to change the information.

    B. **Incorrect:** The Schedule table shows start and finish dates, late start and late finish dates, and free and total slack.

    C. **Incorrect:** The Entry table shows the duration, start and finish dates, predecessors, and resource names. It does not offer a place to change the time remaining for a task.

    D. **Correct:** The Work table shows all of the desired information.

6. **Correct Answer: B**

    A. **Incorrect:** You do this when you want to view Scheduled, Baseline, Actual, and Remaining Costs.

    B. **Correct:** The Earned Value table offers this information.

    C. **Incorrect:** You do this when you want to view the total cost for a task.

    D. **Incorrect:** You do this when you want to view total project cost.

7. **Correct Answer: A**

    A. **Correct:** By turning on AutoFilter in Project and Filtered By, you enable AutoFilter for all of the listed views (and more).

    B. **Incorrect:** There is no AutoFilter option in the View menu.

    C. **Incorrect:** You cannot create a custom filter for a specific table view.

    D. **Incorrect:** You need to click AutoFilter only one time to apply it to the views listed. After it's enabled, clicking it again will disable it.

8. **Correct Answer: C**
    A. **Incorrect:** There is no option when creating a custom filter to Make This A Global Filter.
    B. **Incorrect:** There is no option in the Save tab to save the filter to the Global.mpt file.
    C. **Correct:** This is a valid way to copy the filter to the Global.mpt file.
    D. **Incorrect:** Creating a custom filter will not make it appear in the Project, Filtered By list.

9. **Correct Answer: C**
    A. **Incorrect:** You must sort by group, not by filter.
    B. **Incorrect:** You must create the custom group in the Custom Group dialog box. You cannot open a group, edit it, and then save it under another name.
    C. **Correct:** Create a custom group based on the predefined group Duration.
    D. **Incorrect:** You must work with groups, not filters.

Lesson 2

1. **Correct Answer: D**
    A. **Incorrect:** Project does not know that the task is delayed and needs to be split. You need to make this change yourself.
    B. **Incorrect:** Making this change has no effect on the task in question.
    C. **Incorrect:** There is no reason to change anything that has to do with the entire project, especially the project status date. It's best to split the task.
    D. **Correct:** By splitting the task so that the machine can work on the task before and after the maintenance check, you tell Project not to flag the task as off schedule or modify other tasks because of the delay.

2. **Correct Answer: C**
    A. **Incorrect:** This is not a valid option.
    B. **Incorrect:** This is not a valid option.
    C. **Correct:** This is the correct way to disable the Change Highlighting feature.
    D. **Incorrect:** This is not a valid option.

3. **Correct Answers: A and D**
    A. **Correct:** A Baseline plan saves data for baseline information like Baseline Start, Baseline Work, and Baseline Duration so you can look at slippage when you save additional baselines at intervals.
    B. **Incorrect:** An Assignment report offers a report on who does what and when. It is not used to compare start and finish dates in a project.

C. **Incorrect:** A Workload report offers a report on task usage or resource usage. It is not used to compare start and finish dates in a project.

D. **Correct:** An interim plan saves a set of start and finish dates for a project. This meets the criteria in the question.

Chapter 3: Case Scenario Answers

Case Scenario 1: Monitoring Project Progress

1. Although there are tables (such as the Summary, Schedule, and Variance tables) that display project progress and schedule-related information, you can find the most visual display of baseline data versus actual project progress in the Tracking Gantt Chart.

2. The Project Statistics dialog box provides a quick snapshot of your entire project, including current, actual, baseline, and variance information. You can view the Project Statistics dialog box by opening the Project Information dialog box and then clicking the Statistics button or by clicking the Project Statistics button on the Tracking toolbar.

3. The Task Form offers succinct work information for individual tasks. For a more comprehensive and high-level look at resources, tasks, and assigned work, display the Task Usage view, the Resource Usage view, or both.

Case Scenario 2: Implementing Project Changes

1. In Project you can simply make the change in the Entry table (in Gantt Chart view) to see the change highlighting.

2. Save an interim plan.

3. Split the task this resource was working on to track the work already completed and allow for the downtime in your project. This downtime is created when the resource moves temporarily to another project.

Chapter 4: Lesson Review Answers

Lesson 1

1. **Correct Answers: A and C**

A. **Correct:** You can import tasks from Excel.

B. **Incorrect:** You cannot import filters from Excel into Project.

C. **Correct:** You can import costs from Excel.

D. **Incorrect:** You cannot import views from Excel into Project.

2. **Correct Answers: A and C**

   A. **Correct:** This is the second step. Use the Import Outlook Tasks dialog box to choose the tasks to import.

   B. **Incorrect:** When importing Outlook tasks, you do not use the Import Wizard.

   C. **Correct:** This is the first step for importing Outlook tasks.

   D. **Incorrect:** When importing Outlook tasks, you do not use the Open dialog box or select a file type.

3. **Correct Answers: C and D**

   A. **Incorrect:** There is no Project Viewer available for download.

   B. **Incorrect:** There is no Export command.

   C. **Correct:** You can save basic data such as this in a text file and then send the file in an e-mail message.

   D. **Correct:** Eight rows of data would fit nicely on a single screen, and you can use the Copy Picture button to capture them.

4. **Correct Answers: A and B**

   A. **Correct:** Selecting a mapping field manually is one of the ways to deal with an unmapped field.

   B. **Correct:** Deleting the data eliminates the unmapped field.

   C. **Incorrect:** Selecting All adds all of the available fields to the map. This would result in too many mapped fields and the mapping process would fail.

   D. **Incorrect:** The Export Filter is used to filter fields that are exported, not to map fields that are unmapped.

5. **Correct Answer: C**

   A. **Incorrect:** Although this might work, it certainly is not the fastest way to acquire and send the data.

   B. **Incorrect:** This option does not exist.

   C. **Correct:** The predefined map Cost Data By Task will have the required information.

   D. **Incorrect:** Because there are a lot of tasks in the project, there is a lot of information to send. It's doubtful that all of the information would fit on one page that you could take a picture of and send.

Lesson 2

1. **Correct Answers: A, C, and D**

   A. **Correct:** Creating a centralized location with current resource information that all project managers can access and use is a good reason to use a resource pool.

    B. **Incorrect:** A resource pool is used to manage resources automatically. It is not used for specific project managers to claim resources for their own projects.

    C. **Correct:** Allowing project managers and stakeholders to view cost and material resource data whenever they want is a good reason to use a resource pool.

    D. **Correct:** Resource pools help reduce overallocations by analyzing and managing resources.

2. **Correct Answer: D**

    A. **Incorrect:** The Summary table shows schedule-related information, including Duration, Start, Finish, % Complete, Cost, and Work.

    B. **Incorrect:** Gantt Chart view shows Task Name, Fixed Cost, Fixed Cost Accrual, Total Cost, Baseline, Variance, Actual, and Remaining columns. It does not show resources.

    C. **Incorrect:** The Project Information dialog box shows the Start, Current, and Finish dates, the Status date, the Schedule From date, the Calendar, and Priority data. It does not offer a place to assign resources to a resource pool.

    D. **Correct:** Enter resource information for a resource pool in the resource pool file.

3. **Correct Answer: C**

    A. **Incorrect:** A work breakdown structure is used to organize tasks for reporting schedules and tracking costs.

    B. **Incorrect:** A summary task is a task that is made up of subtasks; it is not used to identify accountability, responsibility, management, and approvals of all authorized work scope.

    C. **Correct:** An organization breakdown structure is used to create a logical framework for identification of accountability, responsibility, management, and approvals of all authorized work scope.

    D. **Incorrect:** An enterprise resource list is a list of resources shared across an enterprise.

4. **Correct Answer: D**

    A. **Incorrect:** This setting should be enabled when you want the resource pool to lose all conflicts.

    B. **Incorrect:** Use Resources tells your sharer project to use resources from another file.

    C. **Incorrect:** Priority, Standard is an option in the Level Resources dialog box, not in the Share Resources dialog box.

    D. **Correct:** If the resource pool is to win every conflict, Pool Takes Precedence must be enabled.

5. **Correct Answers: C and D**

    A. **Incorrect:** There is no Level Now button on the Standard toolbar.

B. **Incorrect:** There is no Level Now option under Project.

C. **Correct:** You manually level resources using the Resource Leveling dialog box.

D. **Correct:** You manually level resources using the Resource Leveling dialog box. You access this dialog box from the Tools, Level Resources option.

6. **Correct Answer: A**

A. **Correct:** Back loaded is the correct answer.

B. **Incorrect:** Front loaded increases the hours scheduled per day from the start to the end of the task.

C. **Incorrect:** Early peak increases the hours scheduled per day from the start to the end of the task, excluding the first day the task is scheduled.

D. **Incorrect:** Turtle schedules work to peak in the middle.

7. **Correct Answers: A, B, and D**

A. **Correct:** Second, you must choose Format, chose Details, and choose Remaining Availability.

B. **Correct:** First, you must access the Resource Usage view.

C. **Incorrect:** There is no underallocation option in the Filter dialog box. There is an overallocation option, however.

D. **Correct:** Third, you must note the amount of underallocation in the Rem. Avail. row.

Lesson 3

1. **Correct Answer: D**

A. **Incorrect:** In the Save As Template dialog box, selecting the check box for a type of data is what keeps that data from being added to the template, not clearing the check box.

B. **Incorrect:** In the Save As Template dialog box, selecting the check box for a type of data is what keeps that data from being added to the template, not clearing the check box. Also, resources rates refer to rates, not to fixed costs.

C. **Incorrect:** Because it's easy to exclude this data using the Save As Template dialog box, it's best achieved there, not by changing all rates to $0.00.

D. **Correct:** In the Save As Template dialog box, selecting the check box for a type of data (such as Resource Rates) is what keeps that data from being added to the template.

2. **Correct Answer: D**

A. **Incorrect:** The only way to make changes to an original Project template is to open the template from the Templates\1033 folder.

B. **Incorrect:** The only way to make changes to an original Project template is to open the template from the Templates\1033 folder.

C. **Incorrect:** The Templates folder is located in the *<hard disk drive letter>*:\Program Files\Microsoft Office\Templates\1033 folder, not the *<hard disk drive letter>*:\Program Data\Microsoft\MicrosoftOffice\Templates folder.

D. **Correct:** To make changes to an original Project template, you must open the template from \Program Files\Microsoft Office\Templates\1033.

3. **Correct Answer: A**

A. **Correct:** You must type the Task ID number of the external predecessor followed by a backslash in the Predecessors data for the task to link.

B. **Incorrect:** You can copy and paste information to cross link data among two projects, but in this question you are creating links for task dependencies, the Task Information dialog box is open, and you must use the box to provide the cross link.

C. **Incorrect:** You keep any already-inserted project from being updated by clearing the Link To Project check box found in the Project Information dialog box.

D. **Incorrect:** You must create the cross link in the Predecessors tab and, in the ID column, type the name of the master project followed by the Task ID number of the external predecessor followed by a backslash.

4. **Correct Answers: B, C, and D**

A. **Incorrect:** You do not have to create a cross project link among projects to create a master project file.

B. **Correct:** To create a master project file, you must view the file in Gantt Chart view, insert at least one subproject, and save the master project.

C. **Correct:** To create a master project file, you must view the file in Gantt Chart view, insert at least one subproject, and save the master project.

D. **Correct:** To create a master project file, you must view the file in Gantt Chart view, insert at least one subproject, and save the master project.

5. **Correct Answers: A and B**

A. **Correct:** After using the Paste Special command, you must select Paste Link.

B. **Correct:** You must select the area to paste the data and use Paste Special to paste it.

C. **Incorrect:** This is how you create a cross link for task dependencies among tasks, not create a simple project link.

D. **Incorrect:** This is how you create a cross link for task dependencies among tasks, not create a simple project link.

Lesson 4

1. **Correct Answer: A**

A. **Correct:** The Schedule tab offers these options, as well as others.

B. **Incorrect:** The General tab lets you set AutoFilter for new projects, configure the Planning Wizard, and set default standard and overtime rates. It is not used to configure how tasks are created by default.

C. **Incorrect:** The Collaborate tab is used with Project Server and allows you to configure teamwork options.

D. **Incorrect:** The Calculation tab lets you configure how calculations are made and how calculations should be applied to other areas of the project.

2. **Correct Answer: C**

A. **Incorrect:** Effort-driven means that new tasks are scheduled so that the work on the task remains constant as you add or remove assignments.

B. **Incorrect:** Automatically linking tasks that have been moved or cut has nothing to do with when the tasks start, so this is irrelevant.

C. **Correct:** Autolink automatically links tasks when you cut, move, or insert them. This applies only to contiguous Finish-To-Start task relationships, however.

D. **Incorrect:** This option specifies that Project schedules tasks according to their constraint dates. This means that constrained tasks won't be moved in negative slack situations.

3. **Correct Answers: A, B, and D**

A. **Correct:** You must first open the Options dialog box, then select the Calculation tab, and finally click Earned Value to apply the changes.

B. **Correct:** You must first open the Options dialog box, then select the Calculation tab, and finally click Earned Value to apply the changes.

C. **Incorrect:** This option does not need to be enabled for the earned value calculation options to be changed.

D. **Correct:** You must first open the Options dialog box, then select the Calculation tab, and finally click Earned Value to apply the changes.

4. **Correct Answer: C**

A. **Incorrect:** Selecting this option distributes the changes to total percent complete evenly across the schedule to the project status date.

B. **Incorrect:** When this option is selected, a task's remaining portion moves forward to start of the status date.

C. **Correct:** Updating Task Status Updates Resource Status meets this criterion.

D. **Incorrect:** When this option is selected, a task's completion portion moves back to finish at the status date. The default status of this check box is cleared, which means that the completion portion of the task is set to finish as previously scheduled.

5. **Correct Answer: A**

    A. **Correct:** The View tab of the Options dialog box offers an option to show the project summary task.

    B. **Incorrect:** There is no option in the Project Information dialog box to configure the display of the project summary task in Project.

    C. **Incorrect:** You do configure the display of the project summary task in the Options dialog box, but in the View tab, not the General tab.

    D. **Incorrect:** The Organizer dialog box is most often used to share custom filters, groups, fields, views, and tables.

6. **Correct Answer: D**

    A. **Incorrect:** Currency settings are changed in the View tab of the Options dialog box, not the Calculation tab.

    B. **Incorrect:** Currency settings cannot be configured in the Properties dialog box. This dialog box is used to manage general data that applies to a project, such as title, author, manager, company, and similar data.

    C. **Incorrect:** Currency settings cannot be configured in the Project Information dialog box. This dialog box is used to offer data like Start and Finish Date, Current Date, Schedule From, and similar data.

    D. **Correct:** Currency settings can be changed in the View tab of the Options dialog box.

7. **Correct Answers: A and C**

    A. **Correct:** Creating a copy of the project will allow you to make changes without affecting the original project.

    B. **Incorrect:** A workspace is a group of files and settings that you can save and reopen when you need to. Project creates a list of current settings, open views, and open projects. It does not create a reversible project file.

    C. **Correct:** By changing the number of undo levels to 99, you will have that many "undos" available.

    D. **Incorrect:** A baseline is a set of data that is used for comparison; it is not a file you can revert to.

8. **Correct Answers: B and D**

    A. **Incorrect:** Rates are input from the Options dialog box and the General tab.

    B. **Correct:** Rates are input from the Options dialog box and the General tab.

    C. **Incorrect:** New tasks do not need to be effort-driven in order for rates and overtime rates to be applied by default.

    D. **Correct:** In order to make these rates default rates for the project, Set As Default must be clicked.

9. **Correct Answer: D**

    A. **Incorrect:** Select this when you want to show successors and predecessors in the current project.

    B. **Incorrect:** This only specifies whether Project should accept external data and update the project based on what it acquires.

    C. **Incorrect:** Changing the calculation mode to manual means only that you'll have to click Calculate Now to update your project. It does not affect anything in this scenario.

    D. **Correct:** This is the correct feature to clear.

10. **Correct Answers: B, C, and D**

    A. **Incorrect:** Advice From Planning Wizard must be selected before you can configure other options. If you clear it, no other options will appear and no advice at all will be given.

    B. **Correct:** To avoid getting advice about scheduling, you must clear this option.

    C. **Correct:** To receive advice about errors you must select this option.

    D. **Correct:** To avoid getting advice about using Project, you must clear this option.

11. **Correct Answers: A, B, and D**

    A. **Correct:** This is a valid option and will enable the use of legacy file formats.

    B. **Correct:** This is a valid option and will enable the use of legacy file formats.

    C. **Incorrect:** This will not change the way legacy formats are handled.

    D. **Correct:** When clearing this option, you are forced to choose either option A or B.

12. **Correct Answers: B and D**

    A. **Incorrect:** Although you could show the Calendar view and group complete and incomplete tasks, you would not be able to display all of the information that would be shown in the Tracking Gantt.

    B. **Correct:** You can customize a view using Window: Split and selecting the panes you want to view.

    C. **Incorrect:** When you edit an existing view, you can create only a single view. You cannot add another view using the View Definition dialog box. You must create a combination view.

    D. **Correct:** Create a combination view to show both views on the same screen.

13. **Correct Answers: A, B, and D**

    A. **Correct:** To rename any customized field, you will need to open the Fields dialog box. Then, to view Resource fields, you select the Resource option near the top. Finally, select the field you want to rename and click the Rename button.

    B. **Correct:** Before you open the Organizer to copy custom fields, both the file that you are copying from and the file that you are copying to must be open. Once open, each will be available within the Organizer.

C. **Incorrect:** Using the Import Wizard will only import project data to your current data file. This includes things such as task and resource names, but not custom fields.

D. **Correct:** After the file you are copying from and the file you are copying to have been opened, you can use the Organizer to copy custom elements (such as fields) between the two open files.

14. **Correct Answers: A and C**

A. **Correct:** With both projects open, the one that includes the formula and the one that you want to import it to, you can import the formula using the Custom Fields dialog box.

B. **Incorrect:** Formulas are not available in the Organizer's Fields tab.

C. **Correct:** To import a formula from another project, the project must be open.

D. **Incorrect:** You do not need to import the entire project; you only need to import the formula to be applied to the resource.

15. **Correct Answer: A**

A. **Correct:** Double-click the Actual Cost heading to open the Column Definition dialog box. There you can type in a new title for the field name, OurCost.

B. **Incorrect:** In the Custom Fields dialog box you can create a custom cost field but you cannot rename default Project fields.

C. **Incorrect:** In the Font dialog box you can change the font, font style, and font size for heading and selected data, but there is no place to rename a default field.

D. **Incorrect:** In the Text Styles dialog box you can change the font, font style, and font size for heading and selected data, but there is no place to rename a default field.

16. **Correct Answer: D**

A. **Incorrect:** You can create custom settings in the Project Properties dialog box, but doing so does not prevent you from making formatting changes later.

B. **Incorrect:** Change Highlighting is a feature that allows you to see what impact changes you make to a project have on other data in the project before you apply the changes.

C. **Incorrect:** Even if you do disable this feature, you can still make changes to the bar and bar text.

D. **Correct:** To make changes to a view's attributes, you must be in that appropriate view first. (If there's no bar graph to edit, there are no options to edit it.)

17. **Correct Answer: B**

A. **Incorrect:** There is no option for Layout under the File menu.

B. **Correct:** You use the Options dialog box and the View tab to change the date format in all places within a project, not just in the bars.

C. **Incorrect:** There is no option in the Bar Styles dialog box to make changes related to date and time.

D. **Incorrect:** There is no option in Format Gridlines to make changes related to date and time.

Chapter 4: Case Scenario Answers

Case Scenario 1: Sharing Project Data

1. Because Project can read data input in Excel, this is a fairly simple import process. However, to ensure that the process goes smoothly, it would be helpful to share the Excel project planning template with the Accounting department. When completed, a workbook based on this template can be easily imported into Project without the need to create a custom import map.

2. The best solution is to have the Human Resources department export the resource information to either a text (*.txt) or comma-separated values (*.csv) file. In this format you can use Project's import feature to read the data in your project file. The field names will probably differ from those that Project uses. If this is the case, you can map the fields as necessary.

3. As you map your fields, save the mapping as a custom import map. This way you can use the mapping for future imports.

Case Scenario 2: Sharing Resources

1. Creating a resource pool would fulfill this need.

2. You can see resource overallocation highlighted in the following views: Resource Usage view, Resource Sheet view, and Resource Graph view.

3. Resource Leveling.

Case Scenario 3: Working with a Master Project

1. Create a master project plan and insert each of three individual subprojects (which are managed by the experts). When you need project information, you can simply open the master project plan to view the linked subprojects.

2. Create a cross-project link using ghost tasks that link a task in one project file with a task in another project file.

3. You can remove the link between a subproject and a master project while maintaining the subproject task list in the master project file by opening the Task Information dialog box for the subproject's summary task and removing the checkmark next to Link in the Advanced tab.

Case Scenario 4: Customizing Project

1. Create a customized field for each set of data that is currently saved in Excel. Then add that field in any table.

2. Create a custom table using the More Tables dialog box that contains only the columns from the Entry, Cost, and Schedule fields that you use. To use it in future projects, use the Organizer to copy the custom table to the Global.mpt file.

3. Double-click a column header and update the field title to text of your choosing.

Chapter 5: Lesson Review Answers

Lesson 1

1. **Correct Answers: A and B**
   A. **Correct:** Creating basic and visual reports in Project offers opportunities to review different sets of data, including reports on overallocated resources, among others.
   B. **Correct:** By filtering the data shown in a basic report, you can create reports based on any single data type, such as Cost Overbudget or Critical.
   C. **Incorrect:** Creating a template will not help you learn anything or gather data. Creating a template will only help start a similar project later.
   D. **Incorrect:** This report does not exist. Although you can create various visual reports, this is not one of them.

2. **Correct Answers: A and C**
   A. **Correct:** To create an Earned Value report, you must first open the Visual Reports dialog box and then, in the All tab, select Earned Value Over Time Report.
   B. **Incorrect:** The desired report is a visual report, not a basic report.
   C. **Correct:** To create an Earned Value report, you must first open the Visual Reports dialog box and then, in the All tab, select Earned Value Over Time Report.
   D. **Incorrect:** The Overview options are part of the Basic Reports dialog box. Overview options include Project Summary, Top-Level Tasks, Critical Tasks, Milestones, and Working Days, but not an earned value report.

3. **Correct Answer: B**

   A. **Incorrect:** AutoFilter can be used to filter data, but it does not filter it in a way that makes printing the data possible.

   B. **Correct:** A basic report that filters the data you want is the correct way to collect and then print the desired data.

   C. **Incorrect:** By default, there are no Task Summary reports available in the Visual Reports dialog box. Even if there were, they would likely not be filtered properly.

   D. **Incorrect:** Switching to Task Usage view does show the tasks involved in a project, but filtering and then printing the results would not bring the desired outcome.

4. **Correct Answer: D**

   A. **Incorrect:** A Basic report is a text-based report and is not colorful or in the form of a bar graph.

   B. **Incorrect:** There is no option in Project to create an Excel Report. You can create a visual report to view in Excel or Visio, however.

   C. **Incorrect:** There is no option in Project to create a PowerPoint report. You can create a visual report to view in Excel or Visio, however.

   D. **Correct:** Visual reports created in Project can be bar graphs and are colorful and vibrant. They can also include information for budgeted work.

Lesson 2

1. **Correct Answer: D**

   A. **Incorrect:** Visual reports offer visual representations of specific data like Baseline Cost, Budget Cost, Earned Value Over Time, and so on. This type of report is not what is needed in this scenario.

   B. **Incorrect:** Basic report categories include Overview, Current Activities, Costs, Assignments, Workload, and Custom. The only resource report offering is the Overallocated Resources report, which is not appropriate here.

   C. **Incorrect:** A custom monthly calendar report offers a filter but not an option to choose periods of time.

   D. **Correct:** The crosstab report, a custom report, offers all of this information and more.

2. **Correct Answer: D**

   A. **Incorrect:** The Page Setup dialog box is where you configure the printout's orientation, scaling, paper size, margins, headers, and footers.

   B. **Incorrect:** The Visual Reports dialog box is where you create visual reports for Earned Value, Budget Cost, Cash Flow, and similar reports.

C.   **Incorrect:** The Print dialog box is where you configure the printer properties, print range, and timescale.

D.   **Correct:** When you create a custom resource report, you configure the report specifications in the Resource Report dialog box using the Definition, Details, and Sort tabs.

Chapter 5: Case Scenario Answers

Case Scenario 1: Displaying Views and Reports

1. Use Project's basic reports to view the Earned Value report. Before displaying the final result, click the Edit button and apply the Costs Overbudget filter to the report. This allows you to enter a value of your choice ($500) to see only tasks costing more than their baselines.

2. Use Project's Visual Reports feature to send the requested data to an Excel 2003 (or later) PivotTable. When changes are made to the data on the PivotTable, the associated PivotGraph will update so that the stakeholder can visually see the effects of any work assignment adjustments.

Case Scenario 2: Working with Custom Tables and Reports

1. You can copy your custom elements into your Globat.mpt file and share that file with others. Doing so, however, will overwrite any custom elements already stored in their personal Global.mpt files. Or simply copy the custom elements using the Organizer into any project file. The other project managers can then open the project file and copy the elements into their own Global.mpt. In any of these procedures the work is done in the Organizer dialog box.

2. Custom reports are easily deleted when they are no longer needed, just like filters and groups, using the Organizer dialog box.

3. Select the report in the Custom Reports dialog box, and then click the Setup button. From either the Header or Footer tab (depending on where the logo will be placed), click the Insert Picture command button to add the image to the printed report's header or footer section.

Glossary

assignment contouring   A process that determines how work for an assignment is to be distributed. For some assignments much of the work must be done before a few final projects can be completed; in other situations work might need to be distributed so that the majority of the work is completed at the end of the project.

AutoFilter   A quick way to view only the task or resource information that supplies only the data you want to see. In order to use AutoFilter, you must turn it on in the Project menu in Filtered For.

AutoLink   When AutoLink is enabled in master projects, linked tasks are automatically updated when you cut, move, or insert them. By default, this is enabled.

baseline plan   A snapshot taken of the original plan and at chosen checkpoints for the project. Baseline plans often are discussed with other baselines, like cost baseline or schedule baseline, and serve as a reference point for measuring changes in your project. In Project you can save up to 11 baseline plans for one project file.

bottom-up planning   One way to plan a project. In this method you define all the tasks you want to include in the work breakdown structure first and later group them into larger summary tasks.

budget resource   A resource that is tied to the project's budget. Budget resources need to be tracked in the project and are applied using the Resource Information dialog box. By default, the Budget check box is not selected on a resource and thus must be selected manually.

calendar   The settings that define the workdays and hours available for a project, including its resources and tasks. These settings include how many work hours are available each day, when those hours occur (day or night), and work-week length. It is also possible to add exceptions to a calendar for company-specific calendar exceptions, such as early-release Fridays or company-wide vacation days. *See also* project calendar.

Change Highlighting   A feature that is enabled by default that allows you to see how the changes you make to a project will affect the project before you save the changes. After you save the changes, the highlighted areas are no longer highlighted.

combination view   A view that displays two views on a single screen, such as Gantt Chart view and Resource Usage view. You enable a combination view by choosing Window and then Split.

constraint   In general, a restriction or boundary placed on a project, task, or resource. A constraint can be a deadline, a budget, staff size, or quality of resources.

cost budget   The process of establishing a budget so that project costs can be maintained and managed.

cost resource   One of the three types of resources (the other two are material and work). This type of resource does not affect the scheduling of a project (but does affects the budget) and is generally something that is not directly used on a project or performs work on it. Airfare, lodging, training, permits, and travel expenses are common cost resources.

Cost table   A table that shows the Task Name, Fixed Cost, Fixed Cost Accrual, Total Cost, Baseline, Variance, Actual, and Remaining fields. Use this table to manage costs associated with tasks.

critical path   A series of tasks that define the finish date of the project. If the critical path tasks do not finish when scheduled, the project finish date is delayed.

decomposition   The first step in creating a project is to create a work breakdown structure (WBS). The project manager uses the WBS to create work packages, which are the smallest sets of work that a project can be broken down into. The process of breaking down the WBS into small work packages is called decomposition.

duration   How much time passes between the start and finish of a task.

Earned Value   A schedule analysis tool you can use to analyze cost information in a project plan.

effort-driven scheduling   A term that describes the theory that adding more resources equals shortening a task's duration. If it takes one person eight hours to perform a task, but two people can do it in four hours, the task is effort-driven. If it takes one person eight hours to drive a car from point A to point B, adding another person will not make the task finish any faster. This is an example of a task that is not effort-driven.

exception   Infrequent variances to normal working times. These variances are known in advance and can be added to a project calendar so that work is not scheduled for that day. Exceptions include vacation days, holidays, personal time, and so on.

exporting   The process of copying data from one application to another. For instance, Project data can be exported for use in Excel, Word, or Outlook, to name a few. You'll generally export data when the person who needs to review or use the data does not have or does not use Project or when you need the information in another application for work that Project can't do.

field   A type of information that contains specific information about a task or resource. Fields include Start Date and Finish Date, Cost, Actual Cost, Predecessors, and more.

filter   A way to display only the desired information in a project. You choose the criteria.

Finish-to-Finish (FF) relationship   A relationship between two tasks where the predecessor task's finish date controls the finish date of the successor.

Finish-to-Start (FS) relationship   A relationship between two tasks where the predecessor task's finish date controls the start date of the successor.

Fixed Duration   A task type where the duration is fixed. Although you can change the duration manually, if units or work changes and Project must perform the recalculation, the duration will not be changed but the other variables will.

Fixed Units   A task type where units are fixed. Although you can change the unit value manually, if duration or work changes and Project must perform the recalculation, units will not be changed but the other variables will.

Fixed Work   A task type where work is fixed. Although you can change the work value manually, if duration or units change and Project must perform the recalculation, work will not be changed but the other variables will.

free slack   The amount of time a task can fall behind, be delayed, or slip, and not affect other tasks in the project schedule.

Gantt Chart   A graphical representation of a project's timeline. The left half of the Gantt Chart is a table listing task names and related information, and the right side offers tasks in the form of a vertical bar chart.

ghost task   A task that acts as a placeholder in your project plan file and links to tasks outside the project in which it is held.

group   A group is a way to order data for tasks or resources. You can specify multiple group levels to sort, filter, and group data.

importing   The process of copying data from one application into to another. For instance, data created in Excel, Word, Access, Outlook, and others can be moved into Project using Project's import tools. You'll usually import data when you need to use data created by someone who does not have or does not use Project or when the data is stored in another application.

import/export map   A group of settings and rules that tell Project how to import or export data from or to another application. These rules help map data from one application to another by letting you define what field in one application will map to another field in a second application.

indent (demote)   Moving a task to a lower outline level (this means the task is moved to the right in the Gantt Chart and becomes a subtask).

interim plan   A task's start and finish values that can be saved and used to compare project progress at various stages.

lag time   The amount of delay in the relationship between the predecessor and the successor. Waiting for paint to dry for three days prior to installing molding or carpet is one example.

lead time   The amount of time that must pass for one task before its successor task can start. In a task where all carpet must be removed prior to painting a room, the task of painting the room can start after half of the carpet has been removed. This is lead time.

leveling   The process of resolving resources conflicts and overallocations by delaying tasks, splitting tasks, and making changes to assignment in a project.

link   A dependency between tasks. In general terms, a link details when a successor task can start in relation to a predecessor task. Dependencies include Start-to-Finish, Finish-to-Finish, Start-to-Start, and Start-to-Finish.

master project   A project file that includes subprojects (inserted projects) and that is used to manage multiple smaller projects from one larger project.

material resource   One of three types of resources (the other two are work and cost). Material resources are consumable items like paper, paint, oil, gas, and concrete.

milestone   A significant event or reference point in a project. It is often a deadline and used to monitor the project's progress. A milestone is represented as a task with a duration of zero days and is shown as a diamond on a Gantt Chart.

Network Diagram   A graphical representation of a project that focuses on task relationships. Each box in the Network Diagram view displays details about a task, and lines show tasks' relationships to one another. The Network Diagram most closely represents the PERT (Program Evaluation and Review Technique) view.

organizational breakdown structure (OBS)   A project organization framework for identification of accountability, responsibility, management, and approvals of all authorized work scope.

Organizer   Available from the Tools menu, a tool that offers tabs that include Views, Groups, Fields, Reports, and more. You can use Organizer to copy custom filters and groups to the global template.

outdent (promote)   Moving a task to a higher outline level (this means the task is moved to the left in the Gantt Chart.)

overallocation   The result of assigning more tasks to a resource than that resource can accomplish in the available time.

PERT formula   A formula that you can use to calculate the estimated duration of a task based on an optimistic duration, a pessimistic duration, and an expected duration. The PERT formula is: Estimated Duration = ((Optimistic + Pessimistic + (4*Expected))/6.

predecessor   An activity or task that controls when a successor task starts or ends.

progress line   A line that shows the progress of your project visually and that is displayed on the Gantt Chart. Progress lines connect in-progress tasks that help you easily see work that is behind and work that is ahead.

PivotChart A chart that summarizes large amounts of data and offers the results in an easy-to-read format. With a PivotChart you can rearrange the data and assign the criteria so that you can easily view the desired data.

PivotDiagram A collection of shapes in a tree-like organizational structure that can help you summarize data using nodes and sub-nodes.

PivotTable An interactive table that summarizes large amounts of data. You can rotate rows and columns, filter data, display different pages, and more.

project A temporary series of tasks that will, once carried out, meet an end product, an initiative, or a venture that a company wants to produce or create. A project can be an office move, the rollout of a new product, the construction of a building, a new initiative (perhaps a new phone or e-mail system), the manufacture of a new product, a new company Web site, or a perhaps even a company buyout.

project calendar A calendar applied to a project that defines work days and hours available for the project, including its resources and tasks. *See also* calendar.

Project Guide By default, a guide that appears in the Task pane of the Project interface to help you set up, create, manage, and finalize a project. The Project Guide offers topics, instructions, controls, and wizards that you can use to manage your project.

project scope The work required to complete a project.

project summary task A project-level task that has an ID of 0. By default, the project summary task is not shown and must be configured in the View tab of the Options dialog box.

recurring task A task that occurs more than once and on a regular schedule. A common recurring task is a weekly or monthly staff meeting.

report A format in which you can print schedule information that is appropriate for the intended recipients.

resource An item used to complete a task in the form of materials, facilities, person-hours, funding, equipment, or people (to name a few). Resources can be categorized as work, material, or cost.

Resource Graph A graphical representation that allows you to see each resource allocation, cost, or work in a project graphed on a timescale. In the timescale the horizontal axis represents time and the vertical axis represents units of resource allocations, cost, or work.

resource histogram A way to view resources, resource requirements, resource usage, and resource availability over a period of time.

resource pool A project file that contains only resource information (such as resource names, rates, and so on), that can be shared among project managers. By sharing resources in a pool, it's easier to find and resolve overallocations because each manager knows which resources are being used when and why.

Resource Sheet A graphical representation that uses a table to display information about your project's resources and tasks. The Resource Sheet view does not tell you about the tasks to which resources might be assigned.

Resource Usage view A graphical representation of a project that shows a summary of resource usage values for tasks in the project. Resource Usage View also offers the total usage of the resource for other projects, shows what resources are overallocated, and shows all of the resource assignments and their percentages of work allocation in a timesheet.

Schedule table A unique table that shows task names, start and finish dates, and late start, late finish, free slack, and total slack fields, along with a timeline.

sharer file   A Project data file that uses a resource pool.

single view   A Project view that shows only a single view, such as Resource Sheet or Task Usage.

split task   A single task that has been split into two or more tasks. Generally a split task is created when there are gaps in the task's schedule.

Start-to-Finish (SF) relationship   A relationship between two tasks where the predecessor task's start controls the finish of the successor task.

Start-to-Start (SS) relationship   A relationship between two tasks where the predecessor task's start controls the start of the successor task.

status date   A date you specify to calculate various project indicators. The Status Date does not have to be the current date.

subproject   A project inserted into a master project.

successor   An activity or task whose start or finish is controlled by another task.

Summary table   A table that shows the task name, duration, start and finish dates, percent complete, cost, and work for each task. There are also options to filter and group and a timeline.

summary task   A task that contains subtasks. Summary tasks often define phases of a project.

task   The smallest activity in a project. Tasks have distinct start and finish points, unique IDs, and, occasionally, their own calendars.

task calendar   A calendar used to schedule and manage tasks. For the most part, tasks are scheduled according to a project calendar, but sometimes tasks need their own calendar—for example, when the task is being performed by a machine that can be run only at night.

task deadline   A date by which a task must be completed.

task dependency   A relationship between tasks where one task controls the schedule of another.

Task Form view   A view in which you can see task IDs, resource names, units, work, predecessors, type tasks, and other task-related information.

task relationship   A connection between two tasks. The relationship can be a dependency, such as Start-to-Start or Finish-to-Finish.

Task Usage view   A graphical representation of tasks in a project. This view lists resources under their respective tasks to which they've been assigned, and the information is organized into a timeline.

template   A project file that has already been created and that contains existing project information that you can use to help you start a project more quickly. A template contains tasks already added in the correct order and might also have milestones, task durations, and task dependencies, among other things.

timescale   An element that typically appears above the Gantt Chart and displays up to three tiers. Each displayed tier can be individually formatted to specify time units, date labels, alignment, and other formatting options.

top-down planning   One way to plan a project. In this method you define all of the larger, summary tasks you want to include in the work breakdown structure first and later break down the tasks into subtasks.

total slack   The amount of time a task can fall behind (slip) without affecting the project schedule.

Tracking Gantt   A graphical representation of a project that shows baseline start, duration, and the critical path using Gantt bars.

Tracking toolbar   A toolbar you can enable to help you collect, enter, and manage a project by tracking task and resource progress. This toolbar offers drop-down lists for Tasks, Resources, Track, and Report, and each drop-down list offers multiple options for tracking.

underallocation   The result of assigning fewer tasks to a resource than that resource can accomplish in the given amount of time. In this instance the resource is idle when not on use.

units   A way of measuring the capacity of a resource to work. When assigning a resource to a task, you also assign units. By default, a resource works at 100 percent. Units are part of the equation Work = Duration * Units.

Variance table   A view that shows task names, start and finish dates, baseline starts and finish data, and start and finish variation data. It also includes a timeline.

visual report   A report in the form of a bar graph, pie chart, line graph, or other graphical representation for summarizing and viewing the data in a project.

work   The total scheduled effort for a task, resources, or project. Work is measured in person-hours and is part of the equation Work = Duration * Units.

work breakdown structure (WBS)   An outline of the project using summary tasks and sub-tasks that help you plan a project. The WBS is organized using the Entry table and is a basic project outline that describes all the tasks that must be completed for the project to finish.

work package   A accountable unit of work listed inside the WBS.

work resource   A resource used to perform work. A work resource can be a person, dump truck, or any other resource that can perform work.

Work table   This view offers task names, work, baselines, variance data, actual and remaining data, and percentage of work complete, along with a timeline.

Index

System Requirements

We recommend that you use an isolated network that is not part of your production network to do the practice exercises in this training kit. The computer that you use to perform practices requires Internet connectivity. If you decide to use a virtual machine instead of standard computer hardware, you can still perform all of the practices.

Hardware Requirements

The computer that you use to perform the practices requires Internet connectivity. Your computer should meet (at a minimum) the following hardware specifications:

- Personal computer with a 700-MHz or faster processor
- 512 MB of RAM or higher
- 1.5 GB of available hard disk space
- 1024 x 768 or higher resolution monitor
- CD-ROM or DVD drive
- Keyboard and Microsoft mouse or compatible pointing device
- Microsoft Windows XP with Service Pack (SP) 2, Windows Server 2003 with SP1, or later operating system

Software Requirements

The following software is required to complete the practice exercises:

- Microsoft Office Project 2007 Professional. Note: Professional Edition is preferable, but it is more expensive to purchase than Standard Edition. If you have Standard Edition, or would prefer to purchase Standard Edition, you will still be able to perform the exercises in this book.
- Optional: Microsoft Office Excel 2003 (or later). (You need this application to display Project visual reports.)
- Optional: Microsoft Office Visio Professional 2007. (You need this application to display Project visual reports.)

CD-ROM Requirements

To use the companion CD-ROM, you need a computer running Microsoft Windows Server 2008, Windows Vista, Windows Server 2003, or Windows XP. The computer must meet the following minimum requirements:

- 700 MHz 32-bit (x86) or 64-bit (x64) processor (depending on the minimum requirements of the operating system)
- 512 MB of system memory (depending on the minimum requirements of the operating system)
- A hard disk partition with at least 700 MB of available space
- A Web browser such as Internet Explorer version 6 or later
- A monitor capable of at least 800 × 600 display resolution
- A keyboard
- A mouse or other pointing device
- An optical drive capable of reading CD-ROMs
- An application that can display PDF files, such as Adobe Acrobat Reader, which can be downloaded at *www.adobe.com/reader*

What do you think of this book?

We want to hear from you!

Do you have a few minutes to participate in a brief online survey?

Microsoft is interested in hearing your feedback so we can continually improve our books and learning resources for you.

To participate in our survey, please visit:

www.microsoft.com/learning/booksurvey/

...and enter this book's ISBN-10 or ISBN-13 number (located above barcode on back cover*). As a thank-you to survey participants in the United States and Canada, each month we'll randomly select five respondents to win one of five $100 gift certificates from a leading online merchant. At the conclusion of the survey, you can enter the drawing by providing your e-mail address, which will be used for prize notification only.

Thanks in advance for your input. Your opinion counts!

*Where to find the ISBN on back cover

ISBN-13: 000-0-0000-0000-0
ISBN-10: 0-0000-0000-0

Example only. Each book has unique ISBN.

Microsoft *Press*

Save 15%
on your Microsoft® Certification exam fee

Present this discount voucher to any participating test center worldwide, or use the discount code to register online or via telephone at participating Microsoft Certified Exam Delivery Providers. See microsoft.com/mcp/exams for locations.

Microsoft

Microsoft | Learning

Good for 15% off one exam fee in the Microsoft Certified Professional Program

Offer expires 12/31/2012

Your voucher discount code

exam voucher

Redeemable at Microsoft Certified Exam Delivery Providers worldwide. For locations, visit: www.microsoft.com/mcp/exams

Promotion Terms and Conditions

- Offer good for 15% off one exam fee in the Microsoft Certified Professional Program.
- Voucher code can be redeemed online or at Microsoft Certified Exam Delivery Providers worldwide.
- Exam purchased using this voucher code must be taken on or before December 31, 2012.
- Inform your Microsoft Certified Exam Delivery Provider that you want to use the voucher discount code at the time you register for the exam.

Voucher Terms and Conditions

- Expired vouchers will not be replaced.
- Each voucher code may only be used for one exam and must be presented at time of registration.
- This voucher may not be combined with other vouchers or discounts.
- This voucher is nontransferable and is void if altered or revised in any way.
- This voucher may not be sold or redeemed for cash, credit, or refund.

X13-92079